The Vulture Investors

THE
VULTURE
INVESTORS

THE WINNERS AND LOSERS OF
THE GREAT AMERICAN
BANKRUPTCY FEEDING FRENZY

HILARY ROSENBERG

HarperBusiness
A Division of HarperCollins*Publishers*

A hardcover edition of this book was published in 1992 by HarperBusiness, a division of HarperCollins Publishers.

First paperback edition published 1993.

Designed by George J. McKeon

The Library of Congress has catalogued the hardcover edition as follows:

Rosenberg, Hilary.
  The vulture investors: the winners and losers of the great American bankruptcy
feeding frenzy / by Hilary Rosenberg. — 1st ed.
    p.   cm.
  Includes bibliographical references and index.
  ISBN 0-88730-555-5
  1. Leveraged buyouts—United States. 2. Bankruptcy—United States. 3. Business
failure—United States. I.Title
  HG4028.M4R67   1992
  332.7′5′0973—dc20   91-58511

ISBN 0-88730-648-9 (pbk.)
93 94 95 96 97 CC/RRD 10 9 8 7 6 5 4 3 2 1

To my husband, Ed Hersh

Contents

Acknowledgments

This book is the product of eighteen months of intensive work and it could not have been accomplished without the help of dozens of people.

I would like to thank the many sources who agreed to be interviewed. In particular, the following people permitted me to call on them more than once or twice, and patiently guided me through the complexities of their stories: Jon Bauer, James Casey, Denis Cronin, Lewis Davis, Steve Davis, Talton Embry, Harry Freund, Joel Friedland, Jay Goldsmith, Shelley Greenhaus, Robert Harrison, Hans Jacobson, Paul Kazarian, Michael Lederman, Bruce McCullough, Ken Moelis, Michael Price, Mark Rachesky, Wilbur Ross, James Rubin, Mikael Salovaara, Bill Scharffenberger, David Schulte, and Martin Whitman.

I am very grateful to my colleagues at *Institutional Investor* for putting up with my half-time schedule during 1991, and to the editors and management for encouraging me (and giving me time) to undertake this project.

I have had more than my share of excellent editors at Harper-Collins. Martha Jewett launched the book and carried me through the initial stages. Jim Childs, Tom Miller, and Eileen Campion each contributed wisdom and invaluable enthusiasm. And the book would have been little but a wistful idea if not for Al Krause, at whose suggestion I contacted Martha.

I never would have made it through this process without my husband, Ed Hersh, who gave me constant support, fresh perspectives, and a steady stream of jokes. Our family and friends supplied plenty of encouragement, understanding of too-brief phone calls and hastily-cancelled visits, and were always there when I needed them. In particular, I need to thank one of my oldest friends, Michele Gasco, who, during a phone call in December 1990, was a sounding board in helping me to find the book's direction. Also, I am greatly indebted to my attorney and friend, Paul Julian.

Finally, I would like to thank Dire Straits, The Moody Blues, and Van Morrison, who, though they are not likely ever to pick up a book about bankruptcy investors, got me through some of the toughest days of writing and editing.

Introduction

Nineteen ninety was a transitional year in finance. After eight years, the economic boom finally ended and a recession began. Wall Street firms reached a nadir in earnings as the stock market sank and new securities issues nearly vanished; the only mention of growth was in terms of layoffs. The junk bond market had collapsed the year before and was groping for direction. Corporations that had borrowed heavily to fund expansion were seeing the folly of their ways. Many declared bankruptcy. Others took every opportunity to retire debt.

As an editor and writer for *Institutional Investor* magazine, I worked with my colleagues to depict the uncertainty and the rampant fear. But we and others in financial journalism also became engaged in a search for the next era. What would be the needs of corporations in the 1990s, and how would financial institutions and the government respond? What would be the priorities for investors? And who would become leading figures during a decade that would certainly be one of frugality?

The last question, when applied to investing, seemed already to have an answer. The corporate raiders who defined the mood of the 1980s by staging hostile raids on major corporations were out of the picture. In 1990, I believed that there was a new group of investors who had begun to emerge. These investors, the so-called vultures, were a much quieter bunch. They did their work in the obscurity of the restructuring and bankruptcy processes and the illiquid markets in distressed bonds and bank debt. In that environment, they made rich returns on their money as either passive or active investors in troubled companies that were struggling to repair their operations and their balance sheets. Some of these investors had been around for years, ignored by the general business community that had been so spellbound with corporate tycoons and raiders. But now, new faces were joining this more experienced core of investors and new money was pouring into their hands from institutional investors looking for the next hot play. At the same time, many vulture investors were becoming pushy, if not hostile. And because larger companies were running aground, vultures were exerting their newfound influence on well-known American institutions like Sunbeam and Bloomingdale's.

But although the vultures were becoming more visible, they were still unfamiliar, even enigmatic, to most people in the business world. Major publications touched on them here and there, when they turned notable profits or became involved with a particularly notable company. But no one had ever taken an in-depth look at them, their motivations, and their activities. For me, the question remained: What kinds of investors actually *choose* to make their living by seeking out troubled companies and becoming mired in the complexities and contentiousness of a bankruptcy or out-of-court workout? I was convinced that the vultures—especially the activist ones who were becoming major forces in the workouts of large companies and in some cases ending up with sizable ownership stakes in rejuvenated companies—must truly be fascinating people as well as astute investors.

I wanted to spend time listening to them and those who work alongside and across the table from them—the lawyers, accountants, investment bankers, and of course, the corporate executives. As I began my research, however, I arrived at a second realization: the best way to describe the activist vulture investors is in action, as characters in the real-life dramas of bankruptcy and out-of-court restructurings. More than simply presenting them and their strategies, a look at the vultures' activities through entire cases would reveal their true effect on the companies and on the other people involved in reorganizations. For it occurred to me that as vulture investors become more powerful, they hold greater potential to delay a restructuring or bankruptcy reorganization indefinitely and in doing so hurt other parties. On the other hand, they also can use their power in a positive way to accelerate the process, although they may also force some parties to accept less than if the case had dragged on.

So I chose to tell the vulture investors' war stories as reenactments of cases. Each of the stories told in this book begins with a vulture's investment and follows his maneuvers through the twists and turns of the bankruptcy and finally to the resolution, where he takes a profit or a loss or a bundle of stock that holds out the possibility for profit in the future. Hopefully, these accounts will serve as keyholes into the world of bankruptcy where technicalities of law and finance lock most people out.

1

Love among the Ruins

On a clear afternoon in May 1986, Michael Price boarded a Lexington Avenue subway near his office in lower Manhattan and rode uptown to the electric razor–topped Citicorp Center. There, in a second-story, glass-enclosed conference room looking out on the atrium lobby, Price took over a $62 million loan from Citibank to the Storage Technology Corporation, a maker of data-storage devices. He paid roughly $41.9 million. When he was done there, he strolled the several blocks to Bank of America's New York offices, where he assumed a $16.4 million loan from that West Coast institution to the same company, for which he paid only about $10.5 million. The two deals together were the last in a string of Storage Technology bank debt and bond purchases Price had orchestrated over the previous year and a half. The three portfolios that made up his Mutual Series Fund had socked $100 million of their $2 billion in assets under management into this one company and now owned about 35 percent of its total debt. The interesting twist here was that Storage Technology was bankrupt. Price is a vulture investor, and he was changing the direction of one of the largest bankruptcy cases in history—and making a killing in the process. To vulture investors today, it was one of the seminal deals in the recent history of their business.

It took Price nine years of buying the debt of distressed companies before he dared attempt a deal of this magnitude, and in 1986, shaky bank loans were still unfamiliar territory for investors. In the early 1980s, Price was one of the pioneer vultures trafficking in bank debt; the difficulty of buying into it and selling out of it kept most people away. In late 1984, he galloped away triumphantly from his first bulk purchase in the case of AM International, a bankrupt maker of mimeograph machines. There is no boasting in his tone, just the facts: "I had zero competition, all by myself, at great prices, with no risk." Price's fund earned annual returns of more than 30 percent on its investment, and he soon began putting those profits to work elsewhere.

That was when he began considering an investment in Storage Technology. The Louisville, Colorado, company had sought bankruptcy court protection from creditors the previous fall when losses became too heavy to bear. With heightened competition from IBM, a rushed installation of disk drives that ended up having faulty parts, and an overly ambitious expansion program, earnings had evaporated. Price scanned the financial statements and saw cash, real estate, and receivables from a respectable customer list. In a word, value. Before year end he started buying bonds.

In January 1985, he called Ryal Poppa. The bespectacled, fifty-two-year-old chief executive of Storage Technology had been on the job just two weeks. A turnaround manager by trade, he'd been brought in by directors to revive the beleaguered company. "Michael introduced himself in his matter-of-fact voice," Poppa recalls. "He said, 'Here's what I do. I seldom get in people's way. I want to profit on your bonds, and I can help you in a reorganization.' I said, 'Why don't we get together?' Then Michael said, 'I just have one question to ask. Why did you leave a secure job in Minnesota for this?' I said, 'Because I believe in this company and its products, and I think I can turn it around.' "

That must have been what Price wanted to hear. In the days and weeks that followed he started adding to his position with heaping portions of bonds and bank debt. Later he explained to Poppa: "If you thought *you* could make money, I thought *I* could make money." He acquired his first bank loan for fifty cents on the dollar and subsequent loans for as little as thirty-seven cents. At times Poppa would ask Price for his assistance in buying out creditors who might hinder the company's reorganization. "When we had creditors who were tired of the bankruptcy or who didn't like management or trust me or whatever, I'd call Michael and say, 'This creditor is in my way. Can you see if you can take him out?' " But Price was always one step ahead of Poppa: "I had a sense as to who was constructive and who was not," Price says. "Ryal and I had a common goal."

He even helped Poppa ward off a bidder for the whole company, Bennett LeBow, whose offer was far below what the CEO considered fair. "Ben, in frustration with me, thought I was stiff-arming him, which I was," Poppa recounts. "He called Michael, who arranged a meeting of the three of us at my hotel in New York, the Park Lane. At one point Michael turned to me and said, 'I know Ben LeBow. Let me handle this.' I said, 'All right, but I'll not take less than nine hundred million dollars.' Bennett went as high as four hundred and fifty, and Michael explained to him that the company was worth a lot more. He helped me hold him at bay."

By early 1986, Price's fund owned more than a third of the Storage Technology bank debt, which gave him considerable clout in the process of developing a reorganization plan—which pays off outstanding creditors and reformulates a company's financial structure to bring the company out of bankruptcy. Since a plan must be accepted by a majority of voting creditors in each class who hold two-thirds in amount of the claims of those voting, Price's holding gave him the power to block any reorganization plan that he didn't like. But he didn't own enough debt to push through a plan if enough other creditors were opposed.

At the time, the head of the creditors' committee was a representative of Citibank who had been spurning the company's proposals for a reorganization plan, holding out for a much higher recovery. He had a paralyzing effect on the bankruptcy—and on Price. "I had all this money tied up," Price says. "There'd be no progress unless that guy was changed." Price was already working on buying him out when Poppa phoned with a request that he buy out the loan, which at $62 million was the granddaddy of Storage Technology's bank loans. It was the very next day that Price took that uptown subway to close the Citibank purchase, and as soon as he was done, he picked up the phone to report to Poppa. "Listen, I just bought out your problem, Citicorp. Let's go do our deal." They made a date to have dinner on June 11.

It was raining that evening when Poppa and his advisers and Price and his attorneys, including the esteemed bankruptcy lawyer Harvey R. Miller, sat down to a multiple-course dinner at The Box Tree, a dark-paneled Continental restaurant located in an East Side townhouse. In between hearty servings of smoked salmon, pâté, salad, duck, and steak, the assembled negotiators sipped on two bottles of Opus 1, the $100-a-bottle cabernet sauvignon co-produced by Baron de Rothschild and Robert Mondavi. The discussion centered on the structure of the bonds to be issued in the reorganization. Late in the evening, when the two sides locked over some crucial points, Price and Poppa left the table so that they could speak freely, one on one. It was eleven P.M. The two men stepped out into the wet blackness of Forty-ninth Street and, stopping under a tree between Second and Third Avenues, they talked for a short while and settled on the amount of bonds to be issued, a call provision, and a thirty-month deferral of interest payments. This last point was especially critical for the company. Poppa told Price that he needed to hold off paying interest in order to have $70 million a year to develop a library storage device that retrieves vast amounts of information for insurance companies and airline reservations systems. Without the development funds, Storage would not be able to jump-start its business. Price was willing.

Poppa admires Price's negotiating savvy. "He could be an emotional, strong-willed table pounder," he says. "But he never raised his voice with me. We went back and forth until we came to a midpoint."

After the dinner broke up, Price and his chief lawyer, Miller, left the others and walked down the street together. Impressed by what he'd just seen and heard, Miller asked Price, "Where did you learn to negotiate? Did you ever work in the garment district?" He knew that when the garment center was thriving, it was full of shrewd traders. A deal was never a deal until delivery. Miller's instincts about Price were right on: Years before, during college vacations, he had worked on Seventh Avenue as an assistant sportswear buyer. He worked for his father, who had not finished his own college education at Wharton Business School because he ran out of money, but who then became co-owner and chief buyer for a West Coast chain of women's apparel stores. After looking over stock and sales figures in the mornings, the younger Price spent the afternoons haggling with clothing manufacturers, trying to get them to ship their "hot" dress or sweater to the stores at a good price. That process was known in the district as *handling* (a Yiddish word pronounced *hondeling*). Says Miller: "I would describe Michael as a 'handler.' Handlers never give up. You could slap him in the face and kick him in the teeth, and he'd come back and say, 'Well, how about another penny?' Irrepressible. Michael was irrepressible. A slowly grinding force." Together, Price and Miller sold the Storage Technology creditors' committee on the reorganization package.

The company emerged from bankruptcy in June 1987 pretty much as Price and Poppa had arranged that night under the shelter of a tree on Forty-ninth Street. Price had paid an average of about forty-seven cents on the dollar for his holdings. In exchange for them he got roughly fifteen cents in cash, forty-five cents in bonds, and 23 percent of the stock in the reorganized Storage Technology. Put another way, Mutual Series got a large minority stake in a company for nothing. The company redeemed the bonds at a premium to par, and over the years Mutual Series slowly sold the stock, which flew as the company flourished. Total annual returns on Mutual Series's investment over five years through the end of 1991: between 35 and 40 percent. Price says it's all in the homework. "Our goal is to do that early work, and then if we think the time is right, to really aggressively go after the banks for a large slug of paper," he explains, as naturally as a hunter describing the operation of his gun.

From Storage Technology, Price went on to forage in the bank loans of Manville, LTV, Western Company of North America, Zapata, Smith International, Maxicare, and Integrated Resources and was a major player in Columbia Gas and Zenith Labs. In the case of Manville, the asbestos manufacturer, a $50 million investment in bank debt, bonds, and preferred stock became cash, preferreds, bonds, and more than three million shares of stock when the company emerged after five years of bankruptcy. Mutual Series scored about 25 percent in annualized returns. But in the late 1980s, the spreads on bank debt began to narrow. "The mid-eighties were really unique in the bankruptcy game," Price says wistfully. "There was a real window. Inefficiency. I had no competition. That doesn't happen as much any more." So he has had to look elsewhere for the big prizes. And he has found them.

Hailing from a middle-class background on Long Island, Price took to investing at an early age. In high school, while playing football and lacrosse, he became intrigued with the stock market, and in college at the University of Oklahoma he studied finance (and the history of science). By the end of college he'd moved from negotiating purchases of clothing stock to negotiating purchases of common stock as an assistant to his father's stockbroker. The following year, 1974, he moved to Mutual Shares, the first of the three Mutual Series funds.

Today at forty, Price is a seasoned vulture and value investor sitting atop a mountain of $4.2 billion in assets under management. He owns Heine Securities, the advisory company that manages the Mutual Series's assets. Based on the rule of thumb that fund operators are worth 2 to 5 percent of assets under management, Heine Securities is worth $84 to $210 million (although the value of a money management firm is intangible and considered worth whatever someone is willing to pay at the time). At Mutual Series's headquarters in posh Short Hills, New Jersey, where the company moved from sweaty lower Broadway a few years ago, Price leads a team of twenty-five analysts and traders plus twenty-five other employees. His private office overlooking the John F. Kennedy Parkway is filled with inviting, cushiony furniture. On one wall, overpowering the room, is a near-life-size portrait of a master of the fox hunt seated stiffly on a horse, painted by Lionel Edwards in the early 1900s. The office appears untouched, as if the last person in it were the interior decorator. Price is usually found several yards away, perched on a hard-backed chair in the middle of a cluttered trading desk, ear pressed to the phone, reviewing a lineup of four computer screens. There, he immerses himself in the funds' major dealings while guiding the ten traders around him.

Medium in height, with receding black hair and a steady voice that can turn a hard edge in an instant, Price runs his office informally, operating on a personal basis with everyone. He is mercurial and can be abruptly critical, but because he is well aware of these tendencies, he makes a conscious effort to confer praise. People like his to-the-point, sometimes glib, manner. Asked at a bankruptcy conference in 1991 how he deals with trade creditors, which are a company's suppliers, Price had this to say: "Trade creditors as a class are normally small. So you pay them too much and get rid of them. It's a cost of doing business, like paying the lawyers." Enough said. Or listen to Price on golf: "It's worse than going to the dentist." (He prefers an occasional polo match and horseback riding with his wife, Bunny, and his three young children near their New Jersey estate home.)

In seventeen years of managing Mutual Series's money, Price has built a solid performance record. The three funds have scored compounded annual returns in the high teens over the long term. The result would be better but for Mutual Series's ownership of some of the bonds and nearly 13 percent of the preferred stock of R. H. Macy & Company. The funds wrote off that investment in 1990, and partly as a result they suffered losses of between 8 and 10 percent. Macy declared bankruptcy early in 1992.

Over the years, a substantial amount of the money under Price's guard has gone into the securities and other claims of bankrupt companies, and the size of these investments rises and falls according to the opportunities. How he has managed to do so well in one specialty, while investing in the vast expanse of other, healthier companies as well, is explained in part by a methodology that seeks out value at every stage of a company's life cycle. At one point, a company may be an undervalued growth stock, later it might become an acquisition target, and, for Price, become an arbitrage opportunity, or at some point it might go bankrupt and become a vulture investment. As he puts it: "You own the cheap stock, it becomes the target of a deal, you do the arbitrage, they screw up the deal, it becomes a bankruptcy, and you play that. We don't forget the companies we trade in. We try to watch companies over all parts of that cycle. We watch the acquisitions, we think about whether they're sensible, and we don't lose track." They are sensible, in general, if they have the potential to earn returns of 20 percent or more. By that measure, Storage Technology turned out to make tremendous sense. In that case, of course, Price showed how taking control of a situation can make a big difference in those numbers.

BEGINNINGS

Modern-day vulture investing has its roots in the rubble of 1929. And Price is a key link between today's activist vulture investing and the pioneering era of bankruptcy investing, for his mentor and longtime partner was Max Heine, a man who many consider the dean of bankruptcy investing in the postdepression era. In many ways, he helped set the stage for the era that would follow. With a passion for investing, Heine took advantage of the gap he saw between the price of a bankrupt company's stocks and bonds and the value of that company's assets—a gap formed by the scarcity of people treading among the corporate wounded. Over time, Heine's involvement as a broker and trader in depressed bonds of distressed companies revealed the opportunities to others. As the numbers and size of bankruptcies grew, the business of investing in them took off. That second generation went a step farther than Heine ever did, taking active roles in the reorganization of companies.

The son of a doctor, Heine emigrated to New York from Berlin in 1934 when he was in his early twenties and soon began sifting through the scrap heap of companies shattered by the Great Depression. When he was married, he and his bride were given a check that the giver specified was to go toward buying furniture. Instead, he invested it in the bonds of a busted railroad. But as a brokerage firm operator, Heine was not obsessed so much with making money as he was with the intellectual rewards of discovering value in the rough. Even-tempered, gentle in manner, he operated above the usual Wall Street frenzy in which traders test their physical limits for every point. "Wall Street is made up of a bunch of pretty greedy people," says Price. "Max wasn't that way. Wall Street's made up of a lot of arrogant people. Max had zero arrogance. He had patience. So he had a very stand-back-and-think-it-over view of companies."

In 1949, Heine and a partner launched the Mutual Shares

Fund—an open-end, no-load mutual fund—as a subsidiary of his brokerage firm. The fund was designed specifically to serve Heine's German refugee friends and their families, for whom he'd been investing for years. Now instead of shelling out huge commissions to invest a few thousand dollars here and there in individual stocks, they could buy shares in Heine's fund. He would remain fiercely loyal to these old friends into their old age, making sure that they continued to get the best, most personal service. With Heine as its broker, the fund concentrated on value investments of all kinds, including bankruptcies. His guiding principle was that of all value investors: Don't Lose Money. In bankruptcies, that meant investing in senior securities that were first in line to be paid off. Most often, too, he would wait to invest until the debtor had filed its reorganization plan in which the recoveries for bondholders were clearly defined. Even then, so few investors pursued bankruptcies that the bonds were trading at bargain prices—much lower than what they would eventually be worth when the company emerged from bankruptcy. It was one of the first forms of arbitrage, which in strict terms is buying a security in one market and selling it in another to profit from price discrepancies.

In the early 1960s, Heine led his brokerage and mutual fund operations much further into bankruptcy investing when he ran across Hans Jacobson, a towering man who had made bankrupt railroads his life. Like Heine, Jacobson was a German Jew who had fled the growing hatred in his native country. When he arrived in New York in 1939, he began working as a trader for A. G. Becker, the old-line Chicago investment bank, but the slow days of a listless stock market soon drove him to distraction. Out of sheer boredom, he enrolled in a course at the New York Institute of Finance on investing in bankrupt railroads, taught by railroad analyst Pat McGinnis. At the time, the vast majority of railroad companies were in bankruptcy: the Central Railroad of New Jersey, the Erie Railroad, Lehigh Valley Railroad, Chicago Rock Island Railroad, Missouri Pacific Railroad, Chicago & North Western Transportation Company, Western Pacific Railroad, Denver Rio Grande Railroad, the Soo Line, and the Texas & New Orleans Railroad, among others. Jacobson was hooked. As the war escalated and drew in the United States, the rail industry was coming alive.

Jacobson and other brokers stirred up investor interest in the bonds. "Most of the railroads were now making real money and would be able to do something for their defaulted bonds," says the eighty-seven-year-old Jacobson with an accent still richly flavored with German. "Then, eventually some of them started formulating plans of reorganization, and then you had some indication of what these securities conceivably could be worth."

Jacobson was actually one of the smaller investors who were then trafficking in broken trains. Trading alongside him in the 1940s and continuing on into the 1970s were some of the men who would become great names on Wall Street. Seymour (Cy) Lewis, the legendary trader and chairman at Bear, Stearns & Company, invested in bankrupt railroads and some distressed public utility companies. Charles Allen of Allen & Company and Gustave Levy, the chairman of Goldman, Sachs & Company, also made boxcar-loads of money buying the bonds of troubled utilities and bankrupt railroads—money that helped them pursue other types of businesses later on. In fact, Levy and Lewis also took the Pat McGinnis course that turned Jacobson into a railroad man.

One day in 1963, shortly after Jacobson had quit a trading job, he was walking near Wall Street when he ran into Heine, whom he had met only once before. Heine recognized him, greeting him as if they were old friends, and asked him what he was doing. Jacobson replied, "Quite frankly, I'm looking for a job." On the spot, Heine offered him a position as a trader in his brokerage shop. He became one of the Street's experts in trading bankrupt railroad bonds and someone on whom Heine relied considerably. Years later, two traders were surprised when they paid a visit to Jacobson to discuss some investments. "We were sitting in a room," says one, "and every ten minutes this other old guy would knock on the door and come in very meek and say to Jacobson, 'Hans, they're bidding thirty for the Erie Lackawanna.' Hans would say, 'Take it.' And this man would go away and come back ten minutes later with another trade. And we thought, 'Who the hell is this guy?' Lo and behold, it's Max Heine asking Jacobson what to do with the railroad bonds."

Working for Heine, Jacobson played the arbitrage game in railroads, sharing a field populated mostly by big brokerage houses like Goldman, Sachs; Bear, Stearns; and Salomon Brothers. Jacobson did not always wait around for the plan of reorganization to be filed. In one case, in the 1970s, he brokered the sale of several million dollars' worth of Erie Lackawanna bonds at about 10 cents on the dollar to a mutual fund. For a year or two, the bonds sat at that level. "They called me in one day and asked what should they do with them? Should they sell them? I said, 'If you want to sell them, I will buy them from you because I'm firmly convinced that the bonds are going to be worth several times over what I'm offering you.' " He bought them back at about the price he'd sold them for, and sold them to yet another investor. Whoever ended up with the bonds at the time of reorganization received $1100 for each Erie mortgage bond—110 cents on the dollar.

THE PENN CENTRAL

But it was the bankruptcy of the Penn Central Railroad in the 1970s that marked a turning point in the practice of bankruptcy investing. Because it was the largest bankruptcy of its time by far and offered dozens of different bond issues, the Penn Central attracted more investors than had any previous case. And because it was profitable for them, it would multiply the population of vulture investors. Heine and Jacobson would no longer be among the relative few, and the returns that they would reap would not be as easy to come by nor as plump as those they took before.

For years, the Pennsylvania Railroad had hauled coal from West Virginia to Ohio, competing almost directly with the Chesapeake & Ohio and the New York Central Railroads. To eliminate the redundancies between them, the Pennsylvania and New York Central Railroads merged in 1968. But the unions insisted on guaranteed jobs for all workers. Worse, inept management created chaos in newly merged operations, and the economy slipped into a recession, draining cash from the company. In 1970, the new Penn Central declared bankruptcy with $3.6 billion in liabilities. Under the Railroad Reorganization Act, the government merged all the railroad operations of the Penn Central and the other bankrupt Northeastern railroads into Conrail in 1976. Without a railroad, Penn Central was left as a conglomerate of real estate, natural resources, and amusement parks. Its financial structure contained multiple levels of debt—much of it secured by mortgages on property or individual tunnels or acreage—and preferred and common stock.

Over the eight years of the bankruptcy, the values in Penn Central emerged gradually. For one thing, real estate, which hit the skids in the early 1970s, began to spring back toward the middle of the decade. Also, Victor Palmieri, a maestro among turnaround managers who had taken charge of the company, added value as he managed the non-rail operating assets and sold off some. As the bankruptcy wore on, a growing horde of investors moved into the various bonds and certificates of participation—especially in the few years before the consummation of the reorganization plan.

One investor in Penn Central bonds was a young Michael Price. Heine hired Price on the very day he interviewed him for a job in 1974. By then, the Mutual Shares Fund had grown to some $5 million, and although that was hardly an astounding amount, Heine needed help handling it. Price, who had recently graduated from college, had been working at the brokerage operation owned by one of Heine's former partners, Howard Spingarn. When he told his boss that he was going to work for Heine, Spingarn said, "That's good. Max is a good man. Plus, they have this little fund." Later Heine would tell *Business Week:* "Finding Mike was like winning the lottery." With three daughters, Heine treated him like the son he never had, and they worked side by side. By 1976 Price was making all his own investment decisions, by the following year he was doing half the work on the fund, and by the mid-eighties he was president. As the managers' performance shined, the money came rolling in to Mutual Shares and later two newer funds, and all the funds ballooned in size. Heine and Price continued their extraordinarily close collaboration until Heine died in 1988 at the age of seventy-seven when he was struck by a car while on vacation in Tucson. In 1991, after a rare down year, Price told *Forbes:* "I wish I had Max around, somebody to give me perspective. There are very few people I can talk to [with his experience]. It's the difference between being a coach and being a quarterback."

Price learned all the basics from Heine and Jacobson. During his first year at the small brokerage-investment firm, he'd listen to them talk about railroad bankruptcies and took reading home to learn more. The first block of bonds he bought on his own was a Chicago & Erie issue due in 1982 and yielding 5 percent, which represented a major section of the Erie Lackawanna Railroad, one of the many Northeast railroads that like the Penn Central defaulted on their loans in the 1970s. For $5000 worth, he paid roughly thirteen cents on the dollar. Not only were they cheap but these bonds were secured for more than their principal amount, or face value (bonds usually carry a face value of $1000 apiece), by warehouses, 2500 miles of track that could be picked up and sold as scrap, locomotives, railcars, and real estate. Four years later, when the Erie Lackawanna reorganized, Price collected roughly ten times his money for the holdings. At one point, at the end of 1978, 7 percent of Mutual Shares's funds were invested in bankrupt railroad securities.

The players in the Penn Central bankruptcy included some of the preeminent junk bond investors of the 1980s and vulture investors of the late 1980s and early 1990s. Vulture investor Martin Whitman put his money down after the reorganization plan was released. He shelled out $100,000 for senior "first mortgage" bonds that were solidly secured by assets, and within a year, he made five times his money when he received the full face value of his bonds in the reorganization. Goldman, Sachs bought bonds when they were trading in the teens and wound up getting 100 cents on the dollar for them. Years later the venerable firm would storm into activist vulture investing with the $783 million Water Street Corporate Recovery Fund and would exit just as abruptly. Talton Embry, head of distressed-securities manager Magten Asset Management, was also a Penn Central player.

New York vulture Balfour Investors bought the bonds of a Penn Central subsidiary, the New York, New Haven, and Hartford Railroad, for twenty cents on the dollar and a few years later, in the late 1970s, sold them for seventy-eight cents to Saul Steinberg. Steinberg, the man who a decade earlier had staged a hostile raid on Chemical Bank and who would later take on The Walt Disney Company, among others, accumulated a 13 percent stake in the newly reorganized Penn Central. He then sold his position to the shrewd Cincinnati investor Carl Lindner, who later took control of the shell of the old railroad.

The broker for Steinberg and Lindner on these trades was a

young man named Michael Milken, who was then investing in bankrupt and near-bankrupt companies and would later achieve fame and infamy as the czar of the junk bond market. Another trader, Randall Smith, Jr., who at the time was mainly a convertible bond specialist at Bear, Stearns, later went on to found the largest brokerage firm trading exclusively in vulture investments, R. D. Smith & Company. Penn Central was his first big hit in the bankruptcy game.

FROM RAILROADS TO REAL ESTATE

The railroad bankruptcies produced the first surge of vulture investing in modern times. But in the 1970s, as Penn Central was in the thick of its restructuring, vultures had a new wave to ride: real estate investment trusts. The REITs were essentially mutual funds that held real estate instead of stocks or bonds. They had grown out of the 1960 legislation that provided exemption from corporate income tax for qualified trusts. By 1974, they had burgeoned in number to more than 200 and in assets to $20.5 billion. The collapse of the real estate market in 1974 brought down hundreds of the trusts. While many of them liquidated their assets, others continued operating by selling off assets to pay off bank lenders. The REITs were not actually in bankruptcy, but they were severely depressed.

Vulture investors romped in the REITs' bonds, some of which had sunk to as low as a tenth of their face value. Among the most enthusiastic was Deltec Securities, which had been a pioneer in such outposts as Latin American debt. The firm's president, Arthur Byrnes, visited about forty REITs. "Their assets were all over the country," he says. "If you wanted to know them well you had to go see the properties." He would buy bonds at twenty and thirty cents on the dollar and collect interest; later, in the out-of-court restructuring, he would trade them in for new bonds or stock. "The REITs were a roaring success in our case because we were right on the trend," Byrnes says. "The real estate market got better. These managements worked themselves out of it—inflation bailed them out of it—and they managed to get the banks satisfied and ended up having an ongoing company with no debt and a big tax loss carry forward and some value for the shareholders."

Some investors like Goldman, Sachs made money by investing in the bonds of REITs that were liquidating. The environment was so inflationary that between the time of the announcement of the liquidation and the completion, rising prices boosted values far beyond original expectations. As the railroad bankruptcies had, the REIT disasters drew new investors into the vulture community. Among them were Stanford Phelps; Morgens, Waterfall, Vintiadis & Co.; and Samuel Zell—a man who would later become known as "the Grave Dancer." And here, again, was Milken. He bought into REITs that were liquidating and REITs that were turning their operations around. Nervous about the firm's investment in such low-grade companies, Drexel's conservative chairman, Tubby Burnham, ordered Milken to withdraw. He complied—but only by buying out the firm's position himself with a group of colleagues. Needless to say he made a bundle. Late in the day, Carl Icahn, then an arbitrageur and soon to become a corporate raider, turned up in this market. In 1978, he gained control of a $30 million REIT by the name of Baird and Warner. He renamed it Bayswater, after his childhood home in Bayswater, Queens, and turned it into a vehicle for staging raids on corporations.

THE MODERN ERA

In the 1980s, the playing field for vultures grew for two reasons. Severe downturns in sectors of the economy such as energy and steel sent many companies reeling. Also, executives at struggling corporations began to realize that the 1978 revision of the bankruptcy code encouraged bankrupt companies to reorganize, and they took advantage of the new system. Before, managements of large companies that entered bankruptcy were obliged to hand over control to a trustee and to obtain 100 percent approval of the creditors in any given class. Under the Chapter 11 section of the new code, managements keep their jobs. And getting out of bankruptcy is made easier by requiring yes votes of only two-thirds in principal amount and half in number of those voting in any given class of claims.

More opportunities attracted even more investors. At the same time, the veterans among these discount investors began to move from passive purchaser to active vulture. They now had the experience, the contacts, and the money to influence companies and their bankruptcy reorganizations. And they also had the need, because the growing competition in their arena was hoisting the prices of busted bonds and squeezing returns on the investments. Here and there, scavenging investors began to throw their weight around in attempts to secure a bigger return for themselves. Michael Price's masterful engineering at Storage Technology was one of the most prominent examples.

Another was accomplished by Balfour Investors, a partnership of two men who had started out as securities analysts, Harry Freund and Jay Goldsmith. Balfour became the principal catalyst in the bankruptcy of Nucorp Energy Inc. Mainly a real estate concern until 1979, Nucorp responded to the sharp rise in oil prices by conducting a massive expansion into the oil and gas business as a drilling equipment supplier. Revenues gushed from $91 million in 1980 to $461 million in 1981—helped, unfortunately, by management's fraudulent accounting practices. The following year, when the price of oil sank in the oil glut, Nucorp was unable to foot the interest on $300 million in debt and filed for bankruptcy. Balfour entered the scene in 1984, buying up the most senior issue of bonds, and right away Goldsmith received a call from the Drexel, Burnham, Lambert trading desk. As he tells it: "Michael Milken's and my relationship goes back to when he started at Drexel Firestone [the precursor to Drexel, Burnham, Lambert] in Philadelphia. I knew him a long time. I always had great respect for him. So, Drexel called me and said, 'Jay you're buying the wrong piece.'" They argued that Balfour was not actually buying a senior class of bonds.

But Goldsmith and Freund stuck to their original inclinations, ultimately picking up $37 million of the bonds for $14 million, and indeed the court did consider their holdings to be senior to the other issue. The task remained of negotiating a reorganization plan with other creditors—among them, vulture investors Ronald LaBow of New York's Neuberger & Berman and Talton Embry of Magten Asset Management—and the banks, led by Continental Illinois. But relations were not always amicable. In one negotiating session with about thirty people, Goldsmith criticized the bank for its past support of the company and spoke his mind so harshly that he drove one woman to tears. She raged at Goldsmith, he recounts, "You New York j-j-j-j-j-junk peddlers!" After that, he says, "They hated me." They worked out an agreement where the banks would get paid cash and equity in the reorganized Nucorp—which was still going to be an oil and gas concern but one with a $350 million tax loss carryforward. The senior bondholders, including Balfour, would take 76 percent of the equity and the other more junior bondholders would receive 6.5 percent of the equity.

But there was a final sticking point. The bank group refused to accept Goldsmith as a director. The bank representatives called Freund at home while he was observing a Jewish holiday to tell him that his partner would not be allowed to serve on the board. As Freund recalls, "They said, 'The whole thing hinges on this, we will simply not accept him.' I said, 'Fine. Then, forget the whole deal.' " They didn't, and when the company emerged from bankruptcy in 1986, Freund and Goldsmith were chairman and vice chairman, respectively. By the end of the year they had sold their stock, in part to Sam Zell who eventually became the chairman. All told, Balfour had quadrupled its money in two and a half years.

Then, there are also cases of vultures exercising leverage in companies that were just on the verge of bankruptcy. Take Marty Whitman. In July 1986 his firm invested $25 million in Petro-Lewis Corporation, a Denver-based oil-drilling outfit that, like Nucorp, was a victim of the energy glut. Struggling to avoid bankruptcy, the company was attempting to convince its bondholders to trade their old bonds in for new ones that would lower the company's debt. Whitman, who owned about half of the two senior issues, went on the warpath against the proposed exchange by launching a formal process of soliciting bondholders to vote against the swap. Petro-Lewis countered with a lawsuit. "I think they thought I was the devil," says Whitman. That's when Freeport-McMoran came along. The New Orleans exploration company, headed by a swaggering Texan by the name of Jim Bob Moffitt, wanted control of Petro-Lewis and wanted Whitman's help in getting it. Moffitt and Whitman negotiated the sale of the two senior bond issues to Moffitt—one for eighty-six cents on the dollar and the other for eighty-eight cents, nearly twice what Whitman had paid. Whitman's $25 million had turned into $40 million in just four months.

By the end of the 1980s, the business and financial world had taken a bad fall. The stock market crash of October 1987 sounded an alarm on the economy, and the collapse of the junk bond market two years later was the final bell: The economy was screeching to a halt. On Wall Street, the mergers and acquisitions business stopped cold and silent, and the pink slips started to fly like so many stock sales slips at the New York Stock Exchange. Throughout the economy, business conditions worsened, and the lines at unemployment offices stretched around the corner. Companies that had been taken private through junk bond–financed leveraged buyouts, the magic carpets of the 1980s, plunged to the ground. The rising cash flows that the underwriters had optimistically predicted never materialized, and the companies could not service their crushing debt loads.

In 1988, corporations defaulted on nearly $4 billion of debt, according to figures compiled by Dr. Edward Altman, the Max L. Heine Professor of Finance at New York University's Stern School of Business. That was more than twice the amount of debt corporations failed to service the previous year, not including Texaco, which defaulted under unusual circumstances. In 1989, defaults doubled again to $8 billion, and in 1990 and 1991 they soared past $18 billion—although the pace slowed in the fourth quarter of 1991. The default rate reached dizzying heights in 1991: 9 percent of the junk bond universe verses a mere 1.3 percent back in 1987. In the meantime, business Chapter 11 filings surged from 18,889 in 1988 to 27,493 in 1991, according to the administrative office of U.S. Bankruptcy Courts.

Altman also has measured the breadth of the vulture market. As of May 1991, he estimated the publicly traded vulture market at $98 billion par value of distressed and defaulted securities, with a market value of about $49 billion. When including private debt, bank debt, and trade claims the market expands to about $390 billion and the market value to $247 billion.

The more successful vulture investing feats of the early and mid-1980s became models to be emulated. People who once made their living investing in takeovers and mergers or junk bonds began to drift toward the new hot market: distressed companies. Brand new vulture investors were recently administrators of leveraged-buyout funds, investment bankers, workout specialists, and junk bond investment managers. Money flowed to them and to veterans alike from both institutional and individual investors. Among the old guard, Marty Whitman raised $45 million; Balfour Investors, $60 million; R. D. Smith's Restructuring Fund, $23 million; and Sam Zell, with the help of Merrill, Lynch, an astounding $1 billion. Meanwhile, more recent entrants, including some big boys of the investment management world, boasted even more impressive sums. T. Rowe Price raised $107 million in 1988; Trust Company of the West, $97 million in 1988 and $330 million in 1990; Goldman, Sachs' Water Street Corporate Recovery Fund, $783 million in 1990; and Leon Black, the former corporate finance head at Drexel, Burnham, Lambert, snared a cool $1.3 billion from Crédit Lyonnais, the huge French banking company, and other investors.

With their pockets bulging, the vultures could exercise greater clout in individual situations. More of them could now afford to accumulate at least a third of a class of debt, enough to block a reorganization plan from going through—the same blocking position Michael Price took in Storage Technology. And more investors could accumulate enough securities to prevent an exchange offer from succeeding, as Marty Whitman set out to do in Petro-Lewis. With their new rich resources, combined with the equally important experience of working through one bankruptcy after another, the vultures have made fortunes for themselves.

In the process, they have played a growing role in the restructuring of corporate America. The mere presence of flocks of vultures in the market has fundamentally changed the dynamics of bankruptcy from one in which management has an overwhelming advantage. Some experts believe the system was designed to be neutral but ended up biased toward management only because of the inexperience of the creditors. Whatever the case, the vultures came along in numbers and learned their way around the Chapter 11 maze. "Now you've got sophisticated bondholders on the committees and trading the claims," says bankruptcy attorney Sandra Mayerson. "They can use the system to their advantage." These and other bondholders even began to band together into committees for negotiating with a company right at the point of default, before the word *bankruptcy* even came up.

They do not always use their influence for the better. As more vulture investors dive into the distressed market, there are simply more people fighting for a piece of the pie. Conflicts develop with increasing frequency between these investors, who have purchased their claims at a discount, and bondholders and lenders who have booked their claims at par. Naturally, those with a lower cost are willing to settle for much less than those who have put up 100 cents on the dollar. The conflicting agendas can prolong a case, forcing even further deterioration of the company's operations and ultimate value. Although they acknowledge the natural conflict and the potential for delay, vulture investors defend the essential role they play in the economy. Their willingness to purchase claims gives suppliers and other creditors the ability to raise cash when they need it, for example. In some cases, they bring equity capital that can make the difference between sickness and health. Most distressed-company investors say they work for not only their own gain but for the reorganization of companies into profitable enterprises, and they try to encourage a speedy reorganization. The bet these investors are making is that the sick business they're investing in will stabilize so that it can be restructured as a healthy company. If a company dies, vulture investors can lose big. Indeed, vulture investors have been great advocates of the prepackaged bankruptcy in which a company's creditors agree to a reorganization plan before the company files for bankruptcy so that the bankruptcy is then only a matter of administrative duties that can take as little as a few months to accomplish.

Bankruptcy investors resent their image in the press as rapacious speculators, and deplore the term *vulture,* which reinforces that image and has stuck as tenaciously as *junk* to high-yield bonds. One investor compares the image problem with that suffered by short sellers who borrow securities and sell them, betting that the price will fall and allow them to buy the same number of securities at a lower price and reap a profit before returning them to the lender. Because they profit on bad news, the short sellers have gained a reputation as cold opportunists. But, says this bankruptcy investor, "If I'm short on the grain market, I'm hoping the price will go down and poor people can buy food. You'd think there'd be some reward for that." There is a reward for vulture investing. And though it's not in the form of praise for good deeds done, it's rich nonetheless.

2

A Field Guide to Vultures

Vulture: *Any of various large raptorial birds that are related to the hawks, eagles, and falcons but have weaker claws and the head usually naked and that subsist chiefly or entirely on carrion.*

—*WEBSTER'S NEW COLLEGIATE DICTIONARY, 1979*

The major bankruptcy investors of our time combine scrutiny of value with strategy as they spin gold from the corporate rag pile. As they interact with the debtor, other creditors and the sundry advisers, the tension can make for high drama. When all goes right—the choice of investment, the strategy to influence the restructuring, and luck itself—the profits can be momentous. The returns, although not as outrageous as those gained via some of the most notorious leveraged buyout investments of the 1980s, are enviable at 30 percent and higher. As Sam Zell, a prominent vulture investor who has called himself "the Grave Dancer" told *Institutional Investor* in 1989: "I like what I do, and society rewards it very highly. Theoretical physicists solve problems too, but society doesn't necessarily commend their endeavors so highly." On the other hand, one bad move or unforeseen event can leave a

21

vulture investor as dry as a wanderer in the Mojave Desert. Either way, the more activist vulture investors can have a major impact on the progress—and outcome—of a troubled company's restructuring efforts.

But before showing the vultures in action, it is important to understand their world. Who are the vulture investors, and what is the framework in which they operate? Vultures are so named because they have a predilection for businesses that are dead or dying. Whether it is a company in bankruptcy, close to bankruptcy, or heading down a road toward liquidation, it has potential appeal for vultures. Such desperate situations present opportunities to buy stock, bonds, bank debt, and other obligations at frighteningly low prices and to collect handsome profits later on when the company distributes assets to creditors and shareholders in its reorganization. That explains the vulture's two other common names: discount investor and distressed security buyer.

Vultures are a rare breed of investor. They are willing to fly headlong against a blizzard of prevailing opinion, betting that a company on its knees will once again stand up and resume walking. In some cases, they bet that the company will be worth much more dead than alive, and that they will profit when it is sold off in pieces. This is the ultimate in contrarian thinking—downright risky business—and indeed vultures can lose big if a restructuring fails. Even with successful turnarounds, vultures can go away from the table still hungry. And when restructurings drag on longer than expected, as they often do, a vulture's initial returns can disappear.

In recent years, the pickings have diminished and the risks have increased with the influx of new scavengers and with the erosion of asset values. But the more creative and daring vultures continue to find ways to dig up riches. These activist vultures don't just buy stocks and bonds and then wait for the check to arrive in the mail. They help sculpt the restructuring programs that determine exactly how creditors and shareholders will be paid and, ultimately, how a destitute company will be financed in its next life. With the promise of greater profits, more vultures who were once passive have taken activist roles, like so many Clark Kents shedding their business suits for a Superman's cape. But to influence the direction of a restructuring, the activists take on much greater risk than the passive vultures. They might maneuver themselves onto a creditors' committee or build a stockpile of bonds, in both cases making heavier-than-usual bets on a company.

To handle these risks, the activist vulture's gambles are highly calculated, based on painstaking research and an encyclopedic knowledge of the bankruptcy code and the bulky system that has grown up around it. And because results can be long in coming, vultures must exhibit swami-like patience throughout the winding processes of restructuring and bankruptcy. But these measures hardly ensure success. Analysis can be a sophisticated guessing game, because the valuation of assets is often largely subjective and can fluctuate madly, reasons that most investors stay away from vulturing. Besides, the most accurate valuation analysis and all the waiting in the world are rendered meaningless if an investor jumps in too early at too high a price—that is, if he or she wasn't patient enough to begin with.

Seasoned vultures tend to have good instincts for valuation and timing. From early 1988 through late summer of the following year, Balfour Investors bought very little. Says Balfour partner Harry Freund: "Prices had gone up, everybody was rushing into our area, and the values that we were used to were not evident. Everything was just flooded with money, and ignorant money. Summer of 1989 there was an implosion—a quiet thing, in which a lot of people in our industry lost a great deal of money, very fast, and where a lot of bonds that were in the forties or fifties found their way into the twenties or the teens in a matter of months, weeks in some cases. Big money was lost, and perceptions changed in our business. Southmark. Southland. Revco. Resorts. Western Union. People bought at levels that seemed to us to be absurd. We just stopped because there was nothing to buy. We're old dogs in this business, so we know when to stop. Not to act in our business is probably a more valuable talent than any other."

Activist vulture investors are the corporate raiders of the nineties. Much like the 1980s raiders, who bought up loads of stock and waged battles for control or greenmail payments, vultures are scrappy characters, always ready for a fight and unrelenting in the worst altercations. Bluntness is a characteristic they tend to share as well. Many are dismissive and often downright insulting toward those who disagree with their notions of value, whether they be managements of bankrupt corporations understating the value of their companies, junk bond investors in 1980s leveraged buyouts (LBOs) who failed to realize their overconfidence until it was too late, or LBO artists who through their mistakes created lucrative vulturing opportunities. As Talton Embry, a vulture veteran based in New York, said of the latter in a rather tongue-in-cheek speech in 1989:

Large amounts of money are no longer available to these assholes. They are still, however, in charge of the businesses they bought and are now behaving like complete shitheads. As a result, my business is "scrapping with shitheads."

And like the corporate raiders, activist vultures are fiercely independent. In many instances vulture investors have labored for years in cramped offices to cultivate their own businesses, despite the criticism that they are making a living off the misfortunes of others. Several of those who have worked within the confines of a large firm have broken off to do their own thing. Randy Smith, the former head of bankruptcy trading at Bear, Stearns, single-handedly built his own formidable bankruptcy trading firm. Others have fashioned highly profitable, self-contained vulture departments at large firms such as Oppenheimer and Fidelity.

Theirs is a tight community, not unlike the ring of corporate raiders, junk bond investors, lawyers, and investment bankers that revolved around Michael Milken and Drexel, Burnham, Lambert—although much smaller and not as interdependent. (Indeed, the junk-bond community that backed the raiders was too close for its own good. Several major players including Milken engaged in insider trading and other illegal activities.) Vulture investors know many of their peers because they have worked alongside or against them, or both, and because they include among their ranks specialty brokers who deal with the lot of them. And although vultures often come into conflict with each other, they tend to respect one another as boxers admire their opponents in the ring. They even have their own conference of sorts in New York—snidely dubbed the Creditors' Ball in parody of the fabled Predators' Ball that Michael Milken hosted in Beverly Hills. More a light-hearted mid-summer picnic than a gala deal-making event, it is hosted by Robert Miller, a bankruptcy lawyer who represented creditors in the reorganizations of Donald Trump's Taj Mahal casino, A. H. Robins, and Continental Airlines. Since 1986, investors, attorneys, and investment bankers have gathered annually at Miller's vacation home in the Hamptons on Long Island garbed in shorts, T-shirts, and sneakers to play tennis, guzzle beer, and sip summer cocktails. The first year he distributed T-shirts that read, "Your loss is our gain."

Although they have much in common, the activist vultures are actually a flock of many differing breeds distinguished in several ways. There are the old hands—not necessarily older people—who have been practising this art since Penn Central days and were the pioneer activists. Most of them are tough birds who made it without the support of a wealthy institution, like Embry who built a vulture and junk bond investment management firm to $550 million in assets under management. Or Ben Walsh, an elderly career vulture investing his own money, who flits from creditors' committee to creditors' committee, playing the gadfly in such cases as the Southland Corporation bankruptcy.

And then there's that new generation of vultures that has begun filling the skies. Some are tied to big money—Fidelity Investments and T. Rowe Price in Baltimore and pension manager Trust Company of the West in Los Angeles. Some have switched identities from junk bond aficionados to vultures. Take Leon Black, who for years was a leader in the junk bond field when he headed the corporate finance department at Drexel, Burnham, Lambert in the heyday of Michael Milken. But by mid-1991, he became the most feared of vulture investors, using his mountains of cash to take monstrous stakes in the debt of such distressed companies as Harcourt Brace Jovanovich and Gillett Holdings and later, demanding top dollar in return. His style quickly earned him the nickname "the Black Prince." One new-generation vulture, Carl Icahn, was one of those corporate raiders of the 1980s who turned to distressed companies when the mergers and acquisitions market dried up. He has since been a driving force in the bankruptcies of Texaco, Southland, and Trump Taj Mahal and in the restructuring of Western Union.

Perhaps the easiest way to understand the vultures is to type them by what they want. By that measure there are two major groups: Migratory Birds and Nest Builders. Migratory Birds, also known as speculators and traders, are the traditional type of vultures who dart in and out of securities looking for a good trade. Although they may be involved with a company for several years, as the restructuring progresses, their investment stands as only a bet that a security bought now will pay off at a much higher price when the company is restructured. When the company is fixed, these investors usually have little more to do with it; for what was once carrion has again become a living being that no longer holds their interest. Although most vulture investors fall into this category, activists are plentiful and range from the big institutions like Fidelity and T. Rowe Price to smaller money managers like James Bennett, who started a fund at R. D. Smith and later split it off, to individual investors like Stanford Phelps and Ben Walsh.

Nest Builders, by contrast, throw their fate in with a company for the long term, staying with it after it has climbed out of the depths. They acquire either the whole company or a sizable chunk of debt that later, in a reorganization, will be exchanged for a big piece of the new stock. These vultures then run the company themselves or bring in experienced management. As restructuring proceeds, they negotiate a plan of reorganization that casts them in the leading role. With their $1 billion-plus bankroll, Zell and his partner, David Schulte, are currently the most well endowed of this predator class. Others range from former Drexel, Burnham workouts co-chief Paul Levy to leveraged buyout specialists Hicks, Muse & Company. Some migratory types, too, become Nest Builders when they see something they like. Ronald LaBow, a longtime speculator with the high-class New York investment firm Neuberger & Berman, used a strategy of buying out much of the senior bank class of debt to acquire Wheeling-Pittsburgh Steel Corporation in 1991.

The activist vulture investors can also be identified by the strategies they employ to achieve their goals. There is, for instance, the Committee Man, whose modus operandi is to get on the creditors' committee in a distressed situation, either before or after a bankruptcy filing. Then there's the Heavyweight, who buys a heap of bonds and piles them onto his plate. Both take advantage of the 1978 Bankruptcy Reform Act, which requires that corporate managements work out a mutually agreeable reorganization plan with creditors that determines how much they will recover of their claims. That means bargaining both with the creditors' committee and with Heavyweight individual creditors who choose not to be on the committee. It's what the bankruptcy code calls a "consensual plan," and as Marty Whitman observes, it is when "people go to meetings, formulate a plan and figure out who's going to be a screwer and who's going to be a screwee. And guess who the people at the table would like to make the screwee? The people who are not at the table." In recent years, the consensual plan process has extended informally to wobbly companies that have not yet had to resort to bankruptcy. In trying to hammer out workable refinancing arrangements and avoid bankruptcy, managements consult with big bondholders as well as steering committees, which have been quickly organized by bondholders. Their professional fees and expenses are paid for by the troubled company.

Certainly, the Committee Man takes the easiest and cheapest route to secure influence in a reorganization. Shortly after a debtor files for a Chapter 11 reorganization, the regional U.S. Trustee in charge of administrative matters names the members of the committee, or committees, that will represent creditors. Experienced vulture investors, major creditors, and bit players alike often apply to serve and often are chosen. In his committee seat, a vulture has the opportunity to help formulate and later argue for the plan that will be to his greatest advantage. In the late 1980s, when LTV Corporation had already been in bankruptcy for a few years and with nary a glimmer at the end of the tunnel, vulture organizations took advantage of the frustration among creditors by swooping in and buying out most of the bank creditors of the aerospace division at steep discounts. When in 1991 they perceived that the attorney for bank-level creditors was not being responsive to their needs, they used their clout to get their own creditors' committee.

There's one drawback. Once they are on the panel, vultures are privy to inside information in the case and usually have to sign away their right to trade in the securities of the debtor. For some it poses a serious dilemma, because they want to show their clients that they are taking advantage of the up and down movements in securities prices. In 1990, just after Federated Department Stores and Allied Stores Corporation filed for bankruptcy, vulture money manager Embry was appointed to the Allied Stores unsecured creditors' committee. But after just one month, before he received any confidential information, he decided to resign so that he could buy more bonds. The chairman of that committee, a representative of Fidelity Investments, however, successfully argued for the right to stay on and set up a barrier, or Chinese Wall, separating committee work from trading activities.

But those who are well traveled in bankruptcy circles might know a committee member well enough to exert influence from afar. They can make their views known without learning inside information in the process. Says James Rubin, a new-era vulture investor with Sass, Lamle, Rubin & Co. in New York, "I was talking to an investment banker in a deal we're involved in where he's an insider and I'm not. I said at the end of the conversation, 'I have no interest in hearing inside information. This is my theory on how a deal should work out on this thing.' And he gave me reasons why my idea was good, why it was bad, and we had a very theoretical conversation. Now he can go back to his fellow insiders and say, 'I was talking to Jim Rubin and he had this idea and I think it's pretty good.' And presto, you'll see it show up in the deal. The longer I've been involved in this business the less necessary it's been for me to serve on committees to be influential."

The Heavyweights take the more macho approach of cutting and carrying big slabs of securities. They don't need to bother with committees, because their size requires that they be dealt with one on one. Often Heavyweights use their big holdings to block an exchange offer or reorganization plan that they don't like. Constructing a blocking position in bankruptcy can be difficult. Approval of a plan requires a vote of a majority of holders carrying two-thirds of the debt of those voting in each class of claims; so an ounce over a third is what's needed to do the job. Or a Heavyweight can just threaten to block, which can be equally effective.

The blocking strategy has been employed time and again since Price and others used it with great reward in the mid-1980s.

To some vultures, these blocking tactics have lengthened the bankruptcy process. "All it takes is a couple of intransigent people to basically block everything, and as this community has gotten enlarged so have the chances of having an intransigent involved," remarks John Gordon, the president of junk bond investor Deltec Securities in New York. In his experience, the bankruptcy process has stretched out to such a degree that it is no longer worthwhile for an investor to do his homework early so he can buy in early. "In the old days of bankruptcy investing the early bird got the worm," he says. "But I would postulate that now it's the late bird that gets the worm, because things take longer and longer than people expect. The frustration levels build up so that securities have a tendency to keep going down right until the very end. And then they suddenly spike back up." Deltec has changed its investment timing accordingly. When it spots a tempting investment, it will wait until well into the revamping process to put its money in. "It actually makes life a little bit easier, because before you had to do all this anticipatory work so that when the announcement came you were there with your basket ready to scoop up the securities. Now, a filing is just sort of like a wake-up call. You're on notice to look at it in the next six to nine months."

Most blocking creditors are from the migratory family of vultures. Marty Whitman is one of the more notorious of these. If he cannot for some reason build the required position in the bonds, he will link arms with other investors whose holdings can make up the difference, as he did with the Public Service Company of New Hampshire. In the Allied Stores bankruptcy, Talton Embry may have been off the committee, but he ended up buying $240 million worth of the 11.5 percent bonds, 34 percent of that class. The plan, therefore, would not pass unless and until he voted for it.

Nest Builders can also be blocking creditors. In 1990, a pair of cocky young ex-investment bankers who go by the name Japonica Partners took over Allegheny International Corporation, the maker of Sunbeam and Oster housewares, largely by taking blocking positions in both senior and junior debt. But in most instances, the Nest Builders are either Heavyweights who work cooperatively with company management or bidders for the equity who work out a deal with the management to acquire the company. The bidders play a low-risk game. Zell and Schulte, for instance, keep their wallets in their pockets until they have worked out a sure deal. Says Schulte, "We are the little old lady in tennis shoes. Sam and I are the most pale, weak-kneed, timid of the whole bunch." They will rarely buy any securities unless they can be assured that they will have a controlling position in the company. "Our way of thinking is, the only way to participate is in the deal," says Schulte, that is, as one of those negotiating and contributing capital to the restructuring. "Fresh cash used to buy an existing security or claim does not change the financial condition of the issuer one iota. Our program is to invest in deals that create cash [for the company] to make the deal happen. If the deal doesn't happen, we don't write the check."

To see all of this in action, take the hypothetical case of Cantkeepup, Inc., a maker of second-class light bulbs that gets into trouble when its chief rival, the Light Up The World Company, introduces a new long-lasting fluorescent bulb. Suffering from a severe cash shortage, Cantkeepup has defaulted on its bond interest payments and appears to be slouching toward bankruptcy. The vultures then begin circling.

Dean O. Treyding, a Migratory Bird, and I. C. Greene, a Nest Builder looking for a perch to build a home, start at the same point, by valuing the company and its debt. The task of analyzing a corporation takes on an added dimension of complexity when that company is distressed. For one thing, this being a company in trouble, its financial statements may not have "good numbers" representing true value. Good numbers on assets, liabilities, and earnings have to be dug out through assiduous analysis, and those numbers may change if the company continues to deteriorate.

Then there are the questions presented by the restructuring process itself. Will the reorganization be resolved out of court as a swap of old debt for new debt or in court as a Chapter 11 bankruptcy? What kinds of disputes might arise among creditors and between creditors and the company? How long will the restructuring take? Bankruptcy with its requirements for creditors' commit-

tees, disclosure statements and reorganization plans and with all
the negotiating that must go on between all the parties, requires a
much longer period to resolve than an out-of-court debt exchange.
What can make the purgatory even longer is the bias inherent in
Chapter 11 toward the debtor. Under the bankruptcy code, the
debtor has a three-month "exclusivity period" in which it is the
only party permitted to file a reorganization plan with the court.
Typically, however, the court extends this term on request more
than once and often several times.

If the issues aren't too complex, the company could be a candidate for a prepackaged bankruptcy, also known as a prepack, a
controlled bankruptcy, or an 1126b, after the section of the bankruptcy code that allows it. In a prepack, a majority of bondholders
holding two-thirds of the voting claims approve a plan *before* a
company files for bankruptcy. By filing Chapter 11 with a preapproved plan, the company is in limbo for a much shorter period—
as little as a few months. But a regular, uncontrolled, bankruptcy
can take three years or longer as all the parties work to reach
consensus on a reorganization plan that determines how the assets
will be divided up and in what form, which in turn sets the new
capital structure. Then the plan must receive the same percentage
approval as above.

After their extensive valuations, our two vultures, Treyding
and Greene, both conclude Cantkeepup, Inc., is worth a throw of
the dice at the right price. They scan the different classes of claims
and stock; there is bank debt secured by assets of the company,
unsecured bond debt, unsecured trade claims, and stock. Each has
a price and each a different degree of safety. Given the value of the
company and the probable convolutions of the restructuring, Treyding and Greene ask what each of these classes will receive in the
end in compensation for their claims. There is a pecking order that
determines which classes of claims are paid off first in the event of
a bankruptcy or liquidation. In the simplest terms: bank loans
backed by corporate assets are first, then unsecured senior debt,
junior debt, and stock, or equity. Under Chapter 11's so-called rule
of absolute priority, a category of claims is allowed to receive
payment only after the levels above it have received 100 percent of
their face value. In reality, though, the rules are not so clear-cut.

Most of the time, junior and equity levels have enough leverage—often by delaying the workout process by such means as a lawsuit—to force the higher-ups to negotiate and cut them in on a deal.

Treyding, the Migratory vulture, chooses to buy bank debt because it is senior and secured—it has collateral backing its face value. In a bankruptcy, he believes it is either "unimpaired," meaning that it will remain in place and be paid off, or it will be swapped for equity, debt, and/or cash equal to full value plus interest. The bank debt, according to Treyding's research, is a "lay-up," a "slam dunk, riskless proposition," in the vultures' vernacular. In other words, he thinks he can get it at very cheap prices compared with what he will collect in the end. Treyding picks up his phone and calls each bank with an offer, and those banks suffering from a sickness called "lender fatigue"—caused by frustration with an unreliable debtor or by negotiating gridlock—take the price offered and sell out.

For Greene, the play is in the unsecured bonds and trade claims. His calculations of the company's full value indicate that if there were to be a bankruptcy, the bank debt would be paid off in full, including interest, but that payment will use up almost all of the available value. To pay the unsecured classes—suppliers, subcontractors, and bondholders—their recoveries, the company would then have to hand over the bulk of new stock it will reissue after reorganizing; the result, those claims holders would have control of the newly revamped enterprise. With the disastrous scaling down of the company's value, Greene figures, the old equity is what is often called "hopelessly under water." He then goes after a "piece" of debt here and a piece there and within several months owns nearly two-thirds of the unsecured class of debt—more than enough bonds to be a blocking creditor either in the case of an exchange offer or a bankruptcy reorganization proposal.

Soon, Cantkeepup's management does propose an exchange-offer refinancing, in which the bank creditors would be "taken out," or paid in cash the face value of their loans plus interest; the unsecured class would get a "haircut," recovering only some of the money owed them in the form of stock and bonds; and the stockholders would retain a majority of the equity. For the deal to go through, the company says that 85 percent of each group must vote in favor. The company's management visits some of the leading bondholders and shareholders to sell the deal, emphasizing that if they don't tender, or exchange their securities for the profferred deal, bankruptcy will be inevitable. Migratory Treyding, happy to cash out, decides to trade in his bank debt. Nester Greene, who by now has bought up truckloads of bonds with the dream of redeeming them for a controlling stake in the equity when the company is restructured, does not tender them, because the plan being offered does not give him enough stock. The company extends the deadline a few times in the hope that holdouts like Greene will come around. But they don't. In fact, three bondholders get together and file with the court to put the company into an involuntary Chapter 11— forcing it into bankruptcy—because the company has been in default now for more than the month-long grace period that is allowed. The company gives up and files voluntarily for Chapter 11 bankruptcy.

Now, Cantkeepup has a three-month exclusivity period during which its management is allowed to develop and propose a reorganization plan. Bank creditors hire a law firm to represent them in negotiations with the company over the reorganization plan—also called "the distribution" or "the deal" or "whacking up the pie." Meanwhile, the administrator of the bankruptcy, the U.S. Trustee, appoints a committee to represent the unsecured creditors, which in turn also hires a law firm, an investment bank, and an accounting adviser. Greene, with his 65 percent of the unsecured bonds, decides not to join the committee but instead to negotiate with the company management and the committee on his own. To reserve his seat at the table, he "becomes restricted," officially barring himself from trading, because of his proximity to inside information. Negotiations proceed slowly. After three months, the company applies for an extension to its exclusivity period and is granted one, and over the course of a year it obtains more extensions.

Finally, the company releases the first draft of a reorganization plan that has been endorsed by the bank creditors, including Treyding, and the unsecured creditors' committee. According to the plan, the company's value remains much less than that envisioned by Greene, and in fact, it is less than what the company estimated before the bankruptcy, in part because of a deterioration of the business while it has been in Chapter 11. Migratory Bird Treyding is satisfied and wants to get his recovery and run because "the meter is running." In other words, the longer he waits for his recovery, the less will be the annual return on his investment.

Greene, the Nester, continues to believe that the values are greater. He and his attorneys refuse to sign onto the proposed reorganization plan. Finally, he agrees to invest a wad of new capital in the company in return for a majority stake in the new equity. The company "emerges." Treyding receives his principle and interest for a healthy 30 percent return on his investment after only two years in bankruptcy. Greene now holds a majority of the stock and brings in new management, who diversifies the business into sculptural light fixtures. Sales take off and the stock flies with it, just as Greene had predicted when he first invested. Both Treyding and Greene, in the idiom of the vulture investor, have just hit the ball out of the park.

WAR STORIES

WAR STORIES

3

Power Play

*The rule is, jam to-morrow and jam yesterday—but
never jam to-day.*

—*THROUGH THE LOOKING GLASS*

In the chain of vacation spots running up and down the New
England shore, Seabrook did not in any way stand out. It was a
sleepy beach resort town on the coastline of New Hampshire a few
miles north of the Massachusetts border. But all that changed in
the 1970s. Seabrook was no longer just another place; it was a
nuclear reactor. And it was not just any nuclear reactor; it was the
one that became the rallying point of the antinuclear movement.

   The groundbreaking took place on a breezy July morning in
1976, on a barren rocky outcrop that extended into marshland.
Among the seventy-five or so business and government officials
was Robert Harrison, a vice president of the Public Service Company of New Hampshire (PSNH), which would have a 50 percent
stake in the reactor, sharing ownership with ten other New England utilities. As the event got underway, the bespectacled Harri-

son, then in his midforties, glanced at a small group of protesters standing behind a rope barrier a few hundred yards away and thought that they looked like "petulant schoolchildren." Holding their picket signs aloft, the small contingent from the Clamshell Alliance looked on quietly as Governor Meldrim Thompson sank a spade into the earth and threw the soil to the side and others followed suit. Afterward, as the attendees lunched at the nearby Exeter Inn, a young woman protester burst into the room and gave out a yell that Harrison could not quite make out. Hotel employees hustled her back outside. A commotion rumbled through the room, then quieted down. It appeared to Harrison, who would become PSNH president in 1980 and chief executive officer in 1983, that the antinuclear movement was something the utility could live with—just petulant schoolchildren—while the Seabrook plant was being built.

But he was wrong. The protests expanded as time elapsed and succeeded in delaying Seabrook's opening for a few years, and that delay in turn put Harrison's company into bankruptcy.

What made the delay so devastating was a law passed by state legislators in 1979, three years after that ground-breaking ceremony. In retrospect, says Harrison, who had been with the company since graduating from college in 1957, the legislation "was the death knell for Public Service." All "construction-work-in-progress" costs would now be excluded in the determination of electricity rates. Seabrook was already three years in the making and several years from completion, but PSNH could no longer charge the public for its construction. PSNH reacted by slimming down its stake in the new plant from 50 to 36 percent, still the largest of any of Seabrook's utility members.

Unable to raise rates sufficiently to finance the Seabrook project from 1979 on, PSNH borrowed—and borrowed and borrowed. In 1984, the utility found itself hanging from the edge of a cliff after its bank lending group, stunned by new estimates of Seabrook's cost, pulled away its support. The company survived by suspending dividends on its common and preferred stock, and issuing $840 million in new bonds through Merrill, Lynch. The nuclear facility was finally completed in 1986; construction costs had blown past the original estimate of $2 billion for two units to a final $5 billion for only one unit. The following year, PSNH's investment in the new plant hit $2 billion, representing 70 percent of the utility's total assets. But the refusal of neighboring Massachusetts towns to come up with contingency plans for an evacuation hamstrung efforts to get the reactor licensed and operating. Some towns went so far as to dismantle emergency sirens to block the startup. Citing the deadly 1986 Chernobyl accident, Massachusetts governor and then-presidential candidate, Michael Dukakis, did his best to prevent Seabrook from being licensed by refusing to authorize the design and testing of plans for evacuating areas in his state that might be contaminated in a nuclear accident.

By 1987, the utility was carrying nearly $1.7 billion in debt and was earning only $130 million before taxes. Another expedition to Wall Street was in store. In the spring, Drexel, Burnham, Lambert launched a private placement of increasing-rate, unsecured notes to raise $150 million of capital in a plan to keep PSNH humming and help bring the seemingly cursed Seabrook nuclear plant on line.

THE NUTTY PROFESSOR

"Just not viable." That was Marty Whitman's terse assessment of the plan. "It was a ridiculous attempt by Drexel to stave off the inevitable." The $150 million, says the veteran vulture in his gritty voice, was "like spitting in the ocean." His conclusion was unforgiving: Public Service Company of New Hampshire was living posthumously. It had to go bankrupt. When Drexel, Burnham's private placement memo landed on his desk, it was like a green light flashing "Go invest."

Whitman is an affable man in his late sixties with fly-away white hair and deep lines in his face. Although he made his way through undergraduate and graduate schools, including a year at Princeton University, and taught for years as a visiting professor of investing at Yale University's School of Organization and Management, Whitman sounds more like a subway conductor than an Ivy League academic. He has retained the unpolished dialect of his Bronx upbringing, substituting *dese* for "these" and *mattirrity* for "maturity." This is not a man who conforms to social convention even for the sake of appearance; Whitman is more than anything, himself. He was the middle child of three children, the only son to Polish immigrant parents who made their living, like so many transplanted Eastern European Jews, in the Seventh Avenue garment district. Together, they ran a company that sold felt bodies to the makers of ladies' hats. In high school, Whitman earned average grades and showed little interest in a career, and when he graduated in 1942, he joined the navy to go to war. During his training in Nebraska, he met the woman he would later marry after a three-year tour of duty overseas serving as a pharmacist's mate—or as he elegantly phrases it, a "pecker checker." His life seemed to have been laid out like a blueprint before him. Once married, he began business classes at the University of Nebraska with the goal of working in the department store owned by his father-in-law. Within six months he realized that all of it—the department store, the school, the location, and the bride—were wrong. He dropped all of them and headed back to New York.

Rejected by top-notch colleges because of a less-than-distinguished high school record, Whitman settled for what he calls "emergency college," the two-year New York State Community College for Veterans in upstate New York (now Sampson College). But in 1948, after one term, he transferred to Syracuse University, and he surprised even himself with his industriousness. "I was on track and I was getting all A's," he shrugs. "I guess I grew up a little." He graduated magna cum laude with a B.S. degree in business and got accepted to Princeton University's economics graduate program, aiming for a career in academia. But after a frustrating year struggling with Princeton's taxing math requirements, he decided to put off finishing graduate school and go to work. Several years later he completed a master's degree in economics through night classes at the New School for Social Research in Manhattan. For a thesis he bore into the heart of the securities business, examining the underpinnings of the free market itself, or as he put it, "the enormous police state that had to be erected in order to try to get this artificial system to work." He described the role that each member of the network—the stock exchange, the Securities and Exchange Commission (SEC), and the securities dealers—plays in bringing about a free market. Such intellectual pursuits are vintage Whitman, who loves to analyze broad issues and extrapolate on the uses of concepts like the pre-packaged bankruptcy. He explains his ideas with fervor, and some-times, friends say, using his own brand of shortspeak. A friend once joked that when Whitman speaks he seems to start in the middle of the paragraph, and when he's spoken "it's like interpret-ing the Delphic oracle."

On the road to his eventual pursuit of bankruptcy investing, Whitman lurched from one corner of the securities business to another. Research was his first career, which he started at Shear-son, Hamill & Company, the firm that eventually became Shearson Lehman Brothers. He ticks off his specialties: "I was a coal analyst, an auto analyst, a steel analyst, a cement analyst." But to him, securities research was only skin deep, failing to probe into a company's marrow. "I used to go to analysts' lunches, and these corporate executives would get up and try to explain to all these analysts what their business was really about. And then there were questions. But all the analysts wanted to know was what the next quarter's earnings were and what pays the dividend." Whitman transferred to the underwriting desk, where he analyzed and wrote the prospectuses for new issues. "Dullsville," he concluded. "Not a lot of money." Then it was back to research, this time for William Rosenwald, the son of Sears, Roebuck founder Julius Rosenwald, who managed a substantial chunk of the family fortune and in-vested occasionally in railroads gone bust. Now on the investing side, Whitman felt closer to a living, breathing corporation than ever before. Rosenwald's operation not only handled portfolios of marketable securities but had a separate group of companies it controlled, like today's merchant banking boutiques. Among the prized holdings were Continental Diamond Fibre, the Banner Steamship cruise line, and Western Union International.

He had his closest personal brush with a distressed company as an investment banker. In 1967, he joined the corporate finance department at Blair & Company, a New York brokerage firm owned by the financier Jay Pritzker and his family. But by the middle of the following year, Whitman says, "I figured these guys had to go down the tubes. They weren't making much money. It was a time of a new-issue boom, and they weren't originating any new issues. It was a grossly inefficient, disorganized outfit, and every time I went to a board meeting I could never understand what they were talking about. I didn't want to leave my money at Blair." A few years later the firm closed its doors. But by then Whitman was running his own advisory firm specializing in both stockholder litigation and bankruptcy, two niches he chose because they were not being heavily exploited by the big investment houses. Among those hiring him for bankruptcy advice in the mid-1970s were the first mortgage bondholders in the Penn Central bankruptcy. He began investing his own and others' money in distressed and bankrupt companies while also running a brokerage and advisory firm, M. J. Whitman. He started out with about $30,000 of capital. Within a dozen or so years his net worth flew past $20 million and kept on flying upward.

For a multimillionaire, Whitman is surprisingly spartan. He drives a seven-year-old cherry red Honda Prelude (license plate: Chaptr11) and lives in a Central Park West apartment decorated, as his partner Kirk Rhein has described it, "like the apartment of an untenured professor." The briefcase he carries, in the words of his other partner, Jim Heffernan, "looks like it's covered with some kind of carpet." On a regular workday Whitman might dress in olive green cuffed corduroys and a tweed jacket that's seen better days. In recent years he's taken to wearing sneakers to work, even with a suit, although around the office he'll often wander around in his socks. At one meeting with representatives of the Columbia University endowment Whitman started out by removing his shoes, revealing huge holes in his socks. "And I'm not talking just a little hole he overlooked when he was putting them on in the morning," Heffernan says. "There was more hole than sock!"

THE WHITMAN WAY

His strategy has many fewer holes in it. When he invests in a rotting company, Whitman buys the most senior security qualified to vote if the company were to file for bankruptcy. He does not want debt that in a bankruptcy reorganization will be "reinstated," or left untouched in the reorganization. Holders of reinstated debt do not qualify to vote on the reorganization plan or participate in the negotiations that shape it. By contrast, any class of debt that will be exchanged for cash and/or new securities—of still-uncertain value—is considered "impaired" and holders do participate in the process. Whitman can reap more attractive returns by buying into what he believes will be an impaired class—that sells at a lower price because of the associated risks—and then actively influencing the restructuring of the company. In other words, in making an investment he finds the greatest degree of safety that holds a position of influence.

But before getting out his checkbook, Whitman sketches a picture of what would happen to the value of his senior holding if there were to be a default and then a bankruptcy filing. "Ninety-eight percent of the people in credit analysis only do it to gauge the prospect that there may or may not be a money default. And the stuff I do is to assume there will be a money default and determine how I will come out. Worst-case analysis." If Whitman determines that, yes, a default is on the horizon and that he as the owner of a senior issue would come out well in that case, he dives right in. He may even go for the senior issue of a company that is already in bankruptcy if the price is reasonable. He prefers to acquire a minimum of a third of the securities in a senior class, which will allow him to block a reorganization plan that doesn't appeal to him.

Whitman didn't always have the resources to pursue this strategy. But in 1985, the year after taking over a mutual fund, Equity Strategies, from Security Pacific Bank, he launched his activist investing career. He began with an investment in the senior bonds of Mission Insurance Company, which subsequently went bankrupt in one of the largest insolvencies of a property/casualty insurer. Most of the details on Mission were handled by the two lawyers who would later become his partners. "One of Marty's shortcomings is that he starts the deal and knows where he wants to end up, but he has no patience for the process," says one of them, Jim Heffernan. "That's where Kirk [Rhein] and I come in." During the five years of Mission's bankruptcy, Whitman orchestrated a number of other major investments including Petro-Lewis and PSNH.

Investing in troubled companies is more than a money-making exercise for Whitman. He also views it as an opportunity to play a meaningful role in society—by providing fresh capital or reorganizing corporations' financial structures to make them strong again. But he insists that he always works with an eye toward what impact the restructuring will have on the general public. Public policy issues have always fascinated him, although his bluntness can get in his way. When, for example, the proportions of the savings and loan crisis became apparent to the world at large, Whitman conceived a plan to reorganize the industry and flew down to Washington to discuss it in person with William Seidman, the director of the Federal Deposit Insurance Corporation. When Seidman dismissed Whitman's ideas, saying they would violate the Glass-Steagall Act, Whitman felt insulted and bit back: "So what? It's a lousy law. Get rid of it."

THE ROAD TO NEW HAMPSHIRE

In PSNH, Whitman says his concern for the public interest greatly influenced his whole approach. His knowledge of the utility industry is extensive. In 1967 he testified before the Senate as a rate regulation expert during antitrust hearings targeting AT&T. In 1979, he had an opportunity to learn more about utility finance when he was retained as financial adviser to the Kemeny Commission, the group named by President Jimmy Carter (and headed by Dartmouth President John Kemeny) to investigate the near-meltdown at the Three Mile Island nuclear reactor. His assignment was essentially to answer a charge made by consumer activist Ralph Nader that the company had rushed the opening of the power plant in 1978 to generate tax savings and raise rates that would ease a critical working capital shortage. In an eighty-one-page report that compared all the electric utilities operating in Pennsylvania and New Jersey, Whitman determined that the allegations were groundless.

A few years later, as he witnessed the deterioration of two utility companies with idle nuclear power plants—PSNH and Michigan-based Consumers Power, saddled with the comatose Midland 2 reactor—Whitman considered the ramifications of bankruptcy for operations, investors, and ratepayers. No utility had filed for bankruptcy in fifty years and none had ever filed since Chapter 11 was created in a revision of the bankruptcy code in 1978. In a 1985 paper, he refuted the conclusions of three financial and law firms that a bankruptcy filing would force a utility to shut down, cutting off a major source of tax revenues to the state, reducing investment income to state pension funds, raising unemployment, and harpooning local business confidence. "As far as we can tell," Whitman wrote with typical candor, "most people in the financial community, as well as in the electric utility industry, have little or no idea of what filing for bankruptcy reorganization will actually mean." In reality, he concluded, a bankrupt utility would keep pumping electricity and at lower operating and capital costs than before filing the petition for bankruptcy. Creditors would be more willing to lend to a company that is working out its problems in bankruptcy than one that is in a state of greater uncertainty (especially because postpetition lenders get a first call on assets), and vendors would feel likewise. As for investors, Whitman maintained that secured lenders and probably others would end up recovering the full face value of their holdings. Only the stockholders, he concluded, would be big losers. And because a utility has relatively predictable earning power and relatively predictable claims, Whitman added, its life in bankruptcy could be relatively brief.

Newly confident, Whitman put his money down. He bought discounted mortgage bonds of both Consumers Power and PSNH, positive that even in case of bankruptcy he would profit. Both utilities succeeded in resolving their difficulties without resorting to bankruptcy—for the time being. Whitman sold out of PSNH in 1986, waltzing home with nearly $15 million, including interest, just about doubling his money in less than two years. Of course, it was as clear to him as it was to everyone else that this utility was far from being out of the thick New Hampshire woods. Seabrook's reactor was still sitting idle, awaiting the resolution of legal challenges posed by protesters. Meanwhile, the debt PSNH had taken on to finance its stake in the plant continued to require payments, which had to be funded through the utility's ongoing operations. Time was the enemy, and time was winning.

When the financial skies over PSNH turned gray once again in the spring of 1987, Whitman began investing his and his clients' money in the mortgage bonds. PSNH had $770 million of first-, second- and third-level mortgage debt that in a Chapter 11 case would have priority over the $786 million of unsecured debt.

Then the opportunity came along to turn this investment into a power play. Whitman was a member of an investment group called Consolidated Utilities and Communications, Inc. CUC had been formed with the purpose of finding utilities to acquire by Steve Davis, a New York utilities lawyer affiliated with LeBoeuf, Lamb, Leiby & MacRae, fellow attorney Sam Sugden, and Roland Betts and Tom Bernstein of the film financier Silver Screen Partners. Earlier in 1987, Whitman had joined CUC to structure a bid that it made for the Virgin Islands Telephone Company, using $100 million from Citicorp's venture capital division. But the partners were outbid.

Sniffing around for another deal, Davis asked Whitman whether PSNH might be a good investment. "I thought, wow, these fellas were nice to bring me into the VITELCO [Virgin Islands Telephone Company] deal," Whitman recalls. "Why don't I bring them into the New Hampshire deal?" After all, if they could get Citicorp to come in with another large sum of money, the big bank and CUC could accumulate the crucial one-third blocking position that would give them a seat at the table in case of a bankruptcy—which Whitman thought was inevitable.

Over a weekend, Whitman wrote a report detailing the strategy that would extract the most value from PSNH: investing in the third mortgage bonds. Whitman figured that absent a huge rate increase or cash infusion, the company would not be able to pay third mortgage bondholders cash interest but instead would be forced to give them stock—in fact, the majority of the stock in the reorganized company. Given the vigorous New England economy at the time, that stock could only head up and up. If instead the company found it could afford to pay third mortgage bondholders in full, he thought the investment would still be worthwhile. In any case, he believed these holders would play instrumental roles in formulating a reorganization plan. And that was something Whitman relished.

The only real risk Whitman saw in the mortgage bonds was a cut in PSNH's high electricity rates to the lower levels of other utilities in the region. It was a risk he was willing to take, mainly because the third mortgage bonds were selling at such an attractive price, sixty cents on the dollar, and carried a nice 13.75 percent yield. His game plan, therefore, was to take a Heavyweight, blocking position in the bonds and urge the company to do what today is commonly called a prepackaged bankruptcy. The bankruptcy code allows creditors and shareholders to approve a plan of reorganization first and then file under Chapter 11; the approval has to meet the Chapter 11 standards of two-thirds in amount and a majority in number in each class of debt. The goal of a prepackaged bankruptcy is to stay in bankruptcy only a few months. Finally, Whitman contacted Steve Davis to report his conclusion, that yes, PSNH was a good play, and that CUC should invest in its third mortgage bonds.

Over at Citicorp, CUC members Davis and Roland Betts discussed the PSNH idea with Steve Sherrill, an executive in the bank's venture capital group and a friend of Betts's. In turn, Sherrill consulted with George Skouras, the head of the brand new Citicorp Turnaround Investments, who had more than $50 million of the bank's money to park in distressed investments. "You know bankruptcy investing," Sherrill said. "What do you think of PSNH?" Skouras was quite interested, and the two men decided to host a lunch for all the prospective investors and the man who would give the investment the preliminary go-ahead, the head of Citicorp's venture capital group, Bill Comfort. At the suggestion of Betts, Whitman sent his strategic plan over to Comfort, a middle-aged, cigar-smoking Oklahoman with whom he had worked years before.

So, one day in June 1987, Whitman and his two partners, Heffernan and Rhein, and CUC's Davis, Betts, Bernstein, and Sugden went over to the Citicorp Center for lunch with Comfort, Sherrill, and Skouras. Over tuna salad sandwiches and sodas, the vulture investors explained the strategy. Half an hour into the discussion it almost looked like a done deal. But Comfort had to dash out to catch a plane to Australia. In the car to the airport he chewed over the idea, and picking up his cellular telephone, he called his colleagues, who were still lunching; after going over the deal a bit more with Sherrill and Skouras, Comfort gave the green light. Provided his superiors agreed, Citicorp would invest $100 million in PSNH—half coming from his group and half from Skouras's turnaround fund—and Skouras would be in charge of managing the investment. On the spot, the gathering drew up a two-page preliminary agreement.

Sherrill and Skouras easily sold the deal internally to the upper echelons at the bank. Citicorp would be invisible in the transaction behind CUC, the spokesman for the investment. CUC would invest a small amount alongside Citicorp and would take a small share of the profits. Its members would advise Citicorp on the deal, and in particular, Whitman, Davis, and Sugden would offer their expertise in utilities. In a sense, Citicorp was hedging its bets, since it also had $4 million in loans outstanding to PSNH as part of a bank lending group. The Citicorp investment people would not consult the bank's utility lending group about PSNH, because of those loans. Whitman and Davis would also direct the strategy that Whitman had plotted, Whitman as chairman of CUC and Davis as president.

BLOCKING MOVES

CUC/Citicorp started quietly buying bonds right away. Ultimately, it held 40 percent of the $325 million principal amount of third mortgages as well as some second mortgage bonds at a total cost of about $100 million—the vast bulk contributed by Citicorp and a few thousand from the other partners. On his own, Whitman invested another $35 million in third mortgage bonds for customers of his brokerage firm, M. J. Whitman, and for other groups. While they were gathering these goods, PSNH's cash supply continued to shrink. In mid-July, the company canceled the private placement Drexel, Burnham, Lambert had planned and began preparing a debt swap with current bondholders that management viewed as a longer-term solution—lowering cash obligations long enough to allow time for Seabrook to get up and running.

But to stave off bankruptcy, PSNH also needed an electricity rate increase, and in July, CEO Robert Harrison consulted with then-Governor John Sununu about an emergency rate hike. Harrison flew to Travers City, Michigan, where Sununu was heading a National Governor's Association meeting, and they met for an hour. "Keep the increase under double digits," Sununu urged. But because of Seabrook's costs, Harrison knew that was impossible. "We really have to go for 15 percent," he told the governor. Harrison now acknowledges that he probably burned an important bridge that day, although he still believes he did the right thing. On

August 5, the company formally requested a 15 percent, $71 million rate boost. If regulators approved the increase, they would run up against that 1979 law prohibiting utilities from charging customers for costs of new construction before operation. So PSNH beseeched regulators to ask the New Hampshire Supreme Court to reconsider the constitutionality of the law. Harrison warned that unless PSNH could raise enough cash, it would miss a $40 million interest payment due on October 14.

Whitman soon learned the details of PSNH's planned debt swap. In essence, the company wanted to exchange the outstanding $325 million of third mortgage bonds and $800 million of unsecured debt for new third mortgage bonds, paying interest initially in stock. If holders of 85 percent of each debt class accepted, annual interest payments would drop by 66 percent and give PSNH a breather. Whitman had two immediate objections to PSNH's whole strategy. For starters, he opposed the rate increase on public policy grounds. "It was fuck the ratepayers, fuck the public. All that a rate increase would do would pay off the common stock, the preferred stock and the unsecured creditors at the expense of the rate payers and at the expense of the economy in New England."

Whitman also opposed the issuance of new third mortgage bonds. Before investing, CUC/Citicorp and its lawyers pored over the complex terms, or indentures, that governed the bonds, and they determined that the company could not issue more third mortgage bonds and thereby allow others to share in the assets backing the existing bonds. But the interpretation of bond indentures is an inexact science. "I read that indenture ten times," Whitman remembers. "I didn't think they could do it. The company thought they could do it, Merrill, Lynch thought they could do it; First Boston thought they could do it; Drexel, Burnham thought they could do it. [All three were PSNH advisers at one time during the process.] And I concluded they couldn't do it." CUC/Citicorp had the clout to make his conclusion stick.

At PSNH headquarters in Manchester, chief financial officer Charles Bayless got a call from a Merrill, Lynch banker who had discovered that Whitman was buying up the bonds, although he didn't yet know about Citicorp. "You're going to hear from this guy Whitman," he told Bayless. "He has a vulture fund, and he's going to try to call off the exchange offer. Don't do it." A few days before the scheduled announcement of the swap proposal, Whitman did call and explained that he had a substantial position in the bonds and that the exchange offer would be injurious to those bonds. Could Bayless postpone the offer while they work out another deal? "No," Bayless said. "We'll put out the offer, and then we'll consider any objections and alternatives you have."

PSNH released its exchange offer on September 18, 1987. On the same day it ran an ad in New Hampshire newspapers warning of the dire consequences of bankruptcy if the company didn't get its emergency rate increase and financial restructuring. The ad, accompanied by a photo of the dour, gray-haired CEO, Robert Harrison, read, in part:

Consider this. Experts see no benefit in bankruptcy because in bankruptcy, the creditors come first, not the typical customer. Not the elderly, nor the needy. Not the business community that employs you. And certainly not the politicians.

As for all the people who lent PSNH the money so that customers didn't have to pay until Seabrook was completed, they, as *creditors,* will line up to get the maximum return from the bankruptcy court (emphasis in the original).

It was signed: "Robert J. Harrison, President and CEO, Public Service of New Hampshire, Resident of New Hampshire, 30 years."

That day, CUC/Citicorp, officially calling itself just CUC, went public with its by-then impressive collection of bonds. "This plan is dead in the water," Whitman told *The Wall Street Journal.* "We have enough bonds to defeat it." And enough bonds to put PSNH into bankruptcy. CUC was not the only creditor to disparage the exchange offer, but it was absolutely the biggest.

Whitman had his own notion about how PSNH should be restructured, and he sent it directly over to PSNH headquarters. The idea was first for the state to freeze rates for three years. That would win the regulators' favor and guarantee that the regulators wouldn't cut rates. "If we were going to make money on the investment, there couldn't be a massive rate decrease," Whitman says. "To this day I think there was a legal basis for one. Nobody else picked up on it. I didn't tell anybody that I was against rate decreases. I didn't want the thought to occur to anybody." With a rate freeze, the utility would have only enough value to pay off the senior two levels of bonds completely and some of the third mortgages. So Whitman reckoned that in addition to cash the third mortgage bondholders would get the bulk of the equity ownership of the profitable, operating power-generation business. Also by his plan, unsecured holders would take a bit of PSNH's stock plus most of the utility's 36 percent stake in Seabrook; the shareholders would get a morsel of that Seabrook stake. Junior-level bondholders and equity holders were appalled that anyone would leave them with only a big piece of a nuclear albatross that at the time few people thought would ever go into operation. Surely, if presented with an exchange offer that looked like this, the juniors and stockholders would not take it. Since an exchange offer would require 85 percent approval, it would fail.

Given the potential opposition, the only way to accomplish the deal in Whitman's eyes was through a prepackaged bankruptcy. Instead of chasing after 85 percent of each class of securities to complete an exchange offer, a prepack requires approval of only a majority of holders with two-thirds of the amount; dissenters would be forced to go along.

Although Harrison rejected Whitman's plan in the press, Whitman called him and Bayless with an invitation to discuss the matter over dinner in New York with himself and Davis. PSNH didn't yet know how much CUC owned or even that Citicorp was involved, but, says Harrison, "We knew Whitman had a substantial position and was a force to be reckoned with." The two Heavyweights treated their guests to dinner at The Four Seasons complete with a $200 bottle of wine. The conversation was pleasant. Whitman and Harrison engaged in chitchat about their tennis games. The two hosts then casually sketched out their plan for PSNH, explaining that they wanted reasonable rates and the prepackaged bankruptcy approach as a way to save management from prolonged agony and expense. But the CEO was unmoved. "My job," Harrison asserted, "is to protect the interest of the stockholders." Whitman and Davis laid down no ultimatums, keeping the evening congenial from aperitif to espresso. "We had a nice time," Davis says, "but we got absolutely nowhere."

The following day they met to continue the discussion at LeBoeuf, Lamb, Leiby & MacRae, which was representing CUC at the Public Utilities Commission. George Skouras, the Citicorp workout fund chief who had $50 million on the line, was out of sight in an adjoining conference room awaiting a progress report. This time, the conversation was more confrontational than it had been the evening before.

"There's a finite level you can raise rates before businesses drop off of the system," Whitman said.

Harrison responded that he still intended to raise rates as high as he could, by the 15 percent requested, and to double rates over five years.

"Bob," Whitman rasped, "may I remind you that the first two words of the company's name are *public service.*"

Again, he and Davis explained their plan for a prepackaged bankruptcy.

Bayless was moved to point out an obvious flaw in the strategy. "This plan seems to be just a little bit unfair to our shareowners."

"Shareowners!" said Whitman. "They're so far under water I can't even hear them when they make those little gurgling noises."

Bayless was annoyed that CUC's attorneys from LeBoeuf, Lamb, Leiby & MacRae agreed that rates shouldn't have to be raised to a level allowing the utility to pay its bills. As he saw it, that view conflicted with LeBoeuf's other position as general counsel for the Edison Electric Institute, the trade association of investor-owned utilities, which holds that when an electric utility spends its money prudently, it should recover its cost in full. Two days later, when he heard a LeBoeuf attorney express CUC's position at a hearing before the Public Utilities Commission in Concord, a furious Bayless ran outside in the pouring rain to use a phone booth to call the LeBoeuf senior partner in charge of utilities. He complained about the conflict he perceived, and within days the firm withdrew from representing CUC.

CITICORP IN THE SPOTLIGHT

On October 14, PSNH defaulted on interest payments to its unsecured bondholders. In its own silent way, this was a threat. If bondholders refused to agree to the exchange offer of old debt for new third mortgage bonds that the company had presented a month earlier, the next step would be bankruptcy.

Toward the end of the month, management discovered Citicorp's involvement. All kinds of rumors had been circulating concerning the source of the funds backing CUC. In an interview with Whitman and his partners, Heffernan and Rhein, an editor at the quirky, right-wing Manchester *Union Leader* said he'd heard that the money behind CUC was Hollywood money connected in part to Madonna. But the real story was somehow leaked to PSNH's advisers, and in October they spread the news to other bondholders and to the company. Livid, Harrison shot off a letter to John Reed, Citicorp's chairman and CEO. How could the bank play both sides of the street, allowing its investment units to block the company's exchange offer? After all, in its other role as a lender to PSNH, the bank had access to confidential material. "And don't talk to me about Chinese Walls," Harrison charged, referring to the bank's supposed separation of lending and investing departments. He never got a reply.

In a filing with the Public Utilities Commission at the end of October, PSNH tried to pull the curtain away from that Wizard of Oz named Whitman. He'd claimed to control nearly $200 million in bonds, the filing said, but he himself owned only $25,000 worth. The real money behind CUC was Citicorp, and it owned bonds with a principal value of $148 million, not $200 million. By now, Harrison was convinced that CUC's prepackaged bankruptcy proposal was simply a hostile raid on the company orchestrated by Citicorp and this wily vulture investor.

Today, Whitman denies ever playing the corporate raider. Yes, by his analysis of the company, CUC/Citicorp would either end up getting paid in full or receiving most of the stock, depending on whether the state increased or froze electricity rates. "As investors we always knew they were either going to pay us or give us the company," Whitman says, "if there wasn't a massive rate decrease and they could not invade our collateral [by issuing new third mortgage bonds]. We either had to get the company or make a lot of money or both. It was ordained. No other scenario could possibly work. As an investor, as a money grubber, I don't think I really cared which way they went." It just so happened, though, that he and Davis thought the more likely outcome was majority control. Still, he claims he didn't want to actually run an electric company. "What we wanted was cheap common stock that would appreciate above the reorganization value. We thought we could make a lot more money if after the reorganization we received readily tradable common stock based on the reorganization value, more than we could make if we received cash and new debt securities. Why would I ever want to be in the utility business? Citicorp felt the same way. We never wanted to run a utility."

Despite the hostile words, PSNH and its advisers—Merrill, Lynch and Drexel, Burnham—realized that if they wanted to get their exchange offer through they had to talk with CUC and convince it to go along. CUC presented a revised version of its pre-packaged bankruptcy plan meant to be more palatable to the junior bondholders. Added to the stake in Seabrook that would go to junior bondholders and stockholders would be a contract to supply 500 megawatts of power to PSNH; that created an extra $200 million or so of value for those holders. CUC also offered to put in $100 million to fund Seabrook's cost for another year. Whitman, Davis, and Skouras believed they were finally starting to get their ideas across. On November 13, *The Union Leader* reported Whitman's remark that PSNH officials were "beginning to cooperate" with him and PSNH's confirmation that its financial advisers had "talked about concepts" with CUC. Pleased, Whitman backed off on an earlier threat that CUC might force the company into bankruptcy. In reality, however, while each side came to understand the other's position more clearly, they hadn't even come close to meeting in the middle.

GUERILLA TACTICS

The Citicorp contingent, deciding that radical measures were called for, made an appearance at PSNH on behalf of the bank's investment. In November, Skouras and Sherrill paid a visit to Harrison at his office in Manchester. The chief executive greeted them coldly. "You forced us in 1984 to go to the junk bond market," he said in an accusatory tone. Harrison blamed Citicorp for being the member of the bank group to speak the loudest about pulling the utility's credit line in 1984, and he claimed that the investing division of Citicorp was now using confidential information that the bank had obtained back then. Nothing else came out of the meeting. The only way CUC president Steve Davis could interpret Harrison's barrage of charges was fear of the unknown. "We were a phenomenon that they'd never had to deal with—activist, aggressive bondholders."

Stalled on its proposal, CUC began waging guerilla tactics. In an appeal to PSNH directors and the New Hampshire public to stand behind its plan or compromise, it ran "An open letter to the citizens of New Hampshire" in *The* (Manchester) *Union Leader* of November 9, 1987. At the top, in big black letters, the ad quoted a PSNH expert witness who appeared before the Public Utilities Commission on September 16: "In Financial Terms, PSNH is Broke." On the next line: "They want *You* to bail them out. That's not fair." Then, below:

We've all seen Mr. Harrison's ads and his "solutions" to their troubles: Big Rate Hikes Today. Bigger Rate Hikes Tomorrow. We're Consolidated Utilities and Communications, PSNH's largest investor group. We want a *permanent* solution to PSNH's problems. We want PSNH to operate profitably with low rates, so New Hampshire and PSNH can grow together. We want the financial burden of Seabrook off the ratepayer's back, while maintaining access to low-priced Seabrook power if it ever comes on stream. We developed a plan that will do all this, and more. Our plan is fair to everyone—investors *and* ratepayers.

Unlike Mr. Harrison's plan, the CUC plan will: Freeze your electric rates for three years; Guarantee you high quality electric service; Prevent you from paying for Seabrook until it works. Mr. Harrison doesn't like our plan. First, he refused to let us meet with PSNH's Board of Directors. Then he tried to keep us from testifying before New Hampshire's Public Utilities Commission. We don't think that's right. We think everyone in New Hampshire deserves a chance to know about our plan, and to make up his or her own mind (emphasis in the original).

The CUC group followed up the ad with a press conference on Wednesday, November 18, at the New Hampshire Highway Hotel, an old-style conference center and watering hole for legislators located on Interstate 93 in the state capital of Concord. (The hotel has since burned down.) The purpose of the briefing was to unveil a study comparing the economic impact of the two plans that were on the table. Side by side on two broad white sheets of paper CUC displayed the differences: PSNH's immediate 15 percent rate increase and 10 percent a year rate increases after Seabrook comes on line and CUC's three-year rate freeze followed by an 8 percent boost and adjustments thereafter by the inflation rate. The key to the disparity was vastly different values placed on Seabrook. While PSNH continued to value the reactor at its cost, $2.1 billion, CUC cut that back drastically to only $500 million. In a final flourish at the press conference, CUC resurrected its threat to push PSNH into bankruptcy. Unless agreement could be reached, CUC would make sure the company was in court by March. PSNH spokesman John Cavanagh dismissed the conference as a "self-serving media event by some slick New Yorkers from Madison Avenue."

In direct response to that news conference, PSNH ran a full-page ad in *The Union Leader*. Depicted in outline was the distinctive Citicorp skyscraper standing in an ocean of water, its diagonal top poking through the surface. Nearby, a family of four sat innocently in a rowboat while below the surface two sharks gazed hungrily up at them. The family, of course, was poor little PSNH. And the sharks? They were the vultures raiding the company. "What you don't see about the N.Y. takeover of PSNH should worry you," the ad began.

The financial plan presented recently by Martin Whitman and his group of New York bankers is just the tip of the iceberg for New Hampshire. Mr. Whitman and his Wall Street partners know it doesn't take a fool to realize that most people will bite at the concept of no rate increases for the next three years. It's what Mr. Whitman *doesn't* say, or answer, or testify to, that should have us all concerned. Is there more to the Whitman plan than meets the eye?

The ad maintained that Whitman was hiding things. Such as:

Why won't Mr. Whitman come clean and admit that he truly represents big Wall Street financial institutions that hired him to do just one thing—get a maximum return for *them?*

Why won't Mr. Whitman melt away his secrecy as to the true objectives of his plan? That is, the complete *takeover* of PSNH by New York bankers— for a whopping profit.

Finally:

We at PSNH hope Mr. Whitman decides to open up about the things he seems to be hiding. In the meantime, when you read his ads and his statements, keep in mind that it's not always what you see that causes the trouble. It's what you don't see that can sink the ship (emphasis in original).

CUC in turn began laying plans for a convocation of the third mortgage bondholders. At that meeting, the giant investor planned to crush PSNH's hopes of issuing any new third mortgage bonds to complete an exchange offer, and it would do so by declaring the company to be in default on the current third mortgage bond payments. PSNH hadn't actually missed an interest payment on those bonds. But CUC claimed that the company's default on the unsecured classes of bonds back in October indicated that it was insolvent and unable to pay its debts including the third mortgage payments; the company was, therefore, in "technical default" on the mortgages, according to the terms of those bonds. "It seemed the only way," Davis says. "We weren't getting through."

On November 25, the eve of Thanksgiving, PSNH pre-empted CUC with a lawsuit. The utility charged that by calling the bond-holders' meeting and by running the "PSNH is Broke" newspaper ad, CUC was engaging in solicitation of bondholders' votes but had not complied with SEC rules for solicitation. PSNH asked the judge to slam a preliminary injunction down on Whitman and CUC, preventing them from holding their meeting with bondholders. The company also asked that Whitman and his associates be ordered to stop making "false and misleading statements" about what it called CUC's takeover attempt. According to the filing,

Whitman and his clan were "a group of New York investors that prey on weakened companies in concert with a giant New York commercial bank."

"We wanted to stop them from going forward," says Harrison. "Their whole effort we wanted to stop." If they couldn't stop the CUC juggernaut in its drive to take over the utility, PSNH management intended to file for Chapter 11. That way, Harrison reasoned, the committee approval process would be sure to force a compromise that would bring rates up and pay off all creditors.

The judge began hearings on PSNH's lawsuit the Friday after Thanksgiving. CUC denied it was trying to rustle up bondholders' votes, either by calling the meeting or running the ad. "How could we possibly be soliciting?" Whitman asks. "We weren't asking for votes, we were describing a plan. If we were soliciting anybody in the ad, we were soliciting the company, the government of New Hampshire, and the citizens of New Hampshire." Nevertheless, a week later, the judge granted the injunction. There would be no bondholders' meeting. But CUC still stood between PSNH and its restructuring plan.

THE BALFOUR BOYS

Like Whitman, Jay Goldsmith and Harry Freund of Balfour Investors had had some experience with utilities and their troubled reactors before they sank their teeth into PSNH. They had started out with General Public Utilities (Three Mile Island), buying senior and subordinated bonds and selling out when the company recovered. Moving on to Consumers Power (Midland), they repeated the maneuver and did the same thing at Long Island Lighting Company (Shoreham). "We were investing twenty and thirty million each in these plays and getting big returns out," says Goldsmith, the rotund vulture whose deal-making dates back to the railroads in the 1970s. Then they heard the rumblings in New Hampshire. Seeing their fellow vulture and old friend Marty Whitman buying up cartfuls of third mortgage bonds, the Balfour partners thought it might be a good idea for them to take a look at this utility. But the conclusion they arrived at was very different from Whitman's. In their view, the value of the enterprise was amply great to pay off

Whitman's class of third mortgage debt in cash and debt instruments. The next debt class down—unsecured debt—would then be the recipient of most of the equity in the revamped company, equity that would later skyrocket in value.

Balfour would have preferred to take a senior position, for safety's sake. Since CUC and others had cornered the market though, the safe class was essentially out of reach. But in December 1987, the opportunity to get unsecured bonds at unparalleled discounts became too good to pass up. That November, the vulture brokerage firm R. D. Smith & Company had released a research report on PSNH saying the junior bonds were worth sixty cents on the dollar, twice their trading value, even if Seabrook never went on line. At the time, the world was still reeling from the October 1987 stock market crash, and a flight to quality was depressing the prices of PSNH bonds. There was a virtual feast of them for those who dared. On some days the Balfour partners would place an order with Randall Smith for $15 million worth of bonds, and he would present them with $30 million that was available. In one instance, Balfour was about to bid twenty-nine cents on the dollar for one institution's stack of bonds worth $22.5 million at face value, but before it could make the bid, the institution offered them 28.5 cents. Bonds rained down like oil from a gusher. With such a surfeit of sellers, the Balfour Investors sometimes suspected that they might really be acquiring mud. "You question your sanity when these things happen," Freund says. His partner, more to the point notes, "You've got to have a great big set of nuts."

The debate over who would get control of this company—the juniors or the seniors—raged across the breakfast table that Whitman, Goldsmith, and Freund shared every few months at the Carlyle Hotel on the Upper East Side. At breakfast late that fall, Freund asked Whitman straight out why he was taking such an overt stance in the press about acquiring a utility. He was specifically referring to a *Business Week* article about Whitman, titled "Who Says Utilities Can't Be Raider Bait?" To Freund, a utility is by its nature a local institution, prized by the communities it serves because of its critical role in the economy. "And here you are, a New Yorker, Jewish, a foreigner. Why do it?" he asked Whitman. Whitman joked that it was all because of CEO Bob Harrison.

"That guy loves me. When he looks in the mirror in the morning to shave, he sees my face coming out at him. He just loves me." The very next morning, the gentlemanly Harrison visited the two partners at their office in Rockefeller Center. And when Freund mentioned Whitman's name in passing, it turned out that Whitman's joke had been close to the truth. "That Marty Whitman," he intoned. "You know, I still shave with a straight razor, and when I look in the mirror and I'm shaving I have this desire to take that razor and go for his throat."

Whitman might not have wanted to run a utility, but he was pretty sure that he and his group were going to acquire control of it. He told the Balfour partners that day that he was confident his plan would prevail, and if they didn't like getting a few scraps plus the Seabrook stake, too bad. In Whitman's view, the judge would put his stamp of approval on the Whitman plan as the best deal—or in bankruptcy parlance, he would "cram down" the objecting lower classes of debt. After breakfast, Harry and Jay gave Marty a ride in their chauffeured car down Park Avenue to his office in the east thirties. Jay sat in front with the driver, and Marty sat with Harry in the backseat. Turning to Harry, Marty poked his index finger at his nose and in a grim tone declared, "You guys are going to be crammed down. We're going to cram you down." He sounded dead serious, but Freund detected a hint of disingenuousness. "He knew we were entitled to something," Freund says. "He just thought it was a lot less than what we wanted."

BACKING OFF THE PLANK

So by December 1987 management had blocked CUC from holding its meeting. Now what? Its exchange offer was still dead in the water because CUC still held the crucial votes. The proposed solution was an exchange offer that would pay off the Citicorp clan so that it would no longer have a say in the case. In mid-December, PSNH presented a new offer: It would pay all third mortgage bond holders 100 percent of their principal value plus interest. Unsecured creditors, such as Balfour, and preferred stockholders would then be the ones to get the major stake in the company. The plan, however, still required the 15 percent emergency rate increase the company had requested in its original exchange offer; a ruling from the state supreme court was pending on whether they could receive such a large increase. As they refined the new exchange offer in December and January, PSNH officers continued to meet with the various parties that would be affected—CUC, creditors, and stockholders. Among those Harrison saw was Balfour Investors's Goldsmith and Freund, the holders of unsecured bonds, who took him to a restaurant he was familiar with from his recent encounter with Whitman. "I met with them at their office, and we had dinner at The Four Seasons. It seemed to be a very popular place," Harrison says. They offered him some advice on how to push through his new exchange offer, something they'd heard Moshe Dayan once say in response to the question "What is the secret to your success?" Dayan quoted a French general: *"Toujours de l'audace!"* Harrison, they said, had to stand up boldly to the pressures against him and the exchange offer.

Meanwhile, strains that had been festering between Citicorp and Whitman produced a marked change in their relationship. Whitman was a man who made quick decisions and could swing into action on a moment's notice, and often he took a hostile stance against a company's management. He became frustrated with Citicorp's ponderous decision-making processes and the tendency of its representatives to second-guess him on strategy. "Marty is a brilliant man," Davis says. "but not long on patience. Maybe the two go together." Citicorp, on the other hand, had a duty to keep close tabs on its $100 million investment, which is a lot of money even for the biggest bank in the United States. As far as it was concerned, Whitman had been ineffective in convincing management and PSNH advisers that CUC's proposal was the way to go. And so the bank took charge of the CUC investment, consulting Whitman only on some strategic issues. For his part, however, Whitman suspected that Citicorp's takeover of the investment was a reflection not of his style but of the bank's business as the largest lender to the utility industry; the bank could not afford to be seen as sponsor of a plan that froze electricity rates. "They were under pressure because my whole plan and all my schemes in the interim between July and December were to keep rate increases in check, for business as well as public policy reasons."

CUC doubted that the company could pull off a restructuring

that paid third mortgage holders in full. And it doubted that the state supreme court would give the utility its 15 percent rate hike. Consequently, Citicorp and CUC's Davis continued to push their own plan in talks with the company's financial advisers. By the end of December, Davis thought that the two sides were near agreement. In mid-January 1988, CEO Harrison visited George Skouras in his office at Citicorp. Skouras implored him, "Don't file for bankruptcy if you're rejected by the state supreme court. Don't make an abrupt decision without thinking it through." Harrison assured him that he wouldn't. On January 26, the court did rule against PSNH, and a rate increase of the double-digit kind that the company wanted became unreachable. The very next day, despite Harrison's pledge to Skouras, the company took its sad story to bankruptcy court. It was virtually out of cash, for although assets exceeded liabilities, $2.95 billion to $1.7 billion, 70 percent of the asset value was tied up in Seabrook, which wasn't generating a penny. But the immediate cause of the bankruptcy was a rush for the company's assets. Other, unsecured creditors were falling over each other trying to attach property to cover their claims, and when the rate ruling came across, PSNH management believed it would lose control of the company unless it filed. "We were backing off the plank until we had to fall off," Harrison says.

In the end, Harrison couldn't blame Whitman and Citicorp directly for the bankruptcy, because the rate ruling was the catalyst. But he does find them guilty to a degree. "I can't say [their block of the exchange offer] was the definitive factor. But it certainly had to be a contributing factor. It cast a pall over the whole thing. If the exchange offer had happened, we arguably could have made it through."

So now it was back to square one. Once the creditors set up their bankruptcy committees and hired their advisers and the advisers became familiar with the case—a process that took a few months—the drama of who would get control of Public Service Company of New Hampshire began all over again.

On the day of the bankruptcy filing, Goldsmith and Freund were in London sitting down to lunch with an investor who participates in many of their deals. "We have lunch with him always in the same place, always at the same time, always the same food,"

Freund says. "He loves to hear our ideas, which amuse him as sort of oddball. We like to get his reaction because if there are any holes in our story we quickly hear them." On this day, the partners could barely wait to tell their friend about what they felt was the imminent bankruptcy of the New Hampshire utility. But the friend was still trying to get over the stock market crash, and before they even finished their drinks, he leaned over and said, "Jay and Harry, this lunch is going to be totally social. I am not interested in any stories. I am not open to buying anywhere in the world. The world is coming to an end, and that's it. Just let's talk about anything you like other than investments." Jay and Harry looked at each other. Here they had what they considered to be one of the two or three best investment stories of their careers, and one of the investors they most revered wouldn't even listen to the story. So they chatted. And finally, Freund turned to Goldsmith and said, "Jay, it's really a pity that we can't pass one of the greatest stories we've ever heard by him, because I was really looking forward to this lunch in order to take what I think is a perfect story and find the holes in it." So, the friend relented. "I'll listen," he said, "but believe me I am not buying dollar one." At the end of the lunch, he committed to buying $5 million worth of bonds and eventually came in for another $25 million. By the end of February, the Balfour group had accumulated $150 million worth of unsecured bonds at an average price of about thirty cents on the dollar.

Other vultures also were swirling around PSNH. Talton Embry of Magten Asset Management owned about $30 million worth of second and third mortgage bonds. And R. D. Smith accumulated a heap of unsecured, junior bonds for its customers. PSNH held something of a special place at the vultures' brokerage firm. It had been the subject of its first big research report after opening its doors in 1985. Like Whitman, Smith bought the bonds that year and got its customers out later with a big profit. And like Whitman, R. D. Smith returned in 1987, picking up bonds and stock. When the utility filed for bankruptcy, R. D. Smith became co-chairman of the creditors' committee as the agent for more than $400 million of the junior bonds it had bought for itself and customers, more than half the class. Bayless, the utility's CFO, went to the committee's organizational meeting scheduled to start at nine o'clock one

64   *Power Play*

morning but was told to wait outside. "We cooled our heels until one P.M. while there was a huge fracas over whether R. D. Smith would be on the committee because they wanted to continue trading in PSNH debt," he says. The broker considered setting up a Chinese Wall between its trading operation and its committee activities, but such a maneuver had never been attempted before and would not be until 1991 when a judge permitted Fidelity Investments to do it in the Federated/Allied bankruptcy. Finally, says committee attorney Joel Zweibel, "As counsel, I had a chat with John Adams [of R. D. Smith] and Randy Smith and explained that in my view you could not be a member and continue trading." The brokerage house decided not to pursue a place on the committee.

Later on in the bankruptcy, Ben Walsh, an individual investor who has made vulture investing his livelihood and whose general modus operandi is to get on creditors' committees, joined the committee. Like other vultures, he argued strenuously for the speedy delivery of an adequate recovery, coming into conflict with those members who bought their securities at full price and wanted to fight for as large a recovery as possible. One adviser characterized him as "very loud, disruptive, very critical." But, beyond behind-the-scenes discussions with management and creditors' committees, none of the vultures' efforts in this case came anywhere near those of Whitman and CUC/Citicorp.

THE METER IS RUNNING

By the time of the bankruptcy filing, Skouras and Davis had taken the lead on the CUC negotiating team. Whitman, weary of the bank's seemingly sluggish style and convinced that he was going to get paid well in the end no matter what happened, had decided to withdraw into the background. The first matter on CUC's courtroom agenda: It wanted to be paid the $42 million in annual interest it was accruing during the bankruptcy.

To Wilbur Ross, this request marked a turning point in the case. Ross is a ubiquitous bankruptcy investment banker from Rothschild, Inc. who represented the PSNH equity holders' committee and became famous in the case for calling the state under Sununu's administration a "banana republic." In Ross's view, money used to pay CUC its interest during the bankruptcy would be money that could not be used to make contractor payments on Seabrook to prepare the plant for licensing. And if Seabrook didn't get licensed, the stockholders could end up with no recovery in the reorganization. "We had no other way to get the money to finish Seabrook," he says. "It would have been finito for us." Bankruptcy Judge James Yacos did not grant CUC's request. So CUC went on to number two on its list of priorities. It launched a campaign to get the case closed as quickly as possible, for the meter on its investment was running. "They knew they were going to get paid full principal and interest in the end," says the utility's CFO, Bayless. "They'd seen the projections like everyone else had. So it was in their interest to get this thing done as soon as possible."

He credits CUC with becoming the peacemaker in the process, whenever disagreement erupted between the creditors' and equity holders' committees. But the Citi group tried to be a driving force in the bankruptcy as well. From the start, CUC opposed the company's effort to hold onto control of the bankruptcy process and continued to oppose it even after June, when the company easily won an extension to its three-month exclusive right to sponsor a reorganization plan. With that eventual plan in mind, CUC met with three New England utilities that had expressed interest in acquiring their New Hampshire neighbor: New England Electric System in Massachusetts, Northeast Utilities of Connecticut, and Central Maine Power. And no matter who ran the reorganization, CUC believed the deal would get done quicker if it was linked to moderate rate increases, which could win the state's support. So it set out to convince unsecured holders to agree to somewhat lower rate increases than they wanted. And its representatives held discussions with state utility regulators about getting what it considered a reasonable rate increase—not a whopper, just enough to guarantee the payment of interest to its own class of third mortgages and to throw a few bones to the lower debt classes as well. State regulators were naturally all ears.

CUC's activities disturbed Wilbur Ross over at the shareholders' committee. "Everybody knew they, CUC, eventually would get one hundred cents and their interest," he says. "So why were they playing around so much? Why were they participating in all the

hearings? A lot of noise for no reason." In particular, he objected
to CUC's efforts to impose lower rate increases, which would keep
the value of PSNH at such a low level that equity holders would
receive a negligible recovery. As for the creditors' committee of
bondholders and suppliers, it wanted a rate hike large enough to
ensure that its constituency was paid in full. The committee held
several meetings with state representatives throughout the year,
which its attorney characterized as "terribly unproductive." PSNH
stood on the side of equity holders, shooting for the highest rates
it could possibly get so as to give something back to them. "We
threw down the gauntlet," says Harrison. He wrote to Governor
Sununu and proposed a meeting for August 2, 1988.

They met at the governor's office in the state's 1819 granite
capitol building in Concord. The country's oldest continuously
occupied capitol, the domed building features three front entrances
and four corner chimneys and is cradled in elms. In a corner on the
second floor is the governor's office, which looks out on the state
library and the legislative office building. The participants in the
meeting positioned themselves as if they were following stage directions for a confrontational scene. Sununu sat behind his desk,
flanked by a U.S. flag on one side and the clipper-ship state flag on
the other and with his advisers grouped around him. Facing him
across the desk were Harrison and his advisers as well as members
of the creditors' and shareholders' committees, the speaker of the
state House of Representatives and the president of the state Senate. As Harrison relates, "One of Sununu's advisers asked me,
'What is your value of the estate?' I said, 'Two point five billion
dollars.' One of the accountants they'd hired laughed, and I became irritated with him. But in bankruptcy our duty was to maximize the value of the estate, and in doing that there would be more
going to securities holders including common stockholders." One
scenario his team presented for obtaining the higher rates needed
to reach that $2.5 billion valuation was for the utility to switch
from state to federal regulation. Roused, the easily provoked
Sununu said, "I want to be blunt," and he was. For one thing, he
said, the state would never agree to a transfer of regulatory control.
Another thing, rate levels, not value, should be the goal, and any
one year's rate increase should be single digit. He lashed out at the

representatives of the state, the debtor and the committees for being so slow to agree on those levels.

In September, Harrison retired and CUC's members sensed an improvement in the company's willingness to work with them. In 1982, the mild-mannered, balding Harrison had what might be called a double-triple-bypass heart operation—two triple-bypass operations performed within a few months of each other, because of the failure of the first one. When in August 1988 he suffered several runs of ventricular arrythmia, his doctor advised him that if he continued to work in a stressful environment he would surely suffer a heart attack. He had to quit. "Once he retired," says Davis, the CUC president, "the relationships improved enormously. I'd got the sense there was personal animosity toward CUC from Harrison."

For the besieged Seabrook reactor, there was good news and bad news in November. The good news: The Nuclear Regulatory Commission eased requirements for emergency planning, Seabrook opponent Michael Dukakis lost his bid for president, and President Ronald Reagan signed an order authorizing the federal government to take over the evacuation planning process, bypassing the state of Massachusetts. The bad news: The antinuclear movement was trying to throw up new obstacles to prevent a startup, such as suggesting that the utility was too ill financially to operate Seabrook.

Just before John Sununu left Concord to take his new post as President George Bush's chief of staff, he met with PSNH, CUC, and the committees for one last crack at forging a rate plan. Under a heavy snowfall, roughly fifty people arrived at the state legal counsel's offices in Manchester the morning of December 17, a Saturday—the only day Sununu could manage while shuttling between New Hampshire and Washington. The atrium-style conference room they used was known by the state's lawyers as the "Cave of the Winds" because of its high ceiling and legendary wind currents. Those currents would rise to the level of gusts during this particular session.

"This is a settlement conference," an attorney for the state announced, and introduced the governor.

Sununu stood and began a speech. "The window of opportunity isn't open wide and it is closing fast. It's a long, hard, uncertain road. But there are advantages in settling and there are advantages in dealing with an outgoing administration." He promised to push through rate increases before leaving office. "I'll take the heat from the public and the legislature," he said. "Seabrook is necessary and safe. By virtue of greed Seabrook will not come on line. You guys have got to differentiate wants versus needs. The time involved in working this out can be measured in days or years. It's your choice."

He reviewed the state's latest proposal, and then closed with a threat. "I have to leave at four this afternoon. Unless the parties have reached agreement by then, I'll go out on the steps of the building and tell the media that the problems of PSNH are the fault of the greed of New York investors."

Attorney Joel Zweibel objected on behalf of the creditors' committee. "Governor, you know that PS of New Hampshire's problems are not the fault of those who have invested in it. They are the fault of your legislature. The state supported construction of Seabrook, because it couldn't have been built without that support. And then it turned around and wouldn't permit PSNH to cover its costs."

There was a general discussion of the issues and the proposal at hand; the company and creditors were put off because the state's proposed rate increases were lower than what it had previously forwarded. The various parties then broke up to huddle in separate rooms of the law offices. At lunch, CUC's Davis, Skouras, and their consultant Mike Schnitzer ran the state's rate proposal through a computer model, using a laptop they had brought along, to arrive at a rough estimate of how that increased the value of the utility. They concluded that the state's proposal approached CUC's acceptable range.

After lunch, the parties reconvened in the Cave of the Winds. Sununu threatened once again to go out to the reporters who were waiting in their cars while it snowed, and tell them that "greed killed Seabrook." James Neidhardt, of the Equitable Assurance Society of America and chairman of the creditors' committee, spoke for the committees and PSNH when he announced that they needed more time to evaluate the state's new proposal.

"We will get back to the governor as soon as possible," he said.
"When is as soon as possible?" Sununu wanted to know.
"As soon as possible," Neidhardt repeated.
"Hours, days, weeks, months?"
"As soon as possible."
Sununu was furious. "You want me to drop dead," he raged. "If you want me to act, you should get back to me within a matter of days."

The meeting broke up at about four P.M. in a cloud of uncertainty. On Sunday, CUC, which had begun its analysis during the meeting, set down in minute detail a somewhat modified version of the state's proposal in an attempt to bring the two sides together. But after presenting it to the state on Monday, CUC heard no response.

PSYCHEDELIC EXPERIENCES

At the same time, the Balfour partners were getting increasingly edgy about Seabrook. Would it ever open? If it were allowed to take the first step into low-power testing, would the test come off smoothly? The way things were going, it seemed more likely that the ultimate success of Balfour's investment would depend on the opening of that plant. And that's why they decided to get out. "We don't like to have our money and our performance hinged on an event over which we have no possible control," Freund says. "It just isn't us."

A visit they made to Seabrook around that time convinced them to sell much sooner than they would have otherwise. The head of Seabrook operations, Edward Brown, invited the partners to come up and take a look at what they had spent their money on. They traveled to the plant, and Brown showed them around. From start to finish, the experience was jarring for the two money men who had never before seen the insides of a power plant, let alone a nuclear-powered one. Everything was new, including the concept that they had to wear hard hats and goggles. "They wanted us to put them on," says Goldsmith. "We said we can't see without our glasses. We have to wear our regular glasses. So they got a permit for us, we could wear our regular glasses." Boarding elevators, the three men sank down hundreds of feet into the bowels of the earth, where three mile-long tunnels are filled with dust and lined with a claylike muck on the bottom. From there they went to the core. As Freund describes it: "You go into this tomblike thing where there's this shiny thing that you couldn't even go near." In the control room, Freund and Goldsmith were appalled to see the young workmen in charge there playing catch with a clipboard. They didn't say a word, but Goldsmith looked at his partner's face and saw that it was ashen. "I knew what he was thinking," he says. "It was the same thing I was thinking. This frigging thing's likely to blow up."

"These were children," Freund says. "Twenty-five- and thirty-year-old boys walking around there. They looked like our sons, pressing little buttons that kept on going red and green and yellow. And we said to ourselves, 'One day one of them is going to press the wrong button, and with our luck all of New Hampshire is going to go into the Atlantic Ocean.' The whole thing was a strange psychedelic experience of sorts for people like us. It really was. And we walked away shaken." On the plane back to New York they agreed: They would sell out as soon as they got home. And they did. Over several weeks at the end of 1988, a broker at R. D. Smith found buyers who would take the entire complement of bonds off their hands at widely differing prices averaging sixty-five cents on the dollar—more than double Balfour's purchase price almost exactly one year after it had bought in. Total profit: $49 million. The buyer of most of these bonds was Fidelity Investments.

SHARE THAT BALL

On December 27, 1988, PSNH filed a reorganization plan that would give secured holders all they had coming to them in the form of new debt, and pay unsecured creditors in full in the form of new bonds and stock. Preferred stockholders would end up with 27 percent of the reorganized company and common shareholders with 18 percent. The entire package was contingent on an immediate 30 percent rate hike—still much too great for the state to accept, but PSNH planned to swing deftly around that roadblock by applying for federal rate regulation. The following month,

Northeast Utilities, after being put off by PSNH for months, announced a $1.2 billion bid for PSNH—sans Seabrook—as part of a reorganization plan it also proposed. Others were preparing competing bids. Unsecured creditors and shareholders didn't like NU's offer of as little as thirty-five cents on the dollar plus PSNH's 36 percent stake in the stillborn Seabrook plant, but CUC, who had been negotiating with NU, was in favor and talked up the bid in meetings with state officials. For the moment, however, an outsider's proposals didn't matter, because PSNH still held its exclusive right to file a plan and, like a spoiled child marching off with his ball, didn't have to let anyone else play. The company's response to NU and all prospective bidders was that no bids would be evaluated until the end of March.

But PSNH's exclusivity period, which had already been extended by the judge, was expiring on February 28, 1989. And outside forces were lining up to oppose another extension—CUC, the state, and Northeast Utilities. Hearings began on February 22 and ran for five days. "We argued that the best way to reorganize the company was to open it up for auction," says Steve Davis, who testified that the company had refused to conduct serious rate negotiations with the state. Judge Yacos agreed. Ruling that the company had not tried hard enough to find a rate compromise, he terminated PSNH's exclusivity, and let others onto the playing field to propose their own reorganization plans. "That act, that the judge was prepared to open up the process, especially to prospective acquirers, was the key that opened the door," acknowledges creditor attorney Joel Zweibel. "CUC's support for an ending of exclusivity was helpful in convincing the judge he should send a signal permitting third-party bidders."

With an end to management control of the process, suitors came out like the leaves of spring to compete for the hearts and minds of the creditors, shareholders, and rate regulators. Creditors and shareholders wanted an offer that would pay them well, but that required rate increases that the state's business community was loath to grant. In March 1989, the state's Business and Industry Association released a report arguing that a 30 percent rate boost would cause plant shutdowns and the loss of as many as 22,600 manufacturing jobs; even a 10 percent all-at-once increase would chop off 15,200 jobs. In May, as Seabrook won approval to begin low-power testing, the bidding volleys continued. In July, the state endorsed a new proposal by NU that increased rates by 5.5 percent a year for seven years.

But the bidding war raged on as four utilities each submitted plans to the court by a mid-September deadline as to how they would reorganize the utility if they got it. NU's $1.9 billion bid, New England Electric's $2 billion bid, United Illuminating's $2.2 billion bid, and management's own $2.2 billion plan. Shareholders, for one, said they would not take anything below $2.2 billion. "We're not trying to gouge, but there is a level below which it doesn't make sense for us," Wilbur Ross told *The Wall Street Journal* on September 18. CUC had already reached an agreement on price with Northeast Utilities. The equity holders' committee then negotiated its own pact with NU, convincing the utility to raise its bid to $2.25 billion and finally to $2.3 billion. That won everyone's applause.

One day at the end of November 1989, Ross found himself handling final negotiations to secure the acquisition by NU by bouncing back and forth Ping-Pong-style between NU's Manchester office and PSNH's office, because the two managements refused to go to the other's office. The unsecured creditors' committee also wouldn't go to NU's office, so after some more shuttling, Ross brought NU management to PSNH's office. And with PSNH not even in the room, he forged the deal with NU and the unsecured creditors. For all his efforts, Ross won a $1 million bonus fee for his firm.

Three years and four months after it filed, PSNH emerged from bankruptcy as part of Northeast Utilities. Fidelity Investments, which had bought most of Balfour's stake at sixty-five cents one year into the bankruptcy, came out better than double that. By getting into the bonds early and taking initiative throughout the process, CUC pocketed more than $80 million in interest and interest on interest over and above its original $100 million investment, of which the CUC partners received $10.8 million and Citicorp the rest. Not bad for an investment that CUC considered virtually risk free. If Whitman had accomplished his prepackaged bankruptcy, the annual return would have been even greater.

By way of celebration, Whitman had navy blue caps made for the CUC partners, each adorned on the front with a vulture standing triumphant atop a cooling tower. And Citicorp threw him a luncheon at which it presented him with a bronze statue of a bull fornicating with a bear. Whitman keeps it on his bookshelf next to a gold-plated pencil sharpener that Drexel, Burnham, Lambert's high-yield department sent out to clients in headier days.

CASUALTY OF WAR

But Whitman's victory wasn't total. His boldness in the case hurt his firm's effort to raise investment funds. In 1986, just before he became involved with PSNH, Whitman had told Heffernan and Rhein, then his attorneys, that he either wanted to become a bigger player or retire. But to become bigger he needed to hook up with people who shared the same vision and who would be willing to go out and raise funds for a blind pool partnership (that the general partner invests however he pleases). "Marty was not a good salesman," Heffernan says, "plus it was not a good use of his time." Heffernan and Rhein were willing, and the three linked names.

The two newcomers to investing didn't realize what they were getting into. "I knew what it is to be humbled, and now I also know what it is to be humiliated," Heffernan says. To raise $150 million for the partnership, he and Rhein crisscrossed the country "basically begging for money." They could show prospective investors their ongoing investment in PSNH, that since they had accumulated the bonds the price had gone straight up. But it didn't seem to help. In one instance, which was repeated in many variations, Heffernan rose at five A.M. to catch a plane to Minneapolis for a 10:45 meeting with an insurance company executive only to sit in the waiting room flipping through magazines for an hour, when his prospect finally showed up, having forgotten about the meeting. He had a lunch scheduled for noon. "That gives us fifteen minutes," the executive said. "What's on your mind?" In abbreviated form, Heffernan presented the blind pool idea, and just as quickly the executive brushed it off. "Oh, we don't do that." End of meeting.

It took months to secure any one commitment, and when they

finally did, it turned out to be unreliable. Then there was a break-through. The restructuring department at Chemical Bank had agreed in late 1987 to contribute $10 million to the new partnership as a lead investor, and allowed Whitman, Heffernan & Rhein to use the bank's name in marketing the blind pool. By the fall of 1988, "we had enough money lined up to do a first closing," Heffernan recounts. They sent out the subscription agreements to investors to start the closing process, but mysteriously they didn't hear back from Chemical. When Heffernan called his contact there, she told him that the bank couldn't make any more equity investments until the end of the year because they might jeopardize a pending acqui-sition of a New Jersey bank. What's more, she had to pass it before top management once again. What Heffernan didn't know was that the August edition of *Corporate Finance* magazine had made the rounds at the bank and was causing some concern. On the cover: the Citicorp tower, with a shark's multitoothed maw super-imposed on its top, accompanied by the headline "Citicorp Turns Raider." To Chemical, Whitman, Heffernan & Rhein—and its involvement with Seabrook—was too controversial a firm to be allied with. "They never intended to call us back," fumes Heffer-nan. It wasn't until June 1989 that the partnership finally closed with only $45 million. Still, Whitman, Heffernan & Rhein thrived as bankruptcies burgeoned.

For his part, Whitman seems more struck by the failure of his hoped-for quick, pre-packaged bankruptcy that he says would have helped the public interest. "With hindsight the constructive things I wanted to do never had a prayer," he says with a half-embarrassed smile. "I mean it was Don Quixote tilting at wind-mills. I thought the thing was so constructive I could make people understand. It would have been terrific for everybody had it been done my way. It would have been a lot more constructive, and the pressure under which New England finds itself could be less severe than it is. They got the rates they wanted. They have as high rates as there are in the country."

As for Citicorp, despite its clear success with this bankruptcy investment, it has since gotten out of the vulture game. (On the lending side, ironically, the bank continued to struggle with loans it made to highly leveraged companies that subsequently went bankrupt.) In keeping with a trend at the bank to retrench from investing activities, George Skouras closed his turnaround fund and launched an operation that trades third world debt for equity in local enterprises. One obscure and risky enterprise replaced by another.

4

The Committee Man's Coup

With money I'll throttle the beast-blind world between my fingers.
Without it I am strapped; weakened; my life is a curse and a care.

—THE LETTERS OF THOMAS WOLFE

James Rubin started circling Coleco Industries in 1986. The toy maker had taken on enormous debt to produce its blockbuster Cabbage Patch® doll, but sales were on the wane. The reality of the toy business is that you're only as good as your next toy, and Coleco didn't appear to have one. Such is the stuff of which vultures' dreams are made. "I really thought Coleco was terminal from the moment I started looking at it," says Rubin, a principal with the New York investment firm of Sass, Lamle, Rubin & Company. "Even terminal things have some value."

At thirty-eight, Rubin is of the young generation of vulture investors. For him, vulturing is a way of life. "I buy my clothes at discount places," he says. "I like to buy dollar bills for fifty cents." A lanky six foot two, he is soft-spoken and energetic. "I don't get stressed," he maintains, sitting behind five neat stacks of bank-

76

ruptcy documents in his cramped midtown Manhattan office. Un-like most of his peers, Rubin entered the netherworld of distressed investing through a corporate door, as a result of his employer's misfortunes. After earning a degree in engineering from Cornell University in 1975, he started in an M.B.A. program there but grew impatient for a role in managing a business. He began working for a small maker of industrial piping as a management trainee and worked his way up to vice president, only to help usher the company through Chapter 11. The company had fallen as a result of low demand from troubled smokestack America and low produc-tivity from a militant union. Rubin helped sell the company's assets to a competitor, where he continued as a vice president. Within a year, however, his new employer's ambitious acquisition campaign led it down the path of doom, and its banks forced it to sell assets.

Through these tribulations, Rubin realized that he so enjoyed the process of tearing apart and rebuilding a company that the idea of working at a going concern seemed excruciatingly dull. "It is very stimulating and very compelling intellectually to fix opera-tions and handle all of the contractual negotiations to set up your balance sheet and your expense basis," he explains animatedly. "But a mundane running of that finished product seemed very boring to me. Worrying about marketing strategies, people's vaca-tion schedules, and fights between sales guys just did not seem to be exciting." Yet, he also discovered that there was little reward in being on a management team that had to go down with a sinking company and then had to attempt to pull it back up again. The ordeal not only consumed a manager's life but, in the end, it could cost him his job, because boards of directors often replace the managements of struggling companies. So, when his second em-ployer foundered, he left with the notion of gaining control of the company by buying its bank debt. That deal fell through, but Rubin would not soon forget the taste he had had of vulture investing. For a while he ran his own management consulting business specializing in the rejuvenation of small down-and-out private corporations. Although he did well, he could not shake the investment bug. It seemed to him an ideal way to maintain an involvement in the rebuilding process while making a lot more money. "I mean, you could make good money by being a professional, but it seemed like you could make even more money, and it would be more exciting still, if you could invest in these things," he says. "The only problem was that I didn't have any money to invest."

In 1985, he traipsed up and down Wall Street to find out whether people invested in soured companies for a living and whether he might join them. As he talked to more people, he repeatedly heard two names mentioned: Michael Milken of Drexel, Burnham, Lambert and Randall Smith of Bear, Stearns & Company. He visited Drexel, Burnham but decided that he did not fit in at the junk bond powerhouse. Drexel, Burnham concentrated on public companies; he knew private companies. It hired people to be researchers or investment bankers; he had had broader experience. Then he happened to see an advertisement in *The Wall Street Journal* announcing the formation of R. D. Smith & Company, Randall Smith's new investment management and brokerage operation devoted exclusively to the tired and the poor of the corporate community. So he called and asked for Smith, who, somewhat uncharacteristically, got right on the phone. They spoke at length. Smith invited Rubin over for lunch, and soon hired him as a consultant for a company that Smith was taking out of bankruptcy. Rubin became part of Smith-Vasiliou Management, the money management arm of Smith's operation that at the time dominated the firm. Within a couple of years, however, R. D. Smith's brokerage business took the leading role, and the next thing Rubin knew he was no longer researching the same types of longer-term investment ideas.

He left and formed a small investment firm, specializing in shaky public companies like Coleco. Then in 1989, while he was looking to hire someone to raise money for him to invest, he bumped into New York value manager Martin Sass. Sass happened to be looking for someone to run money in distressed securities. "And so we decided, why don't we both bag the employment idea and just start a business together?" Rubin recounts. Rubin owns half of the investment and advisory firm they set up and runs the investment side himself. His income is based purely on his performance. As he says, "If I don't make money for my clients, I don't make money." The firm takes a fifth of the portfolio's gains as its revenues, and Rubin takes half of that after expenses. If the portfolio of a dozen or so investments loses value, Rubin collects nothing and continues to do so until the value washes above the high watermark. By mid-1991, however, he had yet to go home with empty pockets. Annual returns on individual deals have often flown beyond the stated goal of 25 percent—striking 41 percent in 1991. These vulture profits, plus quarterly contributions from investors totaling more than $40 million, had built a portfolio of about $70 million.

SOMETHING ROTTEN IN THE CABBAGE PATCH

Like Charlie Chaplin in *Modern Times,* Coleco lived a life that swung from good fortune to adversity and back to good fortune again. In 1977, the West Hartford, Connecticut, company was a middle-aged forty-five years old and prospering with the introduction of the Telstar℠ black-and-white video games. When that product slumped, Coleco rebounded with a line of hand-held electronic football and baseball games followed in 1982 by ColecoVision℠ video games. In 1983, the year that the brutally competitive video game business began a long decline, Coleco wheeled out the Adam Computer℠. The $100 video game system was supposed to become a personal computer with the insertion of modules. Plagued by technical and production problems, it was a major flop and almost brought the company to ruin.

But in stepped the Cabbage Patch doll, a rather homely looking creature with a pressed-in face that had been turned down by several major toy companies by the time Coleco's management stumbled into it at an arts and crafts fair in Georgia. The doll captured the hearts of children across the nation (including Rubin's daughters) and the wallets of their parents. But while Cabbage Patch was not a short-lived fad, it was a phenomenon that was in its prime and would not maintain that strength indefinitely. By 1986 its sales were severely wilted, having collapsed from $600 million to $270 million in one year. In 1987, sales were down to $127 million. In turn, Coleco's losses grew and its cash supply withered. The company had accelerated production of the dolls, creating a bulky cost structure and high debt level to support a product with weakening sales. In the first quarter of 1988, management went hat in hand both to bondholders to offer them a majority interest in the company in exchange for their bonds and to its bank group for a new borrowing agreement. The lenders resisted, and an agreement remained elusive. Virtually all sales activity stopped.

In May 1988, a call for new leadership prompted the resignation of Arnold Greenburg, the chairman and the son of Coleco's founder, and his replacement by executive vice president Morton Handel. The following month, Handel underwent quadruple bypass heart surgery, and from his hospital room he began to review papers the company was preparing for a bankruptcy filing.

Rubin did not choose Coleco from a list of possible investments. The bonds came to him from a professional individual investor who was carrying them among his holdings but didn't know what to do with a distressed bond. He asked Rubin to manage a portfolio of Coleco bonds and cash for him, but Rubin resisted the offer. From what he knew of the company, these bonds were not worth anywhere near the market price in midsummer 1988 of around eighteen cents on the dollar. So Rubin negotiated an agreement that solely for the purposes of determining his incentive commission the bonds would be valued at five cents on the dollar. Based on that value, Rubin would get 20 percent of the profits. If the company did file for bankruptcy and if it emerged fairly quickly, Rubin and his client could reap a handsome return. As for what was in the portfolio, Rubin will only say there were "under ten million dollars" worth of Coleco bonds. Handel's sources told him the vulture investor owned only $200,000 worth of bonds for which he paid no more than $50,000, but Rubin claims the values were much greater.

Rubin was certain that Coleco was on the brink of ruin. In his first review of the toymaker's balance sheet, his eyes were drawn to an unusual entry under the asset column called "barter advertising credits." It was a huge amount: more than $80 million. He did some research and learned that Coleco bartered excess merchandise for credit toward future television advertising time, but that fifty cents of credit had to be matched with fifty cents of cash in order to buy $1 of commercial time. The credits thus represented

$160 million of advertising—an asset that while valuable could not be spent for years and cost money to use. To a desperate company, Rubin mused, this paper was not of much value. "It was one of the reasons I knew this company was going to eventually die."

On July 11, 1988, shortly after Rubin actually acquired his bonds, the company finally pitched into bankruptcy, filing in a New York City court under bankruptcy Judge Prudence Abram. A week and a half later, at a meeting at the U.S. Trustee's office in downtown Manhattan, Trustee Harry Jones appointed Rubin and fourteen others to the committee that would represent all of Coleco's unsecured creditors who held some $435 million in debt. The members, who included institutions like Massachusetts Financial Services as well as suppliers like D&E Packaging, immediately elected Rubin chairman—he wasn't a large holder but he had experience working in bankruptcies and, most important, he was willing to devote a lot of time to the job. Also, at the time he was fairly new to the field of vulturing, and was still making a name for himself.

The creditors' committee is the voice of the creditors in the negotiations over a reorganization plan, and the chairman of that committee is usually the strongest voice. In the mid- to late 1980s, before and after Coleco, Rubin was the stockholders' committee chairman in the bankruptcy of American Health Care Management, helping to engineer the reorganization; the chairman of the official unsecured creditors' committee at Texas American Bancshares; and the chairman of the creditors' committee for the Cardis Corporation. And late in the Coleco saga, in 1989, he would become the bondholders' committee chairman in the prebankruptcy workout of Resorts International, helping to cut the deal that got Merv Griffin's casino company in and out of bankruptcy in a matter of months. But no case would be as bizarre or demanding for Rubin as that of Coleco.

ENTER THE BANK VULTURES

Even before the bankruptcy filing, Coleco's attorneys at Stroock & Stroock & Lavan had begun looking for a hungry vulture investor to buy the company's $85 million of bank debt.

They visited many a monied vulture, including R. D. Smith's Randall Smith; Paul Levy, the former co-chief of workouts at Drexel, Burnham, Lambert; and Isaac Perlmutter, the man who for years had been providing Coleco with the advertising credits Rubin had noticed on Coleco's books, trading them for unsold toys. Perlmutter made his living as a buyer of unsold inventories and also happened to dabble in bankruptcy claims from time to time. Paul Levy took the company up on its offer, but later withdrew in a disagreement with the bank. Shortly after the filing, Perlmutter, with his partner Bernard Marden, snatched up the debt for a song—about $50 million—and didn't stop to haggle over terms. They also agreed to allow Coleco to borrow against the assets that backed the bank loans, providing a critical brace to shore up the wobbly company.

Perlmutter, the more visible member of the partnership and its spokesman, is a New York businessman in his late forties who emigrated from Israel as a young man. Unpolished in manner, his English is coarse. He has no formal education in finance, but those who have dealt with him in business agree that he displays a keen instinct for good value and drives a hard bargain. Perlmutter has a history of investment in bankrupt and troubled companies, namely toy companies such as Child World and Lionel.

The quintessential self-made man, Perlmutter started out in this country by selling toys on the street. Later, with the more refined Marden, he built a business called Odd Lot Trading, a retailer and wholesaler of closeout items. In May 1984, they sold Odd Lot to Revco drug stores for 12 percent of Revco stock and proceeded to challenge management for control. Marden was already on the Revco board, and he and Perlmutter had been more than casually friendly with Sidney Dworkin, one of Revco's founders and at the time its chairman and CEO. A few months earlier, Perlmutter had thrown a surprise thirty-fifth birthday party for Dworkin's son. On the day they sold Odd Lot, May 26, 1984, Perlmutter and Marden were waiting in Dworkin's office for the board's approval, and when Dworkin told them the news he got a response that gave him the utmost confidence. As he tells it: "I said, 'I'm really working for you guys,' and they put their arms around me and said, 'You'll never have to worry about us.' "

Within days, however, the mood soured. The partners asked for a meeting with Dworkin and Revco's store operations manager to go over some matters. When they met on June 7, 1984, Dworkin says, "We were presented with a number of allegations, about one-half to three-quarters of an inch of papers dated June 4, accusing us of almost every kind of crime imaginable." Among them: that Dworkin's younger son, Elliot, had shown favoritism to certain suppliers. Dworkin was stunned. After an attempt to resolve the conflicts, the directors threw Marden off the board and removed him and his partner from their posts running Odd Lot. Hardly enough punishment in Dworkin's eyes. Eventually, Perlmutter and Marden sold out their position in Odd Lot for approximately $100 million, and Dworkin soon found that he was left with a closeout business that was in a shambles. Some people blame Odd Lot in part for Revco's own tumble into bankruptcy court, which is chronicled elsewhere in this book. But the characterization of Perlmutter and Marden as dishonest was a mystery to Morton Handel, who had been doing business with Perlmutter at Coleco since 1984. "I found Ike Perlmutter to be totally trustworthy," he maintains. Neither Perlmutter nor his attorney responded to phone calls requesting comments.

When in 1988, Perlmutter and Marden bought Coleco's bank debt they became senior to Coleco's bondholders in rank. Already skeptical about the barter advertising credits, Rubin felt a vague suspicion about the two men. He was also dismayed with Perlmutter's view of the case, which the bank debt vulture made clear to the committee from the start. In Perlmutter's opinion the value of the company's estate after his senior debt was paid off was a fat zero. There would be nothing left for bondholders. It was not a view that the creditors' committee was willing to accept.

At the beginning of August, the committee finally chose its attorneys. The members met at one of their offices in New York for the "beauty contest" featuring five finalist law firms. After each presentation, Rubin told the contestants that they could wait either in the next room or back at their offices for the committee's decision. Marc Kirschner, a slender attorney with steel-rim glasses and iron gray hair who worked with Jones, Day, Reavis & Pogue, a Cleveland-based firm, chose to wait. It turned out to be a good decision. Before long, Rubin asked Kirschner to come back into the room so that they could get to work. There was a court hearing that afternoon on the company's financing arrangement.

Late in the summer, the committee assembled in a conference room at Jones, Day's New York office for its first strategy session with its advisers. Rubin sat back and listened to a cacophany of conflicting opinions. The suppliers stressed that they wanted the business to continue, bondholders who had bought their securities when they were originally issued at 100 cents on the dollar believed things could not be as bad as management was claiming, and the vultures who had bought at a discount wanted to give management the boot. Except Rubin. He had come into the case with an open mind about management. Yes, they'd screwed up the job, but he knew that replacing the management of a Chapter 11 company is not an easy thing to do. "I do this for a living, and it's the only thing I do in large part, and I know how traumatic it is to try to get rid of management," he says. "There's a real cost in doing that. And so while you might have better people, the expense of getting them in there may more than counterbalance the benefits. In fact it usually does." Not to be dismissed, either, was the ugly possibility that the new management would turn out to be just as bad as the old one. "I know that you tend to be very idealistic on how a company should be run, and emotional, and you typically find out that most humans are about the same." So at this first meeting of the creditors' committee, Rubin merely listened to complaints about management without much comment.

When his turn to speak came around, he raised his greatest concern: Coleco's barter advertising credits. In a low-key, point-by-point presentation, he persuaded the other members of the committee that this balance sheet entry was highly suspicious and could provide them with ammunition for their negotiations with the company. On September 20, Kirschner and his legal team applied to the court for permission to investigate Perlmutter and Marden's barter advertising transactions with the company over the years. If there was something fishy going on with the credits, perhaps the committee could use litigation as leverage to obtain a generous distribution in the company's reorganization plan. Perhaps, too, it would provide some way for bondholders to steal away value from some of Perlmutter and Marden's newly bought bank claims. If indeed the company had too little value to pay the bondholders, they would have some way of squeezing out more for themselves. Kirschner received the go-ahead from the judge on October 28.

An activist vulture investor usually enters a bankruptcy with a good idea of the company's value that holds up as he maneuvers to carve out a big slice for himself. In the case of Coleco, however, Rubin found after much research and negotiation during the fall and winter that there was very little value in the company and that practically nothing would go to his class, the unsecured creditors. That became all too clear when, in January 1989, Coleco released a draft of its proposed reorganization plan to the committee. The proposal was a big disappointment to the group, indicating that the company could not even afford to pay Perlmutter and Marden the full principal value of the bank loans they had bought. To make up the difference, the plan awarded them the lion's share of the equity in the reorganized company, 55 percent. Unsecured creditors would get 36 percent plus debentures. The company valued the unsecured creditors' recovery at around thirteen cents on the dollar, but by the committee's estimate, it was a measly five cents. Unacceptable, the committee told management. There must be greater value here. It was at that point that Rubin began to believe that management did not have the bondholders' best interest at heart. He sensed that Coleco might have a natural bias toward Perlmutter, because of their long-standing business relationship.

THE LEGAL AX

Soon after Coleco presented its plan draft, the committee's advisers began to deliver reports to the panel on their research into the barter advertising credits. Their investigation had been far-ranging, involving the perusal of more than 100,000 documents and depositions or interviews of eight witnesses including Perlmutter, Marden, and Revco's Sidney Dworkin. From their research, they concluded that at a time that Coleco was insolvent, it accepted goods—the credits for advertising time—that were worth far less than their stated value. They believed these findings were grounds for a court case alleging "fraudulent conveyance" of goods. The value of goods they believed were fraudulently transferred to Perlmutter and Marden was $71 million (for the $144 million value of the goods, Coleco received $73 million in cash plus barter advertising credits the committee valued at zero). The committee's attorneys also believed that the payment to Coleco was made "in bad faith," as they explained later in court documents:

both the barter company defendants and the debtors [Coleco] knew that the consideration was not the fair equivalent of the goods transferred by the debtors, both the barter company defendants and the debtors knew that the debtors' revenues were declining at a rate that would severely limit the debtors' need for and financial ability to exercise the barter credits within the foreseeable future and the barter company defendants knew or should have known that the debtors were utilizing these transactions to artificially inflate the debtors' sales and inventory.

If the committee could recover damages from Perlmutter, it could actually increase the value of the entire company. Rubin was the mastermind of this scheme. "Jim," says Kirschner, "had organized the committee's focus on this and he was the one I consulted with in learning more about it and in constructing our case. I consulted with him constantly." Bondholders now had hope of a better payment in the bankruptcy.

At once, the committee prepared a lawsuit against Perlmutter and Marden asking for damages of $71 million plus interest, and that the two senior-class vultures not be allowed to collect a recovery on their claim until other creditors received theirs. But a technicality of bankruptcy law stood in the way. Because a company is the primary damaged party in a fraudulent transfer of assets, bankruptcy law requires that it, not the creditors, be the plaintiff in a lawsuit making that charge. It's as if someone who bought a defective car had to ask the dealer to complain to the manufacturer, since the dealer was the first to receive the damaged goods.

Rubin and Kirschner did not expect Coleco to take on the case.

As they saw it, by filing the lawsuit Coleco would in essence have to investigate its own management on its accounting treatment of the barter advertising credits. But procedure had to be followed, and in January, Rubin and Kirschner met with Coleco CEO Handel and Coleco's legal representatives to request formally that the company file the lawsuit. And indeed they were rebuffed—even quicker than they had expected. "We felt that if the management was legitimately interested in enhancing the value of their estate [the company in bankruptcy]," Rubin says, "they would show both the professional and personal courtesy of hearing what amounted to hundreds of hours of research and then spend at least twenty-four hours thinking about it before reacting." Instead, he and Kirschner got the iciest of shoulders. The company thought that the lawsuit was a waste of time and money because the allegations simply weren't true. Handel insisted that the company's barter advertising accounting had been correct and that the transactions with Perlmutter had benefited the company. "Our auditors had reviewed the barter advertising credits in exquisite detail and had reached the same conclusion," he says. Besides, he argued, filing a lawsuit at that time would hurt the company because the industry's annual toy fair in New York was coming up the week of February 13.

Coleco's sharp reaction cemented Rubin's feeling that management was not acting in the interest of bondholders in the bankruptcy proceedings. He now knew that the committee had to create all of its own value in this case—and that meant following through with the lawsuit on its own. On February 3, Rubin and Kirschner took their brief to U.S. Bankruptcy Judge Prudence Abram, a heavy-set woman with straight brown hair and glasses. Handel didn't file an objection to the committee's attempt to sue, although he did tell the judge that he thought the suit was groundless. "If they were successful, it would be to the advantage of the company," he says today. "But we didn't believe they could win. We didn't believe their case had sufficient merit." But Judge Abram gave the committee the go-ahead to file the litigation, and it did so on February 14, 1989. All of the allegations were vigorously denied by both Perlmutter and management.

FROM COMMITTEE MAN TO CORPORATE RAIDER

Rubin and his committee were out for blood. They did not trust Coleco's management, and nothing would have pleased them more than to replace it with another. They soon got their chance when other toy companies began exploring the possibility of acquiring Coleco. The committee was not only willing to help them. It would lead the charge.

Selling the company was initially management's idea. At the tail end of January, Coleco hired Norman Brown of Donaldson, Lufkin & Jenrette to help decide whether to put the company up for sale. As he became involved, Brown witnessed firsthand the severe acidity that had developed between management and creditors. "I felt sort of like the waiter who mistakenly walks in through the out door and gets slammed in the face with a tray," he says. Shortly after the unsecured creditors had filed their lawsuit against senior creditors, Rubin and Kirschner were meeting with the company and its advisers on the latest proposed reorganization plan, which was not much better for Rubin's group than the original one. Again, as they had done repeatedly, Rubin and Kirschner complained about the amount that they would get in the distribution of assets. But this time, instead of repeating the litany of why it was unable to give more, management announced its intention to put the company up for sale. Its investment banker, DLJ's Brown, would showcase Coleco to prospective buyers. Rubin listened wide-eyed. At the end of the meeting, he turned to his attorney, shocked at the turn of events. "This is the beginning of the end of this case if we can just get them to follow through." Once Coleco was "in play," prospective acquirers might place a higher price on the company than Coleco itself did because they would value the company without the management team that had the soiled record. So here was a chance for bondholders to realize the value they had originally envisioned. Even if it turned out that the market did not provide greater value, at least the creditors would know for certain and could quickly bring the bankruptcy to a close. Bondholders would not suffer more than they had to.

During the toy fair in New York in mid-February, Coleco's management had begun quiet, casual discussions with the company's chief rivals—Hasbro, Tonka, Mattel, and Tyco—about the possibility of a merger. Once management informed the committee of its intentions, DLJ's Brown began working on the formal sales process by preparing a brochure describing the company. At once, the distrust that had been brewing between the creditors' committee and management for so long swirled around the issue of how the company was going to handle the sale. Rubin made it clear that he wanted the committee to have input into the process to make sure Coleco was marketing itself as aggressively as it could. And Brown agreed to give the committee an opportunity to review every step that he made.

But then, in mid-March, management backed off. It had reconsidered its strategy and was not going to continue looking for a buyer. Assured of the borrowed funds to make it through another several months, and intent on revising the proposed reorganization plan to give bondholders a larger share of the equity, Handel believed Coleco could conduct its own rehabilitation.

But it was too late. When Coleco would no longer answer the calls of its prospective suitors, some of them contacted the committee to see whether creditors would help them. Barry Alperin, a senior executive with Hasbro, wrote to Kirschner, who years before had been in his fraternity house at Dartmouth. The toy company wanted to know whether the committee would be interested in perhaps going up against management together. Would they ever.

The committee assigned its investment banker, Wilbur Ross, to take a look at the various bidders. Ross is the senior banker from Rothschild, Inc. who was also involved in PSNH and who during the recession could be found involved in several major cases at once. His small, twenty-ninth-floor office in One Rockefeller Center is nothing if not a museum of "tombstone" advertisements announcing Ross's numerous completed assignments. Some thirty-five framed specimens hang on or lean against the wall and fifty or sixty others are encased in Lucite℡ and stand on a low bureau. At his desk, Ross, round, pug-nosed, suspendered, sits partially obscured by the confusion of papers in his in-box.

Once he had signed on to the Coleco case, he set out to strike a deal with a bidder in which the committee would pledge to support a bid that formed the centerpiece of a plan of reorganization. The price would be subject to the bidder's due diligence, which is an investigation to confirm the values of a company's assets and liabilities. He and the committee decided that Hasbro was the only viable potential purchaser. Here was a company that was not only well off but in the same business as Coleco and could incorporate a new toy business at great economies of scale. The Coleco assets were worth more as part of Hasbro, and Hasbro, therefore, would presumably pay a high price for them. As a final point, Ross found that Hasbro, unlike most other toy companies, had had minimal business dealings with Perlmutter.

One Sunday morning in late March, Alperin met Rubin and Kirschner at Kirschner's home in a northern suburb of New York City. In the hour and a half that they sat over coffee on the screened-in porch, Rubin and Kirschner made the prospective suitor comfortable with the idea of acquiring a company that was mired in bankruptcy and doing so by joining forces with people who were not the owners—two factors that would have scared most buyers away. They eased his mind with their theory of how this deal would get done. Here was their scenario:

Coleco had by then received multiple extensions to its exclusivity period (the three months in which only the company can file a reorganization plan) and had already moved for another extension. The creditors sensed that the judge had become frustrated with the company and was ready to let the creditors submit a reorganization plan of their own. And, he says, "she seemed to be sympathetic to our frustration over getting information out of the debtor, and she seemed to be sympathetic with the fact that we were getting completely wiped out in the case." As Rubin and Kirschner explained to Alperin, they believed the judge was likely to accept a plan of reorganization from the creditors that would include the sale of major assets. At the end of the visit, the three men shook hands on a preliminary agreement. Hasbro would move ahead to determine a bid.

Within a few weeks, Hasbro returned to the committee with a $95 million bid for Coleco's operating assets, including the rights to the Cabbage Patch doll, the games division, receivables and inventories. Hasbro insisted on receiving the goods in time for the Christmas selling season—the only way to save the Cabbage Patch doll from extinction. But bankruptcy being the unpredictable and bureaucratic creature that it is, no one could guarantee that the plan of reorganization could actually close on time. Coleco would have to sell the assets to Hasbro while it was still in bankruptcy, before a plan was confirmed by the court. Bid in hand, the creditors and Hasbro put together a joint plan of reorganization to that effect: The sale would go through, the cash from it would go to the company, and then the company's assets would be distributed to creditors.

The wild card in this plan was the lawsuit against Perlmutter. Sure, the litigation could be handled after a reorganization and any awards distributed later. But in that case Perlmutter and Marden would be paid the full $85 million plus interest due to them as the bank creditors and would return some of it later if the creditors' committee won the lawsuit—but that could take years. To Rubin, that just didn't seem fair. "It seemed pretty weird that we would have to, as a part of the Hasbro sale and eventual plan, ship money over to him and then sue him to get the damn money back," he points out. "Why should this guy get rich at the expense of the estate when he may eventually be owing the estate money?" With the judge's approval, the plaintiffs wanted to place Perlmutter's $90 million bank debt claim into escrow so that he would not see a dime of it until the litigation was resolved. If the unsecured creditors reaped anything from the lawsuit, says Rubin, "instead of having to chase Perlmutter all over the world to get him to write us a check we could just simply draw it out of the escrowed money." The intended effect of this arrangement was to put Perlmutter in a bind: Either negotiate a settlement to give up some of your claims or forget about seeing any recovery for an indefinite period of time while you cope with a major lawsuit.

CHECKMATE

While the committee was plotting strategy with Hasbro, Coleco's management was working on a revision of its reorganization plan. On April 6, it announced a proposal that by its estimate would give unsecured creditors sixteen to seventeen cents on the dollar for their claims. But it would still give Perlmutter majority equity control, and the committee valued the revised offer at only ten cents on the dollar. No deal.

Late that month the committee filed its request to terminate Coleco's exclusive right to propose a plan. And then it dropped its bombshell. Just after the committee signed its final agreement with Hasbro—which happened to be at about two A.M.—Kirschner called Coleco attorney Daniel Goldman, waking him up at home, to let him know about Hasbro's bid. It was a courtesy call, because the committee planned to release the story to the press the next day.

The committee asked that Hasbro be allowed access to Coleco's records and officers to do its due diligence. Rejected, Kirschner took the request to Judge Abram the following morning. The company objected.

Soon, however, Judge Abram intervened in the dispute. All the attorneys, for the company, the committee, and Perlmutter, met in her chambers. She finally ruled that because the Hasbro-committee plan would give unsecured creditors more than twice the recovery offered in Coleco's plan, she was going to direct the company to let Hasbro perform its research. She urged Coleco's advisers to reach a consensus by adopting that plan as its own. Within days, all contention evaporated. The company decided to sponsor the committee's reorganization plan and carried out the sale to Hasbro itself.

The matter of the Perlmutter litigation remained up in the air. Hasbro wanted the conflict resolved before the acquisition took place; otherwise Perlmutter would have a claim on the Coleco assets it was acquiring. Perlmutter had reason to cooperate, because he faced the risk of litigation and its inherent costs and delays, and he no longer had any hope of getting control of the company. For its part, the committee worried that the case would drag on and Perlmutter, as senior creditor, would ultimately take all the value. Hasbro's Alperin initiated the talks. Toward the end of May, Rubin, Kirschner, and Ross spoke with Perlmutter and his attorneys over the phone and finally at Hasbro's offices in New York's semi-seedy toy district in the twenties near Sixth Avenue.

That last meeting was a grueling session in which Perlmutter finally began to budge.

At first, Perlmutter offered what the creditors considered to be scraps, practically zero, while the creditors were demanding $75 million. As time passed, Perlmutter dished out more and more. During breaks, an exhausted Rubin amused himself by wandering through the showrooms viewing Hasbro's collection of GI Joe™'s and games. Finally the committee and Perlmutter settled on $26 million. That meant that Perlmutter and Marden had to pay $26 million to the Coleco creditors, although they still denied the charges of the lawsuit. The way they paid up was to subtract the amount from their claim, which had grown to $90 million including interest. Rubin had wanted to push for more. "I, speaking for myself, thought that we could have gotten him up to about $50 million." But others were thankful to get as much as they were being offered, for that $26 million went directly into the bondholders' pockets. "I might have chaired the committee, but I only had one vote, and it was clear that the committee was willing to settle at that level," Rubin says.

To this day, Rubin maintains that Perlmutter's fatal error in this case was buying the bank debt in the first place, which he'd done less than a year before. Because Perlmutter had an unusual business relationship with the company, he was open to litigation. By buying the bank debt, he held a claim in bankruptcy that could be held up by that litigation. As Rubin put it, "he threw his money in prison." He had to fight to get it out.

On June 1, 1989, Coleco announced both the settlement with Perlmutter and the agreement to sell out to Hasbro for $85 million plus warrants to buy one million Hasbro shares. The sale closed on July 12.

In the end, the bondholders took twenty-five cents on the dollar in cash and Hasbro warrants—a far cry from the five-cent value the unsecured creditors placed on Coleco's original offer. Yet then-CEO Handel, who now runs a consulting firm for troubled companies, believes that the creditors could have made out even better if they had handled the Hasbro negotiations differently. "They gave Hasbro a better deal than it had to have. For example, there were prepaid royalties on Cabbage Patch, and the creditors never got the benefit of them. They didn't have the knowledge. They negotiated the agreement without our being part of it."

For their part, Perlmutter and Marden did not make out badly at all. Having acquired an $85 million secured claim for $50 million, they pulled away with a $14 million profit even after the settlement, and the fraudulent conveyance litigation with respect to the barter credits was dropped. That's a quite impressive 28 percent return on their money—although in percentage terms not nearly as good as Rubin's 400 percent.

As part of the reorganization plan, the creditors' committee had to appoint a management team for Coleco's successor company—a shell company with $170 million in net operating tax loss carryforwards. Management's main duty would be to find an equity investor to pour money into the shell; that money would then be used to buy businesses whose profits could be applied against the net operating losses. Creditors on the committee identified Rubin as the best candidate for the management job. After all, he was an investor and he had done the bulk of the committee's work on the Coleco reorganization with gleaming results. They decided to offer him the position. "It was not something I was really wild about doing," he says. But, he adds, "it sounded kind of fun," which is one of his criteria for doing anything, and it did not look like so much work that it would take time away from his regular job. He started with no salary, but when it became clear that the work was going to be fairly involved, he was awarded an annual salary of $50,000. One issue remained to be resolved. In selling its assets to Hasbro, Coleco had also sold the rights to its name. The successor company needed a new one. "Anyone have a name for this company?" Rubin asked at one of the committee's final sessions. Someone replied, "It's your case, you get to name it. Why not your street?" He chose his dog, a collie. Today, vulture investor Rubin is chairman of the board at Ranger Industries.

5

The Three-Headed Monster at Wheeling-Pittsburgh Steel

He that dies pays all debts.

—THE TEMPEST

Paul Whitehead still has the poster hanging on the wall of his office at United Steelworkers of America's thirteen-story headquarters in downtown Pittsburgh. It was the picket sign for the strike that never happened in the summer of 1990 when he, the USWA assistant general counsel, and other union leaders were embroiled in contract talks with bankrupt Wheeling-Pittsburgh Steel Corporation. On top, in flaming red letters, the poster reads: "On Strike. Who gets what from the Wheeling-Pittsburgh plan of reorganization?" Below that is a bar graph with two black bars shooting up from zero and one red bar diving down. Printed beside the first bar: "LaBow Group, $102 million profit." The second: "Oppenheimer, $50 million profit." And the third: "Your steelworker claims, $80 million loss." And at the end, the clincher: "That's why the company and its creditors hope you'll accept the plan of reorganization."

That campaign poster captures the essence of the Wheeling-Pittsburgh bankruptcy. The reorganization of the nation's seventh largest steel maker revolved around the vultures and the union. The union's action to block a bank refinancing plan was what led to the Chapter 11 filing in the first place in 1985. The vultures came in a few years later. As one particularly resentful union official put it, these investors "bought the ability to step into someone's shoes and pretend they've been hurt." Ronald LaBow; Oppenheimer & Company; and Goldman, Sachs & Company were the three major New York vultures who landed on Wheeling-Pitt in search of sustenance. As they tussled with each other and with others in the bankruptcy, they dramatically shifted the course of the reorganization—and some say they delayed it by several months. LaBow bought bank debt, then took control of the process to bring Wheeling-Pitt out of the abyss, and ended up running a steel company.

But before he could carry his goods away, and before any creditor or shareholder could take their recoveries, the union had to be dealt with. During the summer of 1990, the union was trying to negotiate both a new contract to take effect when the bankruptcy ended and a better recovery for union bankruptcy claims. Dissatisfied with what they were being offered on both counts, they prepared to strike. The picket sign was planned as a way to keep the membership angry and inspired. What was on it was just as important as what was omitted. The recoveries of shareholders like Goldman, Sachs and other creditors, including suppliers and bondholders who bought at par, are conveniently missing. Like the union, they all suffered losses in this case. The union's leaders are sophisticated politicians, and this battle was as political as they come. They view bankruptcy as the ultimate clash between labor and capital. The best way to sway the membership, as they saw it, was to contrast those who lose with those who are gaining the most. Really, vultures are the only constituency that ever *makes* money in a bankruptcy, and that's no sure thing either.

When the reorganization plan came up for a vote, union members were overwhelmingly against it. But the votes were never tabulated. Instead, LaBow revised both the plan and the labor contract to give the union what it wanted. The strike didn't happen, and Wheeling-Pittsburgh emerged from bankruptcy.

* * *

The bankruptcy of Wheeling-Pittsburgh Steel had a long and tempestuous history before the vultures swooped in on the scene. The company was founded in 1920 in Wheeling, West Virginia, and merged with Pittsburgh Steel in 1968. It set up headquarters at the Gateway Center, a complex of stainless-steel office buildings and tree-lined walkways tucked into a corner of downtown Pittsburgh. The steel company's modest executive offices occupied a few floors of the building, each bearing the Wheeling-Pittsburgh U-shaped logo, a "ladle," used to transport molten iron and steel, capped by a red dot representing steel. By chance, the international headquarters of the United Steelworkers of America was in a neighboring building.

The story really begins in 1978 when Dennis Carney became chairman and chief executive officer. Ruthless in his management style, he also possessed uncanny foresight in launching an aggressive program to modernize the steelmaker's antediluvian plants. Unfortunately, his timing was disastrous. During and after the 1982 recession, America's steel industry buckled under the pressures of high labor and manufacturing costs, weak demand, and surging imports. Losses flowed like workers from a factory at the five o'clock bell. All the major steel manufacturers lost money— U.S. Steel, Bethlehem Steel, National Steel, Armco, LTV Corporation, Inland, and Wheeling-Pittsburgh. But Wheeling continued to update its nine plants in Pennsylvania, West Virginia, and Ohio. From 1980 to 1985, it spent $700 million for new facilities and equipment, nearly twice the amount invested by other U.S. producers and even 40 percent above Japanese steelmakers' rate of investment.

A showcase of Carney's work was the rail mill in Monessen, Pennsylvania. He put hundreds of millions of dollars into the plant, which included blasting furnaces, a continuous caster for shaping the steel, and a rail-making unit. Some work was also done on the company's sprawling flagship plant in Steubenville, Ohio, which like Monessen produced raw steel. Encompassing buildings on both banks of the Ohio River, it features great bins of iron ore pellets, mountains of coking coal, and four rust-colored blast furnaces the shape of upside down bottles that turn the ingredients into molten iron—all of which dwarf the railroad boxcars nearby. Up-to-date oxygen furnaces turn iron into molten steel, which is then poured into a continuous caster. Rolling mills grab hold of steel slabs and blooms, assaulting the senses with crashing noise.

By 1985, there were few girders left to support the enormous debt the company had assumed to accomplish Carney's ambitions. Attempts to reduce costs through labor concessions and a bank loan refinancing failed miserably when the union refused to go along with an agreement the company had reached with the banks. That left bankruptcy reorganization as the only recourse. When it filed for Chapter 11 on April 16, 1985, the company reported $1.09 billion in assets and $933.9 million in liabilities.

Wheeling's immediate goal was to lower wages and benefits by a brutal 30 percent. When the union soundly rejected this demand, management asked presiding Judge Warren Worthington Bentz for permission to cancel the outstanding labor contract. The fifty-nine-year-old former bankruptcy attorney from Erie, Pennsylvania—who came to the bench the day after Wheeling-Pitt declared bankruptcy—granted that request in July 1985. "It is clear that a reduction in labor costs is . . . necessary if the company is to have any hope of reorganizing," he wrote. Presented with a revised request for a more modest but still severe reduction in labor costs plus fewer job protection provisions, the union appealed Bentz's decision. But rather than wait for a judgment, that month the USWA leadership sent 8200 Wheeling employees out on strike in the industry's first major walkout in twenty-six years. (Bentz's ruling was reversed in 1986.)

Workers stayed off the job for ninety-eight endless days. The union demanded the resignation of Dennis Carney, and finally, he was forced out. To save an estimated $450 million over twenty years, the new management terminated the severely underfunded pension plan and handed over the liabilities to the Pension Benefit Guaranty Corporation (PBGC), the federal agency that backs the promises of corporate pension funds. Union and management then negotiated a small wage and benefit cutback, but the lender banks objected that the contract didn't provide for the flexibility to close the Monessen rail-making plant. The banks argued that the company was losing some $30 million a year operating the facility because of shrinking demand for rail as railroads were consolidating. After agreeing that the company could close Monessen and relieve workers, the union had its contract, and the steelworkers returned to their mills and furnaces. To answer the union's demand for a role in the bankruptcy reorganization of the company, Judge Bentz ruled that the new pact would stay in effect until ten days after completion of the reorganization, when a new union contract would take its place. Negotiating a reorganization plan with creditors and shareholders is difficult enough for a bankrupt company; adding the highly contentious ingredient of union contract talks greatly complicated the case.

Little headway was made toward a reorganization plan in 1986. The company cut costs by shuttering plants, including Monessen, and made plans to move corporate headquarters from Pittsburgh to the city of Wheeling, which had grown up with the coal, rail, and steel industries and had suffered through steel's dry years. On a regular basis, management met with the bank creditors and the committee of unsecured creditors, consisting primarily of suppliers, to report on the status of the case. But with the lack of progress, creditors began to get edgy.

A management shakeup in 1987 delayed things further. At the end of 1986, board chairman Allen Paulson sold the 34 percent stake he'd acquired for $50 million to his friend and Wheeling director, Lloyd Lubensky, for an astounding $100,000—a sale that would become significant later in the bankruptcy. Early in January, Paulson resigned and Lubensky ascended to the chairmanship. But within a few weeks, he clashed with existing upper management on compensation issues and, in what became known as the "Saturday Night Massacre," he fired the CEO, president, and general counsel.

The creditors' committee suggested bringing in William Scharffenberger as chief executive to head the company and get the reorganization plan on track. A gentle-mannered accountant by training who in the 1960s was the assistant controller at Wheeling, Scharffenberger was a professional turnaround executive who made a career of wandering from one forlorn company to the next like the financial world's version of a Mary Poppins, fixing operations and arranging reorganization plans. He maintained reorganization headquarters at the company's old Pittsburgh offices, and his schedule quickly became crammed with meetings. He sat down with the Pension Benefit Guaranty Corporation to work on a compromise on the $496 million claim the federal agency had filed after Wheeling-Pittsburgh had terminated its pension plan. And he started settling the claims of suppliers, particularly iron ore mining companies, with which Wheeling had broken contracts. Union negotiations, meanwhile, were put off while the United Steelworkers diverted much of its energies toward assisting the quixotic election campaign of Michael Dukakis.

THE QUIET TYCOON

In June 1987, Ronald LaBow stepped into this brightening scene. LaBow was the captain of vulture investing at the old-line New York investment firm of Neuberger & Berman, his base of operations for a dozen years. That month, he culled $80.3 million in secured Wheeling bank debt at a bargain-basement price just shy of $40 million. By his analysis, he was sure that he would be paid the full $80.3 million plus interest when the company emerged. During the summer, he continued probing the company and its prospects. In particular he weighed the odds that Wheeling could make a "reasonable" settlement on the looming claim of the pension agency. He concluded that because Wheeling discontinued its pension fund in 1985, it would elude the tendrils of a law passed in 1986 that had strengthened the agency's hand. That would save the company and its creditors hundreds of millions of dollars.

For assistance evaluating the operations side, LaBow called on longtime Neuberger client David Hains, an engineer and one of the wealthiest men in Australia. As the owner of the private investment banking firm Portland House Group, Hains, who is now sixty-one years old, had been a driving force in industrial reorganizations in his native country. Once he took a good long look at Wheeling-Pittsburgh, he teamed up with LaBow to invest and take an active part in the bankruptcy.

Now with greater confidence, LaBow began negotiating to buy out more of Wheeling's bank lenders. He wanted it all. But, along the way, he found that two banks already had sold out to someone else. That someone else was the Wall Street brokerage firm of

Oppenheimer & Company and specifically Jon Bauer and Shelley Greenhaus, two up-and-coming migratory vultures in their thirties. LaBow called Bauer and offered to buy the pieces of debt, but he was turned down. Because the purchases had yet to close, LaBow then went to the two selling banks and topped Oppenheimer's forty-seven-and-a-half-cent bid by ten cents on the dollar. "Those were the first pieces of bank debt that we had ever traded," Bauer says. "And both banks had never sold anything before. Back then, in the early days of bank debt trading, there were no formal commitment letters signed when you had an agreement in principle. For both of our pieces, it took a long time between when we committed to buy and when we actually closed. Now it's much more professional. The day you come in to buy it you have the bank put in writing that they are going to sell it and usually close down in two weeks." But at the time, he could not prevent LaBow from outbidding him, and he did not want to raise his original bid. "In both cases we had to go high up in the bank and convince the chairman of the bank that he had a moral obligation to sell it to us," Bauer says. And they did. Just because there was no more bank debt up for grabs did not deter Bauer and Greenhaus from becoming more deeply involved in this bankruptcy. They would soon surface again, as buyers in the lower-ranked, unsecured level of debt.

As LaBow was gathering in his purchases, he got a call from Jay Goldsmith of Balfour Investors, whom he'd known for years as a fellow bankruptcy investor. "I was trying to find a way in desperately," Goldsmith says. "Ron LaBow's my friend, and I went to Ron LaBow. 'I want to come into this thing.' Ron said, 'Stay out, this is my deal, and we have a lot of the bank debt. Please don't do anything that's going to upset the apple cart.' I said, 'Okay fine,' because I have great respect for him and I think he's one of the most decent guys around and brilliant also. We go back to the beginning." In October, just a few days before the crash of 1987, LaBow and Hains closed the purchase of $182 million worth of bank loans at an average cost of more than $95 million, bringing his stake to 86 percent of Wheeling's bank debt at a total cost of nearly $140 million. Now Ron LaBow and David Hains controlled the powerful secured class of Wheeling-Pittsburgh debt.

Backing the investment was money from three partnerships

going by the nondescript names of DR Capital Partners, RM Capital Partners and General Holdings, Ltd. LaBow and Hains were investors in the partnerships, as was LaBow's employer Neuberger & Berman. As to the other partners, some were junk bond traders from Drexel, Burnham, Lambert, and the scuttlebutt during the case was that one was their chief, Michael Milken. Oppenheimer attorney David Strumwasser jokingly speculated that RM Capital Partners stood for Ron and Mike. LaBow says he doesn't know what it stands for, and all he'll say about Milken's involvement is he "may or may not" have invested in RM with the Drexel, Burnham group. Later in the case when LaBow released documents detailing the members of his partnerships, those listed were all other partnerships with similar letter names, leading a somewhat discomfited Strumwasser to conclude that "LaBow was fronting for the Alphabet Soup."

LaBow assumed that within a year or so when Wheeling-Pittsburgh emerged from bankruptcy, his claims would be paid at par plus interest, more than doubling his money. And that would be that. He would wipe his hands of this rust-belt metal manufacturer, as he had done with virtually all the other investments he'd made in his career. But Wheeling would be different for LaBow. He would be like someone who goes on a vacation to Bangkok and enjoys himself so much he decides to settle down and raise a family. LaBow was going to become very attached to Wheeling-Pittsburgh Steel.

In his midfifties, LaBow is tall with gray-blue eyes accentuated by a colorless complexion and thinning white hair. He is one of the older generation of vulture investors, going back to the railroads in the 1970s, and more recently, he has invested heavily and profitably in the bankruptcies of Tosco, A. H. Robins, and Todd Shipyards. In the case of shipbuilder and industrial equipment manufacturer Todd Shipyards, bankrupt in 1987, LaBow bought 48 percent of the bonds from the company's major bondholder, its vice chairman, at fifty to sixty cents on the dollar. Early in 1989, he was one of a few parties vying to sponsor a reorganization plan. Essentially, he proposed paying creditors and shareholders cash from the company and his own pocket in order to get his hands on the vast majority of the stock in the new company—a plan, it turned out, that was markedly similar to the one he put together at Wheeling-Pittsburgh that gave him control of the company. In Todd, Labow did not end up as the plan proponent, but he also did not get paid 100 percent plus interest on his claim, as most everyone else did. The company and the creditors' committee both objected to the claim on the grounds that he bought it from an insider. LaBow settled for something less than a full recovery, but still made a killing.

Early in 1990, LaBow left Neuberger & Berman to start his own vulture firm called Stonehill Investors after the street he lives on in the affluent Westchester town of Pound Ridge. His spacious office on East Fifty-ninth Street is flooded with light from the floor-to-ceiling window that runs along two walls and features a lustrous wood L-shaped desk, a formal sofa, and a television set. From his Wheeling investment alone, his group is worth nearly $80 million, and he personally owns a piece of that. An intensely private man, he and his second wife also have a home in the winter resort town of Sun Valley, Idaho.

Those who know LaBow say his negotiating style can be rather unnerving. He is all business, no small talk. But in meetings he is soft-spoken and at times can be almost completely silent. One banker told of an initial meeting in which LaBow brought along associates who did all of the talking, while occasionally he whispered into their ears. Oppenheimer attorney Strumwasser echoes others in describing another peculiarity of LaBow's. "He'd sit with you, chitchat, there'd be an agreement on some points, not on others. He'd leave that meeting and think he had an agreement. He used to tell us 'We have a deal with the committee,' and then we'd ask the committee and they'd say they had nothing firm." Whether these were misunderstandings on LaBow's part or canny negotiating ploys no one could discern. What was certain was LaBow's tenacity. Once he decided that he wanted to control the reorganized Wheeling-Pittsburgh Steel Corporation, he slogged through tedious and difficult negotiations with the company; creditors' committee; PBGC; Goldman, Sachs; Oppenheimer; and the union with remarkable patience and determination.

RADICAL INVESTING

By the end of 1987, Oppenheimer's Bauer and Greenhaus were increasingly eager to invest more funds in Wheeling. After a visit to the company, they came home convinced that operations were on the mend and that cash was going to pour in through every door and window. Now that the rest of the bank debt was locked up in LaBow's strongbox, they scouted around for unsecured debt to buy—perhaps from Wheeling-Pitt suppliers who had been left in the lurch by the bankruptcy. In January, they caught a big one.

Greenhaus and Bauer made a perfect fit. Bauer was the trader with a trader's hyperkinetic personality and a quick analytical mind that can absorb an onslaught of price and value data. Trained in economics at Rutgers University and Harvard Business School, in 1982 Bauer became the first analyst for Randall Smith and Basel Vasiliou's flourishing business trading the bonds of troubled companies at Bear, Stearns & Company. In his first big assignment, Bauer analyzed the recently bankrupt Revere Copper & Brass and then helped Smith buy out a major holder of Revere stock and bonds. A Bear, Stearns partnership ended up in control and later sold the company. For a $17 million investment, it took away more than $65 million in value. As a member of the partnership, Bauer shared in that profit: "I was promised a piece of the partnership, but I didn't know how small a piece could be." In 1986, Bauer went over to Oppenheimer to run its junk bond trading department— which in addition to official junk (high-yield, low-rated bonds of solvent companies) specialized in the research, sale, and trading of "busted" bonds and bank debt of troubled companies.

He also joined Greenhaus, who was investing money for the firm. A short, cherubic thirty-nine-year-old with a boyish enthusiasm, Greenhaus is the deal maker of the two, immersing himself in the give and take of negotiations over the recovery. Born in Brooklyn and bred in Queens, he became what he calls "a typical 1960s radical," growing his hair long while in college at the City University of New York. In preparation for a career in New York City government, he studied political science and spent his summers working in the city's consumer affairs and legal aid offices. Graduating in 1976, he went on to business school on a full scholarship at New York University, because he believed "a business back-ground would help me restructure the city government." But after meeting a senior partner at Lehman Brothers, who showed him the bankruptcy and risk arbitrage operations at the firm, he was never the same. That initial spark flared into a passion after a graduate course on bankruptcy. Out of NYU, he went straight to the arbi-trage department at Loeb, Rhodes and then went on in 1981 to invest with the Rosenwald family of the Sears Roebuck & Com-pany fortune, which in the 1970s was one of the earliest groups to spot the sheen in the murk of bankruptcy investing. In 1983, he joined Oppenheimer, putting the firm's money into bankruptcies such as Wickes, Lionel, Texas Air, and Storage Technology. Four years later, he and Bauer raised a $70 million partnership fund to invest in their specialty.

A $75 MILLION CATCH

Bauer and Greenhaus did not have to look far for a good investment in Wheeling unsecured debt. It came to them from a small Wall Street trading firm by the name of Cowen & Company. There, analyst Phil Schaeffer had been thinking along exactly the same lines as Bauer and Greenhaus: Wheeling was recovering, and despite dire prognoses by the experts, there wasn't any persuasive reason to think that the patient would fall back into a coma. In 1987, Schaeffer and his associate Marc Lasry started picking up the bankruptcy trade claims of small suppliers to Wheeling-Pitt. As a bankrupt company often does, Wheeling had broken supply con-tracts it didn't need and then negotiated an amount that the sup-plier could file as a damages claim in the bankruptcy. Late in the year, Cowen stumbled on a not-so-small claim. An associate, Maria Mendelsohn, had the job of contacting Wheeling's larger suppliers to find out if they wanted to sell their trade claims to Cowen at a certain price. One day she called up Maxus Energy Corporation, a natural resources company that by the court rec-ords was owed $300,000. The company confirmed that, yes, it was claiming the amount indicated in the court papers. But Maxus also said that it had claimed more. A lot more. In fact $75 million worth. Mendelsohn was incredulous. She ran around the corner into the office Schaeffer and Lasry shared and breathlessly told them what she'd found. "Guess what? There's this huge piece, a $75 million piece."

Wheeling had canceled a coal contract with Maxus, and the two companies had come to an accord on damages, which Maxus then filed as the $75 million claim. Because Cowen only had a few million dollars to invest in distressed companies, Schaeffer and Lasry could not keep the claim themselves. So Schaeffer placed a call to Bauer, a classmate at Harvard Business School. "Look, we found this piece. Are you interested?" Schaeffer asked. It was like a gift floated down from heaven. Lasry and Bauer worked on pricing the debt, negotiating with Maxus a dirt-cheap price of sixteen cents on the dollar. Then Lasry handed the whole bundle to Bauer for a finder's fee of half a cent, leaving it to him to negotiate the exact terms of the sale.

This matter of terms was hardly routine. Attached to the claim like moss to a log were potential pollution liabilities from a coal mine Maxus had operated with Wheeling. If the government wanted them to clean up any pollution at the mine site, the cost could be subtracted from the claim. That explained why Oppenheimer could buy the claim for such a skimpy price. Bauer wanted to reduce Oppenheimer's risk on the claim as much as possible, which he and his attorneys did by negotiating an option; if liabilities were charged to the claim, Oppenheimer could sell the claim back to Maxus for a bit over cost, plus expenses. But really Oppenheimer wanted to keep the cheap sixteen-and-a-half-cent claim, gain enough leverage in the bankruptcy to negotiate away the liabilities on it, and then take a high recovery of eighty cents or more. "We knew that through the reorganization plan process we would have to use our influence to make sure that Maxus became a free and clear claim," Bauer says.

But that would come later as Oppenheimer fortified its position in the case. Now, in January 1988, Bauer and Greenhaus had made the biggest trade of their careers. Oppenheimer kept part of the $75 million and, while continuing to hold the claim in its name, sold chunks to brokerage clients, including Balfour Investors. When Balfour's Jay Goldsmith first heard from Bauer, he called his friend Ron LaBow, as a courtesy, to tell him he planned to invest.

"Hey, I might be able to buy this piece," he said.

"Well it's speculative," LaBow remarked, "and it may come against us."

"I would never want to come against you," Goldsmith said. "But I want to buy this piece."

LABOW TAKES THE WHEEL

A bankrupt company's management usually handles the reorganization process. But with the lion's share of the secured bank debt in their hands by the start of 1988, LaBow and Hains held enough of the cards to drive much of the action. Slowly, LaBow took an interest in corporate affairs, making increasing contact with chief executive Scharffenberger and his advisers. "He started in a very low key way," says Scharffenberger. "He was interested in certain things we were doing, like bringing in a chief operating officer." LaBow and Hains also contacted the union's leaders to talk about how to get labor negotiations on track. Andrew (Lefty) Palm, the crusty director of USWA District 15 who was the union's chief negotiator on the case, spoke with Hains early on. "I am not one for first impressions," Palm growls. "Usually I really put someone through our litmus test. But I just trusted this guy." Even so, the union wasn't ready to talk turkey, whether it be with LaBow and Hains or the company or anybody else. "Our strategy was for everybody to be settled with what they were going to get out of the bankruptcy. We wanted to be the last at the plate. Then we had a better shot at getting what we wanted. If we'd gone first, others would mess with our deal." Of course, by being the last out of the gate, the union could mess with the deals the others had made.

In early 1988, the LaBow team turned its full attention to the Pension Benefit Guaranty Corporation's $496 million claim. Either by phone or by traveling to Washington with his attorney, Denis Cronin, LaBow met with the pension agency's point men. By April, the company was offering the PBGC an unsecured claim, which would be lumped in with all the other Wheeling unsecured claims. When the reorganization plan was set, all unsecured creditors would receive the same percentage recovery, and at the time the unsecured creditors' committee was estimating a recovery of at most twenty-five cents on the dollar when the bankruptcy ended. One evening in mid-April, when its negotiations with the company had stalled, the agency called LaBow. He advised the pension regulators to take a straight-out $85 million cash settlement to be paid in full at the end of the bankruptcy. It came out to eighteen cents on the dollar—less than the twenty-five cents, but at the time the twenty-five cents was far from a sure thing. And, more important, it was the largest bankruptcy recovery the PBGC had negotiated to date and, therefore, an excellent precedent for its purposes. The agency took the idea to Wheeling and the company signed on.

Hearing of LaBow's involvement, Wheeling-Pitt attorney Bruce McCullough was somewhat frustrated: "The LaBow group was unofficial [not an official negotiating committee in the bankruptcy]. They were free to wander around without accountability. They could say to the union, 'Throw your support our way.' The same with the PBGC. They were dealing separately with the PBGC." As to whether LaBow deserved credit for the pension settlement, McCullough says, "The PBGC kept changing its mind almost hourly as to what it was looking for." Even so, LaBow gave the agency the formula it finally took. Later, the company would have to settle yet another issue with the pension agency. But for now it had leapt a major hurdle, leaving the path clear for management and creditors to sit down and begin preparing a reorganization plan to pay off all of Wheeling-Pittsburgh's debts.

Chief executive William Scharffenberger, knowing that the secured and unsecured creditors as the two top classes of debt had the right to the majority of Wheeling-Pittsburgh's value, insisted that the two parties work out key issues on their own while he oversaw the process. LaBow, as the chief secured creditor, sat down with the unsecured creditors' committee, which represented the entire group of nonbank creditors holding $600 million in claims (including Oppenheimer's $75 million Maxus Energy claim). "We recognized LaBow as a legitimate creditors' group, albeit not an official committee," Scharffenberger says. "We urged the two groups to try to get together and come up with a plan." Intensive negotiations filled the spring and summer of 1988, often taking place at Wheeling's reorganization headquarters in the

Gateway Center and sometimes at various lawyers' outposts in New York. Scharffenberger set a deadline of December to have a preliminary reorganization plan ready to submit to the court.

QUESTIONS OF VALUE

In bankruptcy, fortunes are made and lost on technical issues, and in this case the talks between the secured and unsecured creditors revolved around a technical issue. The two parties were arguing about whether the bank class was fully secured. In other words, was the value of the collateral that was backing the $304 million of outstanding bank loans (owned substantially by LaBow) less than the face value of the loans? That collateral consisted of Wheeling-Pittsburgh's physical assets—its property, plant and equipment—but not liquid assets such as cash and receivables. The committee said the collateral value was less than that of the loans. In that case, the bank class should not receive its interest—a huge amount after a few years—and in turn the unsecured creditors would receive greater value. LaBow said the collateral value was more, much more, than par. So he believed the bank class should recover the full amount of its loans *plus* accrued interest.

But money was only one aspect of this dispute. Another was who would control the reorganization of this massive steel maker. If the collateral value was less than the loan value, the claim would have to be split into a secured portion and an unsecured portion. The secured portion would be paid in full and would not have a vote in determining who gets what in the reorganization plan. The unsecured portion would become part of the much larger unsecured pool of claims and would, therefore, have little say in the reorganization process. Translation: If his claim was substantially unsecured, LaBow would have lost his leverage in this case and the unsecured creditors' committee would have a lot of power. What it would do with that power would be to draw up a reorganization plan that gives its constituents a cash recovery. The unsecured creditors were mainly businesses that need cash, and if they had to take stock, as lower-ranked creditors often do, there was no assurance as to when they could sell it and at what price.

The only way to resolve this difference of opinion about collateral value once and for all was through a valuation hearing before the judge. But that could take many months, and neither group of creditors had the patience or wanted to take the risk that the ruling would go against them.

In the fall of 1988, the two sides reached a compromise. It was fairly simple. LaBow wanted his accrued interest and he had now decided that he wanted to control the stock of the reorganized Wheeling-Pittsburgh. The committee wanted cash. So they agreed to swap. LaBow would take his principal and interest in the form of notes and stock, and the unsecured creditors would receive their recovery in the form of Wheeling's available cash—although they would have to take some stock because there wouldn't be enough cash in the till to pay them enough of a recovery. That stock portion ended up being another important matter for negotiation. The amount of stock LaBow wanted to give the unsecured creditors was 37.5 percent of the new company's equity, which he argued was adequate, because he was predicting a $15-a-share trading value for the stock. But the committee was predicting a value of only $8 a share.

LaBow and committee financial adviser Robert Conway thrashed out this issue in several sessions at Conway's Seventh Avenue office at Ernst & Young. Sitting with LaBow at a coffee table there one day, looking toward the Hudson River, Conway proposed that if LaBow really believed the stock was going to trade at $15, he should guarantee the value. He should buy the stock of any creditor that wants to sell it to him for $15 a share. "That took a while to negotiate," says Conway, "but ultimately that was the thing I believe that closed the deal, because it gave the unsecured creditors liquidity. And they knew exactly what they were going to get in the way of dollar return as long as they exercised the put [took the option to sell stock]. Any creditor who felt it would be worthwhile to ride with LaBow would have the opportunity to do that. As soon as that got resolved, we had a deal." So based on Wheeling's cash holdings at the time and 37.5 percent of the stock at $15 a share, the unsecured creditors' recovery came to about sixty cents on the dollar. The two sides drew up a three-page "term sheet" outlining the agreement and handed it over to Scharffenberger and his staff, who used it in preparing the company's preliminary reorganization plan for delivery to the court by year end.

Oppenheimer's Greenhaus and Bauer didn't yet know the recovery amount that the committee had negotiated. They were not allowed to receive inside information on the talks unless they agreed to stop trading in Wheeling's debt and securities. But the two young vultures had their own opinion about what the recovery should be; given Wheeling's ongoing earnings revival, they thought all unsecured creditors should get eighty to ninety cents on the dollar. Although the two Wall Street sharpshooters didn't know that their target price was much higher than what was being negotiated, they got an indication when they paid a visit to LaBow and Hains. Asked what level of recovery they were looking for, Bauer and Greenhaus said eighty cents. LaBow says he responded that there was no way to give them a number because the company still had to settle with the union on its contract and its employee bankruptcy claims. As Bauer recalls, LaBow told them to "get real." "We were practically laughed out of the office." Remarks LaBow, "We laughed that they were so naive they just didn't understand."

In December 1988, the company presented its preliminary reorganization plan to the court. Wheeling-Pittsburgh would issue twenty million new shares. The unsecured class of debt was in line for $250 million in cash and 37.5 percent of the new stock. LaBow's bank class would recover $225 million in bonds and half of the new stock of the reorganized company; the value of LaBow's share of that would be $323 million, nearly tripling his group's original investment (assuming the stock did start trading at $15 a share as he expected). LaBow also would buy out the unsecured creditors' stock allocation for $112 million, giving him a majority stake in the new company. As for the current common stockholders, they got a measly 7.5 percent stake and preferred shareholders 5 percent.

But the plan was not yet a full-fledged, formal reorganization plan because it did not reflect input from either the stockholders or the USWA. This preliminary plan was submitted to the court as what had been accomplished so far; two important parties had reached agreement, and now the other two would look the pact over and the company would attempt to bring everyone to a consensus. Sounds easy. But, alas, it was not to be so. At different times over the next year and a half, the stockholders, the steelworkers, and Oppenheimer would all attempt to derail the LaBow-committee plan. For Wheeling-Pittsburgh, 1989 was going to be a tumultuous year.

THE ENIGMA CALLED GOLDMAN, SACHS

At least one shareholder decided not to hang around and hope that the final plan granted him more than the preliminary one did. In January 1989, Lloyd Lubensky, the chairman of the Wheeling-Pittsburgh board for nearly two years and its largest shareholder, abruptly resigned and sold his 34 percent stake. His decision opened a door for yet another big vulture to step onto the stage. Buying him out at $8 a share, for a total of $14 million, was one of the pillars of Wall Street—Goldman, Sachs & Company. For Lubensky, the sale was a bonanza. He had acquired the position two years earlier for only $100,000. Ironically, a year after he bought the slab of stock, he offered to unload it for $5 million to Oppenheimer and its client Balfour Investors, but had found no interest and withdrew the merchandise from the market. For a while he considered alternative ways to help haul Wheeling out of bankruptcy while maintaining his big ownership position. He hired advisers from Prudential-Bache Securities to come up with a strategy, and in the fall of 1988 they presented their game plan to the reorganization committee of the board: The company could borrow funds to buy out LaBow at a small premium to the investor's $140 million cost. But the board rejected such an onerous assumption of new debt. So Lubensky decided finally to sell, and he jumped at Goldman, Sachs's $8 a share offer. "His wife wanted him to hold out for a higher figure," Scharffenberger recalls, "but Lou sold it for eight bucks a share. And he was right. He was dead right. He made the right decision and got out."

A few observers thought that Goldman, Sachs would also make out well on this deal. "I think it was a terrific buy for Goldman, Sachs," Chriss Street, managing director at a West Coast investment banking firm specializing in bankrupt companies, declared in *The Wall Street Journal*. "Wheeling-Pittsburgh has real value, and people are going to start taking a look at that." But most people were puzzled as to why Goldman, Sachs was taking such a giant step into this bankruptcy, especially given that the just-announced LaBow-committee plan gave shareholders a Lilliputian recovery. Even if Wheeling-Pittsburgh turned out to be worth more than envisioned by that plan, the creditors and preferred shareholders were first in line to benefit; if strictly kept, the rules of Chapter 11 would demand that the unsecured creditors' recovery rise from 60 cents on the dollar to 100 cents before shareholders had a right to get anything at all. Scharffenberger was among the mystified. "I'll never understand why Goldman bought it." LaBow was flabbergasted. "Denis [Cronin, his lawyer] and I spent days trying to figure out what they know that we don't know. After all, this was Goldman, Sachs." It seemed that the only way Goldman, Sachs could have any hope of profiting from this situation was by taking the considerable risk of sinking a lot more money into Wheeling in return for a big ownership stake. That was what the firm indicated it would do.

He might not have understood Goldman's move, but Scharffenberger was probably the firm's best ally. Even though he had just submitted a preliminary plan to the court, Scharffenberger remained open to a plan that dealt a better hand to current stockholders, and it looked as if Goldman, Sachs was the shareholders' last best hope. The first impression Goldman, Sachs made on him was less than awesome, however. Fred Cohen, Goldman, Sachs's man on the case, burst on the scene like a heavy-metal band in a wooded glen. Scharffenberger was offended by what he considered Cohen's "bombastic" approach. "Fred became very aggressive in the beginning, girding for war, and I fought back a little bit with him in an exchange of letters. He wrote to me that we were favoring LaBow. I wrote back, 'Stop the nonsense. If you've got something to say, come on down.' I invited him down to start working with us. 'Help me develop a better plan. Now it's your turn.' I welcomed Goldman to come in with a plan that would do more for the equity. That was really my hope, that here's this great big powerful organization that has the ability to borrow money here and there, and is able to approach all the steel companies in Europe—because operations were improving and we were beginning to get attractive" as an acquisition. But within a few weeks, Cohen left Goldman and vanished from the scene. His replacement was Douglas Dethy, a member of Goldman's arbitrage department, who impressed

Scharffenberger as calmer and more reasonable. Dethy became the chairman of a new committee formed to represent all stockholders in the ongoing battle over Wheeling-Pittsburgh Steel.

THE PLAN IN TROUBLE

LaBow feared that Goldman's arrival in this case would delay, if not shatter, the plan he and Hains had assembled with the creditors' committee and that the company had submitted to the court in December. That spring, LaBow attorney Cronin repeatedly insisted to Wheeling's lawyer Bruce McCullough that the company should "embrace the plan." McCullough suggested that LaBow put up some money, in the form of a letter of credit, to prove his commitment to the plan. In the meantime, McCullough told him, the company intended to give Goldman, Sachs a "reasonable" amount of time to come up with its program for restructuring the company. When pressed on how long "reasonable" might be, McCullough responded that he and Scharffenberger probably would give the Wall Street firm until August. For now, LaBow did not tie up his money in a letter of credit.

The company still was the only party the court allowed to file a reorganization plan. But that didn't mean it had a free rein. If creditors became impatient with the lack of progress, they could move to end the company's advantageous position so that others could file plans with the court and creditors could vote on those plans. That year, Scharffenberger did what he could to give Goldman, Sachs as much time as it needed to evaluate the company and draw up a plan proposal. "I was glad to stall as long as I could to give equity an opportunity to come up with a plan. *Stall* is maybe not the word, but you prolong it, you try to help, you call meetings or have them make a presentation to the board." But LaBow, like any vulture investor who sees his investment shrinking with the passage of time, was not one to wait around too long.

His patience began to wear thin in May when two things occurred. First of all, Oppenheimer purchased another very large claim. Bauer and Greenhaus had been searching for ways to increase their influence in the reorganization process. For one thing, they wanted greater power to push for a recovery north of seventy cents on the dollar and preferably eighty cents. For another, they wanted to be able to negotiate away the pollution liabilities from the $75 million Maxus Energy claim they had acquired the year before. So they bought a $46 million claim from an affiliate of Hanna Mining, whose representative chaired the creditors' committee, for fifty-seven and a half cents on the dollar. (The Oppenheimer vultures had told that chairman that he'd sold out for too low a number in the December plan—sixty cents. "We said we would put our money where our mouth was," Greenhaus recounts.) That catch would bring the total amount of Wheeling debt under Oppenheimer's auspices to about $180 million—$35 million owned by Oppenheimer itself and the rest by clients. Minus bank debt, the firm now spoke for about $140 million of the unsecured class of debt. It wasn't the one-third of the class needed to block a proposed plan of reorganization, but it was close. Additional Wheeling claims that some Oppenheimer clients held in their own names lifted the broker's clout to a virtual blocking position. Not that Greenhaus and Bauer wanted to block a plan, but the fact that they potentially had enough ammunition to do so meant that when they talked people were going to listen.

LaBow and his attorneys believed that Oppenheimer ultimately would take any deal offered without much complaining, because its investment had cost so little. But they also knew that with its potential blocking position, the firm could delay the passage of the LaBow-committee reorganization plan. "We thought Oppenheimer was trouble," says one of his attorneys, Thomas Mayer. "We had a deal, and we viewed these people as people who might make trouble for us." So when Oppenheimer filed with the court in June for official sanction to transfer the $46 million Hanna Mining claim into its name, LaBow took action. "That was the cannon at Fort Sumter," says Jeffrey Sabin, an Oppenheimer attorney. LaBow began laying plans to challenge the official transfer of the claim.

The second thing that happened in May was more ominous to LaBow than Oppenheimer's claims purchase. Goldman, Sachs's Doug Dethy announced a conceptual reorganization plan that involved buying out LaBow, and he asked the secured creditor to name his price. But LaBow had no interest in selling out. "I had told the court and the union I was in the company for the long haul, and I couldn't back out of that." But this was only Goldman, Sachs's first attempt. It meant to try again to come up with its own reorganization plan, and LaBow had every reason to believe it would. After all, Goldman, Sachs had invested $14 million in Wheeling-Pittsburgh, and if it didn't do something, the LaBow-committee plan would all but wipe out that investment.

LaBow doubted that Goldman, Sachs would actually carry through with a plan. "We knew Goldman was not going to throw good money after bad," Cronin says. "It was too risky." But by proposing a reorganization plan, Goldman, Sachs could seriously hold up the case; that was its bargaining chip for a material recovery in the bankruptcy.

LaBow needed to get rid of Goldman, Sachs, and one way to do that was to nail down Scharffenberger's support. So that summer, the vulture investor began pressuring Scharffenberger to toss Goldman, Sachs to the winds. LaBow met with Scharffenberger on June 27 and reported what committee representatives recently had told him: They wanted to move ahead with the December 1988 LaBow-committee plan but were concerned that Scharffenberger was no longer standing behind it. Both the committee and LaBow believed that Scharffenberger had pledged to support that plan. But Scharffenberger told LaBow that he'd never fully supported the plan and that the only way he would was if LaBow convinced the union and the shareholders' committee to sign onto it. Period.

On July 29, LaBow and Scharffenberger spoke again, this time over the phone. LaBow warned that on August 10 he intended to move to terminate the company's sole right to file a plan—unless Scharffenberger consented to go forward with the LaBow-committee plan on an accelerated schedule. If the judge granted the motion and allowed others to file competing plans, LaBow said that he and the committee had drawn up a new plan that they would submit in the latter half of September. Before closing, LaBow suggested that they meet before that hearing to discuss the matter more fully.

On August 2, Scharffenberger, LaBow, and Stan West (the new chairman of the creditors' committee from the mining company Cleveland-Cliffs), each accompanied by his chief attorney, met for dinner at the prestigious Duquesne Club in downtown Pittsburgh.

Just off Mellon Square Park, the staid businessmen's club is a labyrinth of dark-paneled public and private dining rooms each bearing names like the Walnut Room and the Pine Room. Sculpture graces the hallways and paintings adorn the walls, including august portraits of such Pittsburgh business legends as George Westinghouse and Andrew Mellon. The six men, who in subsequent meetings would call themselves the Gang of Six, took a private dining room for their discussion.

Again, LaBow insisted that back in December 1988 Scharffenberger had made a deal with him and the committee to support their plan, but that now he had broken that promise. The vulture investor wanted the executive to endorse the plan once and for all. Scharffenberger again retorted that he'd never committed himself to the initial plan because neither the stockholders nor the union had subscribed to it. All right, said LaBow. If that was Scharffenberger's final word, then the unsecured creditors, the union, and LaBow himself would go ahead and co-sponsor a plan after September 15—without the blessing of the company. Then he described that new plan. Compared with the initial plan, unsecured creditors would get more cash and less stock, increasing their total recovery from about sixty cents on the dollar to sixty-eight and a half cents on the dollar. Whether current stockholders would receive more than in the original plan and how much that might be would have to wait until the union contract was set in stone.

During the entire evening, committee chairman Stan West remained unusually quiet. But a few days later he came down on Scharffenberger's side, saying publicly that the chief executive had never agreed absolutely to support the plan. Still, as promised, the LaBow group went into court and moved to end the company's exclusivity, and hearings on the matter were due to begin shortly.

OPPENHEIMER WANTS A WAR

With their large holdings, the vulture duo at Oppenheimer could have joined the official creditors' committee. But they did not want to feel a duty to represent all creditors rather than just themselves and their clients—a position that could have bound them to the sixty-cent deal that the group had already cut and that they wanted to raise. So in the summer of 1989, Oppenheimer pulled up its own seat at the bargaining table; Greenhaus and Bauer stopped trading in the debt and securities of Wheeling-Pittsburgh so that they could receive inside information in negotiations without potential conflicts of interest. They and their attorneys, David Strumwasser and Jeffrey Sabin, plunged into negotiations with LaBow, the committee, and Goldman, Sachs.

Their virtual blocking position failed to impress the committee. To these coal and iron ore mining folks, Bauer and Greenhaus were outsiders, Wall Street sharks. The Oppenheimer team insisted that the committee had accepted a low-rent deal in relation to Wheeling-Pittsburgh's true value; in part they blamed the committee's willingness to settle for less in exchange for a cash recovery. To Greenhaus, it was his most grueling fight yet. "It was a constant battle, an agonizing battle to try to convince the creditor's committee that they had sold out too cheaply." Committee members didn't want to squabble over price; they had negotiated their cash payment and that was their priority. Now they wanted to complete the reorganization plan as quickly as possible, for better than anyone else they knew that the steel industry is a cyclical one and could curve downward at any time. To them, Oppenheimer was just slowing the process down. It was as if the committee were about to take off on a planned trip to the moon when a new passenger began trying to convince them to set a course for Mars. That was out of the question.

Oppenheimer's confrontations with LaBow were hardly easier. LaBow simply did not want to raise the amount that he and the committee had shaken hands on. It seemed ludicrous to him to give the unsecured creditor class twenty cents more when no one yet knew what union members would be getting, because negotiations over a union contract had not yet begun. Oppenheimer tried to apply pressure by resurrecting the touchy matter of the collateral value backing LaBow's claim, the same issue LaBow had settled with the committee the year before. Oppenheimer agreed with the committee that the value of the collateral was less than the claim and held that by right the so-called secured creditor group should not receive full face value or any interest. If it chose to, Oppenheimer could move for a valuation hearing that would challenge LaBow's claim and put the reorganization on hold indefinitely.

However, just as LaBow had suspected, Greenhaus knew that practically speaking he and Bauer didn't have any real weapons to use against LaBow. "An asset is worth as much as somebody is willing to pay for it," he says, "and he was the only game in town until Goldman put another bid on the table." Blocking the LaBow plan would only hurt Oppenheimer by postponing the day the brokerage firm would receive payment. For that reason, Greenhaus and Bauer began meeting with Goldman, Sachs's Douglas Dethy to urge him to declare a bid for Wheeling. "I spent months," Greenhaus recounts. "I went over to Goldman to encourage them. And Dethy said, 'Let us think about it.' " But why didn't Oppenheimer as a major debt holder put forward an acquisition offer itself? "We really thought about it, but didn't want the equity of a marginal steel maker," Bauer says. "We wanted the cash instead." Adds Greenhaus: "Oppenheimer is not an investment banking house. We could not raise the necessary funds to do a deal this big. This is Goldman, Sachs! It could. My idea was to get Goldman, Sachs in there. I wanted a bidding war."

THE BATTLE OVER CLAIMS

Although Oppenheimer clearly owned the claims it had purchased from Hanna Mining and other small suppliers in recent months, it did not own the votes attached to those claims. The court had not yet given its permission for Oppenheimer to put the claims in its name. LaBow was trying to keep the brokerage firm from getting that permission by challenging the claims transfer in court. He and his attorneys knew it was a long shot. But, says Cronin, "We wanted the judge to know that Opco was being a profiteer" and was delaying the case. "LaBow was a speculator too, but he was getting the company out of Chapter Eleven."

The hearing on LaBow's objections to the transfer of claims was scheduled to take place on September 7. He was arguing (1) that because Oppenheimer bought claims from the chairman of the creditors' committee (Hanna Mining), it had had illegal access to inside information and (2) that the sole reason it bought those claims was to stop his plan from going forward. On September 7, the courtroom was packed with gray-suited lawyers representing buyers of $200 million worth of claims—including such other vultures as

R. D. Smith, Cowen & Company, and Boston-based Baupost—as well as the LaBow group. Judge Bentz called for Oppenheimer attorney Jeffrey Sabin to speak first about why Oppenheimer should be able to vote the claims:

MR. SABIN: They accuse Oppenheimer of purchasing claims with mal intent. What intent they say? Intent to block a plan. What plan, Your Honor? Their secret plan. . . . Here the facts will show that Oppenheimer simply requested the publicly available information, used its business judgment, and made a decision to invest in claims which they thought would earn an economic return. That's their business. . . .

I find it even more curious, Your Honor, that the Hains LaBow group makes this argument in light of its own activities in this case. When we examine what the objectors purchased over the period of June 1987 and the many months thereafter, they purchased not a blocking position, but a position with respect to the bank claims in this case, sufficient and calculated so that they could control acceptance of that very class.

Once Sabin had finished, the judge turned to LaBow attorney Thomas Mayer and said, "We're going to take a recess. And then I want you to give me your best reason why the transfer of these claims should not be approved." During the recess one of the LaBow team members approached Mayer excitedly in the hall. "This is great. We've really got a shot here." Frowning, Mayer replied, "You don't understand. He's winding up to knock us over the head." Standing before Judge Bentz a few minutes later, Mayer then argued his case:

MR. MAYER: We think Oppenheimer bought its claims, not with any con-structive purpose, Your Honor, and not with the purpose of proposing their own plan, not with the purpose of moving this case to conclusion, but with the purpose of holding things up. . . .
THE COURT: How are they any different than your clients?
MR. MAYER: My clients bought long before there was any plan.
THE COURT: So what?
MR. MAYER: Your Honor, we think that's important.
THE COURT: The plan that's on the table now may not be the plan that ultimately is approved.
MR. MAYER: Your Honor, we think there is a difference between people

who buy before this plan and who work towards creating a plan getting
out of this case . . . and the people who buy for purposes of stopping a
plan and delaying a case. . . .

THE COURT: If Oppenheimer believes that an unsecured claim is worth
more than the existing draft plan provides, it seems to me they have a
right to buy a claim and assert the right to get more money. . . .

MR. MAYER: Your Honor, I think that the intervention of a new party who
comes in to upset the deal from materializing into a plan damages everybody who has a different view of the time and value of money than
Oppenheimer. You have lots of people in the Chapter 11 case, and you
have people who have been in from the beginning and maybe they want
out now and Oppenheimer's internal calculus is they can wait.

The argument was not going in Mayer's favor, but the issue was
continued until the next scheduled hearing, two weeks later on
September 21. But before this first hearing closed, the Oppenheimer group decided to try a new means of pressuring LaBow. It
asked the court to force LaBow to reveal the names of his partners,
who were suspected to be some of Drexel, Burnham, Lambert's
crack junk bond traders, including Milken. The Oppenheimer team
believed that LaBow would rather negotiate on price than release
all of his partners' names, because Drexel, Burnham and Milken
were then being investigated for insider trading. If the company
and its creditors saw that potential criminals were backing LaBow,
they might not put much faith in his plan of reorganization. But the
following week he produced an enigmatic list of more nondescript
partnerships that made up the three primary partnerships, and the
matter was closed.

GOLDMAN, SACHS'S BID

Throughout the summer, as LaBow was seething with impa-
tience and trying to win Scharffenberger to his side, Goldman,
Sachs had been researching Wheeling-Pittsburgh's operations and
financial information to prepare a bid for the company. Just before
the September 21 hearing, Goldman, Sachs had given Scharffenberger a confidential document outlining its upcoming bid and
reorganization plan proposal. Scharffenberger had sent it along to

creditors' committee chairman Stan West with a letter indicating that this plan might be better than LaBow's. When LaBow and his advisers learned about these communications from the creditors' committee, they concluded that Scharffenberger had now definitively disavowed the agreement he'd made to support the December 1988 plan—or at least the agreement they thought he'd made. Denis Cronin decided to surprise eveyone by describing Goldman, Sachs's offer at the hearing, with the press in attendance. Calling it the "nuclear plan" because "it leads to litigation meltdown," he said,

It provides for 45 percent of the existing equity of this company to go to the existing stockholders. . . . A large amount of money in excess of $200 million would be available to finance this plan of reorganization which contemplates taking out the principal secured creditors by cash payment. . . . The plan is filled with conditions.

Predictably, Cronin's commentary inspired a violent objection from David Strumwasser, the attorney for Oppenheimer who had been trying so hard to convince Goldman, Sachs to make a bid.

MR. STRUMWASSER: The debtor is putting some new ideas and thoughts on the table and trying to get people to talk about it, and Mr. Cronin is somehow using this document, and I think very dangerously because this is a public company.
THE COURT: I'm not really pleased with the fact that nobody has seen fit to advise me of this issue before we got here today, but I am going to hear the arguments. So to the extent that what you are saying is an objection it's overruled. To the extent you want to interrupt Mr. Cronin's argument, you are to cease.
MR. STRUMWASSER: I would just ask that Mr. Cronin give Your Honor a copy of the document. That's all at this point.
MR. CRONIN: Your Honor, I have no further—

At this point the judge, deciding that the argument had gone on long enough, became enraged:

THE COURT: I don't know how deeply I have to get into this, but to the extent I have to get into it, I have to obviously see some papers. I will call a five-minute recess, and I want to see Mr. McCullough and Mr. Cronin in my office.

In the judge's chambers, Cronin himself was angry about Goldman, Sachs's maneuvers in the case, and he characterized its offer for Wheeling as an illusion. He wanted to convince the judge of both this and the delaying effect that Oppenheimer was having on the reorganization. So the attorney suggested that Judge Bentz begin holding periodic status conferences with every major party involved in the bankruptcy so that he could see who the major players were, which ones were moving the process along, which ones were the holdup artists, and what was Goldman, Sachs's true role. It was the best way that Cronin could conceive for flushing Goldman, Sachs out. The judge agreed.

Returning to the courtroom, the judge extended the company's exclusivity period for another month, abruptly suspended the hearing, and ordered all key advisers to meet him in his chambers at once. Bruce McCullough for the company, Denis Cronin and local counsel Joel Walker for LaBow, Jeffrey Sabin and David Strumwasser for Oppenheimer, Larry Handelsman and Robert Sable for the committee, Paul Whitehead for the union, and equity committee attorney David Murdoch filed in and sat down. According to Sabin, in essence this is what the judge said: "Boys, this is not how this case is going to go. First of all, the claims transfers are going to be allowed. Oppenheimer is going to have a say in the case. Also, if Goldman, Sachs is going to have a plan, we're going to work out a mechanism for them to have a plan. Now, here's what we're going to do. I hereby want everybody who's got a real interest in this case to attend status conferences that I will begin to hold in two weeks. I want to hear what's going on in this case."

It had been dramatic, but now Oppenheimer had its potential blocking position and Goldman, Sachs had made the announcement everyone had been waiting for: It intended to finance a reorganization plan that topped LaBow's. In the plan, everybody except the bank creditors would get more than what the LaBow-committee plan offered. But Goldman, Sachs's promises could only be met if it were able to issue enough Wheeling-Pittsburgh securities to raise more than $200 million. That was a big *if*. The securities markets at the time were rapidly becoming unreceptive to junk bond quality companies. And, as LaBow attorney Cronin points out, "No one had ever raised that kind of money in a Chapter Eleven." In any case, Goldman, Sachs began discussions with the various parties to firm up the deal.

The creditors' committee rebuffed Goldman's bid because, unlike LaBow's, it neither paid them in cash nor had firm financing. "We said to Goldman, 'Forget it,'" recalls Lawrence Handelsman, the committee's chief attorney from Stroock & Stroock & Lavan in New York. "If you come up with a better deal, we'll consider it. Offer us more cash, you've got it."

Still, LaBow was concerned. Goldman, Sachs's plan might not be viable. But his own plan could be in trouble, too, or at least delayed, given Oppenheimer's opposition. He asked one of Oppenheimer's clients, his old friend Jay Goldsmith, to mediate in their dispute. Goldsmith and his partner Harry Freund had a direct economic interest in peace: the meter was running on their investment. They hosted a few powwows between Greenhaus and LaBow in a conference room at their Rockefeller Center offices that looks out on the skating rink, and they were able to deflate some of the posturing on both sides. "It got very heated between us because we wanted north of seventy and LaBow didn't want to pay us anything near that," says Greenhaus. "Ron was sitting there saying, 'How can you do this?' And Harry and Jay were saying to LaBow, 'Who are you kidding? You guys should be able to work this out.'" LaBow argued that if Oppenheimer wanted to free its $75 million Maxus Energy claim from pollution liabilities, perhaps it would have to settle for a lower recovery. Goldsmith took a gentle approach, as he describes it: "We were pleasant. We said, 'You guys gotta give a little, gotta take a little.'"

But the give and take at Balfour's offices did not lead to any change in the numbers. Oppenheimer continued to believe that the only way it was going to get any more money out of this investment was through a bidding war, and it was doing its best to keep Goldman, Sachs's reorganization plan alive. "Our strategy," says Oppenheimer attorney David Strumwasser, "was to try to keep Goldman and LaBow on the same level in the case, LaBow with his plan and Goldman with its plan, to try to get them to bid against each other. We encouraged Goldman. We had serious doubts that they could do it. But publicly we supported them." A major part of the campaign involved standing up in support of Goldman, Sachs's plan at court hearings and the monthly status conferences the judge began to hold in October. On the other side, LaBow's team proclaimed the opposite: that Goldman, Sachs's plan was nothing more than a pipe dream.

The status meetings were quite out of the ordinary in a bankruptcy. At ten A.M. on the designated day, some thirty people assembled in a double banquet room at the Vista Hotel across the street from the bankruptcy court in Pittsburgh and sat at four rectangular tables configured into a large square. All the key groups were represented by members or advisers: the union, the salaried employees, Oppenheimer, the unsecured creditors' committee, the PBGC, the LaBow group, and Goldman, Sachs. The judge sat on one side of the square, flanked on the left by a law clerk and on the right by a secretary. Going around the room, each party took turns reporting their current position in the case, which often became a speech justifying their side. After a buffet lunch, the parties reassembled in the courtroom for a hearing.

Many of the participants found the conferences ineffective in advancing the case. Greenhaus was almost amused by what he saw. "There were a lot of people walking out of meetings, and there were a lot of times where the judge said you have to negotiate. We'd all sit in the room and look at each other and not negotiate. I mean it was one of those meetings: 'You're unreasonable.' 'No you're unreasonable.' " Relations were so strained between Oppenheimer and LaBow that one time when LaBow encountered Greenhaus and Strumwasser in an elevator at the Vista, he turned and took the stairs instead. Everyone knew that the status conferences were important for what the judge himself gained from them, because he learned a great deal about the case beyond the narrow issues he dealt with in court. Greenhaus and his advisers made sure that the judge understood that they supported Goldman, Sachs's plan. And LaBow's attorney, Cronin, repeated an opposing message at every status conference. "Their offers are an illusion," he said. "They should put up or shut up."

Despite Oppenheimer's strategy, as 1989 headed toward a close

LaBow continued to hold firm on the recovery amount in his plan. And Oppenheimer was becoming concerned because as the stock and junk bond markets slumped, Goldman, Sachs's bid, with its dependence on securities offerings, began to look less and less viable. Thinking that Goldman, Sachs would be more effective if it didn't own Wheeling stock—because stock has absolute last call on a company's assets in a bankruptcy—Bauer offered an alternative. "We actually told Goldman, 'Why don't you guys buy our claim and you'll have a blocking position?' I think we offered it at eighty cents." But Goldman, Sachs turned him down. Then, late in the year, Greenhaus took a short hike across the foot of Manhattan to visit Dethy and encouraged him to find a strong buyer who could go up against Ron LaBow. Dethy responded that the firm was continuing to look for a partner to join them in financing its bid and for a management team to run the company.

UNION TALKS

While LaBow, Oppenheimer, and Goldman, Sachs were circling around each other that fall of 1989, the union began preparing to negotiate for its next contract. During the spring and summer, Scharffenberger had been concerned that he would not have the labor contract by the time a reorganization plan was set, and without that agreement it would be impossible for the company to emerge from bankruptcy and resume regular business. A new contract was scheduled to take effect ten days after the reorganization. If Wheeling emerged without it, a strike could throw the new company into chaos. As Scharffenberger correctly read the union's strategy, "They were waiting to get contracts with the other steel companies, because if they had had to make compromises with us it would have compromised them with the other major companies. They wanted to get those done and treat us last."

In its industry contract talks, the union was struggling to establish what it calls a "pattern," in which all the major steelmakers agree essentially to the same terms. Logically, then, it played its strongest hands first, locking in generous terms that form the basis of talks at other companies. After signing the Bethlehem Steel contract in April, the union signed similar agreements with Armco,

Inland and National steel companies and began negotiations with LTV. (The contract with industry leader USX was not due for renewal until 1990.)

On October 12, Jim Smith and Paul Whitehead from the union and their adviser, Eugene Keilin, flew to New York to present their demands to the LaBow group and the following day to Goldman, Sachs and advisers to Wheeling management. Their message: Give us the pattern agreement and good treatment on our bankruptcy claims.

Still, the union was hesitant to plunge into full-fledged talks with the company because it was confused as to who the next owner of Wheeling-Pittsburgh was going to be. The negotiators weren't happy with the current management, which wanted a low-cost contract, and they were not bowled over by Goldman, Sachs. Goldman representatives had met twice with the union. The first time, shortly after the firm purchased its stock in January of 1989, they paid a visit to USWA president Lynn Williams and other union officials at at his office. The second time it was just the union negotiators at Pittsburgh's elite Three Rivers Club perched on the east bank of the Monongahela River. District director Lefty Palm was one union negotiator who was not impressed with the venerable Wall Street house. "We were very apprehensive and concerned about what their motives were. We met with them, twice. It was borderline, a joke. They just didn't understand. It seemed they wanted to meet with us to get an education about the steel business. We thought that it was like a seminar. And they were always looking at their watches, because they had to catch a plane. They wanted to meet and talk while they were eating and then catch a plane."

The longer they waited, the union leaders figured, the more likely that LaBow would assert his position as the new leader of the company. And that would be good news for the union. "We didn't feel comfortable negotiating with Wheeling-Pittsburgh Steel management," recalls Lefty Palm, who headed up the Wheeling bargaining team. "We categorized them as the hard guns—and they'd be gone. We wanted to negotiate with whoever would be the owner. We felt we could do a deal with Hains and LaBow, that we could do the pattern with them."

He had a chance to test his hunch in October when Hains and LaBow, with the creditor's committee, decided to initiate their own union talks without informing the company. "LaBow and the unsecured creditors felt that they had a deal," explains Scott King, an accounting adviser with Ernst & Young stationed in Pittsburgh who was part of the creditors' committee team. "The only problem was the steelworkers. We decided to go off on our own to try to cut a deal." Hains and a few advisers huddled for two days with union negotiators at USWA international headquarters on the fifteenth story of Five Gateway. But the discussions led nowhere, recounts King. "We realized they wanted the Bethlehem contract. The numbers they put forward were straight from Bethlehem. And we felt the company couldn't afford the Bethlehem contract." Scharffenberger was annoyed when he found out about Hains's end run around management—although he did understand Hains's position: that the current management was temporary and if he and LaBow wanted to replace it they had to take action.

Formal labor contract negotiations with the company finally got started in late November, held mainly at the downtown Hyatt Hotel. Palm sat at the main negotiating table with the union's four other chief negotiators. There was Jim Smith, a towering Texan with a drawl and a silver white mane of hair that led the LaBow team to dub him "the Silver Fox." A former boilermaker in a Houston steel plant who earned a degree in economics, Smith headed up the USWA's research department and developed a reputation for leather-skinned and tireless negotiating. Then there was the other district leader, Jim Bowen, along with assistant general counsel Paul Whitehead and USWA benefits attorney Karen Feldman. Across from them at the main table sat Anthony Verdream, Wheeling's human resources vice president, who came to the company the past September.

A month later, as a spur to get the process moving, other constituencies were invited in. Palm gazed beyond Verdream into a sea of lawyers, including Joseph O'Leary, LaBow's labor attorney, and thirty or so others, representing the various constituencies. They were allowed only to listen, because Verdream was the official spokesman for the company and its creditors. So this was the beginning. The end was not yet in sight.

DOUBLE VISION: TWO PLANS

Toward year end, everyone's patience with the lack of progress in the case was nearly drained. In closed-door sessions with Oppenheimer, LaBow bumped up the recovery price for the unsecured creditor class in his plan—although he says he didn't grant Oppenheimer anything he hadn't planned on anyway. But Oppenheimer continued to lend its support to Goldman, Sachs. On December 22, the company filed suit against Oppenheimer in connection with the $75 million Maxus Energy claim the brokerage firm had bought a year earlier. Wheeling-Pittsburgh now wanted to be indemnified against any potential pollution liabilities tied to the claim. "We were annoyed," says Oppenheimer attorney Sabin. "Number one, we thought LaBow was behind it, that he had put the debtor up to it. Number two, we thought that the debtor's papers were terrible and legally not right. And number three, we thought the suit was filed for vexatious reasons and didn't have grounding in good faith. We decided, 'You make a move like that, and we go for the jugular.' " (Wheeling-Pittsburgh attorney Bruce McCullough says that LaBow had nothing to do with the lawsuit. It was filed as part of an effort to eliminate liabilities for the new, reorganized company.) But before he had a chance to file a countersuit, Oppenheimer, LaBow, and the company started discussions on a settlement of this and other issues between them.

"The sessions in January were very heated, more so than before," Sabin recounts. "Now it was clear that the [LaBow and Goldman, Sachs] plans were getting closer to reality, and that upped the ante. It almost pushed us to going to Goldman and saying, 'We'll get into bed with you, and we'll fund the plan.' " At one session with LaBow, which went late into a Friday evening at Sabin's office in midtown, the normally staid LaBow suddenly began screaming at Greenhaus for no apparent reason and stormed out of the room. At a subsequent meeting, David Strumwasser started out by presenting LaBow with a large bag of Hershey Kisses™ as a peace offering.

Meanwhile, Scharffenberger invited Goldman, Sachs, LaBow, and the unsecured creditors' committee to make separate presentations to the board so that it could decide whose plan to support. On

February 27, the board voted to go with the LaBow-committee
reorganization plan. But before it could take its decision to the
judge, he ordered that both LaBow's and Goldman, Sachs's plans
be submitted to the company and then to the court by the end of
March so that they *both* could be put to a vote:

The debtor shall propose to the court a procedural plan and proposed
schedule under which: Debtor shall consult with and receive from the LaBow
Group and also from the Equity Committee: a proposed plan of reorganization; 2) a summary thereof on not more than two pages; 3) a disclosure
statement. All such documents shall be brief and understandable. Surplusage
and verbose explanations will not be tolerated.

The LaBow group was relieved. To them, this order meant that
Goldman, Sachs should put up or shut up. They gave Judge Bentz
credit for a measure that would help move the case along but was
also fair.

Through March, the company's advisers scrambled to get the
two plans printed up and mailed by the deadline. LaBow, the
creditors, and the company together proposed a plan similar to the
December 1988 plan but that now gave unsecured creditors seventy-two cents on the dollar instead of sixty cents in cash and stock.
The plan submitted to the court by the equity holders' committee
led by Goldman, Sachs depended on the completion of a $100
million stock offering and a $200 million bond issue. That done,
Goldman, Sachs would pay unsecured creditors seventy-five cents
in cash and preferred stock and stockholders would not be diluted
nearly as much as in the other plan. Both plans required the ratifi-
cation of a labor pact.

But Goldman, Sachs's plan was pretty much dead on arrival at
the April 5 court hearing—given the opposition of LaBow, the
creditors' committee, and others. Of course, Oppenheimer could
still block LaBow's plan. But since January, LaBow and Oppenheimer had been working on settling their differences. And both
were increasingly eager to reach agreement. The LaBow group was
concerned that if it didn't make peace with Oppenheimer, the
brokerage firm would sell its position to another vulture at a high
level, and because that vulture would have a higher cost than

Oppenheimer had, it would be looking for a greater recovery and would delay the case indefinitely. But Bauer was afraid that if Goldman, Sachs settled with LaBow before Oppenheimer did, Oppenheimer would have no more leverage to use against LaBow. Greenhaus says that in late March LaBow agreed to raise the return to the unsecured creditors one last time, from seventy-two cents on the dollar to seventy-five cents. In addition, he cleared all potential liabilities from the $75 million Maxus Energy claim. Now Oppenheimer and its clients could receive a seventy-five-cent recovery free and clear and celebrate a tremendous rate of return on their sixteen-and-a-half-cent investment. "If they hadn't gone along with this [deal], it wouldn't even have been worth seventeen cents," LaBow says. "The claim would have been reserved for years until all the liabilities were settled," In return, Oppenheimer agreed to lend its support to the LaBow plan.

In fact, Jeffrey Sabin for Oppenheimer and Denis Cronin for LaBow nailed down the final details of the agreement in the hallway outside the courtroom just as the April 5 hearing on the two plans was getting under way. They then entered the courtroom and, with Lawrence Handelsman, the attorney for the creditors' committee, presented the accord to the crowd of two dozen attorneys. Handelsman broke the news:

MR. HANDELSMAN: I am happy to report that that motion (to proceed only with the LaBow-committee-company plan) which I handed out about two hours ago, is already out of date because it does not include the agreement of the Oppenheimer group to also support the joint plan. We think for the reasons set forth in that motion now made even more compelling by the fact that virtually all of the major unsecured creditors support the joint plan not only is that plan destined for confirmation, but the plan proposed by the equity committee can't possibly be confirmed.

Then Jeffrey Sabin spoke.

MR. SABIN: I am very happy to report that Oppenheimer in their capacity as unsecured creditors holding claims in excess of $142 million in this case have reached an agreement in principal this afternoon with the unsecured committee, with the debtor, with the Hains LaBow group, or the so-called principal secured creditors, resolving the treatment of those secured claims and resolving the treatment of the unsecured claims, which will require some modification to the debtor/unsecured committee plan as filed currently. . . .

We're certainly happy to report that we think the Hains LaBow group, the debtor and the committee all believe it is a major break-through.

Arthur Field, the attorney representing Goldman, Sachs, stood to register his objection to all that he'd heard.

MR. FIELD: The creditors' committee apparently believes that the appro-priate course for a fiduciary is to block the bidding proc-ess. . . . The creditors' committee seems to suggest that this [Goldman plan] is not a real plan, and accordingly it is against this plan even though it is a higher bid. . . . We will shortly ask the Court to take specific action with respect to certain of the votes of parties involved in this. There is simply a lack of good faith in dealing with these matters. If we are to set up a bidding process to get the unsecured creditors a higher return, that will hardly be facilitated by an attempt by the unsecured creditors' com-mittee itself to thwart that.

JUDGE BENTZ: Are you familiar enough with the dollars involved to know whether [with] the LaBow claim voting against you and the Oppenheimer and the creditors who are actually on the creditors' committee voting against you, is your plan dead?

MR. FIELD: I am not sure it can surmount that, Your Honor, unless some of those votes are disqualified. That is what we would present to you.

MR. CRONIN: Mr. Field, what is the issue if I may?

JUDGE BENTZ: Well, he thinks you can be disqualified.

MR. CRONIN: I understand that. He raised that at the last conference. I didn't understand it then. I haven't heard anything today that would help me to further understand it.

JUDGE BENTZ: Absent such disqualifications, are there [uncommited] votes in a sufficient amount to make possible the confirmation of the equity plan?

MR. FIELD: The plan cannot be confirmed if they are all entitled to vote.

MR. HANDELSMAN: Your Honor, Mr. Field and the equity committee seem to have a strange view of what the fiduciary obligations of the creditors' committee is. It is not to vote for a plan that gives more to the equity and less to the creditors. . . . The debtor analyzed that plan and compared it to the LaBow plan and found that it presented a much lower payout. It is not 75 cents. It is 65 cents, in cash, as opposed to 72 cents in cash plus preferred stock. . . . I think the equity committee just doesn't like the answer it's hearing.

MR. MURDOCH: Your Honor, David Murdoch on behalf of the equity committee. . . . It is premature for this Court to accept an announcement from Oppenheimer, Cleveland Cliffs (creditors' committee chairman) and LaBow that they have all agreed to block an equity plan or to vote their own plan when the disclosure statement process barely started. . . . Notwithstanding Mr. Sabin's announcement that he has an agreement in principle, it is conceivable that Goldman, Sachs in its wisdom [could say], now Mr. Greenhaus at Oppenheimer, here is a higher number that can be bid on the unsecured. It is not too late in this process for that to happen.

But shortly afterward, Goldman, Sachs, LaBow, and the committee spent two solid weeks—night and day at the offices of Cronin's firm, Wachtell, Lipton, Rosen & Katz in New York—negotiating an agreement in which Goldman, Sachs also would back the LaBow-committee plan. In return, common stockholders would receive 8.7 percent of the new stock, plus warrants to buy more, up from 7.5 percent in the LaBow-committee plan. And the company and the committee would not object to the reimbursement of $1.5 million of Goldman, Sachs's fees. "They didn't get very much," says LaBow. But they did get something. "It was costing me two to three million dollars a month to stay in bankruptcy [in fees and opportunity costs]. If I saved three months [by settling] it was worth it."

LABORIOUS LABOR

This financial decathlon was hardly over. There were two last hurdles in the bankruptcy, and they were both labor issues. First, LaBow settled a final dispute with the pensions agency involving the legitimacy of Wheeling's supplemental pension plans. This was no small matter. "We could not have gotten out of bankruptcy without [resolution of] the follow-on pension plan," LaBow maintains. The company, as well as LaBow, had been working on it for years and had come within a hair's breadth of settlement before.

before. This time, the U.S. Supreme Court was about to rule on a similar matter involving LTV Corporation. On Thursday June 14, 1990, LaBow's labor attorney, Joseph O'Leary, placed a call to the negotiators at the pensions agency, and during the conversation he learned that the ruling was coming down at any time, possibly the next day. But the agency was willing to bargain through the night to put a Wheeling agreement in ink before the Supreme Court set a precedent. Everyone got on the conference call that afternoon at around three—O'Leary, attorneys for the salaried employees, the attorney for the unsecured creditors, and Stan West (the chairman of the committee from where he was doing business in Dusseldorf, Germany), and the company's labor negotiator Anthony Verdream. At midnight, they reached an accord on the plans for salaried employees, which provided a basis for the future settlement with union-represented workers. That Monday, the Supreme Court ruled against LTV, ordering that it take back its responsibility for all of its pension plans at a huge cost. But Wheeling had come in under the wire.

The next and final item on the agenda was the labor contract. Things had not been going well since the beginning of the year. The union was dismayed that the question of who was going to own and run Wheeling after bankruptcy remained up in the air, and both Goldman, Sachs and LaBow continued to court the union. "There are times when it's like dealing with a three- or four-headed monster, and we don't know who's in control," Lefty Palm told *The Pittsburgh Press.* More important, the company was holding firm on its demand for a low-cost contract. In a phone conversation between Verdream and Palm in late February, Verdream said that the company would never meet the union's demands that Wheeling-Pittsburgh adhere to the standard labor contract. Moreover, he said the company would never file its reorganization plan until the union accepted a labor contract that met management's requirements.

In response, the union suspended talks. And then the union negotiators went directly to the rank and file to report the state of affairs. The leadership was gathering the support of its troops. It held a press conference at headquarters on March 12 at which officials accused the company of trying to bully the union into a cheap contract by dragging out both the labor talks and the bankruptcy.

What the union leaders didn't reveal was their conviction that Scharffenberger and McCullough and other advisers were delaying the reorganization so that they could continue to collect their compensation as long as possible (McCullough dismisses the charge, remarking that this is a common complaint in bankruptcies). Palm and his colleagues were frustrated at their inability to prove these suspicions. But they complained loud enough. It was not unusual for a dozen or so union members to attend the monthly court hearings and hurl catcalls at the lawyers, blaming them for delaying the case. At one hearing, on March 15, a host of about twenty steelworkers and union officials showed up dressed in their usual garb of dungarees and T-shirts. They sat together in the gallery and, before the hearing began, taunted the lawyers entering the federal courtroom "How much are you making?" sneered one. "If any one of you lawyers are ethical, would you please stand up?" another asked derisively. And someone else called out, "If anyone here is making less than five hundred an hour, please let us know." During the proceedings, whenever one of the lawyers looked over at them, some of the union members made menacing gestures such as raising and shaking a fist. When the discussion turned to fees, this exchange occurred:

JUDGE BENTZ: It is an outrageous amount. I don't know what you do about it. You have to get the work done. I am addressing these remarks to the labor constituents. Without your work, there wouldn't be any company, but without the work of these fellows (pointing to the lawyers), we wouldn't have gotten this far on the claims. Instead of being worth 15 cents, they would have been worth zero, and now, they are worth 60 cents or 65 cents.

JIM BOWEN FROM THE FLOOR: And we are working for them.

JUDGE BENTZ: Well, you're working for the creditors, and they loaned credit to the company.

MR. BOWEN: May I say something, Your Honor?

JUDGE BENTZ: Yes.

MR. BOWEN: I review the reports every time Mr. Scharffenberger submits them to this Court. It is a shame that I find that about 45-plus million dollars are the fees that are presently in existence in this case. . . . I would suggest that after this approval today of the request made to you on fees that from now until this case is completed, there will be no cash payment of fees to anyone.

Then, a burly steelworker in a fishnet jersey asked to make a statement, and surprised everyone in the room with his eloquence.

MR. BARNETT: With due respect as one of the guys that works down there, . . . as far as the workers down there that have time and time again answered call when it went out to us to understand and be patient, we did, and this whole time we have suffered. We drive cars that break down on the average of every three months. We can't look forward to buying a new car. I can go on and on. . . .

Our man hours per ton is one of the best in the industry. In other words, less people are putting out more steel. We have answered the call time and time and time again. The Court gave us 50 cents (an interim raise). We appreciated it, but we are so far behind. Like a volcano that erupts, it is close to that point. I wish someone would understand. We can't come in here and comprehend these litigations. The only thing we comprehend is the money received on payday for a job done.

In mid-April, the company ran newspaper ads urging the union to return to the bargaining table. Two days later, the same day that Goldman, Sachs finally announced its support of the LaBow plan, union members staged a rally in front of company headquarters in Wheeling, insisting that the company resume talking, and it ran a response in the newspaper:

Our wages and benefits have been frozen at low levels for five long years. And Wheeling-Pitt and its creditors demand that we agree to be frozen into second-class status for three more years. That's not right.

The union threatened to strike if it couldn't get the pact it wanted—even though it's illegal to strike while still under contract. But, really, who was going to prevent them from walking off the job?

The steelworkers also objected to their treatment as creditors in the now-prevailing LaBow-company-creditors plan. They were claiming $71 million for a rejected wage moderation agreement and

$27 million for a suspended stock plan that had been given in return for concessions.

On May 31, labor negotiations got back on track, but they broke off again two weeks later. At that point, the union leaders began to garner support for a strike from the presidents of the thirteen locals, representing 5500 Wheeling workers, and at the beginning of July they took the unanimous decision to USWA president Lynn Williams for his formal permission. On July 16, the union announced a date: August 16 at 12:01 A.M. Unless the company agreed to the pattern labor contract and increased the recovery on the bankruptcy claims, the union would go out on the second strike of the Wheeling bankruptcy. Scharffenberger asserted that he would sell Wheeling in the case of a long strike, but the union dismissed the threat as a bluff.

Talks resumed on July 24. Again, it was the company's labor negotiator, Tony Verdream, who was seated at the main negotiating table, even though by now it was obvious that LaBow was Wheeling-Pittsburgh's next boss. "Tony Verdream was playing hardball to get us to agree to an agreement that wasn't the pattern," complains Lefty Palm in his gravelly voice. But when it became clear that the union was as stubborn as the company, Verdream finally consented to the union's and the LaBow group's wishes to move LaBow's man Joe O'Leary from the back of the room to sit beside Verdream at the main table. Now he could negotiate directly. Still, Verdream refused to budge, and on Sunday, August 12—four days before the strike deadline—everything came to a standstill. That's when the union called in LaBow. The bargaining committee agreed to negotiate with him alone.

LaBow's team—consisting of himself, David Hains and his son Richard, O'Leary, Scott Faust, and Neale Trangucci, along with Scott King and David Weisenfeld, representing the committee—wrangled with the union through the afternoon and night at the union's Five Gateway Plaza headquarters. In the back of LaBow's mind was a story he'd recently read in a 1988 book about the steel industry titled, *And the Wolf Finally Came*. It relayed the USWA's encounter with Carl Icahn, the corporate raider who in 1986 bought up a large block of USX stock and bid for the company. At one point, he met with Lynn Williams and Jim Smith (one of the men who was now in the room negotiating with LaBow). "He didn't know anything about the steel business," Smith later said of Icahn. "All he knew about were the numbers. I made a minimal effort to explain some of the governmental policy problems on the future of the steel business, and he was totally uninterested in that. He didn't indicate any interest in being a steel tycoon. He was coveting the cash flow from the steel business. We left there with our mind made up that we didn't want him in our industry." The union decided not to give Icahn the concessions he needed to get the company. That weakened his stance considerably, and he soon canceled his bid. Recognizing the power the union held over him, LaBow gave the steelworkers pretty much what they wanted: by including them in the unsecured creditors' group, he gave them a better recovery on their bankruptcy claims. The union also got a labor accord that was generally comparable with those signed with other major steelmakers. At 7:30 A.M. Monday, LaBow emerged from the building with a deal in his hand, walked down the street to Wheeling-Pittsburgh, and delivered it to Scharffenberger.

To pay for what he had just given to the steelworkers, LaBow spent two months trying to convince the creditors' committee to take a lower recovery. "We didn't believe that was the reason," says creditors' committee attorney Lawrence Handelsman. "The union agreement came in within the parameters we expected." Handelsman suspected that the bankruptcy had gone on so long that the rate of return on LaBow's investment was slim; he simply could no longer afford the agreed-on price. "We knew what he paid for the bank debt," Handelsman says. "We were constantly calculating his internal rate of return, and that return was going down with time." Now, LaBow wanted to buy back only some of the stock that unsecured creditors were to receive. That idea got a resounding no from the committee, which held fast to its demand to be bought out completely. But because the committee had lowered its expected value of the company, it agreed to lower the buyout price from $15 a share to $11.25—for a total recovery that was back down to seventy-two cents on the dollar.

If LaBow thought the labor agreement was his final headache, he was in for a surprise. In December 1990, during the hearings to confirm the reorganization plan, three federal agencies objected:

the Environmental Protection Agency (EPA), the Economic Development Administration, and the Farmers Home Administration. They wanted more money, and to get the company out of bankruptcy LaBow put a large sum in escrow as a reserve for their claims as they were settled. (As it happened, the escrowed amount was greater than the settlements.) Some time later, Joel Gross, an EPA lawyer, told LaBow attorney Mayer: "Tom, I don't expect everybody to agree with the government. But you should never ignore the government, and you ignored the government."

How did the vultures' investments come out in the end? Goldman, Sachs spent $8 a share for 1,747,796 shares, a total of $14 million. For each of its shares it received about one-third of a share for a total of 594,251 shares. Wheeling's stock began trading at around $7 a share. At $7 that's a value of $4.2 million. So Goldman, Sachs recouped less than a third of its investment—and its loss is even more severe when considering the $4 million in fees it reportedly shelled out to advisers and the fact that its money was locked up for two years.

For their $20 million investment in bank debt, Oppenheimer and its customers received about twice that. And for about $46 million to buy unsecured debt, they received close to $100 million. So they more than doubled their investment, for a total profit of about $74 million—some spread over three years, some over two. Last year, Greenhaus left Oppenheimer to set up his own shop specializing in the purchase of private and trade claims of bankrupt firms and by the end of the year had $100 million in assets and was raising another $200 million in a fund called Vega (Arabic for *vulture*) Partners. Today, Bauer heads a junk bond trading department of twenty-four people and continues to co-manage Oppenheimer's $160 million vulture fund.

What pushed the unsecured creditors' cents-per-dollar recovery up from sixty cents at the end of 1988 to seventy-two cents became and remains a matter of dispute. Both the committee and Oppenheimer agree that the growth of cash at the company coupled with a falling amount of claims (as some were settled for less than expected) contributed greatly. Oppenheimer's two vulture investors insist, too, that the pressure they created by keeping Goldman,

Sachs's plan alive forced LaBow to raise the recovery to all unsecured creditors more than he would have otherwise. But LaBow says he didn't raise the amount more than he would have if Oppenheimer hadn't been there, and committee attorney Handelsman maintains that the only real effect Oppenheimer's strategy had was to add an extra six months to the case, and the LaBow group believes it was as much as nine months. "We told them they were making a mistake, prolonging things to no avail," says Handelsman. If in that time the steel industry went into a cyclical slump, he says, "We were very concerned that LaBow would wake up and say, 'You know what? This was a mistake. I want to go back to the traditional way of doing things in which I get the cash and you get the stock. I want out.' "

As for LaBow, he invested $140 million initially and after the reorganization spent $45 million to buy out some stock held by the unsecured creditors—at $11.25 a share when the stock was trading at only $7 a share in the market. So in all he spent $185 million. In return, his investor group received $193.5 million in notes plus 54 percent of the stock—at $7 a share, a value of $76 million—for a total value of about $270 million. When considering that most of his investment was tied up for three and a half years, the return is hardly exceptional. But consider this: the $45 million for the stock buyout was borrowed, as was a large chunk of the original investment. The LaBow group won't say exactly how much, but it is not unusual for investors to borrow up to half of their investment. That can be risky if an investor loses money and owes the bank. But in this case, LaBow made enough to pay off his loans plus interest. And his overall return, if he did indeed borrow a large amount, appeared to be impressive.

By November of 1992, the stock was trading below $4 a share. The company, like other steelmakers, was losing money, largely due to competition from imports. For Ron LaBow, the investment in Wheeling-Pittsburgh Steel continues.

6

Fixing Revco

Boswell, lend me sixpence . . . not to be repaid.

—THE LIFE OF JOHNSON

Running a drugstore seems like a simple enough business. Good times and bad, people don't go without medicine and toiletries. Even the ancillary items—candy, condoms, and cigarettes, as the industry calls them—are in constant demand. As a base, the prescription drug pharmacy in a chain drugstore brings in up to 50 percent of the business, depending on the size of the store, at 20 to 30 percent markups. But the sprawling discount drugstore chain Revco D. S. did not have an easy time of it in the 1980s. The company, based near Cleveland in Twinsburg, suffered from a combination of bad luck, bad acquisitions, and a bad leveraged buyout.

Sidney Dworkin and other investors founded Revco in 1956 and built it to more than 2000 stores cutting across more than half the country. It thrived on the policy of "everyday low prices" that attracted masses of consumers. Its troubles began in 1984 when

141

Dworkin diversified out of the basic drugstore business with the purchase of Odd Lot Trading, a seller of merchandise purchased from struggling manufacturers. The Odd Lot Trading stores did poorly, and the two men who had sold out to Revco for stock—one of whom was on the board—threatened a hostile takeover and demanded Dworkin's ouster. The two men were Isaac Perlmutter and Bernard Marden, the same two entrepreneurs who turn up in the Coleco bankruptcy as the buyers of bank debt. The Revco board supported Dworkin and kicked Marden off the board. While this boardroom drama was disrupting management, losses at Odd Lot and liability payments for infant deaths linked to a vitamin E supplement severely damaged Revco's earnings.

To Dworkin, three little letters—LBO—were a magic formula that could reverse the slide in earnings. Or so it seemed in 1986 when the leveraged buyout as a financial tool was soaring in popularity. Two days before the start of 1987, after working on the LBO for a year and with the blessing of Salomon Brothers, the company's attorneys and accountants, and fellow investors, Dworkin took out his checkbook and paid $1.28 billion to his shareholders for the right to boost his family's share of Revco. The only catch was the $150 million a year in interest plus principal payments he had to come up with to service the $1.1 billion he'd borrowed. Dworkin was counting on ever upward profits to pay those bills— despite one ominous event during negotiations over the buyout. In 1986, Revco missed its earnings projections by 20 percent, like a pitcher who aims for the plate but throws the ball into the stands. In response, the company and its advisers from Salomon Brothers simply scaled back their near-term forecasts, keeping the rosy longer-term numbers in place.

That was a bad idea. Competition intensified in the drugstore industry, with new discounters opening up and enterprising supermarkets forging deeper into the business. In early April, the LBO just three months old, Revco's board replaced Dworkin with a younger CEO, although the founder retained the chairmanship. The company stocked shelves with general merchandise, including everything from lamp oil to video recorders and cheap furniture, in an unsuccessful attempt to transform itself into a minidepartment store. The cuts Revco made in its management staff and drug inventories just made things worse by hurting customer service. As a result, the company again proved its errant aim in undershooting the optimistic sales and earnings targets.

In September, Dworkin resigned his post on the board, replaced by Boake Sells, a tall, outspoken former president of the Dayton Hudson Corporation department store chain. But the downward spiral spun ever faster. On April 15, 1988, Sells announced that Revco would not be able to make a $46 million interest payment on its $703.5 million in junk bonds that June. When that prediction became reality, the company earned the dubious honor of being the first major LBO to fail. Management launched a full-scale drive to restructure and lighten the crushing weight of debt. Boake Sells was hopeful. "If everybody works together, including our bondholders and other investors, we can solve our problems and control Revco's destiny outside the courts," he said in what later seemed a terribly naive sentiment.

The restructuring plan, designed by the aggressive and soon to be indicted brokerage firm Drexel, Burnham, Lambert, was to swap outstanding junk bonds for equity in the company. The crucial question was whether there would be enough time to accomplish it. There was a month-long grace period after the default. Then, in mid-July, bondholders could demand payment, and three of them could file to put the company into what is called an involuntary Chapter 11. Just knowing of those possibilities, suppliers might bolt. So Drexel, Burnham wanted bondholders to sign a standstill agreement pledging that they would not demand their interest payments until January 5.

They didn't figure on Talton Embry, a veteran vulture investor with his own Magten Asset Management. Embry, who resents the use of the term *vulture* to describe what he does, had a major stake in Revco that was a scant month old. Around the time of the default, Embry had bought up $100 million worth of Revco's 13 1/8 percent junk bonds, nearly one-quarter of the class of senior subordinated bonds, for which he paid what then seemed an attractive price of about 50 cents on the dollar. To Embry's dismay, because of his substantial position in the class, all of Revco's 13 1/8 percent senior subordinated bonds soon acquired the nickname "Tally bonds." He tried to organize an unofficial committee with two other institutional investors, Fidelity Investments and Keystone Custodian Funds, to negotiate with management. But at the time, this kind of prebankruptcy organizing was unusual, and Revco balked at paying for the group's lawyers and other advisers. Still, Magten presented an enormous obstacle to the Drexel, Burnham-devised restructuring program.

Embry refused to play along with Drexel, Burnham's game plan. The way he saw the situation, it was his right to be paid his interest; and if Revco couldn't come up with the cash at once, it was his right to take the company by the arm and lead it into bankruptcy court. As he explained to a Drexel, Burnham representative, "If you put five thousand down on a mortgage on a house and you can't pay the interest, they come and take the house. If Revco can't pay the interest on these bonds, I'm coming to take the house. I own the business."

On Friday July 22, Embry told Revco that he was preparing court documents to demand full and immediate payment of interest and principal on all of the company's bonds—a hefty $108 million. CEO Sells knew that faced with that impossible demand, he would have to file for bankruptcy. "I was in the office until ten thirty that Friday night and spent the whole weekend making phone calls trying to save the company from Chapter Eleven," he said. He pleaded with Embry to reconsider, but the bankruptcy investor was noncommittal. Sunday, Embry received another call, this time from Nathan Meyohas, chairman and CEO of Transcontinental Services Group N. V., a European investment company that owned 60 percent of Revco's stock. Meyohas suggested a meeting to discuss the situation at hand. But as a reward for his effort to move the restructuring along, Meyohas only got an earful of tough talk. "I told him I'm just a lender," Embry later recounted. "I told him, 'Just pay me the money. I haven't been paid for four months. Don't come to me after four months and tell me you want me to stand still.' I told him it was too late." The following day, Transcontinental wrote off its entire $9.6 million investment in Revco stock.

That Thursday, Revco, its $1.2 billion in assets cowering beneath $1.5 billion in liabilities, filed in Akron, Ohio, for protection from creditors under Chapter 11 of the bankruptcy code.

RAILROAD ROOTS

Talton Embry is in his mid-forties, with a medium build, caramel-colored hair, and tortoiseshell glasses. Easygoing in manner, he might wear corduroys and a blue blazer to work at Magten's offices in the east Twenties—a residential neighborhood that is more relaxed and more hip than midtown. His father was a stockbroker who inherited his father's two-hundred-acre dairy farm in New Jersey, which raised golden Guernseys, chickens, and bees, and that was where Embry grew up. An English major at Rutgers University—where his eighteenth-century literature professor engaged his interest by standing on his desk to sing selections from *The Beggar's Opera*—Embry today has eclectic literary tastes ranging from Swift to the mysteries of Ed McBain.

In 1968, Embry began trading common stocks at Fiduciary Trust Company, an institutional money management firm in New York. After ten years there, he decided that the best way to make money for his budding family was to start his own specialty investment business. And he did, putting his initial funds into short-term government instruments then yielding 14 percent. But he had no idea what area of investing he should specialize in.

He read a research report put out by Bear, Stearns's Randall Smith on the Penn Central railroad, which was then about to emerge from bankruptcy, and that got him thinking. Bankrupt railroads were something he knew about, and something he knew could make money on. His great-grandfather Leonard Loree had started out as a teenager laying track on the Mexican National Railroad and ended up heading or helping to run some forty small railroads at the turn of the century—including the Delaware & Hudson, the Baltimore & Ohio and the Chicago Rock Island. At one point he considered building a third transcontinental railroad, but eventually was talked out of it. In 1908, Loree created a trust to invest solely in railroad bonds and other then-premium-quality securities, but over time, every railroad bond in that trust lurched into bankruptcy. As it happened, however, that was a great boon to Embry's family because, rather than earning the typical 2.5 percent on a typical 100-year railroad bond, the trust now owned stock that could appreciate when the railroads switched to an elevated, profitable track. They did, and the fortune was made and dispersed among Loree's eighty or so heirs. Around him, too, Embry saw examples of wealth made in the rails, including his uncle, a stockbroker who worked for Charles Allen, the financier who once invested in bankrupt railroads and utilities.

So here was Embry in 1978, and it was all happening again. Embry jumped at the opportunity and started investing in railroad bonds, including the Penn Central, Chicago Rock Island, and the Chicago Milwaukee. Later he branched into other distressed securities such as Itel Corporation, various real estate investment trusts, Nucorp Energy, and other oil bonds. Today, Magten manages $550 million in institutional assets and has chalked up a ten-and-a-half-year record of 13.2 percent returns. But along the way there have been very high highs and very low lows. A low point was Manville Corporation. Embry paid forty-five cents on the dollar for the senior bonds of the asbestos manufacturer on the day it went bankrupt in August 1982, on the theory that the case would be a relatively brief one of maybe two years. But the process of settling with the asbestos claimants dragged the case out for more than twice as long.

Embry had a great deal more success in the bonds of Robert Campeau's reeling U.S. retailing empire—Federated Department Stores and Allied Stores. Campeau had acquired Allied and Federated by way of two leveraged buyouts in 1986 and 1988, respectively, believing that a rising tide of earnings would carry all debts. But the earnings projections were an optimist's best-case scenario, and the U.S. operations collapsed into bankruptcy. In his largest investment ever, made over a period of several months, Embry paid $83 million for four levels of Federated and Allied debt. That included $45 million in Federated, $21 million for $60 million worth of one issue of Allied bonds and $17 million for $240 million worth of 11.5 percent Allied bonds—34% of the class. That one-third stake was a crucial blocking position; a reorganization plan could not go forward without his say-so. Embry joined the Allied creditors' committee, but with no intention of staying on for long. He wanted to be assured that the creditors hired attorneys who were going to pursue litigation against the company, charging fraudulent conveyance—that in buying Allied through an LBO, the company and its advisers had put on so much debt so as to render the company insolvent. Once the committee had hired a law firm and Embry saw that the attorneys had the resolve and the staff to do the litigation, he left so that he could continue accumulating bonds.

In early 1992, the Federated/Allied creditors approved a plan of reorganization. Embry will recover bonds and stock for his Federated holdings, giving him a 75 percent return on his investment. For the Allied holdings, he will receive all stock, and if that stock trades at a minimum of $15 a share as expected, he will have doubled his money. Embry planned to plow some of those profits into another form of discounted debt—Latin American and Eastern European government bonds.

THE UNEXPECTED

The booklet describing the philosophy at Embry's firm says the following: "At Magten, we view bad financial news as a signpost for potential opportunity. The fact is, if a troubled company has able management and a business that is fundamentally sound, it may offer higher returns at less risk than other investment vehicles, including investment-grade bonds."

In mid-1988 Embry had bullied Revco into bankruptcy with reasonable confidence that he would see eighty cents on the dollar within two years—$80 million for his $50 million investment, a 60 percent rate of return. After all, Revco had a fresh management team and in bankruptcy it would avoid paying a lot of bills. Customers were all but oblivious to the company's dire financial status because the shelves remained full; even if they knew of the bankruptcy, customers would have no reason to shy away from buying such small, no-risk items as brand-name toothpaste, soap, aspirin, and other toiletries and drugs.

But because of conflicts that developed between creditors and management, creditors who had bought the bonds at par and creditors like Embry who bought at a discount, and creditors and shareholders, and because of a general deterioration of the business, this bankruptcy was destined to drag on and the hope of a good recovery would vanish. By the fall of 1988, Embry had already lost a good deal of confidence in Revco's ability to compete in the cutthroat discount drugstore business, describing the company as "the equivalent of an Olds ninety-eight competing in the Indianapolis five hundred."

In 1989, the company released a preliminary formula for a reorganization plan that gave the majority shareholders a generous 55 percent of the stock in return for a $150 million cash infusion and unsecured bondholders only a minority position and some bonds adding up to a scanty twenty-five cents on the dollar. (Senior creditors were to be paid in full.)

In response, Embry, chairman of an unsecured bondholders' committee—one of three creditor committees, the other two representing trade creditors and banks—and other bondholders began fighting the plan in court and closed-door negotiating sessions. As he asserted in a letter to the board of directors, Revco "belongs to its creditors." Embry helped fashion an alternative plan of reorganization—even though the company was still the only one who could file a plan with the court—that gave junior-level creditors 94 percent of Revco's stock in return for raising $75 million and converting more than $750 million of claims into equity.

At the same time, the committee's advisers were responding to calls coming in from companies interested in possibly bidding to buy Revco. One of the chief financial professionals on the team was David Schulte, the turnaround consultant from Chilmark Partners and soon to be Sam Zell's partner in the Zell-Chilmark vulture investment fund. The committee's advisory crew met with only those who seemed serious about exploring a bid. Only one party actually made an offer. In November, Acadia Partners and the Robert Bass Group laid down a $925 million bid. But for various reasons, management and the creditors' committees turned Acadia away. At the beginning of 1990, Embry handed over direct responsibility for the committee to his associate Pam Cascioli, so that he could devote more time to Magten's other pursuits.

Management, led by Boake Sells, took dramatic action by announcing a program to sell off 712 of Revco's 1900 stores, representing 36 percent of its total sales. Management soon made contacts with some 100 prospective buyers. By the end of October,

Revco had sold 620 stores and closed and liquidated 92 others, collecting a total of $250 million, which it immediately channeled into store improvements. Among the buyers were a company owned by former Revco bidder Acadia and rival druggist Jack Eckerd Corporation, each of which took 220 outlets off Revco's hands. Later in the bankruptcy Eckerd would be back for more—much more.

Also in 1990, an investigation began into Revco's 1986 leveraged buyout. Bondholders had already filed suit in April 1989 against Salomon Brothers, Revco's adviser on the LBO, charging the firm with failing to do proper analysis in assessing Revco's prospects and, therefore, making unrealistic earnings projections. In June 1990, Ohio bankruptcy Judge Harold White appointed Barry Zaretsky, an attorney and law professor, as an examiner in the case to determine whether the buyout involved fraud. His research would determine whether the company and its creditors had grounds for a lawsuit in which the charge would be that the LBO saddled Revco with so much debt that it crippled the company. In July, Zaretsky issued his preliminary opinion that the company and its creditors appeared to have a case, and he continued working toward a firm conclusion.

That October, the company's three creditor committees combined efforts to urge an end to management's exclusive right to file a reorganization plan. They wanted to submit their own plan, which would settle any fraudulent-conveyance litigation that might be filed, give creditors all of Revco's stock, and leave equity holders dry. Late that month, the court gave its nod and terminated management's exclusivity. Now the field was open for anyone who wanted to compete with management in filing a reorganization plan to take Revco out of bankruptcy.

On November 5, the trade creditors' committee did file a fraudulent conveyance lawsuit, seeking a $1.25 billion recovery against more than 2000 defendants—including former shareholders who sold out in the LBO, banks who financed the transaction, and advisers who masterminded it. At stake were the ex-shareholders' profits; the banks' fees as well as their collateral, which lower-ranking creditors could claim for themselves; and the advisors' fees. In January, Zaretsky confirmed their right to sue in his final report, although he urged the parties to settle rather than slugging it out over a protracted period and at great expense.

GOING FOR THE TALLY BONDS

In the third quarter of 1990, Balfour Investors, the New York–based vulture specialty firm, took a liking to Revco. They saw a company that was just beginning to show better results and Tally Bonds trading in the market at a price they considered irresistable. At varying prices averaging thirteen and a third cents on the dollar—a far cry from Embry's fifty-cent cost—they gathered up about $130 million worth of these junior-level bonds and in the process became the largest bondholder in the bankruptcy. They did not join Embry's committee, loathe as they are to limit their flexibility to act in their own interest and buy and sell bonds on fairly short notice. But after a few months, they did begin to take part in negotiations on a final reorganization plan along with the banks and other creditors.

Harry Freund and Jay Goldsmith have been together so long at times they seem almost to blend into each other. If one of them pauses in conversation, the other finishes the thought, and they interrupt each other freely to argue a point, make a correction, or embellish a description. Yet the two middle-aged men are a study in contrasts. Jay is Rodney Dangerfield—heavyset, his white hair combed back behind his ears, a cigar protruding from his mouth, his feet crossed on the table. In manner he is as plainspoken as anyone can be, but also good-natured. The son of a shoe salesman, he grew up in a $27-a-month two-room apartment with his parents and a brother in Brooklyn's rough-edged Bedford-Stuyvesant neighborhood. "We were poor," he says with a shrug. "We didn't have a car, we didn't have a television, there were no vacations." Attending the University of Buffalo on an athletic scholarship for basketball and baseball, he studied medieval history and then spent a year in law school. Although he'd had no academic training in business, he went to work at a small brokerage firm on Wall Street where for seven years he was the assistant to an avid bankruptcy investor named Louis Yaeger.

More refined in manner and speech, the silver-haired Freund is the Jack Benny to Goldsmith's Dangerfield. He was brought up across the river from his future partner, on the Upper West Side of Manhattan, in a vast eleven-room, $180-a-month apartment that required a maid to keep up, and he vacationed with his family in their country home. Not exactly rich, but not far from it. His father was a clothing manufacturer and his mother an active Zionist leader as the national president of Hadassah, the Jewish sisterhood organization. After Wharton Business School, Freund returned to New York, where he worked in real estate syndication and shared an apartment with college buddy Michael Steinhardt, who was then at the Wall Street firm of Loeb, Rhodes. When Steinhardt started the hedge fund he is famous for today, he encouraged his friend to go to Loeb, Rhodes and gave him an introduction. "I went down there not knowing a bull from a bear and I got the job. It was the good old heyday of Wall Street when they hired just anybody." He worked in research there for a few years, went on to do the same at another firm and then became the one-man research department at a new firm launched by Gerry Tsai, the investor who made his name in the "go-go" growth stocks of the 1960s.

Freund and Goldsmith met in 1975 through a mutual friend who wanted to start a three-man brokerage operation. When the friend pulled out at the last minute, they decided to start the firm on their own with investments of $25,000 apiece. For Freund, it was all that he owned; for Goldsmith, it was borrowed. Although they did not intend to focus on distressed securities, a shared attitude toward risk led them in that direction. "Buying something that is depressed, if you analyze it well enough and you know what you're doing, is much less risky than buying IBM, because nobody knows anything about IBM," says Goldsmith. "If somebody says to me, IBM in a year is going to earn x, he's throwing darts on a board as far as we're concerned. If we can get involved in a piece of paper that's been heavily discounted by panic or by market conditions or by unknowledgeable owners, and we can look at the balance sheet and say that the assets are such and such and the cash flow will be such and such, we'd rather make that bet."

"Besides which we're not so smart," Freund interjects. "So why try to compete with those who are much smarter than we in analyzing numbers that are publicly available? Why join the ranks of scores of people who have computers and all the other things—we can hardly manage a light switch—and can gauge the numbers and the trends? We'd rather poke about where nobody else is poking. And for most of our careers, nobody else was poking. Now, of course, we have company. But in those days the cemetery was a lonely place to spend one's time."

One of the few arguments the partners have ever had was over what to name their firm. Freund wanted their own names on the door, but Goldsmith, objecting that Goldsmith, Freund & Company or the reverse sounded like a butcher shop, insisted on something with a British ring for a cast of Old World prestige. One day while reading a story in the *New York Post* on the train going home, Freund came across the name Rabbi Balfour Brickner, a leader in the Jewish Reform movement. He gave out a yell, startling the passengers around him. That was it. Balfour Investors. It had the Jewish flavor of their own names that he wanted and the British quality to please his partner.

Purely by coincidence, the majority of Balfour's investment funds have come from British sources. In fact, much of it stems from a vacation the partners took together in London after they had been in business for two years. In the interest of developing their business contacts, they arranged to meet with three institutions the day after they arrived. One of them was Akroyd and Smithers, the largest jobbing (or market-making) firm on the London Stock Exchange, and they went to their offices in the musty financial section of town known as the City of London. On the way there, Jay muttered complaints about having to spend time surrounded by such dreary buildings and in such "peculiar taxis."

They sat down in an office with the head of Akroyd and Smithers's American trading desk and described their investing style and their current stake in the New York, New Haven and Hartford railroad. Then they repeated their story to someone else at the firm and then to a director. He, in turn, insisted that they meet the chairman, David Leroy-Lewis, who happened also to be the chairman of the London Stock Exchange. "We didn't know who he was," Freund says. "And we were exhausted. We'd told our story three or four times, the rooms were vastly overheated, we were jet lagged, and they put us into—I don't how old the chairs were, but you sank to the ground in a balloon of leather." Leroy-Lewis joined them, and they launched into their story once again. But then, although they tried desperately to prevent it, both of the hot, exhausted travelers began to drop off to sleep. The cherubic Leroy-Lewis tapped them awake and suggested they come back the next day after a good night's sleep and would not hear their protests. They thought they'd botched up a once-in-a-lifetime opportunity. But the next day when they returned, Leroy-Lewis expressed his wish to become one of their clients and committed a sum of money on the spot.

It would be the first of many such London relationships. A year later, Akroyd and Smithers gave the firm just under $1 million in return for 25 percent of Balfour's profits. And the partners noted that the day the London firm made its commitment was November 2, the anniversary of the British government's establishment of a Jewish home in Palestine through what was called the Balfour Declaration.

HELLO, IS THIS PARIS?

As with Talton Embry, the Balfour partners got their start in the railroads. The Chicago Milwaukee railroad was their first home run. It had gone bust three times, in the late 1800s, the 1920s, and 1960. In the mid-1970s, it was skidding once again. For six months, Balfour's Goldsmith watched the company's decline, and in May 1978, the railroad filed for bankruptcy with $76 million of first-mortgage priority debt and $60 million of junior debt. Because a lot of institutions that owned the bonds could not own the securities of bankrupt companies, they sold—fast. In a matter of days the senior bonds swooned from seventy-five cents on the dollar to twenty and the juniors, from forty down to five. At once, Goldsmith flew to Chicago to examine the indenture (terms) on the senior bonds and the composition of the collateral behind them. What he found backing up the senior debt was $13 million in cash and a first unimpeachable lien on all the assets of the railroad. Breathless, he called his partner, Freund, waking him up in Paris where he was vacationing. They agreed that Goldsmith should pick up some of the senior bonds. And with Charles Allen's Allen & Company as the major partner, they bought about half the issue— $38 million face value—at the twenty cents price and a lot of the juniors as well. "We were just kids," Goldsmith reflects. "We didn't know what we had. We could have controlled the whole fucking railroad. We knew we had something good. We bought it on the marketplace at twenty, twenty-one."

But at a meeting of management and the bondholders in Chicago, the chairman of the board of the company insisted that the senior bondholders' lien on the assets was flawed and could be invalidated. "You're not going to get paid," he declared. But as time progressed, the railroad's cash flow improved and the bonds were safe. Balfour sold out from late 1979 through late 1980, unloading bonds that cost nearly $10 million for $24 million. "We try to create an environment in which we can get taken out," says Goldsmith. "Or, if we're not going to get taken out, we want to have a significant influence on what goes on. The idea is always to get out. Get your money out. Don't be a hero. We identify the value, we put up capital to create the position, negotiate the deal, and then we look for an out at a good profit."

Probably Balfour's most disappointing experience was its investment in Global Marine, an offshore drilling company based in Houston that had used debt to build a fleet of rigs all over the world (hence the name Global Marine). At just about the time the fleet was finished in the early 1980s, the market for oil evaporated, and the company filed Chapter 11 bankruptcy. On the theory that the drilling business would turn around, Balfour invested $50 million in Global Marine junk bonds in February 1986—buying up a one-third, blocking position in one bond issue and portions of three others. But the turnaround took much longer than they expected. The value of the company was about half that of the collateral backing the senior level of debt, which didn't leave a whole lot for junior, junk-bond creditors. "If the lien-holding creditors come up short," says David Schulte, an adviser to the company, "what everybody else gets is almost exclusively a function of their negotiating acumen, because the only way junior creditors and equity holders wind up with anything is as a concession for making the process smooth. The power to disrupt becomes essentially what the juniors have to go by. And what that's worth is a function of how much disruption and how well they can play it. The juniors in Global Marine maintained the pretense of tough past the point where they were relevant. There was a moment when the secured lenders would have left a lot more of the company for the juniors. And if at that moment the juniors had said, 'Thank you God for this gift, I'm with you,' they would have had a much bigger piece of the company."

As hard as the junior creditor committee and, separately, Balfour fought, they managed to get only 8 percent of the stock of the new company. At one point the price of the stock was such that if Balfour had sold then it would have sustained a $15.9 million loss. But Balfour was fortunate enough to sell into a very strong rally that lasted only a couple of months, which chiseled the loss down to a more bearable, but still severe, $8.3 million. Balfour blames itself for an erroneous valuation, but for the severity of the loss it took, it also blames the Texas courts for a strong bias toward the company and unfair treatment of the creditors.

TURMOIL AT REVCO

It was a good thing that Balfour bought into Revco at a low average price in the third quarter of 1990, because the business continued to lose money. As one bondholder succinctly described the problem plaguing the company: "They simply do not fill the stores with goods that people want to buy." Operating losses widened. The October 1990 creditors' committee reorganization plan was rendered infeasible by the declining operating performance and cash flows. As a reflection of that, according to Schulte, the market value of Revco's bank debt, junk bonds, preferred stock and equity had fallen from $900 million at the time of the bankruptcy filing to $340 million in May 1991. Sells complained of not having had enough time to concentrate on the business because of the demands placed on him by the bankruptcy. In turn, creditors complained that management was continually revising its business plans and projections, making it impossible to formulate a reorganization plan with any credibility. In Embry's words, the Revco restructuring had "taken on a life of its own." He faced the possibility of taking a large loss. Yet, he stuck with it, because selling out would force him to take a major loss anyway. Besides, he hoped to cut his losses by pushing through a creditors' reorganization plan as quickly as possible. As he said in Magten's strategic publication, "If you learn that the company has real problems, you can either sell, or you can stay and help work them out." He hoped to work out a deal that would give him a slice of the new company's equity—and the chance for a payoff down the road when the business improved.

In the first quarter of 1991, the creditors faced three choices. They could wait to see if management could repair the company. They could try to push in a new management team. Or they could find some drugstore operator out in the world who for a piece of the equity would come in and revive the business. The unsecured bondholders' committee chaired by Cascioli of Magten decided to try for the third option, and its members directed their advisers to find out what companies might be interested in such a deal. But they made it clear that they didn't want to sell the company; they wanted to give up only a minority stake. Schulte and Joel Friedland from his firm brought the idea to executives at the Walgreens and Osco chains, who turned him down. He also contacted Jack Eckerd, which had already bought a passel of Revco stores, and the Rite Aid Corporation. As it turned out, they were very interested in Revco, but did not want to settle for just a piece of the action. They made intimations that they wanted the whole company. This didn't sit well with the bondholders' committee.

That spring, Eckerd decided to make a quiet bid. The Florida-based chain, which also had been taken private in an LBO in 1986, had no cash or public securities to offer creditors in a reorganization. So Eckerd offered to merge with Revco and then issue stock in the public markets that it could distribute to creditors. Both Revco and the creditors rejected the idea in May. The following month, Revco filed its own reorganization plan that distributed stock to junior creditors and existing stockholders. Creditors snarled at it, primarily because it saddled Revco with too much debt.

But also, they now wanted to sponsor their own plan. The company's operations had begun picking up steam, and the bank

creditors agreed to convert about a third of their claims—about
$100 million—into equity. Now junior creditors could end up con-
trolling the company without a burdensome amount of debt; stockholders would receive nothing. So in the spring and summer of
1991, the creditors prepared their reorganization plan.

The Balfour partners, meanwhile, were not happy with the way
things were going in the bankruptcy. The creditors were sparring
viciously with management, and neither the company's nor the
prospective creditors' plans appealed to them because they did not
believe them to be rich enough. Goldsmith and Freund had made
some effort to beat the bushes in the United States and Europe for
potential bidders who would offer a higher value. Certainly, Balfour's partners were glad when they heard that Eckerd was bidding, but they were dismayed that the company had not brought its
bid public.

While lobbying for the support of other creditors during the
summer, Eckerd's chairman, Stewart Turley, visited Balfour Investors at Rockefeller Center. Balfour's assessment of the situation
was that both the trade creditors and Embry wanted to maintain
an independent Revco. The trade creditors were afraid that new
owners would use their own sets of suppliers. And, according to
Balfour's theory, Embry wanted to control a new Revco so that he
could help nurse the company back to health and thereby raise the
value of the stock over the long run to make up for the losses he'd
suffered in the short run. The only way that Eckerd's bid might
succeed, as Balfour saw it, was if it were made official.

"You have to go public with it and force these people [on the
trade and bondholders' committees] to respond to their constituencies," Freund told Turley. "You have to circumvent the people
who are sitting there representing the constituencies, and go to the
constituencies themselves by making a public announcement."

But Turley was hesitant. He believed a public bid would only
inspire Rite Aid Corporation, the nation's largest drugstore chain
that certainly didn't want another jumbo-size chain to compete
against, to join the bidding and push up the price.

Besides, said Turley, eyeing Goldsmith and Freund across their
conference table, "You guys have a self-interest in what you're

telling me because you're in it for the money. You have a low cost, and you're just going to use our announcement to get the hell out."

And Goldsmith responded with his usual candor. "Yeah, we might do that. As long as the bid is public information and everybody knows about it, why not? And if we do it, it'll go into the hands of the arbs [arbitrageurs are traders who buy securities and who believe that when a takeover occurs they'll collect more]. So what's so terrible? The arbs are truly economic creatures and will respond to your deal and anybody else's deal based on the values presented. The only way you're going to get into this game is to come out with a real serious bid that says to the world, 'I want to buy this company.' "

IN PLAY

Still, over the summer Eckerd continued its private discussions with creditor groups and continued to encounter stonelike resistance from most of them.

On September 6, the bondholders', trade, and bank committees released the reorganization plan they'd spent the summer working on. Ownership of Revco would pass to its junior unsecured creditors, and if all classes approved the plan, Magten itself was slated to own 13 percent of the new company. But precisely two weeks later, Jack Eckerd finally went public with a bid, filing a reorganization plan with the Ohio court that included an offer to acquire Revco for $970 million. All creditors would receive bonds, and after the companies were merged, the trade creditors and subordinated bondholders would be able to convert their bonds into a 22 percent stake in the new company. One of Revco's bond creditor groups—holders of unsecured 12⅛ percent bonds—joined Eckerd in cosponsoring the proposal. But the plan didn't sit well with all the other creditors, who held that their own plan simply contained better recoveries. (Although the $970 million Eckerd plan looked generous, that number included the face value of zero-coupon bonds, which appreciate over many years from discount to face value.) In October, all three of Revco's creditor committees formally rejected the Eckerd plan, and the company strengthened the creditors' position by announcing that it was going to stand behind *their* reorganization plan.

But Revco was not yet destined for stability. Just as Eckerd had suspected, Rite Aid jumped into the competition. In its $585 million offer made at the tail end of October, senior creditors would get cold, hard cash and juniors would immediately get Rite Aid stock; they would not have to wait for their stock, as in Eckerd's package deal. Five insurance companies holding Revco 11.75 percent bonds (which were not represented by the official bondholders' committee) cosponsored the plan with the drugstore operator. It was hardly surprising when a week later Eckerd sweetened its offer, and a month later Rite Aid responded by enriching its bid. Finally, Judge White ordered that all three plans go to the creditors for a vote, on three separate ballots, all due on January 3, 1992.

By the time the judge issued his order, the Balfour Investors were long gone. After the Eckerd announcement, the price of Revco's bonds rose in the market and Balfour waited a week or so to see whether Eckerd would make its bid even better or Rite Aid would step in. Then Balfour started slowly feeding its bond position out to buyers in the market. Within about six weeks, Balfour had sold all of its holdings at a variety of prices averaging twenty-seven cents on the dollar. "We made a pleasant little double on our investment," Goldsmith says matter-of-factly of Balfour's year-long stay in Revco bonds. Why didn't they stick around a little longer for a bidding war? "We're not big risk takers," Freund said late that fall. "This is a big risk. What if the deal falls through? What if Eckerd is finished bidding, Rite Aid is turned down, and the company-creditor plan prevails? We don't think the bonds are worth twenty-seven if that's the case."

Indeed, there was plenty of risk as January 3, 1992, approached. The company and most of its creditors continued to support the creditor plan. There was the chance, however, that none of the plans would receive the number and dollar amount of votes necessary to pass. During the week before the deadline, the three contenders ran advertisements to help win votes. Rite Aid pointed out that Revco's current management had lost $520 million in the last four years. Likewise, the Eckerd ad noted that the company-creditor plan "offers you common stock in a stand-alone Revco whose past performance raises serious doubts as to its future prospects." It also mentioned, "You should know that many trade creditors, *including most of those represented on the Trade Credi-*

tors' Committee, have indicated to us that they will support the Eckerd Plan" (emphasis in the original).

Finally, the company used its ad to report that its operations were undergoing a recovery. "The Creditor Plan allows you to benefit from the dramatic improvements and growth Revco is enjoying," it stated. And for those who were experiencing debt hangovers, it imparted the information that "Rite Aid has yet to disclose the source of over half a billion dollars it will need to borrow. That amount would be added to its existing half a billion dollars of debt." And if that weren't enough to scare them, how about the prospect of further delay? "Your time and money have been tied up long enough. Both the Rite Aid and Eckerd plans are loaded with serious antitrust implications."

In the voting in early January, none of the plans received enough votes for a confirmation. Frantic efforts began to make adjustments to the plans that would attract the requisite amount of support. Because the senior subordinated bond holders had voted the creditor-company plan down for the reason that they didn't like the lack of certainty in owning Revco stock, the bondholders' committee quickly found a way to guarantee them a value for that stock. Its adviser, Chilmark Partners, came to the rescue with the Zell-Chilmark vulture fund, offering to buy out up to $160 million of stock at a set price.

But then the creditors began making progress in behind-the-scenes negotiations with Eckerd. Eckerd agreed to improve its bid a third time, and some major creditors decided to go with it. One of those creditors was Leon Black, the former Drexel, Burnham, Lambert head of corporate finance who now ran a billion-plus vulture fund. In 1991, Black's Apollo fund had purchased part of Wells Fargo & Company's portfolio of loans to high-debt companies and with it a chunk of Revco debt that made it the company's largest bank creditor. Believing that the Eckerd offer was now the best on the field, Black and others encouraged fellow creditors to back it. And they did. Rite Aid stepped out of the competition on January 10, and Eckerd began to quickly assemble a revised plan to submit to the court. It looked like the winner.

But, alas, Revco's woes would not end. Only two weeks later, management surprised the creditors with a gussied up version of its own plan.

The following week, the Zell-Chilmark fund gave the Revco plan the glitter it needed to outshine Eckerd's bid: an offer to furnish up to $250 million in cash to those who wanted to avoid holding Revco stock. Zell and Schulte were glad to help end the bankruptcy and take up to 18 percent of the stock in a company that appeared to be on the mend. In mid-February, Eckerd took its leave, paving the way for Revco to emerge as a new company in the spring. (In June, Zell and Embry, as the company's largest shareholders, ousted Sells, citing differences between him and the board. Meanwhile, enhanced marketing and customer service as well as improved cost controls continued to boost financial results through 1992.)

Embry and Magten had endured a painful period of nearly four years. He had managed to reduce Magten's cost through some deft trading with other insiders. By the end of the bankruptcy, his average cost was about thirty-four cents on the dollar—$40 million for some $118 million worth of bonds. And his profit at that point looked to be about $18 million, for a compounded annual return of around 10 percent. "And this case was a disaster," he marvels. "If this is the worst we do, I'm happy."

7

The Raid on Allegheny International

It was common, when two yahoos discovered such a stone in a field, and were contending which of them should be the proprietor, a third would take the advantage, and carry it away from them both.

—*JONATHAN SWIFT*

Sunday evening, September 30, 1990, Michael Lederman flew from New York to Pittsburgh to take possession of the Sunbeam-Oster Company. He was the company's new general counsel. Japonica Partners, an investment company run by Paul Kazarian and Lederman, had just acquired the maker of household appliances and other consumer products that was once called Allegheny International. Early Monday morning, Lederman and Sunbeam's treasurer, Tony Munson, walked the few blocks from the Vista Hotel downtown to Sunbeam headquarters at Two Oliver Plaza, a black octagonal hulk smack in the middle of the downtown cultural district. Across the street, a sleek thirty-two-story tower seemed to stand taller than ever. In the mid-1980s, that granite structure was to be named after Allegheny International and serve as the corpo-

162

ration's headquarters. But by the time it was finished, Allegheny had begun to sink into a financial bog, and it bailed out of the deal. The building now bears the name of the Consolidated Natural Gas Company: the CNG Tower.

Lederman's first act when he arrived at Two Oliver Plaza that October morning in 1990 was to visit the eighteenth floor, the old executive suite that he and his partner Kazarian had nicknamed "The Imperial Palace." It was once the domain of Robert Buckley, the man who became notorious for allegedly driving Allegheny to ruin through mismanagement and extravagance. That extravagance was visible everywhere. Branching off the hallway that curved around the floor were a series of alcoves, which opened into sitting areas furnished in plush couches and Chippendales and in turn led to the executives' offices. The most lavish of these was Buckley's. It featured parquet floors, brass doorknobs, a full bar with liquor cabinets, a marble bathroom suite complete with shower, and a private conference room. For large meetings, down the hallway there was the Officers' Conference Room, wood paneled and well appointed in antiques. For Kazarian and Lederman to oversee the company from these offices as if they were the new imperial kings struck them as being against all the arguments they'd been making that frugality was part of what Allegheny needed to thrive. So Lederman asked all those stationed on the floor to move their belongings to Sunbeam's two remaining floors, and when everyone had gone, he locked the doors. Now the only thing left to do was to turn the company around.

By the time Allegheny entered bankruptcy in February 1988, it had already endured years of jarring changes in which it was refashioned from a steel company into a maker of appliances and other housewares. Buckley, the man who had engineered this reincarnation from industrial to consumer company through acquisitions such as Sunbeam in 1981, was gone, forced out after a 1986 *Business Week* cover story accused him of egregiously wasteful management practices. The article claimed that in the five years since 1981, even as profits became losses and debt mounted, Buckley continued to dole out sumptuous perks to top executives. According to the article, there was a fleet of five jets sometimes used for personal jaunts; there were management meetings for up to 100 executives and spouses in such places as the Bahamas and Boca Raton, Florida, that cost hundreds of thousands of dollars; and more than $30 million in personal loans were made to officers at 2 percent rates. The article also said that in the early and mideighties, Buckley was sinking AI money into high-risk oil and gas and real estate deals that stumbled badly, including a Florida condominium development in which Buckley and other AI executives happened to own units. And it was fast becoming clear that he had vastly overpaid for Sunbeam; the small-appliance business was not performing up to optimistic projections, and the cost of the debt taken on to make the acquisition was weighing heavily on earnings. Even as the company's fortunes foundered, Buckley's compensation remained in the stratosphere. In 1984, he took home more than $1 million in salary and bonus, about 7 percent of the company's net income for that year. Buckley sued *Business Week* for libel. The suit is still pending.

The company's problems continued to mount, even after Buckley resigned in August 1986. In 1987, management attempted to sell the company to the First Boston Corporation, the big New York investment bank, but preferred stockholders led by New York investor group Spear, Leeds & Kellogg blocked the sale by refusing to tender their shares. The Oster/Sunbeam Appliance Company, Allegheny's pride-and-joy appliance subsidiary, continued to swoon with ever-greater losses stemming from an errant focus on one or two products like the Oskar minifood processor and an automatic-shut-off iron.

Now it was February 1988. The company was unable to convince its lenders to refinance their debt on easier terms. Cash was becoming scarce. Finally, saddled with liabilities of $845 million that overpowered the $735 million in assets, Allegheny filed for bankruptcy court protection from creditors and began the grueling process of reorganization. So grueling was this particular bankruptcy that participants came to refer to it as "the case from hell." A divided board and a particularly contentious set of creditors and shareholders combined to doom one reorganization plan after another. Once again putting itself up for sale, the company attracted the likes of Donaldson, Lufkin and Jenrette (DLJ), the Wall Street brokerage firm, Victor Kiam of Remington shavers fame, Black & Decker, and Paul Levy, the former codirector of workouts at Drexel, Burnham, Lambert & Company who was now part of an investment boutique called Joseph, Littlejohn & Levy. Agreements were struck with DLJ, then Black & Decker and then DLJ again. But in the end, all the buyers backed off like so many disillusioned suitors as they saw operations continue to decline. A year and a half into the bankruptcy, the company and its creditors were finally agreeing on something: putting the company up for sale was not the answer. They would have to come up with their own, internally generated plan to reorganize. But just as the parties finally began to come together, Michael Lederman and Paul Kazarian showed up at the door with an alluring $700 million offer that seemed much too good to be true. Few believed that two former midlevel investment bankers in their thirties who went by the mysterious name of Japonica Partners could pull off an acquisition that more venerable names had failed to do. For that reason, they didn't invite Japonica in. But because they could not get inside the company and were in reality backed by two powerful vulture investors—Michael Price's Mutual Series Fund and Michael Steinhardt's Steinhardt Partners—Japonica Partners took the risk of a hostile tender offer and didn't relent until they had the company in their grasp.

Japonica stalked Allegheny with a double-barreled strategy. On the one hand, it purchased bank loans and bonds and private debt from three classes of debt holders, building a huge stake that would give it great influence over the way in which the company would be reorganized. But also, because the judge had earlier allowed parties besides the company to file reorganization plans, Japonica filed its own, all-cash plan of reorganization to compete against the all-stock one that management was presenting to creditors. By sponsoring its own plan, Japonica could acquire control over the management of the company. In the end, the company plan won out, but Japonica had bought enough claims—while the bankruptcy code constrained the company from buying claims—to control both it and the company.

The young, pugnacious partners, who acquired the nickname in the bankruptcy as "the Twins," pursued their goal single-mindedly as raiders are known to do. It was a huge undertaking and a larger risk, but ultimately, after endless battles for information and litigation on both sides, it worked. They and their backers captured the company they'd coveted, and today even their enemies acknowledge a stroke of genius in their work.

THE EDUCATION OF THE VULTURES

Paul Kazarian is a wiry man with an acute analytical mind that seems never to stop humming. Speaking with an accent strongly flavored by his Rhode Island upbringing, he is passionate, sarcastic, and profane. Here is his only half-facetious description of how his investors grilled him on his analytical work during the Allegheny drama: "They'd push the shit on me, like you'd get in a room and they'd beat me up and yell at me and try to intimidate me and ask me a question six different ways, and then challenge the numbers, 'Take them back.' " The passion infuses his work. When hovered over financial reports, Kazarian often has his radio on, blaring rock music, and he tends to yell sporadically over the music to associates working in nearby offices.

In public, Kazarian is mischievously eccentric. A vegetarian for health reasons, he will not hesitate to order a peanut butter and jelly sandwich in a posh French restaurant. Yet, as Peter Langerman, a Mutual Series Fund analyst, points out, "He goes overboard to tell you he's a regular guy. He'd tell you how they'd pack up in the wagon, the kids screaming, to go to Rhode Island [from their home in Brooklyn]." Both Kazarian and his partner, Michael Lederman, disdain wearing ties and have been known to wear baseball caps to meetings. Up until a few years ago Kazarian's fine ink-black hair flowed nearly to his shoulders. He got a crewcut in the fall of 1990—right after Japonica finally snared Allegheny. Now with his gold-rim glasses and pocket protector, he has the appearance of an engineering student. Friends and foes alike consider Kazarian's unorthodox behavior disconcerting—from quirky to downright annoying. But what they all agree on is that he is smart, calling him a "computer," an "encyclopedia," and a "financial animal." Ultimately, people describe him as a "brilliant financial analyst."

Kazarian founded Japonica Partners in late 1987 in Pawtucket,

Rhode Island, naming it not after some land in the Far East, but after the street he grew up on in that town. Japonica Street was the nucleus of a thriving Armenian immigrant community that had sprung up in the early part of the century. In 1915, Kazarian's grandfather Charlie escaped the Armenian genocide in Turkey, where he'd been forced to watch his first wife and their two children tortured to death. He married another refugee, and they moved into a house on Japonica Street, where they raised three sons and two daughters. Kazarian, too, grew up in that house, with sisters, brothers, parents, and grandparents. On the porches and sidewalks of that street in the summers, the Armenians from the blocks around would gather to relive the tragedies they'd endured. And on that street, Kazarian's grandfather founded a small ice-making company, which his three sons built into a hodgepodge business of real estate, retailing, and oil distribution.

Earning a political science degree at Bates College in Lewiston, Maine, Kazarian obtained a masters degree in that field at Brown University before entering Columbia Business School. He went on to practice investment banking at the prestigious Wall Street firm of Goldman, Sachs & Company. For most of the seven years he worked there he was stationed in the corporate finance department, often working on mergers and acquisitions in a variety of industries. In 1986, Kazarian hit it off with Michael Lederman, a bankruptcy lawyer a few years his elder—he is thirty-nine and Kazarian is thirty-six—who had just arrived at Goldman, Sachs and sat next to him. Reedlike and balding, Lederman wears black wire rims and a short-cropped black beard, which was something of an anomaly at the austere investment bank.

Calmer in demeanor, he's a good intellectual match for Kazarian. The son of a printing company worker and an interior designer, Lederman grew up on Long Island and went to the University of Pennsylvania, fully intending to major in religion. But later he switched to South Asia regional studies with an emphasis in multinational enterprise, hoping somehow to help third world nations develop economically. He even learned to speak Hindi. After graduating with honors, he changed course yet again, earning law and graduate business degrees from the University of Virginia in 1980. After working as a railroad lawyer for a couple years with the Washington, D.C., firm Sidley & Austin, he returned to his New York City roots to start work as a bankruptcy lawyer at Shearman & Sterling before joining Goldman, Sachs in 1986 to help launch its workout practice. Coincidentally, one of the projects he took on was to make a presentation to Allegheny International about how it should restructure its finances and reduce its debt. Management responded somewhat superciliously that the company had "other options." A few weeks later Lederman found out what those other options were when First Boston announced its offer to acquire the company—the offer that then failed.

In the fall of 1987, Kazarian left Goldman, Sachs to return to Pawtucket to take care of the family business after his father had been forced into retirement by a heart attack. Within months he'd buffed up the company for sale and found a buyer. Some of the proceeds went into founding Japonica, which Kazarian intended as a vehicle for making sizable investments in companies. The advice his father gave him was characteristically direct. "Don't blow it. Don't be a dope." Back in New York, Kazarian found temporary quarters in the Park Avenue office out of which Lederman—who'd just left Goldman, Sachs—and another ex-Goldmanite were running an advisory firm for companies in need of restructuring.

Scouting the field for bargains, Kazarian became entranced with CNW, the holding company for the Chicago & North Western Transportation Company. Having worked on the Conrail privatization while at Goldman, Sachs, Kazarian knew railroads. CNW's stock was trading in the low twenties following a failed $31-a-share bid for the company, and Kazarian was convinced the stock was trading at less than half of its intrinsic value. Lederman reinforced his enthusiasm. As a lawyer in Washington he had represented the Burlington Northern Railroad in its unsuccessful effort to keep the CNW out of the Powder River Basin in Wyoming and Montana. Intimately familiar with the line, Lederman confirmed Kazarian's sense that the market was not recognizing the abundance of cash it was producing and its large depreciation.

Kazarian took his analysis to another old Goldman, Sachs buddy, Chuck Davidson, formerly a bond trader who left in 1984 to become a general partner at Steinhardt Partners, the $1.5 billion hedge fund run by Michael Steinhardt. Davidson had always shared Kazarian's boyish zeal for value hunting, and in this case he bought the argument, and then the stock—by giving money to Japonica, which became part of a group that acquired just under 5 percent. Expecting that management would not welcome Kazarian, Davidson advised him to charge at the company with a hostile bid. But at that time Kazarian was not spoiling for a fight. He was convinced that once management heard his ideas for reconfiguring the company, it would enthusiastically deploy them, hence raising the value of the stock. On November 15, 1988, after spending months putting together a business plan, Kazarian—with Lederman, who had become increasingly involved with Kazarian's project although he did not yet work for Japonica—flew out to Chicago to meet the senior officers. They set up a second meeting for a month later, but shortly before, the company canceled and rejected Japonica's business plan.

That's when Kazarian finally took Davidson's advice and decided to turn hostile. In March 1989, Kazarian and Lederman—who had just formally joined Japonica and moved with him into an office across the street from where they were—launched a proxy fight to replace the eight-member board at the May 16 annual meeting. To prepare an effective bid, the Japonica group raised its stock holding to a level that would be adequate to accomplish an LBO—and to scare the wits out of CNW management. Kazarian approached Michael Price for backing. Kazarian had met the famous value investor in his Goldman, Sachs days, and Price held him in high regard. With Mutual Series funds, some smaller investors contributing, and Steinhardt upping its investment, Japonica Partners boosted its stake from 4.9 percent to 9.9 percent. In April, they placed a $44 bid and in May commenced a tender offer for all CNW shares at that price. Soon after, Japonica lost the proxy fight for the board seats, but it continued the tender offer. Then on June 6, the Blackstone Group, a merchant banking boutique run by former Commerce Secretary Pete Peterson, came in with a $50 bid. Japonica lost the company, but the group's investors were rewarded with a $30 million profit.

The next morning, Davidson called the partners, who were in their small, sparely furnished office assiduously researching other possible investments. "Okay, we didn't win CNW," he told them.

"But I've got another target. Allegheny International just had another plan of reorganization go down the tubes. Let's take a look and see what's going on."

FRIENDLY BID, UNFRIENDLY WELCOME

Since the fall, Davidson and his bankruptcy lawyers had been combing through the growing numbers of bankrupt companies like a shopper at a rummage sale looking for good buys. The problem, he found, was that most bankrupt companies were bankrupt for good reason: They were lousy companies. But his instincts told him that Allegheny was not a lousy company; it was a good company with good products and a lousy management. "I follow the Peter Lynch theory of investing," he says, referring to the legendary former manager of the Fidelity Magellan Fund. "Think of yourself as a consumer and you're probably a reasonable proxy for the world. Allegheny was Sunbeam and Oster. I'd actually heard of the products. My wife had an Osterizer. It was simple." Products that people know and trust make a solid foundation for investment. He bought a few bonds and in the spring, when the CNW fight was still raging, he called Wilbur Ross, the investment banking adviser from Rothschild, Inc. who was representing the unsecured creditors' committee in the bankruptcy. Ross told Davidson that in his opinion there was great value in Allegheny. He encouraged Steinhardt Partners to bid to acquire the company, but he also had a word of advice: "You are going to have trouble with Allegheny," he said, "because we have been through the rounds with Paul Levy, with DLJ, with everybody you can imagine, and it seems pretty clear to us that the debtor is quite hostile to anybody taking it over." Shortly afterward, Japonica's run at CNW ended, freeing up the one-project shop for a new assignment.

Kazarian agreed to review the company's public documents for a few days and make a judgment on the values. But the supposed financial wizard found the public documents to be impenetrable, mainly because accounting changes had made historical comparisons meaningless. "If you looked at all their financials, you figured instinctively that it had to be malicious," he exclaims, his eyes burning with intensity. "They made the company so totally incomprehensible—changing the calendar year, recombining units, pulling them back apart, changing accounting assumptions. The first conclusion was, How the hell could the company's financials actually be interpreted?" Lederman visited Allegheny with a team of three researchers and reviewed more documents there, but what they saw only clouded the situation further. Kazarian reported to Davidson in his usual style: "Look, this thing is a piece of shit. The numbers are horrible." For instance, there was the bottom-line number: In the first half of 1989 the company reported a net loss of $18 million. But it was almost too horrible to be believed. In fact, Kazarian began to think that the ugly numbers were obscuring a prize property. "What initially intrigued us was we couldn't believe any company intentionally could be so screwed up as they were trying to show it." he says. A more substantial lure was the solidity of the brand names, which Kazarian saw as clearly as Davidson had—Sunbeam irons, toasters, mixers, barbecue grills, and warming blankets and Oster blenders.

In late June, based on their preliminary work, Davidson and Japonica made an exploratory offer for the company. Steinhardt would commit $60 million in equity and the rest would come from bank loans. They wrote a letter to the board announcing the preliminary offer of $700 million in cash and notes and asked for access to company files to allow them to do "due diligence," in-depth research to confirm the bid. But it was like a stone dropped into a canyon. The board showed no interest at all. The company recently had been abandoned by DLJ for the second time and was not receptive to another potential buyer. "Information, limited as it was, on Japonica provided no basis to believe they were viable," says Bruce McCullough, the company's bankruptcy attorney from Buchanan, Ingersoll in Pittsburgh.

The company and its creditors had been left without either a proposed bankruptcy reorganization plan or a business operating plan. Under CEO Oliver Travers, Buckley's successor, operations were deteriorating, especially within the core Oster/Sunbeam housewares unit. In earnest, the board and some senior creditors turned to James Milligan, a turnaround expert, to manage the company. An accountant by training, Milligan had restructured the Borden foods company in the 1970s and followed that up by rebuilding a conglomerate called Questor around its main business, Spalding sporting goods and Evenflo Juvenile Products, and more than doubling its value. By the spring of 1989 Milligan already had been advising the board's executive committee based on a strategic plan he'd developed for DLJ. And his advice carried weight. According to Lewis Davis, the company's chief corporate lawyer who worked with McCullough at Buchanan, Ingersoll, "whatever Milligan suggested in terms of running the company the board did." He called for the closing of some plants and the termination of many executives and rank-and-file employees throughout the company's sprawling operations. Because of his decisive action and his prior achievements, Milligan had credibility with the creditors. The board needed him. In June, the directors hired Milligan as a special adviser with the assignment of assembling a business strategy for the company that would form the basis of a stand-alone reorganization plan. His reward, he thought at the time, would be the keys to the company when it finally emerged from bankruptcy.

AN OPENING

Five blocks up Liberty Avenue from Allegheny headquarters, in the Federal Building, Bankruptcy Judge Joseph Cosetti had dramatically different ideas for the company. Cosetti, a white-haired, outspoken former economist given to colorful metaphors from the bench, reacted to DLJ's withdrawal with three dramatic measures intended to get the reorganization moving. That June, as Milligan was beginning his work, he deferred the payment of fees to all legal, financial, and accounting advisers working for Allegheny and the creditors' committee (although not other creditor groups) as an incentive to speed up the process. He also eliminated the company's exclusive right to file a reorganization plan, opening the field to others. And he invited U.S. Trustee Harry Jones to move for the appointment of a Chapter 11 operating trustee to replace Allegheny's management, a move that would instead, indirectly, create another opening for Japonica.

Officially, Jones is the U.S. Trustee for Region 2, which consists of New York, Connecticut, and Vermont, but for a while in 1989 and 1990, he was also the U.S. Trustee for Region 3, consisting of

Pennsylvania, Delaware, and New Jersey. As U.S. Trustee, he plays an administrative role in bankruptcies, including appointing committees, reviewing fees, and filing applications in court to appoint a Chapter 11 operating trustee. The judge rules on such applications, and Cosetti certainly appeared to want a trustee named. But the blunt Jones had his own way of doing things. His first task, as he saw it, was to evaluate the situation at hand. Jones arranged a meeting of the representatives of all the various constituencies at his offices in the cavernous, granite-columned U.S. Customs House at the southern tip of Manhattan. Starting out, he got everyone to agree to abstain from filing reorganization plans, as the judge had just allowed them to do, and instead to try to reach a consensus. One participant was Charles O'Hanlon, the representative of Mellon Bank, the lead bank in the twenty-six-member bank group who became an important force in the bankruptcy. "Jones banged heads in a room sort of like a labor mediator. He in effect brought everyone together, made them stay in the room and said we're not going to leave this room until you've worked out a deal. Everybody just aired their grievances and nobody wanted to make a deal." Still, after that initial meeting, Jones was convinced that the case was not yet so out of control that it required an operating trustee. What it needed was a focal point. He set up a series of meetings that summer in New York to keep the parties talking and nudge them toward agreement.

At one of the sessions, Jones gave Japonica a chance to present its bid. Wilbur Ross from his seat advising the unsecured creditors' committee had encouraged Jones to give Japonica a hearing. "We felt the case was setting a terrible precedent against the whole idea of outsiders coming in and bidding for companies in Chapter 11. And since we're in so many cases we really were interested in encouraging people to come in and help out the creditors." Besides, because he'd met with Davidson and knew that Steinhardt was solidly behind Japonica, he believed that Japonica's bid was "very real." As for the other creditors, their contempt for the company was at such a high pitch that all were willing to hear from an outsider.

Right before the session with Japonica, the various creditor groups and the company met in a conference room at the offices of bank creditor attorneys Milbank, Tweed, Hadley & McCloy in the Wall Street district. Each creditor group sat in a different part of the room—the banks in one cluster, the insurance-company unsecured creditors in another, the subordinated debt holders in yet another cluster, and the company in the middle. The creditors pelted Allegheny's advisers with invective like a target at a stoning, complaining about what had befallen the company and its operations.

"We're going to file to liquidate this company, and whatever happens happens," threatened one member of the bank group.

"We're here to discuss ways to reorganize the company, if you want to talk about that," said Allegheny attorney Lewis Davis. "But if you want to liquidate we can't stop you. Go ahead. Have a good time."

However, one of the company's advisers, Leonard LoBiondo of the accounting firm Zolfo, Cooper & Company, then explained that liquidation would probably reduce, if not wipe out, recoveries for some of the creditors below the bank level. And that would lead in turn to years of litigation between the banks and the other creditors.

After an hour or so of bickering, they trudged the few blocks to U.S. Trustee Jones's office, walking through the swelter of a summer rainstorm into the arctic air-conditioning of the U.S. Customs House to listen to Kazarian. All the advisers in the case were present—the company's attorneys, Wilbur Ross and the creditors' committee's attorneys, the company's financial advisers, the banks' advisers, the advisers for the Sunbeam creditors, and the adviser for the shareholders' group.

Here was Japonica's opportunity to win over the agents for the creditors and the board. Instead, he turned them off. Kazarian told the gathering that Japonica, with $60 million in equity financing from Steinhardt Partners and bank loans, was prepared to offer $700 million for the company. But as John Mueller, the representative of the equity holders' committee relates, his manner was brazen and presumptuous. "He was anything but a salesman. He basically came in and said, 'This process is out of control. We're here. We can do it.' He didn't stand up and speak. He sat there.

Never smiled. The message I got was: You're dealing with a bunch of flakes. We're the pros from Dover. Stand back, you might get hurt. People at the meeting were offended."

On the whole, the creditors were unimpressed with the young man and his numbers, especially because he offered no firm equity or bank financing agreements. But Trustee Jones, seconded by Ross, argued that Japonica should be given access to information that would allow it to firm up its bid, because two buyers were unquestionably better than one, the company itself being one. He asked everybody to agree to it and after some discussion everyone did. Then he gave Ross the job of being the one to furnish Japonica with the flow of information coming from Allegheny.

Lederman and Kazarian soon paid a visit to headquarters in Pittsburgh. "The controller threw us in a room with no organized information, a bunch of unmarked boxes," says Kazarian. And the numbers remained opaque, unintelligible. But to Kazarian, the company was like an Armenian woman practicing the art of Naz, in which she entices a man by telling him to go away. The poor treatment they received and the bad numbers they saw were only a tease. Underneath lay a valuable company that was crying out for new management.

Meanwhile, Allegheny's current management was attempting to restart their engines. By the end of July, Milligan had plotted a course for the company that involved shrinking its infrastructure to meet its already shrunken sales capacity. One goal was to remove $100 million of working capital by reducing inventories, accelerating collection of receivables, extending payment terms on payables, and closing down plants. With less investment tied up in plants and inventories, working capital needs would decline and presumably cash would pour in. In a conference call with U.S. Trustee Jones and Allegheny attorneys Davis and McCullough in August, the creditors urged the company to proceed with the Milligan plan. The message was clear: They trusted Milligan and feared that bringing in an outside party would lead to yet another disappointing experience that would drag the bankruptcy out and the company's operations down.

Davis and McCullough obtained the company's permission to stop shipping information to Japonica. "We didn't see any purpose in it," Davis says. "The creditors weren't interested. The company's attitude was they didn't have the ability to do it. They didn't check out. They weren't a DLJ or a Paul Levy. They didn't have a history of having financed deals and put them together. And they didn't appear to have the money," since Steinhardt would contribute only a portion. So in August 1989, except for answering some questions about the information they had received, the company cut Japonica off. And to most of those concerned in the case, they vanished from the scene.

All the constituencies turned their attention to constructing a stand-alone reorganization plan that would please everybody. By borrowing $400 million from Wells Fargo, the banks and Prudential (the senior-secured creditor of the Sunbeam subsidiary) would be able to go home with their pockets stuffed with cash. Since the senior-unsecured creditors—including major insurance companies such as Equitable and Aetna—also wanted cash, work began on a plan to issue junk bonds and give the proceeds to that class of creditors. The subordinated debt holders would get a major stake in the new company's stock. But holders of the old stock would receive only a smidgen of the new stock.

In September, Japonica's Lederman appeared before the company and creditors at another of the U.S. Trustee's meetings in Manhattan. He reported that Japonica had now done enough research on the company to know that it definitely wanted to acquire it. And he also had some commentary on the company's stand-alone plan: "I said it's impossible," he recalls. The reason he cited was the recent weakness in the junk bond market.

The junk bond market's dive that fall did puncture the proposal to raise cash for the insurance companies that made up the senior-unsecured class. They would have to take stock. But the basic Allegheny plan to give cash to the banks and Prudential also went out the door when on November 8, the eve of the first scheduled hearing on the reorganization plan, Wells Fargo withdrew its commitment to lend $400 million for the deal. Now even the banks and other senior creditors faced the reality that they might have to accept a large portion of stock in the reorganization. Whatever cash they could get depended on how much cash the company generated and how much the company could borrow. For banks, taking stock as a recovery in a bankruptcy is anathema. Their business is not running companies or becoming shareholders in the companies they lend to; they can't unload large stock holdings right after a bankruptcy reorganization because such a stampede would depress the price. Ultimately this distasteful prospect gave Japonica its key opportunity.

A FINANCIAL ANIMAL AT WORK

The day after Wells Fargo withdrew, Japonica, who had not been heard from since September, sent the directors a second, firmer bid: It would buy the company for $683 million, mostly in cash. Kazarian, assisted by Lederman and two associates, had spent the fall of 1989 digging deep into the company's financial morass to nail down the values and formulate a business plan and a bid price—the same months-long research process they'd undergone before approaching CNW. Here is how they arrived at their bid. Japonica brought in a number of consultants, specializing in such areas as pensions, real estate, and environmental risks, to evaluate assets and liabilities. Arthur Andersen set up computer models that swallowed numbers and spit out cash flow, income statement, and balance sheet scenarios. At one point Japonica had more than ninety people performing sundry analyses on the case.

Kazarian himself separated out the Sunbeam and Oster housewares companies from the rest—lawn furniture, clocks, electric blankets, and barbecue grills—and saw that nonhousewares generated about $80 million in annual cash flow. "But we didn't know what was in the housewares yet because the numbers were so pathetic you couldn't get to the bottom line." The Oster/Sunbeam housewares business had been hemorrhaging money for several years. Japonica couldn't tell whether a business that averaged $250 million a year in sales had any real value. Would it ever produce a profit? If not valuable in itself, was it valuable for the brand names it could give to Allegheny's other products? Searching for answers, Japonica talked to analysts, called retail stores and consulted for-

eign companies to discuss how much they might pay for the division. "We started learning little bits and little bits and little bits,"
Kazarian says. They even got a tentative offer. Matsushita Electric
Industrial Company, the Japanese conglomerate, presented a letter
of intent to acquire the housewares unit from Japonica for $325
million. First, of course, they had to acquire the company.

That fall, the four-man Japonica team began spending some
nights in the office in a routine that would repeat itself in spurts
throughout the campaign to acquire Allegheny. They'd work until
they could hold their pencils no longer and then stretch out on the
nearest available space for a few hours sleep. For beds, there was
a couch, the floor, and a futon and blanket that Lederman's wife
had donated one day out of pity. Kazarian, squeamish about the
mice that had been seen in the office, usually preferred the shelf in
his office to the floor.

Realizing that at some point they were going to have to negotiate a plan of reorganization, Japonica needed a bankruptcy attorney. In October, they went out and got themselves a high-powered
bankruptcy lawyer, Herbert Minkel of Fried, Frank, Harris,
Shriver & Jacobson. Fried, Frank is one of the country's three top
mergers-and-acquisitions law firms, and Minkel at forty-three was
codirector of its bankruptcy practice. Allegheny was not new to
Minkel. During the auction phase of the company's bankruptcy in
the fall of 1988, he'd represented one of the bidders, Victor Kiam.
In early October, he met Japonica's two partners at a midtown
Manhattan restaurant and was surprised to see them wearing no
jackets or ties and Kazarian sporting a Pittsburgh Pirates baseball
cap. "I thought they were doing it to just sort of shake me up. I
think they were probably a little concerned about my manner since
they thought they were hiring somebody who had a reputation for
being very tough and I came across as being a gentleman. I think
that was of some concern to them." But on the contrary, the
partners were quite aware of the strategic value of Minkel's stature,
and as Lederman said, "We used his credibility when we needed
it." For his part, Minkel was impressed. "There are people out
there who've always wondered why Fried, Frank and Herb Minkel
would be involved with two guys who didn't seem to have two
nickels to rub together. But I never viewed this as being a highly

contingent engagement because they had a real commitment from a real player [Steinhardt] who had very large dollars behind a project that they had put a lot of time into before they retained Fried, Frank." And they were soon to have two real players.

ENTER MICHAEL PRICE

During the fall, Japonica's partners became convinced that they should finance their acquisition of Allegheny a bit differently than originally planned. Instead of funding only $60 million from equity capital (cash contributed by a source that would take an equity interest in return), they would double that to $120 million and reduce their reliance on bank debt. Among their reasons: the debt markets were drying up, banks were becoming reluctant to lend for takeovers, and it takes less time to acquire a company when there is less bank debt required. Where they were going to get the extra $60 million was a question that already had an answer. Because Japonica had reaped a windfall from its CNW investment earlier in the year, Kazarian spoke regularly with one of his chief backers, Michael Price. "When you make a lot of money for somebody, you develop a real friendship based on that," Kazarian notes. Naturally, they talked quite a lot about Allegheny International.

Price knew a thing or two about Allegheny. Over the years, his Mutual Series Fund had owned stock in various companies that were later acquired by Allegheny, including Schenuit Industries, Chemetron, and Sunbeam. When it bought these companies, Allegheny paid their shareholders cash plus Allegheny securities of one kind or another. But Price did not particularly want to own an interest in Allegheny International. "We never really liked Buckley, and we never really liked Allegheny and the prices of the securities," Price says. "So we got out of them."

But as he was prone to do with all companies he had invested in, he watched Allegheny. He raised one eyebrow when the board kicked Buckley out and the other when such a reputable party as First Boston attempted to acquire the company. When First Boston failed and well-known investors lined up to invest in the troubled company, his interest grew. But he could find no compelling reasons to invest in Allegheny himself. "We looked at it and looked at it, and we concluded this makes no sense at all, there's no value. We watched [money manager] Mario Gabelli load up on it, we watched Spear, Leeds and Kellogg load up on the preferred, and it was lunacy." Then after Allegheny filed for bankruptcy, "We watched all the different groups come in and say, 'nice business, nice business, nice business.' " He didn't understand it. So because he knew Allegheny's CEO Oliver Travers from the days when Travers ran Schenuit Industries, Price traveled to Pittsburgh to see if he could answer the key question: Was there real value here? But Price came away unenlightened and decided against making an investment. For a while he followed the company through the newspapers. "It was kind of a back-burner item that we were watching. Like every night at eleven o'clock you sit down to watch the next episode of 'Cheers,' I watched the Donaldson, Lufkin group go in and Paul Levy go in and all these guys go in and try to buy this business or that business from Allegheny or the whole company, and in each case there was a different story of why the purchase didn't close."

When Kazarian became enmeshed in the company, Price suddenly had a much more intimate view of the situation. He and Kazarian often spoke about the company, sharing knowledge and impressions. By the fall, Price became persuaded by Kazarian's analysis that there was value buried deep inside Allegheny's numbers. Before long, Price made a preliminary commitment to supply the needed $60 million in funds for Japonica's planned acquisition. As the Mutual Series Fund's point man in the case he assigned Peter Langerman, a bankruptcy analyst who once practiced as a bankruptcy lawyer. Although Price and his staff were impressed with Kazarian's insight, they kept close tabs on the progress of the young financial dynamo. For one full day, Price grilled Kazarian on his analysis in a room at Japonica's offices on Park Avenue. "He pounded me for a day, tried to shoot holes in my analysis, and he couldn't," Kazarian says. The younger vulture began working to determine the amount of cash that would be in the company's coffers when the company emerged from bankruptcy—if Japonica's bid was accepted it could use some of that cash to help pay for the acquisition. Allegheny's management was then projecting

$100 million; Kazarian boldly projected about three times that much. "If you look at things that we kind of put our ass on the line for, that was a big put-your-ass-on-the-line," he jokes today. Price challenged him on the assumption, pressing him to make sure it represented the most likely scenario. "Mike would call me from a car, like try to catch me off balance, see if I was fucking around," Kazarian recalls. Finally, Japonica put all its numbers together, inked in its bid for Allegheny, and sent it out to the board that day in early November 1989.

REBUFFED

When they heard about Japonica's bid, the creditors were still dumbstruck from the events of the day before. Wells, Fargo had abruptly announced it was not going to fund the company's plan with $400 million, leaving the prospect that creditors including bank lenders would have to take the bulk of their recoveries in stock. Still, the creditors shrugged off Japonica's offer of real green cash. They'd been the mergers-and-acquisitions (M&A) route before, and it had led nowhere. Why should Japonica be any different? Besides, Paul Kazarian and Michael Lederman seemed to have even less going for them than former suitors DLJ, Paul Levy, and Black & Decker had. They were financiers with no operational management team, no apparent plan for raising the funds they would need, and no proof of any commitment of equity financing from Price and Steinhardt. The phrase that was becoming a refrain among creditors was Japonica wasn't "for real." One of the banks' lead attorneys, Joy Conti, advised her clients to go with the most realistic deal—one that gave stock to all classes and some cash to the bank class. "Everybody said, 'Are we going to waste more time chasing these [acquisition offers] or are we finally going to sit down and say what is really financeable and how much stock are we going to get and what's the value of the stock?' " That was where all the creditors began to focus.

The only group to show real interest in Japonica was the committee representing Allegheny's current shareholders. Although stockholders are the group with the least amount of influence in a bankruptcy, at least they were a voice of support and hope. John

Mueller, the committee's financial adviser, saw in Japonica's bid a potentially serious competitor to Allegheny's reorganization plan. If Japonica became a serious bidder for the company, perhaps the company would ultimately find some way of raising the recoveries for everyone, including stockholders. Mueller met Kazarian and Lederman for dinner at Donald Trump's Grand Hyatt Hotel on Forty-second Street. Mueller recalls that he and Lederman ordered steaks, and Kazarian asked for a plateful of beans. "We don't serve just beans," the waiter intoned. Taking a cue from Jack Nicholson's character in *Five Easy Pieces,* Kazarian scanned the menu and said, "Give me the lamb chops with the beans, and hold the lamb chops." The Japonica partners wanted the shareholders' support for their bid, and Mueller took them more seriously than anybody else did. Still, he had misgivings because their only previous acquisition attempt was the aborted raid on CNW.

Japonica was putting most of its effort into winning over Allegheny's directors and was trying to get a hearing with them. Kazarian and Lederman assumed that even in bankruptcy a board of directors faced with an offer has an obligation to evaluate that offer and respond to it. But the Allegheny board simply did not want to meet with Japonica, because the directors didn't believe the young firm had solid financing. The board had assigned the company's attorneys and financial advisers to check into Japonica, and so far they had found that it had no capital to speak of and no written agreement with Price or Steinhardt to finance its proposals. "If they had the money, my attitude was let them take the company," says James Milligan, the board's special adviser. "But there was uncertainty as to whether they had the money or whether they just wanted to get in control of the process."

The refusal of the board to hear their case in person infuriated Kazarian and Lederman. They started their own campaign against the board. They wrote scathing letters to the directors, pointing out that their refusal to meet with Japonica was a breach of their obligations. Japonica even reported the company's bankruptcy counsel, McCullough, to the Pennsylvania Disciplinary Board for comments he'd made that Japonica claimed were inconsistent with his fiduciary duties. (However, although McCullough had seen a copy of the letter, he says he never heard from the board. When he later inquired about the alleged report, he says the disciplinary board wrote him confirming that it had never received a complaint.)

Even after reporting him, the Japonica duo with their typical chutzpah lobbied McCullough to take their acquisition offer seriously. Kazarian called him repeatedly to set up a meeting to discuss the bid, and finally the lawyer agreed to meet—but on his terms. The December day they were going to be in Pittsburgh he was flying to Cleveland; they could find him in the USAir Club at the airport. On the appointed day, McCullough, a beefy man in his early forties with a mouth that curves into a frown, arrived at the USAir Club to find what he describes as a short man with a beard standing near the doorway. It was the first encounter in what would be a stormy relationship. As McCullough remembers it, this is what ensued:

"Are you Bruce McCullough?" the man inquired.

"Yeah," said McCullough.

"Well I'm Paul Kazarian."

They shook hands.

"Your partner doesn't like me very much," McCullough said. "He tried to write the disciplinary board to say I wasn't representing my client." (Lederman claims that Japonica, not himself personally, wrote to the disciplinary board.)

"Well, that's my partner, Lederman. He's a lawyer, you know, and these things happen."

The conversation went downhill from there. Kazarian asked McCullough whether he would cooperate with Japonica in its effort to buy the company.

"Look," says McCullough, "we've already looked into you. You're not for real. If you can show us green dollars backing your bid, we might be cooperative."

"We're going to do this," Kazarian countered. "We'll do it without you. If you want to call Michael Price or Steinhardt they'll answer the phone and tell you that they're ready to go ahead."

"Yeah," McCullough laughed derisively, "and I could be calling the Bronx Zoo, too. I don't know Michael Price or Michael

Steinhardt's voice. I don't have any way of identifying who I'm talking to. I've been conned by some of the best. I can't just make a phone call and rely on that goddamned phone call."

McCullough rose to leave and catch his flight, and the two men said a quick, icy good-bye.

About two months later, McCullough made a startling discovery. "I realized that the person I'd been talking to was not Kazarian, but was his partner, Lederman. He knew he'd sent me a copy of that letter to the disciplinary board. So he was purposely passing himself off as Kazarian. He was only about this high"—McCullough illustrates by raising his hand to the level of his chest—"and he'd heard I'm pretty big, so he was probably concerned for his well-being, having challenged my integrity." (Actually, at five foot ten, Lederman is not that short.)

For his part, Lederman denies passing himself off as his partner. "I remember meeting him at the airport. I remember him introducing himself and saying, "Hi Paul.' And I said, 'No, I'm Mike.' He must have thought he was meeting with Paul. I have no idea. Paul and I don't look at all alike. We'd been in court observing the bankruptcy proceedings for a while. I don't think the arrogant lawyer cared who was who."

Shortly after, in December, Japonica finally received the board's official rebuff to its bid, which by now was not much of a surprise. It was contained in a letter penned by CEO Oliver Travers that said, in effect: The board had tried to auction off the company and had failed. Now the company was going to do the reorganization on its own, Travers said, and the only way Japonica could challenge that would be to file a competing plan. That was certainly an option, although a difficult one. For now, the Japonica team continued to hold out hope that ultimately it could persuade the board to either hold an auction or withdraw its stock plan and negotiate a cash plan with Japonica.

The banks, senior unsecured creditors, and junior creditors proceeded to negotiate the company's new all-stock reorganization plan and finally reached agreement on a distribution formula. They predicted that the stock of the reorganized Allegheny would start trading at as high as $7 a share after the bankruptcy. The banks would get 55 percent of that stock, and they tried to act as if they were happy about it. That's what Charles O'Hanlon, the representative from the lead bank, Mellon Bank, advised them to do. His theory was that if the banks, which supposedly knew Allegheny better than anyone else, acted as if they really wanted to control the company, that attitude in itself might attract a major, serious buyer. "We were prepared for the eventuality that we would have to own the company," says O'Hanlon. "But we knew nobody would ever buy us out in any way shape or form unless we acted like we really wanted to own it first." The banks and other creditors then wound up two remaining issues—issues that would hinder Japonica later in the game. Issue number one: Environmental, product liability, and pension claims that were unresolved at that time would be paid in stock as they were settled. And issue number two: As a safeguard against the possibility that the banks would sell their majority stake in one piece at a premium price, creditors adopted a "poison pill." Anyone buying more than 30 percent of the stock or anyone acquiring more than 45 percent of the stock *through the reorganization plan* would have to offer to buy the remaining stock at the highest price already paid. The company's proposed reorganization plan was filed December 29, and the hearings on confirming the disclosure statement for a vote proceeded into January 1990.

HOSTILE STRATEGY #1: BUYING BANK CLAIMS

Paul Kazarian and Michael Lederman wanted to own this company, and as the CNW fight showed, they weren't easily discouraged. In December, the partners continued to dog the company for information in the hope that they could do enough due diligence to secure bank financing and in turn win the support of the board and the creditors. And they continued their efforts to meet with the board on their bid and its financing—unsuccessfully.

At the same time, Japonica saw a huge opportunity to get a jump on buying the company by purchasing a chunk of claims at a big discount. Under the company's own all-stock plan, these claims would eventually translate into a stake in the new Allegheny. Michael Price encouraged them to go this route, even if only to assure themselves of some reward for their time. In bankruptcy, he said, "the only way to be certain of having some profit is to buy out banks or the public bonds. If you just make a bid for the company and you lose, but you own nothing, you don't make any money after all this work."

The second issue was how much to buy. "Enough to have a say in the way things come out," Price advised. What that means is enough to have a potential blocking position. This is where buying claims becomes hostile. From Kazarian's perspective, Price's first point made the most sense. "You never want to lose money. It's one thing not to make a helluva lot, but to lose money you're the world's greatest schmuck. If you ever lose money, you're disgraced and you should never come back onto the football field. If we bought the bank debt at least we knew we had some protection." It also wouldn't hurt to put some teeth in their bid by showing the company and creditors that they had substance behind them and a commitment to the company—that they were "for real." And certainly, big purchases of bank debt would shake everybody up just a little bit, especially if they happened to be big enough to give Japonica the power to block the reorganization plan proposed by the company.

Their timing to pick up bank loans (or claims) at sale-days' prices couldn't have been better. Kazarian sensed that the banks, for all their pretense, desperately wanted to get out with cash. "The jamokes, as we referred to the management and their attorneys, had actually convinced the banks that there wasn't enough cash available in the company, so they had to take stock. That's what created a huge opportunity for us." Japonica spent the month of December working through the details of how to go about buying bank debt—analyzing the purchase of claims and the legalities of it from the perspective of both the bankruptcy laws and the laws governing publicly traded securities, because the debtor's plan would convert bank debt into equity. Lederman would handle the negotiations, and with Kazarian, he drew up scripts containing the presentation he'd make to the banks plus the questions the banks might throw back at him and the responses he would then deliver. To be sure of themselves, they read their lists of questions and responses over the phone to Steinhardt Partners' Chuck Davidson and to Michael Price, who had been buying bank debt since the early 1980s. They copied the scripts onto about a dozen jumbo-size sheets of sketch paper and hung them on the walls of Lederman's office.

Finally, Lederman started dialing. At first, the conversations with the banks were exploratory: If they were interested in selling out, how much would they want? In January, the conversations turned into intense negotiations. More sheets went up on the walls listing every prospect and their responses and concerns. Every phone call was documented: the contact's name and the time and substance of the call, so that he could keep track of the complex give and take. There was $186 million in bank loans; Japonica had $120 million to draw from, and perhaps could get more if the buying got hot.

Their first offers were low, but not too low, using strategy mapped out by Price. "What I said to them was start low. Buy a guy. Word will get around. Make your next bid a few cents lower. It psychologically blows their minds. Then they'll all rush for the fire door." Why didn't Price just handle the transactions himself as he'd done so many times before? "Once we show up as a buyer of bank loans, the word goes around that Mutual's buying the bank loans. They know we're big, they know we're a buyer, they know we have a good track record in the stuff, and they're less likely to sell at good prices. Some guy named Michael Lederman, soliciting a bank, they don't know who he is." Price adds: "Now they will."

By the middle of January, Lederman's negotiations with the banks were progressing nicely. Then, abruptly, he put everything on hold. Japonica was about to launch the second phase in its strategy to acquire Allegheny.

HOSTILE STRATEGY #2:
THE COMPETING PLAN

Back in May 1989, Judge Cosetti had taken away the company's right to be the sole proponent of a plan, and at the insistence of U.S. Trustee Jones nobody followed up on it by filing competing plans. Now Japonica, having failed to budge the board with its acquisition bid, was going to be the first to challenge the company in this way. The Nest-Building vultures would position themselves squarely against the company by filing an all-cash plan of reorganization to compete with its all-stock plan. There wasn't much time: their last chance to file would be January 24, 1990, the day before the final hearing to clear the company's plan for a vote. This was a crucial matter. By bankruptcy law, once a plan is approved for a vote, no other plan can break into the process until the creditors and shareholders had finished voting.

While still negotiating bank claim purchases, Lederman plunged into a process of translating the company's stock plan into a cash plan. That involved taking the securities that the various classes of creditors and the shareholders were to get under that plan and determining what the distribution would be if cash were substituted for securities. "We had to work out the formulae which would apply since different people would get different amounts based on different contingencies under the debtor's plan," says Japonica attorney Minkel. "The amount of stock the banks got depended on how much cash they got, which was a variable [depending on how much cash the company held at the time]. You wound up with several variables, so the cash distribution under the Japonica plan was determined by an equation that had three unknowns." The entire process was the bankruptcy version of a marathon. During the month of January, Lederman, Minkel, and his associate Cynthia Baker labored over these calculations and over the preparation of plan documents for a minimum of twenty hours a day at either Japonica's or Fried, Frank's offices. "But," says Minkel, "we cracked it." Japonica would pay $650 million in cash for Allegheny International.

To qualify to file a plan, Japonica needed to own some Allegheny securities. So right away the vulture firm snapped up a $10,000 face amount bond for $2,700 from Chuck Davidson's portfolio at Steinhardt Partners. It was a tiny acquisition, but it was enough. A few days before Japonica filed the plan, Lederman stopped negotiating to buy bank debt, because he didn't want to close any deals before the banks had had a chance to review Japonica's plan and see what it offered them, namely 103 cents on the dollar (principal plus some accrued interest).

The Japonica plan reorganized Allegheny into two parts. Because it wasn't yet certain whether the Sunbeam/Oster housewares division was positive, negative, or neutral in value, Japonica would own it with another company in a joint venture. At the time, Japanese conglomerate Matsushita was its prospective partner. As for the company's other businesses, Japonica saw such enormous value in them that it intended to run these on its own.

The eleventh-hour filing of Japonica's plan on January 24 came as a shock to the entire ring of players in the case. To Lewis Davis, one of the company's attorneys, it was the surprising solution to what had become a riddle. "We knew they were watching every hearing we were at, so we knew they were still around. We didn't know what they were going to do." In court, after Minkel had presented the plan, Lewis's partner, McCullough, thumbed his nose at it:

Your Honor, the debtor (company) has heard from Japonica for these many months and has had a number of communications with them and their representatives as well as other constituencies. The continuing nagging question is where is the money? It reminds you of the old ad campaign about where is the beef. . . . So Mr. Minkel and his crew may proceed as this court is willing to have them proceed, but until we see more than a bunch of printing that's just copying of what we've done, we're not going to be very excited.

Somewhat reluctantly, the judge agreed to expedite the hearings for approving Japonica's plan for a vote so that creditors would be able to consider both plans at once. On February 5, the judge stamped the company plan's disclosure statement with his approval and set March 30 as the last day for voting.

Now that they had filed a third bid, this time in the form of a plan, Kazarian and Lederman had renewed hopes of meeting with the board to convince them they had solid backing. They were invited by director Joshua Angel—a curmudgeonly New York bankruptcy lawyer who had been appointed to the board at the start of the bankruptcy and who played the part of a renegade—to present their cash plan and its financing to the board. But the partners and their attorneys showed up at Allegheny headquarters on Friday, January 26, only to spend the day cooling their heels in a conference room and were not allowed into the board meeting. The board insisted that Japonica's representatives first explain their financing arrangements to the company's financial adviser (Smith, Barney) and attorneys (McCullough and Davis at Buchanan, Ingersoll). As McCullough noted in a filing dated January 29, Japonica's disclosure statement included "a form of commitment letter which purports to have the consent of three money center banks, specifically Money Center Bank No. 1, Money Center Bank No. 2 and Money Center Bank No. 3. These banks are not identified." But Kazarian didn't trust Buchanan, Ingersoll, given its refusal to believe Japonica had equity financing commitments. He said, "I will meet with the board and I will show the board."

TOUGH TACTICS

In reality, however, Kazarian's hopes of meeting with Allegheny's board had by now just about evaporated. Now, he and his partner directed their energies to the dual tasks of competing with the company's plan for votes and buying up bank debt. The day after Japonica filed its proposed plan and distributed it, Lederman picked up the phone to resume his bank loan negotiations. He placed his first call to Canadian Imperial Bank of Commerce (CIBC). "I said, 'Do you want to sell or do you want to wait for your hundred and three cents in our plan?' " That is, if Japonica's plan came out the winner. Still, the wait could be long for final court confirmation of whichever plan prevailed. The bank wanted to sell. After some discussion, CIBC agreed to sell its $12.6 million loan for eighty cents on the dollar. That sale and one other closed on February 23, and three days later Japonica sealed two more for a total so far of $25.8 million paid for $32.2 million in claims. It would be a week before these sales would be publicly disclosed.

Lederman insists that his calls were just as methodical and reasoned as he and Kazarian had planned. He explained to the banks on the other end of the line how Japonica valued the bank claims and then asked the banks how they valued the claims at that point in time, and he discussed Japonica's reorganization plan and its financing. But Charles O'Hanlon—the Mellon Bank representative who had advised the banks to act like they wanted to take the stock that the company's plan was offering them—says the banks told him that Lederman played on their fears. "Lederman called them up and said, 'The debtor's plan is going to fail [to win enough votes]. Our plan may fail too. You guys are going to be stuck in this case for years yet. You ought to cash out now. We're offering eighty cents. Do you want to be mired in this case for years? You've already been in it so long, why don't you just give us your claim?" Whatever the true tenor of Lederman's presentation, bank group attorney Joy Conti was impressed by Lederman's persistence in calling each bank daily and repeatedly asking how much they would take for their loans. "That's why they ultimately won," she says.

To promote their reorganization plan to those creditors who were going to stay in this case and vote, the partners met with some of the key players. Creditors didn't like Japonica's plan because of the low return they were to get—the $6.42 a share before a large reserve for disputed claims compared with stock the company said would be worth as much as $7 a share—and the lack of firm financing. In an effort to win over the lead bank, Japonica took Mellon's O'Hanlon out to dinner in New York at the Brasserie, a bustling East Side eatery that is a hive for deal makers. O'Hanlon recalls the conversation as follows.

"We don't think this company should be run by Milligan," Kazarian said. "We don't think this company should be owned by the debt holders. We think we should own it. We can get the maximum value out of it, so that's why we want it."

"Well, that's fine," replied O'Hanlon. "But all we've asked you for is to show us the money, and we'll let you in. And you haven't done it. You haven't been forthcoming, you've been very secretive about it. If you had the money, and you could show us the wherewithal to do it, my guess is that we would talk to you."

Soon after, O'Hanlon met Japonica Partners again, this time for dinner at the restaurant in the Atrium Club, the health club near their Park Avenue office where they worked out every afternoon. He told them that he had given Milligan his support because it was the surest deal of the two. But again he emphasized, if Japonica acquired the financing to do its plan, the banks would be glad to have a choice of two plans. The two partners cast aspersions on Jim Milligan in an attempt to sow doubt in his mind that this was the man to go with as Allegheny's new CEO. They pointed out that Milligan was pushing a reorganization plan that gave bank creditors nothing but stock, an anomaly in bankruptcy, and that in their view the company had much greater cash-generating ability than Milligan was revealing. O'Hanlon reacted with annoyance. "Results speak for themselves," he told them in a resolute tone. "He was very successful at Spalding. He was very successful at Borden. He's probably the kind of manager that the company needs." At one point O'Hanlon became particularly inflamed, Kazarian recalls. "He said, 'People like you don't ever get financing.' "

Japonica at this early stage also hosted meetings for banks and senior-unsecured creditors at Bankers Trust Company on Park Avenue to explain their bid and assure them that it was a serious one that was likely to get financing. Bankers Trust was then one of four banks who were considering financing Japonica's plan, although Japonica had not yet released the names of its prospective banks. "We took them to Bankers Trust," Kazarian says. "So, ya know, guess. Guess who the bank is. But if we mentioned Bankers Trust's name, we had to pay them a million and a half bucks as a commitment fee. So we were trying to save some money." To many of the creditors, Japonica's reluctance to tell all about their financing plans was merely a psychological ploy aimed at buying up bank claims as cheaply as possible. If the banks were at all nervous about the Allegheny plan yet couldn't tell if the Japonica plan was viable, they faced the vacuous prospect of no plan at all. So, the theory went, they'd sell out for whatever they could get.

At the Bankers Trust meeting with the bank creditors, Japonica exhibited the tough tactics of hostile players. About a dozen people, including the two attorneys for the bank group—Joy Conti and John Jerome of Milbank, Tweed—and representatives of individual banks crowded into a conference room in the international department of the bank. Out of two large document bags, Kazarian and Lederman pulled eight six-inch-thick black binders and placed each of them with a thud on the conference table. "These books contain months of research and analysis we've done on the company, by product line and by division," Kazarian explained. "We know the company better than anyone else." He flipped through one of the binders, stopping to display a page of numbers, but he declined a request to pass the books around for inspection. So the questions began. As O'Hanlon tells it:

"Who are you going to get your financing from?" O'Hanlon said in a demanding tone.

"We're not going to tell you," replied an unflappable Lederman.

"Is it Bankers Trust?"

"We're not going to tell you."

"Who's your equity?" O'Hanlon asked, referring to those contributing financing in return for a stock interest in Allegheny.

"We're not going to tell you."

Others broke in with questions, but O'Hanlon continued to ask persistently about their financing. Each time the banker posed a question, Lederman looked at him and either didn't answer or answered someone else's question.

At one point, bank group attorney Jerome asked a question about existing management in which he referred to Jim Milligan as "Mickey Mouse and his management team." As Lederman began to respond to the question, O'Hanlon blurted out incredulously, "Mickey Mouse?" Then he turned again to Lederman.

"Mike, I'm asking you a question. The equity, how much equity are you going to raise?"

Lederman paused a moment. "I'm not talking to you," he said.

"If you're not talking to me, why am I at the meeting?"

"I don't know," Lederman shrugged.

"Fine, I'll see you guys when you get done," and he packed up his briefcase and left the room.

Lederman followed him to see if there was anything he could do to get O'Hanlon to come back to the meeting.

Outside the conference room, he found O'Hanlon sitting on a couch. "Why don't you come back to the meeting? John Jerome asked me to come out here and ask you to come back in."

"Look Mike, I just want to ask you some questions," O'Hanlon confronted him. "If you guys don't want to answer that's fine. But the last two weeks I've caught you in at least one lie." (Lederman had claimed that the banks were calling Japonica trying to sell their debt. But the banks told O'Hanlon that Lederman was harassing them.) "In this business, you trade on your word. We don't have written contracts in bankruptcy. There's only one contract and that's when you have a reorganization which is confirmed. I can't deal with people who don't tell the truth. So there's no reason for me to sit in there. If you want to tell those other people whatever you want to tell them, spread whatever fertilizer you want to spread, go in and do it. I'm not going to participate in this charade. Go on back in."

In a somewhat different version of this episode, Lederman says, first of all, that by then everyone knew the sources of Japonica's equity financing. They were, of course, Steinhardt and Price. Also, he says, at the end of this episode, O'Hanlon yelled an obscenity at him and Kazarian and stomped out of the room with tears of rage welling in his eyes. Lederman then went out and found O'Hanlon sitting in an outer room holding his head in his hands, crying. Says Lederman: "He told me he was a total failure and that he couldn't face the group again. I went back in and asked Joy Conti to go out to calm him down."

About a week later, O'Hanlon got a call from Dick Daniel, his superior at Mellon. Daniel had just received a letter from Japonica telling in grim detail Lederman's version of O'Hanlon's behavior. As O'Hanlon relates: "The letter said I should be replaced on the account because obviously I'm on the verge of a nervous breakdown, I couldn't adequately represent the banks and now that they held a bank claim, they thought that was detrimental to their interest being realized." He told his boss that the story was an exaggeration and says that Daniel confirmed that with lawyers and bank representatives who had been there. None of this surprised bank group attorney Joy Conti: "Japonica was out to win at all costs. They had a campaign, if they could not get somebody to go along with them they would use whatever tactic possible to get them to go along. They were writing these letters constantly asserting we had fiduciary duties to them and implying that I was violating my fiduciary obligations. They were attacking all the professionals that had adverse positions to them, trying to get them to be afraid of them in terms of what they were going to do. My response to Mike Lederman at all times was you're not my client,

I'm acting in the best interest of my clients, period, end of story."

Even those who were rooting for Japonica acknowledge that its tactics were unusually combative. "They were very aggressive and a little abrasive," says Wilbur Ross. "A lot of people in the case said they were very 'New York.' That became a pejorative term in the case." But Ross, for one, considered Japonica's behavior justifiable. "Suppose they were a little abrasive, and they probably were. *A,* nobody was helping them, and I think that made them more abrasive than they would have been. *B,* in the hostile bid area that's how people are, and this really was a hostile bid."

Japonica continued pressing O'Hanlon in early March to support its plan. In between creditor discussions on Japonica's plan at the Vista Hotel across from the courthouse, Lederman met O'Hanlon in the cocktail lounge. Lederman argued that because Mellon Bank's former president had sat on Allegheny's board before the bankruptcy, the bank could be held solely responsible for creditors' losses. In addition, he contended that O'Hanlon could be personally liable for those losses if he opposed the plan that offered creditors the greatest recoveries—namely, Japonica's plan. "That didn't frighten me," O'Hanlon says. "I let him know I was judgment proof. I said, 'Mike, unlike you, I make fifty to sixty thousand a year, that's the most I've ever made. I've got a house with two mortgages on it. All my property is liened up. I don't have anything. You can sue all you want, I'm not going to raise a defense. Because I couldn't afford to raise a defense. So do whatever you're going to do. You could get any judgment in the world, I could not satisfy a one-dollar judgment.' "

8

Closing In

To firm up the bank financing for its proposed acquisition of Allegheny International, Japonica Partners needed to get inside the company, tour its divisions, and check over its books to verify the financial information it had been given. Then it would pass its analysis along to prospective lenders so that they could decide whether to back Japonica. For months, Paul Kazarian and Michael Lederman had been hounding the company and its attorneys with written requests for documents. For instance, Japonica wanted a corporate appraisal report, which Allegheny agreed to give only if Japonica reimbursed it for the $250,000 cost of doing the evaluation—which Japonica did not want to do. The pair of vulture-raiders also wanted James Milligan's projections for earnings and revenues for various divisions and the whole company, and after much nagging, the company sent some along. But Kazarian says that the reports omitted the housewares division, which was the big question mark. "Then you'd ask for it, you'd like pressure them, and they'd laugh at you," he says. "Then when we finally got housewares, what would they do? They'd leave out crucial pages so you couldn't piece together what the numbers were. They'd actually go in and strip out, white out, their projections. On some material they sent us, ninety percent of it had been whited out. It was as if they were saying, 'Here, you got it, you got it, go ahead, smart ass.' " When he asked for help confirming the publicly reported 1989 results, the company agreed to let him confer with its auditors. "Then we went down to Pittsburgh," Kazarian says, "and they had a junior-level guy who said he's not going to call the accountants, that he doesn't have to. I said, 'I can't just call them, you gotta do it.' 'No.' "

Reluctant to reveal trade secrets to an outsider, management refused to give Japonica anything before it could determine that Japonica's plan was viable, that is, "for real." Attorneys for Allegheny demanded that Japonica disclose its financing plans in an examination under oath. As Bruce McCullough told the judge:

These gentlemen are very vassal in selecting the truth and what they want to say. One of the things that you can't do is let them be in one room with one group of people and another room with another group of people because they've got nothing to anchor them to reality. And part of the reason you need to do it under oath and with everybody else present is so they have to say the same thing the same time the same way today, tomorrow and the next day. We've had that experience with them.

Japonica opposed such an examination, preferring to present its financing plans to the board. The judge, however, gave his sanction for McCullough's firm, Buchanan, Ingersoll, to subpoena the two partners. Kazarian, who was meeting with potential bank lenders in an effort to secure acquisition financing, and Lederman, who was busy negotiating the purchase of claims from Allegheny's bank creditors, eluded Buchanan, Ingersoll's grasp for nearly a month. Although the law firm sent clerks out to stalk the partners at their homes, their offices, and a favorite hangout—their health club, the Atrium Club on East Fifty-seventh Street—the brat-pack merger-and-acquisition players could never be found. Whenever subpoena servers came to the door of Japonica's Park Avenue office, someone warded them off by saying that Mr. Lederman or Mr. Kazarian was not in—whether or not that was true. In one case, a server hung around outside Kazarian's home in Brooklyn two days in a row—from 7:30 P.M. to 11:30 P.M. on February 23 and the next morning from 5:00 A.M. to 9:00 A.M.—but in neither case did he find anyone at home. Finally, on the morning of February 26, someone emerged from the house, as the law clerk relates in court documents:

At 8:15 A.M. deponent observed a male exiting above mentioned location answering to the description of Mr. Kazarian. Deponent approached the individual and asked him if he was in fact Paul B. Kazarian, he answered yes. When deponent displayed the legal documents to the individual, the individual denied himself. As deponent handed him the documents, he let them fall to the ground and walked away.

To Lederman, this game of dodge ball was simply necessary. "Every time they occupied a day of my time and a day of Paul's time, we could not make progress on this deal." But in part it was also sport. "Do you like playing hide-and-go-seek?" Lederman says, grinning. "It was fun. I wake up in the morning and for me, I come out and play with my gang. I play with Chuck [Davidson of Steinhardt Partners], I play with Paul. I have fun. Every day, I have the time of my life. There's rules. You slap me, you slap me. You get me, I have to come. Tag, you're it." McCullough tagged Lederman in the court room. "It was significant that I finally learned who Lederman and Kazarian were," he says, referring to the mix-up at the airport, "because I served Lederman in the courtroom one day when he was visiting and had to double-check with everyone there to make sure that I wasn't being flimflammed again." Japonica scheduled its first deposition for February 28 at the Intercontinental Hotel in New York, but because Japonica had named the date late the day before, there wasn't enough time to inform all the creditor representatives who wanted to take part. But true to their damn-the-bastards attitude, the Japonica kids went ahead with the deposition anyway—with one of their own lawyers asking the questions. A more balanced session was arranged for March 12 in Pittsburgh.

REAL MONEY

Between the two sessions, the company learned that Japonica did have some real money behind it, because on March 1, all four of Japonica's bank claim purchases were filed with the court. The reaction at the company was surprise and concern. There seemed to be no good reason for Japonica to be buying bank claims except to block the company's plan, and that was aggravating. But Lewis Davis, McCullough's partner at Buchanan, Ingersoll and the other chief Allegheny attorney, was also impressed. "It takes a lot of guts to buy claims, even the senior group of claims, because things can go wrong," he says. And for the first time, Allegheny's directors began to see that Japonica was not to be easily dismissed, despite what McCullough, Smith Barney, and other advisers had told them. McCullough himself acknowledged that Japonica had won a point. "You can't ignore thirty million dollars. So I was losing a little bit of the confidence of the board that these guys weren't for real. Some of the board members began to say, 'Even if we can't prove they're for real, we can't ignore thirty million dollars.' " At the same time, however, he and others still doubted that Japonica would end up acquiring the company. Sure, it had some money, but its supply couldn't be limitless. Besides, once they did their due diligence and got a close look at this damsel in distress, Kazarian and Lederman would see the warts and, like all of Allegheny's suitors before them, flee the scene. At least that was the prevailing theory.

Now that Japonica's new status as a sizable bank creditor was official and out in the open, Kazarian decided to use that status aggressively to obtain some information about the company. When he learned that Japonica had been barred from an Allegheny-hosted meeting with the banks and other senior creditors on March 5, he decided to crash the event, insisting that as the owner of bank claims he had a right to attend. The meeting was in Tampa, which happened to be where Jim Milligan—who by now had accepted the position as the Sunbeam subsidiary chief executive officer and was Allegheny's prospective CEO after the reorganization—was thinking of relocating Allegheny; it was also near Milligan's home in Sarasota. As Kazarian tells it: "Bobby [Setrakian from Japonica] and I went down with Herb Minkel—you know, 'Fuck you, we own this and we're coming to sit in.' " They checked into the Tampa Hyatt at Westshore where the following day management was going to give creditors a preview of its presentation to Wall Street securities analysts. Creditors wanted the preview, because they hoped that this presentation would convince brokerage firm analysts to recommend Allegheny's stock on reorganization (under the company's plan). Therefore, demand for the stock would be strong and creditors could then sell their newly acquired stock quickly and for a good price. At the direction of the creditors' committees, management did not invite Japonica to the meeting; they were afraid that the vultures, as the proponent of the competing reorganization plan, would be disruptive.

When he settled into his hotel room, Kazarian decided to give Milligan a call. He had never met Milligan in person but had called him many times at home in Sarasota and at his Colorado ranch. The hour was past midnight when he picked up the phone. It is hardly surprising that when one asks two people as different as Kazarian and Milligan to recount the same conversation, one gets a Roshomon-like result: Two completely different conversations. To wit: Here is how Kazarian remembers the conversation.

Milligan answered the phone. "Huh?"

"How you doin'?" Kazarian said cheerily.

"Who the hell is this?"

"It's Paul Kazarian."

"What the fuck do you want?"

"We want to talk. You know we're big holders."

"Look, if you were my kid, I'd take your fucking head and stick it under the water and drown you, you little bastard."

Kazarian held the phone away from his ear so that his associate, Bob Setrakian, could listen in.

"Look," Milligan said, "You keep on coming after me I'm going to blow the fucking company up."

"In any case," Kazarian said, "we're here and we're going into the meeting tomorrow."

"No, don't go into the meeting," said Milligan, now calmer. "I'll meet with you outside."

The next day he met with Kazarian and gave him copies of the presentations.

As the more subdued Milligan remembers the conversation, the phone woke him from a deep sleep, but it took him only a few seconds to recognize the voice on the line.

"Why in the hell are you calling me at this hour of the night?" Milligan asked.

"I'm here for the meeting," said Kazarian. "What are you going to do with me?"

Milligan then explained why he didn't think it was appropriate for him to attend the meeting because he felt Japonica might be disruptive, but that he would be happy to furnish him with the information that would be presented. They made arrangements for Milligan and Sam Iapolucci, Allegheny's chief financial officer, to come to Kazarian's room the following afternoon. There, the two executives gave Kazarian copies of the presentation.

KAZARIAN TAKES THE STAND

On March 12, at six P.M., twenty people gathered in a windowless, round conference room at Buchanan, Ingersoll offices, located in the leaden USX tower that is balanced on stilts on the eastern edge of downtown Pittsburgh, to conduct the deposition of Paul Kazarian. Earlier in the day, Lederman's deposition had gone relatively smoothly. Because Kazarian was handling Japonica's bank financing, his testimony was more pertinent—and, it turned out, more impertinent. "Paul's deposition at BI was unlike anything I'd ever seen in my entire life," says his attorney, Herbert Minkel.

In true form, Kazarian appeared tieless with the usual Pittsburgh Pirates cap perched on his head. When the questioning began, he lit a cigar, bit off the tip and spit it onto the carpet as everyone looked on in amazement. After many of the questions, Kazarian paused for as long as thirty seconds before answering and then as often as not asked that the question be restated. For example:

Q: Are you familiar with the disclosure statement filed by Japonica Partners in the Bankruptcy Court regarding Allegheny International?
A: Which one?
Q: Are you familiar with the one filed dated February 2, 1990?
A: How do you define "familiar?"
Q: Have you, or had you, read it, either prior to or after it was filed?
A: Portions? All? to be more specific.
Q: All?
A: I have not read all of it.

Q: Have you read portions of it?
A: Yes.

Minkel believed Kazarian was just being a very careful witness. "People ask their clients in the course of preparing them for a deposition to really think about the question before they answer it, so they don't assume they understand what the question meant. Paul does that, but, like a lot of things he does, with a little more *vigor* than some people." In the nearly four-hour grilling, Kazarian named four banks who were thinking of lending Japonica the money to acquire Allegheny, two of which eventually became part of the financing. Earlier, Lederman had produced copies of Japonica's freshly inked equity partnership agreements with Michael Price's Mutual Shares Fund and Steinhardt Partners. After revealing this information, the two bankruptcy raiders and their staff finally were allowed into the company to complete their due diligence. Kazarian led the troops in.

By now it was clear that due to delays creditors would not be able to vote on Japonica's and the company's reorganization plans at the same time. Votes on the Allegheny plan were due March 30, while the court had yet to approve Japonica's plan for a vote.

JAPONICA ENCOUNTERS A RIVAL IN BUYING BANK LOANS

Back in New York, Lederman continued to buy Allegheny bank claims. On March 13 he locked up two more. But he was running into resistance from the remaining banks. He and Kazarian, who became involved in some of the negotiations, began to feel frustrated with banks that did not want to make a deal. "We were told basically to go to hell so many times," says Kazarian. One bank that was particularly recalcitrant was Morgan Guaranty. "We had one kid from Morgan Guaranty," Kazarian recalls. "We were trying to buy his piece for like ten million bucks. It was a young kid. He said, 'I am unwilling to accept the credit risk' [of Japonica's commitment to buy his bank's Allegheny loan]. And I'm looking at him, like, how stupid are you? And then he said to Chuck Davidson from Steinhardt, 'How much do you have under management?' And Chuck looked at him and said, 'One and a half billion dollars.' And he said, 'Yeah.'—meanwhile we're talking about a ten-million-dollar piece—he said, 'Yeah, but how much do you have in Treasuries, in what's liquid?' And Chuck looked at him and said, 'Six hundred million dollars.' The guy goes 'Oh.'—Oh? Oh? I mean, how stupid are you? Oh. And everybody's sitting here looking at this guy like what world did he come from?"

As for other banks, they were happy to talk, but they wouldn't deal. A major reason was that by mid-March they were being courted by another group of investors that Jim Milligan had brought in. Allegheny's bank creditors had asked Milligan to find a sure way that they could unload the stock at a guaranteed price. Milligan had connections to a group of investors known as GKH Partners—representing Harry Gray, the former chairman of United Technologies; investor Melvyn Klein; the Pritzker family, owner of the Hyatt chain of hotels; and Daniel Lufkin, cofounder of onetime Allegheny suitor Donaldson, Lufkin & Jenrette who had left that firm. Some of the GKH partners had backed Milligan in his turnaround of Spalding and Evenflo, and because they had made out extraordinarily well in that case, they were quite willing to support him in this venture. The plan was for them to make commitments to buy creditors' stock in the new company. GKH would attempt to buy just under 30 percent of the new company's stock (according to the bylaws contained in the Allegheny reorganization plan, anyone owning 30 percent or more has "control" and would have to buy out, at a premium, anyone who wanted to sell their stock) on consummation of the reorganization plan. To handle the negotiations, GKH partners brought DLJ back into this bankruptcy yet again to broker the new deals with the banks and other creditors. On March 16, DLJ's Norman Brown and Lawrence Schloss began offering to buy out bank creditors at $6.25 a share when the stock was issued under the company's plan.

Japonica still had the tactical advantage, however, because it was willing to take the greater risk of buying out the banks' claims here and now, during the bankruptcy. GKH wanted to wait until the bankruptcy was over, leaving creditors with the risk that the case would drag on longer than expected. Japonica's advantage proved valuable when on March 19 this rivalry moved to Zurich.

JAPONICA'S END-RUN IN SWITZERLAND

Swiss Volksbank was the agent representing a group of Swiss investors who held almost a third of the senior-unsecured debt of Allegheny. Those investors had to decide whether to vote for the company's stock plan by the March 30 voting deadline, but they were having trouble understanding the deal. "The Swiss had no interest in American bankruptcy," explains Robert Martin, one of Allegheny's investment bankers from Smith, Barney, Harris, Upham. "If a company is in trouble in Switzerland, it is liquidated. So, the concept of a bondholder taking stock was beyond them." They wanted Allegheny to describe exactly what they were going to be getting in this reorganization and explain why it was in their interest to vote for it. Swiss Volksbank invited Allegheny executives to fly over to give a presentation.

DLJ decided to go along as well, and it wasn't long before Japonica found out. As Minkel recalls: "I got a call from Swiss Volksbank's U.S. law firm. They said they thought that DLJ was going to Switzerland with the company to meet with the noteholders to make them an offer. It would have made it very difficult for us to get our plan." In other words, if the Swiss committed to sell the shares that they would get as a recovery under the company's plan, they would naturally vote for the company plan and against Japonica's plan. And because the Swiss held 30 percent of the senior-unsecured class, they had virtually enough to block Japonica's plan (a third is needed for a block, but there were so many bondholders in the class that many would fail to vote). Minkel relayed the information to Lederman, who then called the U.S. lawyer for the Swiss and expressed an interest in purchasing the notes himself. As long as the Swiss already had the meeting set up with the company, he inquired, why not let Japonica come over and make an offer at the same time? Fine, the Swiss's lawyer said. The company would make its presentation on Monday morning; Lederman would have his chance the following day.

He and an attorney, Andre Weiss, flew to Zurich that weekend. By coincidence they checked in at the same hotel as the Allegheny and DLJ crews. It was in the hotel that Lederman first met Allegheny's treasurer and the future treasurer of Sunbeam-Oster,

Tony Munson. In greeting him, Lederman didn't miss a chance to try to win over someone from the other side. "You don't really want to move to Tampa, do you?" he asked, referring to the talk going around that Jim Milligan intended to move the company to Florida. Japonica had stated publicly that if it won control of the company, it would maintain headquarters in Pittsburgh.

After the Allegheny team walked its audience through the company's reorganization plan in a conference room at Swiss Volksbank, DLJ's representative spoke with the noteholders' agents about buying their shares when they were issued at the end of the bankruptcy. But DLJ never made a formal offer, reportedly fearful that they might be violating laws governing publicly traded securities by offering to buy the debt at a discount to what was in the plan.

The next day, Lederman and attorney Weiss met Swiss Volksbank's four negotiators in a conference room and offered sixty-five cents on the dollar for the notes. The Swiss bargaining team then left the room and consulted with management for more than an hour before returning. Lederman recounts the events upon their return:

"No deal," said one. Lederman responded simply by beginning to pack up his briefcase, and Weiss followed his example. Their preparations to leave greatly upset their Swiss hosts, as Lederman was hoping it would.

"Look, there must be something you can do here," the lead negotiator implored. "You can't come in and say this is it."

"It really is," Lederman said with a shrug, knowing all the time that he had the authority to go considerably higher in his offer than he had.

"Even seventy-five. We'll do it at seventy-five."

Lederman paused from his packing and said, grimly, "Sixty-six."

"A penny?" said the other, incredulous.

"Yeah, and I'm making it an official bid. So it's sixty-six. You'd better run it up to your senior management. I'll sit here for fifteen minutes."

They left the room and within minutes they were back. They would take the offer.

Lederman flew home with a new Swatch⒯ⓂⒶwatch on his wrist and 30 percent of the senior unsecured class of bonds in his pocket. A virtual blocking position. Japonica, however, denies that it ever intended to thwart the company's plan; its aims were to buy the company as economically as possible and to prevent DLJ from blocking its own plan. And the Swiss deal was undeniably economical: Ultimately, the reorganization plan that the judge consummated gave the senior unsecured class of bonds (of which the Swiss were once a part) ninety-three cents on the dollar.

TO BLOCK OR NOT TO BLOCK

Lederman insists that it was for the same economic reason that he continued to try to lure claims from the banks. But as it turned out, he happened to acquire just the percentage needed to block the company's plan—a *definite* blocking position as opposed to the nearly certain one the Swiss purchase gave him. Here's how he did it. On Friday March 26, Lederman clinched the purchase of a $9.8 million claim from the First National Bank of Boston at 85 percent of par and later in the day snapped up a $12.6 million claim from Continental Illinois Bank at 95 percent of the face value. That pushed Japonica's stake over the 33.33 percent threshhold.

All along, Joy Conti, an attorney for the bank creditors, had been watching. She saw the price Japonica was paying spurt up to ninety-five just before the close of balloting on the 30th, indicating to her the vultures' desperation to secure a blocking position and beat the company plan so that its plan would be the creditors' sole alternative. But Lederman continued to insist that the fact he obtained a blocking percentage before the voting deadline was mere coincidence. "We wanted to acquire the company. That was the fundamental goal. Those bank claims represented stock in the company at an attractive price. To buy the company, you end up crossing thirty-three percent."

Then there's the question that if Japonica wanted only to block the company's plan, why did it continue its efforts to buy bank debt even after reaching the one-third level? After he sewed up the Continental claim, Lederman procured the Bank of Hawaii's $2.2

million claim. And Lederman didn't stop there. Having just agreed
to shell out ninety-five cents to Continental, Lederman went back
to all the banks who'd turned him down before and offered ninety,
and when every one of them rejected that, he came back with
ninety-five. "Then we said, what price do you want? And they went
into their speech about how they want to get one hundred cents
plus interest for the period of time in bankruptcy." Almost every
one of them said the same thing, indicating to Lederman that they
had banded together, perhaps intending to negotiate as a group.
He didn't yet know that many of them had already committed to
sell their "when-issued" shares through DLJ to the GKH group.

March 29, the eve of the voting deadline, rolled around, and
Sunbeam CEO Jim Milligan called Paul Kazarian to urge him to
vote for the company's plan. In a phone call to bank representatives, Lederman said Japonica still didn't know how it was going
to vote. "But we actually knew how they had voted," Conti says,
amused by the recollection, "because somebody had told us that
the votes were in and that they had voted no. He was on the phone
saying, 'I still don't know what we're going to do.' We're all sitting
there laughing and saying, 'Oh Mike, please.' They were trying to
keep up an illusion that they weren't buying these for control and
that they were looking at which was the best plan, their plan or the
AI plan."

So if they didn't acquire their claims to block the company's
plan, why then did they vote no? Says Lederman, "The recovery
going to the creditors did not reflect the value of the company. By
that time we knew how management had been manipulating what
the company's true value was, and it was not being paid out to the
creditors. It was not there. So we voted no."

Japonica was in for a fight. Within days of losing its hard-
fought campaign for a reorganization plan, the company on behalf
of its creditors filed a motion to disqualify Japonica's votes on the
grounds that they were cast in bad faith—i.e., to block the plan to
acquire the company. "We didn't have much time to think about
it," says Mellon Bank's Charles O'Hanlon. "We didn't know they
were going to get a blocking vote till the very, very, very last
minute. So the next week we said, what can we do to get this plan

confirmed? I mean everyone in the case didn't want Japonica to make the plan fail. They wanted that plan to succeed even if Japonica's plan was there. They still wanted two plans at the finish line because they knew the debtor's plan was confirmable and they didn't want to be left with no plan. So everybody started the legal research on it."

(The obvious precedent to use was a case from several years earlier involving hotelier Conrad Hilton, who had held stock in a corporation that owned a bankrupt hotel. When a proposed reorganization plan effectively stripped Hilton of his ownership, he bought up a blocking position and voted the plan down. But the court disqualified his votes, ruling that he acted in bad faith in that he didn't vote as a creditor, but as an equity holder with a motive to control the outcome.)

In April, McCullough and his crew began loading their guns to win the lawsuit. "The litigation started fast and furious all over God's half-acre," he says. "There were three, four, five, and six depositions going on at the same time in different cities all to get ready for the litigation to disqualify."

Japonica shot back with a motion to disqualify all others' votes *for* the company's plan on the grounds that the GKH group's purchases of when-issued shares were not publicly disclosed and, therefore, violated securities laws. Curiously, Lederman says that once Japonica had blocked the company's plan, he began to receive calls from banks that had committed to sell their Allegheny shares to GKH. They wanted out of those commitments. Now that the company's plan was enmeshed in litigation, they couldn't tell when or whether it would ever take effect, and that was scary. Could Lederman help them wriggle out of the contracts so they could sell out to Japonica? After reviewing them, however, he decided there was nothing he could do. These were very tightly worded contracts, he found. Without a formal release from GKH, the banks appeared to be locked in.

The stalemate in the bankruptcy sent a chill through Allegheny operations as well. Morale sagged among suppliers, buyers, and employees alike. Says Milligan, "Everyone was feeling up in the air. They thought, what are we going to do? What's going to happen?"

INCH BY INCH, TOWARD A JAPONICA PLAN

Meanwhile, Japonica was moving ahead on its own reorganization plan, continuing the analysis of Allegheny's operations and financial statements that it needed to present to prospective bank lenders. By now, a small Japonica team was comfortably ensconced in one of the offices on the company's lushly decorated executive floor. But Kazarian continued to believe that the company was obstructing his team's efforts to obtain information at every turn. He even found artificial barriers in the hallways—plants, chairs, and partitions obstructing his way, placed there, secretaries told him, by the management. That was the least of his problems. The company allowed Japonica to interview managers at headquarters and the divisions, but only with an attorney present. "And every time you'd ask a question, she had to say whether they could respond to the question or not," Kazarian complains. Often, he says, the lawyer did not allow a response. In Portland, Tennessee, at Almet, a maker of casual outdoor furniture, Kazarian stood by while in the adjoining room Earl Maxwell, the division president, and Allegheny financial executive Sam Iapolucci wrangled over what numbers to give Japonica. According to Kazarian: "There was a fight going on in the other room like you wouldn't believe. Finally Earl got so pissed off, he said, 'Let's leave.' We went out into the factory and he started giving us a lot of the real poop, which was great."

At the Northern Electric subsidiary, a maker of electric blankets, the company had told Kazarian that they'd had a huge number of returns after the publication of reports linking electromagnetic fields from some appliances to cancer. "So we had our auditors go down there to ask them where the returned blankets were," Kazarian says. " 'Well,' they said, 'they're on a truck.' 'Okay,' said the auditors, 'How many blankets can you fit per truck? Does that mean you have fifty trucks? Where are the fifty trucks?' They said, 'They're up my ass.' "

The company acknowledges that there was a fairly heavy battle over what information was given to Japonica and how it was given to them. But management had been hearing disturbing stories from personnel about the conduct of Japonica's principals and employees inside the company. In turn, management reported these stories to Allegheny attorney Lewis Davis: "We had calls from top management saying they got a call from the insurance guy who was placing casualty insurance for one division. Japonica had said to him, 'Don't go forward, we can find a better price.' The guy was confused and asked senior management who he was working for."

In another instance, the person handling bankruptcy claims was told by a Japonica representative that he was too generous in the settlements; so the employee consulted senior management on whether he still had authority to settle claims. Similarly, one of the managers negotiating asset sales reported that a Japonica team member told him he should be getting better prices. And yet another Japonica researcher showed up at one of the properties Allegheny was preparing for sale, the Dover Hotel in Manhattan, and demanded to be shown around.

All of that may be true. But Lederman maintains that while he was inside the company, junior managers would approach him and his team with complaints and ideas. "I think we were very well regarded and well received by the employees, who had no faith or confidence in existing Pittsburgh management. They liked the fact that we were really interested in what was going on in the company and how to make it better. They sought us out. They'd find us, they'd want to talk, they wanted to tell us things. They wanted to be helpful." Of course, they may also have wanted a job if Japonica ended up owning the company. Having pleaded to be able to do on-site research and analysis that would take no longer than a week, Japonica ended up staying for months. "We weren't dragging our feet," insists Steinhardt Partners's Chuck Davidson. "We were moving as fast as we could. It was sort of like we were supposed to read Tolstoy's *War and Peace,* and they're sending it to us a page at a time, and the pages are out of order. I mean it makes it awful tough reading."

Also, as sales and earnings slid, Japonica had new information to evaluate nearly every day. In the quarter ending April 1, Allegheny reported sales of $254 million down from $268 million the year earlier and a $20.7 million operating loss, more than quadrupling the 1989 first-quarter loss. Almost all of its major businesses were now losing money. Kazarian was puzzled as he saw the company make sharp turns such as accelerate the recognition of over-head and write off receivables. "Pow! They never told us. All of a sudden the numbers start going down. What's going on? The company can't be doing that badly. Sales are basically okay. Everything's falling out of bed." (The company's explanation was that Milligan's working capital reduction plan was taking effect. As a result, earnings declined but cash began to increase.)

While Kazarian devoted all his time to getting enough information to secure bank financing for Japonica's plan, Lederman and attorney Herbert Minkel were trying to get the proposed plan approved for a creditor-shareholder vote. The experience was frustrating, to say the least. When Japonica's latest revised documents were handed out just before one court session, Douglas Campbell, the attorney for Sunbeam subsidiary creditors, flipped through the pages one by one. Each time he came to a page with numbers on it, he said in a voice loud enough for Lederman to hear, "Not in my language," and he placed it in a separate pile.

By mid-April, the hearings on Japonica's plan disclosure statement had been going on for a month and a half. Minkel was at the end of his tether. "We'd start at nine o'clock in the morning and I'd still be on my feet at nine o'clock at night, in court. Just hearing after hearing, revision after revision. It was just an effort to make it as painful as possible by people who didn't want us to get out there with our plan and who used the disclosure statement [hearings] as a way to try to box us in. It was without question the most painful hearings on disclosure ever, because the focus wasn't to get a disclosure statement out. The focus wasn't even adequate information. The focus was to prevent us from getting a disclosure statement out."

There were hundreds and hundreds of pages of objections that Japonica was obliged to resolve. The company, for example, argued that Japonica's proposed level of bank financing wouldn't be enough because Japonica was counting on using at least $125 million of the company's cash in addition to it and the equity money from Price and Steinhardt. But the company said there might not be $125 million of cash at the company. Others wanted more information included in the disclosure statement such as the unabridged partnership agreements Japonica had struck with Price and Steinhardt. Unsecured creditors lobbied for clarity. "Information regarding its mechanics and effect is as rare and illusory as water in the Sahara Desert," Odyssey Partners wrote in an objection filed with the court in late February.

Apart from the hearings on the minutiae of the disclosure statement, the creditors were driving for a better deal from Japonica. The bank creditors kept pressing for cancellation of the provision in Japonica's plan to hold back a certain amount from their recovery to fund a reserve for disputed claims. The unsecured creditors' committee continued to complain that Japonica's plan offered no better value than the company's plan. "We were convinced they'd put more on the table so we wanted to keep them in the process," Wilbur Ross explains. "But we surely didn't want to endorse their bid."

ENLARGING THE STAKE: THE TENDER OFFER

On Saturday, April 14, Judge Cosetti opened his newspaper and saw to his amazement a full-page announcement of an SEC filing for a tender offer by Japonica Partners to buy all the subordinated bonds of Allegheny and its Chemetron subsidiary—unsecured debt worth $134 million at face value. The offering prices were twenty-eight to forty-one cents on the dollar for Allegheny bonds (depending on the type of bond) and eighty-four cents for the Chemetron bonds. Japonica had deliberately launched the tender on the day before Easter Sunday. "To really rattle them," Kazarian smirks. "In fact, the printer actually sent us a copy with the Easter Bunny on it, with coattails and top hats kind of dancing on the bottom." A tender offer for debt in a bankruptcy setting had never been done before.

In court the following week the judge was livid, insisting that Japonica had an unfair advantage over the company because it could purchase claims—and votes for its plan—whereas the company by law could not. He declared that if someone moved to enjoin Japonica from carrying out the tender offer, he would grant the motion. Representatives of all the holders of the subordinated bonds were in the court room, but no one spoke up. Kazarian says the offer was made because Japonica believed it could buy the debt at a good price, not to buy votes for its plan. "The tender was done for profits, to make money," he insists. "That's what we told the judge. We were out to make more money. I had told the judge, 'We own this, we own that, we're out to buy basically anything that's for sale. Any and all.' We did it because we were buying it at such an unbelievable price. The return was basically five to one." The offer was to stay open until 5:01 P.M. May 14. On May 3, the judge finally approved Japonica's disclosure statement, which had been amended to make reference to the tender offer. Now Japonica would solicit votes for its plan until the close of ballotting on June 8.

As the tender offer deadline approached, what was a first in bankruptcy began to look like a bomb. No one was biting. Davidson and Lederman had discussions with the unsecured creditors' committee all through the twenty-one-day offering period but roused little interest in the offer from them or their advisers. "We did not endorse their tender," Ross says. "We just felt it was not a very good bid. So we were actively telling people not to do it. We were saying that there was only one reason to take the bid, if you had to get out in a hurry, because it seemed clear you'd get more ultimate value."

Japonica told the committee that it would consider raising the price it was offering, and among themselves, Japonica Partners and Steinhardt's Chuck Davidson discussed raising the offer to fifty cents on the dollar. But no one seemed to want to deal at all. Then, May 14, deadline day, everything changed.

A few hours before the five P.M. deadline, Kazarian called Mike Halpern, a former associate of his from Goldman, Sachs days who now ran money for David Murdock, owner of pineapple grower Castle & Cooke in Hawaii and a major holder of Allegheny subordinated debt. Kazarian recounts the conversation:

"Mike, why aren't you tendering?" Kazarian said.

"You're going to strip our votes," the voice on the other end objected. He had heard a rumor that Japonica wanted to get the bonds, strip the voting rights off of them, and then return the bonds to the holders without paying.

"Where'd you come up with that?" said Kazarian, alarmed.

"The company told us."

Kazarian was exasperated. "I'm not going to strip them. You tender them, I'll buy them."

"So, you promise me you're not going to do it?"

"Look, you've seen the offering document. I'm not going to do it, period."

Halpern tendered the Murdock bonds, and within the hour, the three other major holders followed suit. "The Goldman network," says Kazarian. "Having been there for seven years, I had this relationship. It really helped us out. That was a real plus." In all, the partnership bought 36 percent of the Chemetron debentures and 62 percent of the Allegheny subdebt. One of those who tendered was Odyssey Partners, the major holder of the class. "In that case," recounts Japonica attorney Herbert Minkel, "their counsel said their client would not take not a penny less than fifty cents." But they settled for many pennies less.

To Chuck Davidson, the vote-stripping rumor wasn't the only, or even the major, explanation for the last-minute rush. "They all wanted to play coy," he says. "We ignored what they were saying and just knew where their hearts really were. It came at the end. It always came up to these eleven fifty-nine P.M., *Perils of Pauline* endings. That seemed to be how they liked to negotiate. I hated this process."

SHOPPING FOR MORE DEBT

The resounding response of the subordinated debt holders to the tender offer echoed menacingly in the ears of the two senior classes—the banks and the insurance companies. What did it mean for them? They called a strategy session with the company's attorneys, who told them that Japonica's subordinated debt purchase meant that the vulture firm had secured a controlling, although not a majority, position in the reorganized company if the company's plan was ultimately approved—40 percent versus the 19 percent that Jim Milligan's GKH group had managed to pick up from the bank creditors. "So we talked about how to fence them off," recalls Allegheny attorney Lewis Davis. How were they going to keep Japonica from ultimately winning control of the company? The insurance company creditors suggested implementing cumulative voting, which could have kept Japonica from winning enough board seats to secure real control. Davis and his partner McCullough suggested classifying the board of directors—dividing it into three classes with only one up for election each year—to keep Japonica from controlling the board in the immediate future. They also thought of striking a deal with Japonica to meld the company plan with the Japonica plan. "And we told the creditors we were talking with Japonica to see if we could get Japonica and Milligan under the same roof," Davis says. That seemed to be the most promising option.

Japonica had by then huddled with Milligan a few times. The partners figured that one way to end the bankruptcy swiftly was to recruit Milligan, the CEO-elect in the company's plan, onto their team. And they believed that their substantial ownership gave them the leverage to do that. So each side had its own motivation for coming together.

Kazarian and Lederman arranged a clandestine rendezvous midweek in late May at Nemacolin Woodlands, a resort near the West Virginia border. Once a Rockwell family retreat, Nemacolin had been bought in the mid-1980s by lumber magnate Joe Hardy, who turned it into a vacation spot and convention center. Milligan and Davis made the two-hour drive and, ironically, were greeted in the entranceway by a sign that read, "Nemacolin welcomes the Mellon Bank group"—a completely unrelated event, but an amusing coincidence given the hush-hush nature of the Japonica meeting. The resort is a sprawling expanse of golf courses and condominium units. Because it was a weekday, the complex was mostly empty. "We were in this enormous place, and it was virtually deserted," Davis recalls. "We were in one set of condominiums at one end, they were in another set at another end." They met, had dinner, and talked. The two Japonica partners discussed their ideas for running the company. Milligan would fit in as chief operating officer and president and would primarily work on Sunbeam and Oster operations; Kazarian would be chairman and concentrate on the nonhousewares businesses. It was late at night when they broke up, having resolved nothing. Because Milligan was intent on getting back to Pittsburgh, he and Davis headed back at around two A.M.

The next day they met again, this time for lunch at the grand, brick-faced William Penn Hotel in downtown Pittsburgh. Davis outlined the demands: Milligan would become CEO, the board of directors would be a balance of his people and Japonica's people, and there would be parity ownership of both GKH Partners and Japonica. In essence, the encounter was the start of a negotiation process that would end a few weeks later with each side concluding that they couldn't work with the other. "They obviously wanted control," says Milligan. "I think it was clear from that discussion— and it wasn't adversarial in any way—that it was a control issue. If they wanted to control it, it wasn't a situation I wanted."

Japonica, meanwhile, was negotiating with the banks, both on why they should vote for its plan and on the possibility of buying them out. The banks stood their ground: They wanted Japonica to cancel the reserve for disputed claims that reduced their recovery in its plan. They'd sell out, but only for 110 percent of their principal (the principal plus some of the accrued interest). Japonica held at 104 percent, and talks broke off on May 24, two weeks before the voting deadline for the Japonica plan. The following day, in a surprise move, the banks' attorneys announced in court that the banks were going to vote against the Japonica plan. Although that declaration appeared to doom the plan, Japonica feverishly continued to bargain with both the banks and the insurance companies. After all, there was always the hope that the banks would change their minds about the plan or sell out before the voting deadline.

Japonica couldn't sway the banks, but it did capture the insurance companies' claims. The vultures were elated. Although Davis denies it, the Japonica partners say that he told them that if they acquired the insurance company creditors' debt, they would effectively own 51 percent of the reorganized company and he would feel "duty-bound" to turn the company over to them. Whatever the case, in rapid-fire negotiations, Japonica agreed to take the insurance companies out for 93 percent of the value of their claims—the equivalent of $7 a share under the company's plan, which was soon going to be a very important number in this case. Japonica also agreed to raise the recovery for the rest of that debt class in its plan, from 86 percent to what it had just paid the insurance companies. Japonica completed the purchase on June 7, the eve of the deadline for voting on its plan.

Before agreeing to sell out, however, the insurance companies had cast negative votes on Japonica's plan—votes that would be enough to block the plan. But now they hurriedly arranged a conference call on June 8 with the judge to request permission to reverse their votes. The judge turned them down. Both plans now had been blocked. But most participants thought that Judge Cosetti would disqualify Japonica's blocking vote on the company plan, allowing that plan to go through.

LAYING TRAPS FOR EACH OTHER

At first, Japonica didn't care a whole lot about losing its plan. By now, under the terms of the company's plan, Japonica held the equivalent of 51 percent of the stock of the reorganized company. Based on at least what they say Allegheny attorney Davis had told them—that they'd have the company if they bought out the insurance company claims—Japonica decided to suggest what they called "an orderly transition process." On Friday, June 8, Lederman phoned Davis and suggested in a firm tone that as of that Monday morning Oliver Travers resign as chairman and CEO and Kazarian step in to take his place. Until the plan was consummated and Japonica took full control, Milligan would work with Kazarian, and Lederman would be general counsel. Taken aback by the call, Davis relayed the communication to his partner McCullough, who took the matter to the executive committee of the board in a conference call. The board concluded that enough was enough. Japonica had not yet won the day. The vulture investors didn't yet own the company. And they certainly weren't in a position to dictate who the chairman was going to be. To avoid any further confusion in the management ranks as to who was really in charge, the executive committee decided to show Japonica the door.

That was McCullough's assignment for Monday, June 11. He first informed bank attorney Conti, because the bank creditors were the company's most senior creditors. Conti interpreted Japonica's move as an attempt to play its trump card. If it succeeded in taking control through such a transitional process, Japonica wouldn't have to raise a penny of bank financing to buy the 49 percent of Allegheny it didn't already own. With a controlling position in the pro forma stock and control of the management, it would effectively have bought the company for a song.

Next, McCullough instructed Earl Maxwell, president of the Almet furniture division in Tennessee, to expel Japonica's people from the property. At 4:30 McCullough walked over to the company and rode the elevator to the eighteenth floor where Japonica had been camped out for nearly three months. In his account of the story, he found Kazarian alone in the room:

"Hi, how are you?" Kazarian greeted him.

"I'm fine," McCullough said. "You've got till the close of business to be out of here."

Kazarian looked surprised. "Wait a minute. I've got to get Mike." He left and a minute later returned with his partner, closed the door, and explained to him what McCullough wanted them to do. Lederman asked why.

"Because we don't want any confusion as to who's in charge here," McCullough explained.

Kazarian then stepped up to McCullough and looked him squarely in the eye, their noses only inches apart. "You know, Bruce, I dream about you day and night, every night. Now hit me, hit me. You know you want to hit me."

A thought flickered in McCullough's mind that it would be so nice to hit Kazarian if he could. But the lawyer was satisfied knowing that he was in the position of power and that Kazarian was obviously frustrated by that. Kazarian then told McCullough to leave the room.

"No, I don't think I'm going to do that," the attorney replied easily and walked over to the window, sat on the sill, and crossed his arms over his chest.

Now Kazarian became insistent. "I told you to get out of here."

"It's not for you to tell me. I'm here to tell you to get out. I'm not going to move." He didn't move.

"Fine, you can stay all night."

Then, Lederman broke in. "Bruce, look, we don't need this. Will you just give us a little time to talk it over and decide how we're going to respond?"

McCullough rose to his feet. "That's a fair request," he said and left. He went to the other side of the floor to report to Travers. "They have until five o'clock, but if it takes them longer than that I'll be happy to hang around," he told the CEO. (Kazarian says that he never dared McCullough to hit him. "I would have been crazy to do that. He's a lot bigger than me." But Lederman recalls that Kazarian did confront McCullough with such a challenge when the lawyer said something to the effect of, "I've been relishing the moment to slam Japonica.")

A little while later, Kazarian and Lederman asked to see Travers, and he headed over to their office with his lawyer in tow. Kazarian addressed Travers.

"Ollie, Bruce tells us we're kicked out of here. Is that true?"

Travers confirmed that the executive committee had directed it.

"But Ollie, we plan to have a good smooth transition here, we don't see how this can contribute to that."

Before Travers could respond, McCullough spoke. "I don't think it works that way, guys. There isn't a transition in place here, and when the time comes, we'll do it as best we can."

After pleading with Travers once more, the partners gave in. Within the hour, they and their team were gone. "We collected our troops," says Lederman, "like the Armenians leaving Turkey in the Diaspora or the Jews leaving Egypt in the Exodus, and we crossed Liberty Avenue, which we analogized to the Red Sea." They resettled in the office of their Pittsburgh attorneys, which was across the street. Tuesday morning, June 12, Japonica had the following memo handdelivered to a number of lower-level AI employees with whom they had been working:

Certain words come to mind as we recall the image of our band on Liberty Avenue at 7:00 P.M., literally surrounded by dozens of briefcases, suitcases, cartons, etc. These words are: exodus, diaspora and exile. Although we do miss you and the homeland, our temporary relocation, we concede, does not rise to such biblical proportions. After all, we are only across the street on the 26th floor of the CNG Tower. Some of you have reached us already this morning. Our telephone number is 338-2900. Mail, packages, faxes and our ongoing work with you should be directed to us here. Thanks. See you soon.

THE BANKS LAY A TRAP AND GET TRAPPED

On June 13, Lederman was about to fly from New York to Pittsburgh for a three P.M. meeting where he was going to offer the bank group more money for their claims. But shortly before he left for the airport, the banks called to cancel and announced that they were filing suit against Japonica. The purchase of the insurance companies' debt had put the banks at a terrible disadvantage. Now that Japonica had 51 percent of the reorganized company under the company's stock-for-debt reorganization plan, the banks reckoned that Japonica would simply sit tight and let the reorganization go through. In that case, the banks would be stuck with a minority position. "When one group controls fifty-one percent of the company, the [remaining stock] is never going to have the same value as the stock would if it were all on the market," Conti says. "And we would become involuntary shareholders in *their* company, which isn't the company we voted for."

In searching for an out, the banks grabbed hold of the "poison pill" antitakeover provision that the company had adopted for its plan that past December. According to the provision, Japonica as a party who through the plan would receive more than 45 percent of the common stock would have to buy out everyone else at the highest price paid. And the highest price paid in this case was the ninety-three cents, or $7 a share, that Japonica had just paid the insurance companies. "Once they went over forty-five percent we had them," Conti says. "We went in and said you have to buy us out in cash. That was much more money than they were going to pay in their plan, because their stock price in their plan was less than six dollars a share—lower than the company's plan because it gave effect to the holdback [for disputed claims]."

Now Judge Cosetti had several issues on his plate to decide, and he would settle everything all at once. Would he disqualify Japonica's votes against the company's plan as was expected? Or would he disqualify everyone else's votes, as Japonica had moved? Finally, would he order Japonica to comply with the antitakeover poison-pill provision and pay off creditors at $7 a share? He did not appear to be leaning in Japonica's favor. In a hearing on June 21, the judge remarked that he was "flabbergasted" by Japonica's tactics. "Whenever they run into an obstacle, they run out and purchase it!"

Behind the scenes, Japonica resumed negotiations to buy out the banks. Finally, on July 11, they reached a verbal agreement in principle, and all of the officials of the committees submitted letters to the court requesting that the judge not issue his decisions until there was a status conference to discuss a compromise. The following morning, Japonica attorney Herbert Minkel and the committee chairman appeared in court, expecting to participate in that very conference. But when Conti approached the bench to discuss the settlement, the judge turned her away and handed out his opinion. It was a 114-page order. In it, the judge gave the company what it wanted by disqualifying Japonica's votes and confirming the company's plan. He gave Japonica a semivictory by canceling the GKH agreements to buy when-issued shares from bank creditors. And he also gave the banks a victory of sorts by presenting Japonica with what seemed a Hobson's choice: either pay off all remaining shareholders at the price of $7 a share or, when the company emerges from bankruptcy, Japonica's shares would be held in a trust for three years and they would not be allowed to vote on the election of board members or any other matter.

Kazarian claims he wasn't fazed. "Our biggest fear was the judge was going to tell us we were going to have to pay ten to fifteen bucks a share to make the payment truly onerous, because at seven bucks a share we knew it was a steal. So the big laugh was that after the judge came out with his opinion and said we had to buy it at seven bucks a share, we all sat back and were saying, 'Such a penalty? We should get such a penalty every day.' " Still, they didn't just pay up. Japonica was looking for an even better deal. It staunchly refused to honor the poison-pill provision. Would it allow its shares to be put in trust? Or would it appeal?

Whatever Japonica decided to do, the banks felt caught in a corner. If Japonica's shares were held in trust for three years, the uncertainty would depress the price of the stock the banks held. And Milligan might leave for fear of what Japonica might do when its shares were released. If Japonica appealed the judge's ruling, the stock would sit in another sort of limbo waiting for a judgment.

Two things could then occur. First, Japonica could lose the

appeal but still refuse to honor the poison pill, whereby its stock would be held in trust for three years. "What would be the value of our stock on the marketplace with that kind of overhang?" says Joy Conti. "It can be devastating." Second, if Japonica won the appeal, the banks would be minority shareholders in a company run by Japonica—not a management they found particularly appealing—and the value of their stock would be depressed by Japonica's controlling position. To Herbert Minkel, the banks were left with an untenable situation. "So they had litigated and they had won," he says, assessing the situation. "Now they were going to go back and tell their managements that they had a high probability of making [maybe] a sixty-cent recovery in a transaction where other people had sold out for as high as ninety-five cents. And they, geniuses that they were, were going to ultimately take a forty-cent write off in a circumstance where they had passed up a dollar four, insisting on a dollar ten."

The banks wanted to negotiate.

Actually, Japonica had no desire whatsoever either to leave their shares in trust or to appeal Cosetti's ruling. They also wanted to negotiate. But to keep the banks on edge, the partners didn't reveal their intentions. They told the banks that they would only make a deal with them if the opinion was withdrawn. "It just tortured the banks, because they knew if they couldn't get the opinion withdrawn they were on the verge of taking a huge write off," Minkel says, almost gleefully. If it could not reach an accord with the banks, Japonica would appeal the ruling.

But the banks knew the judge would not reverse his ruling. Instead, they offered to accept something less than the $7 price the judge had ordered if Japonica would just agree to pay the $7 to everyone else. Because the bank group was so small and the other groups so large, it was the only one that could negotiate a lower price without having to hold another plan vote. So the haggling started again. The banks wanted $1.10 on the dollar, but Japonica held at its $1.04 offer. Ultimately, on July 25, the parties settled on $1.05 ($1.06 with interest) which for the bank class translated into an equity value of $6.60 a share. Japonica agreed to pay $7 a share for all the other classes. Kazarian and Lederman had negotiated the cheapest price they could. They had to weigh it against the cost of appealing the opinion and allowing the $125 million investment

Japonica and its backers had made to sit idle, and they decided to pay up and get on with managing the company.

LOOSE ENDS

Now that it had settled with the banks, Japonica reached quick agreement with the other constituencies. For the unsecured debtholders, it would offer an option of cash or stock. Then it had to tie up loose ends with the company. Japonica called Davis over the weekend, Davis says, "to say that they wanted to own the company, that they thought we wanted to reorganize the company—which of course we did—and that the only way to end this without years of litigation is to settle this. I said, 'Fine, we'll set up a meeting.'" A few days later Davis and Eleanor McNulty, an attorney from his office, Kazarian, Minkel, attorney Andre Weiss, and Mutual Shares's Peter Langerman got together for dinner at Christopher's, a swank restaurant perched on a hill overlooking the convergence of the Allegheny and Monongahela rivers into the Ohio. It was mainly a social event, the smoking of the peace pipe.

The next day they reconvened in Davis's office and went over the list of things he wanted. First, severance for Milligan of an amount to be determined later (Milligan later negotiated over the phone with Kazarian for a $1.5 million severance), which reimbursed him for the money he'd spent out of his own pocket and work he'd done without pay. Travers would get $900,000 and chief financial officer Sam Iapolucci $800,000. At the last minute, the company came in with one more request. They wanted the directors to receive severance equal to six months' compensation: $650,000 in all. "They'd been through a lot, worked pretty hard themselves, been threatened with all kind of lawsuits, and upon consideration they concluded that something akin to a severance fee was not out of order," McCullough explains. Minkel was furious. "This is the only bankruptcy case where directors got severance. Ever. It's outrageous." A steaming Lederman called Chuck Davidson at home, as Davidson recalls: "I just said to Mike—I wasn't even mad—I said, 'You knew this was going to come.'" To push through the company's plan with the amendments that gave Japonica control, Japonica agreed to these conditions.

On August 2, all the parties gathered in the courthouse to present the settlement to Judge Cosetti. "We still weren't that sure they'd come up with the big pile of money," McCullough says. Japonica's banks were in fact nearing the end of their due diligence. The main question was how much they were going to lend given the changing level of the company's cash. Milligan's cash-raising strategy was paying off better than he had expected. The company was brimming with cash, $270 million, and the flow was still strong. Because the company needed only so much cash to operate smoothly, the rest could be used to help pay for Japonica's buyout. Japonica knew, however, that going into September the company would start to need much more cash; many of its products—grills and garden furniture—were spring items and the process of building inventories had to begin in the fall. Any delay in the bankruptcy could mean a difference of tens of millions for Japonica.

At the August 2 hearing, Minkel interpreted the following as McCullough's effort to try to delay the settlement:

MCCULLOUGH TO THE JUDGE: There is [sic] a number of other procedural and non-financial matters that are involved in this and they should not go unnoticed because one of the problems with money is it tends to blind one to other things. I'm assuming the court has read all of those various things, such as the fact that Japonica will be taking control of the debtor as of the signing of this. . . . I don't mean to be an old fuddy-duddy, but the court obviously noticed that there are major changes to the debtor's plan. I would look to any guidance that the Court has with respect to notice and due process and I would look to any guidance the court has to offer with respect to financial issues because I'm sure a lot of questions will be asked of me and Lew Davis by our executive committee. . . .

(Davis rises)

DAVIS: Your Honor. Although as Bruce says we, of course, appreciate guidance, I believe we have to rule on the substance of what is there, first, before worrying about the technical issues, which perhaps we could deal with at 4:30 or 5 when the court reconvenes.
MCCULLOUGH: That's fine, too.

Bearing in mind that Herbert Minkel was not McCullough's greatest fan and endured a long struggle with him, here is how Japonica's attorney recounts that exchange. "Bruce McCullough stood up, and he tried to persuade the court in his backhanded way that there still were issues that should be of concern to the court. He tried to sabotage it. Bruce was so bad that even people who were his friends came up to me afterwards and said they were shocked and were prepared to acknowledge that his conduct could not be justified. He was so bad that Lew Davis stood up in the middle of the hearing, interrupted him and took over the hearing, something I had never seen before and I trust I will never see again."

The judge approved the settlement, giving the parties ten days to close. August 15. On August 14, McCullough called Minkel with some information that for Japonica was potentially devastating. It had come to his attention that Allegheny's Chemetron unit was the holder of a Nuclear Regulatory Commission license for a plant in Ohio with a potential waste cleanup problem and that, according to federal law, NRC approval was required for a transfer of that license. Again, Minkel was outraged. "Now I will tell you that the need for NRC approval to transfer a license is not an issue that comes to somebody's attention on the day of the consummation of a settlement of a reorganization that's been going on for two and a half years." He was convinced that McCullough was trying to single-handedly derail the plan—a notion that amused McCullough. "Some people said that I was so mad at Japonica that I'd stayed up late at night reading regulations to find out how I could stall the deal and stumbled across this regulation. I am not that good. I'm not that good to plan it this way. But I appreciate the compliment."

NRC approval was not a matter of a phone call and a faxed signature—especially in August when Washington is on vacation. The company believed that getting that NRC stamp on the license could take three months. As far as Japonica was concerned, the effect of a ninety-day delay would be that the company's internal cash would go down. Japonica would not be in control, so it would not be able to take action such as selling assets to raise cash. It would therefore need to go back to its bank for more money—if they'd agree to lend more. The delay would hurt not only Japonica but the creditors as well. "These are not people who are trying to see that creditors get what creditors are looking for," Minkel charges McCullough and the management. "Vietnam was the last war played with these rules."

Japonica did have an effective battle plan, though. After hearing from McCullough, Minkel called Marcus Rowden, a partner at his firm who also happened to be a former chairman of the NRC. Rowden hastily set up meetings with the NRC. Working with Allegheny's NRC counsel and Rowden, Lederman managed to get the NRC's okay in less than a month. The judge approved modifications to the settlement on September 14.

The closing of the acquisition took place on Friday, September 28, at a law firm in Manhattan. Kazarian's father roamed about the room snapping photographs. A number of tie-ups prevented the proceeding from starting before 4:30. A loan officer from CIT Business Credit, which was going to lend $65 million for housewares working capital, was having last-minute jitters because the operating numbers were still somewhat vague. "At one point he had his head under the sink running water on the back of his head," Kazarian recounts. "Ended up, we never borrowed a penny." As the afternoon waned, Kazarian became nervous that some of the people in the room who were observant Jews would have to leave because it was the eve of Yom Kippur, the holiest day of the year. After consulting with one of the Japonica bankers on this problem, he decided that the best thing to do was to draw the shades so that that contingent wouldn't realize the sun was setting.

Under the terms of the plan, the Sunbeam creditors, the Almet furniture creditors, and the Sunbeam holding creditors got 100 cents. The banks got 105 percent of their principal (plus interest). Other debtholders had the right to elect within forty-five days of consummation to get $7 a share or $1.53 per stock warrant (an option to buy stock), and equity holders got 16 cents a share in stock warrants. Some industry players called Michael Steinhardt to express their surprise that Japonica was overpaying for Allegheny. "That was the prevailing opinion when this deal was done," Chuck Davidson says. Steinhardt himself hadn't been intimately involved in the deal. "But Mike heard these calls and of course it would agitate him. We would discuss it, and I'd say they don't know what they're talking about." In fact, Japonica's two equity backers wound up paying out only $210 million for the company—$125 million for all debt purchases before the closing and $83 million for the rest. The Japonica-Steinhardt-Mutual Series partnership borrowed only $125 million from banks because they were able to use an astounding $325 million in cash from the company. The total paid: $660 million, a good chunk less than the $683 million Japonica had bid for the company the past November. Their costs—fees for consultants, auditors, appraisers, attorneys, and bank lenders—amounted to less than $15 million dollars. Well worth it, Michael Price says, "for getting a single-A-rated balance sheet." Now, the partnership owned 99 percent of the new Sunbean-Oster Co. (with 1 percent held by the public)—and Mutual Series and Steinhardt owned the majority.

In retrospect, Price thinks that Japonica went overboard in the bank loan and bond buying it did during the spring. "A third of a class is enough to block a plan. You don't need any more than that," he says. Because Japonica's purchases ended up exceeding 45 percent of the when-issued stock, the banks and the judge were able to nail them with the poison pill. Responds Kazarian: "Philosophically, we have little strategic differences here. It's like the only point in our entire relationship."

The Sunday after the closing, Lederman flew to Pittsburgh, and the following morning he took charge of a company that was much changed from the one Japonica had found in the spring of 1989. As many as a fifth of the employees—several thousand—had been eliminated through plant closings and consolidations and cost-cutting layoffs. Where in the Buckley days there had once been 600 employees at headquarters, Japonica found 60, partly as a result of Milligan's streamlining. What was a 45-person mergers-and-acquisitions department under Buckley is now a 1-person department consisting of Kazarian.

In its first year, Japonica cut headquarters staff to about fifteen, mainly by sifting out what it considered ineffective employees, and moved them into a new more modest building downtown. In the summer of 1991, Kazarian and Lederman moved Japonica Partners from Park Avenue to Providence, Rhode Island, near the town where both had vacation homes. And in the fall, they decided also to move Sunbeam-Oster headquarters to Providence—apparently breaking their promise to maintain the former steel company in its original home of Pittsburgh. "At the time the statement was made, that was the intention," says Lederman. "The company could not shake the taint of being Robert Buckley's company. It could not shake the taint of being Allegheny, a Chapter Eleven failure. It could not shake the taint of having been subject to a hostile takeover. And it could not shake the name Allegheny International." Japonica moved ten of the fifteen employees to Providence, and there it began to hire some seventy additional workers, rebuilding departments it had thinned out and creating a new market research division. "We kept it in Pittsburgh for over a year," says Lederman. "We gave the city the chance to be what was best for the business. It wasn't."

Compensation became more incentive oriented. At the subsidiary operating companies, Japonica raised about forty midlevel people up and gave everyone stock. As for the two vulture-managers, Kazarian began earning $1.5 million a year and Lederman, $260,000. But Kazarian didn't take any of the $923,000 fee the vulture partners and its team collected from the bankruptcy; Lederman took a sizable portion of that. Both will get a lot of stock.

By the spring of 1991, they'd introduced ten new products, including two new Osterizers, a cabinet-stand mixer, and new irons. In the first nine months of 1991, the company earned $35 million, a far cry from the $40 million loss the year before. In the months following the reorganization, Japonica began finding riches it didn't know it had. During a trip to Paris in December, Kazarian and Japonica staffer Robert Setrakian met an acquaintance in Offenbach. As Kazarian recalls their encounter:

The man said, "Have you been to the Paris office?"

"We don't have a Paris office," Kazarian responded.

"You have a Paris office," the man said with assurance.

"Look," Kazarian began, "it's not on the balance sheet, it's not here."

The man shook his head. "Go down there. It's twenty miles away," and he gave Kazarian directions and a map.

Kazarian and Setrakian got in their car and drove. As Kazarian relates: "And there it was: big office, a warehouse. Another warehouse up in Stockholm that nobody told us about. Bank accounts filled with cash. Literally, three-quarters of a million dollars in cash nobody knew about. Total net we found cash squirreled away in escrow accounts not included on the balance sheet—property that we didn't know we owned—of sixty to sixty-five million dollars. We had no way of knowing it was there." Japonica was convinced that the old management had been hiding it. According to Price, hiding cash through various accounting means is very common in bankruptcy. Managements are so protected in Chapter 11, he says, that they take measures to put themselves on as good a footing as possible when the company emerges from bankruptcy. Milligan dismisses the notion that he was hiding cash and says if any assets weren't listed on the balance sheet, it was the result of the time it takes a new management (meaning himself) to locate every asset.

Would the vultures make money? By the end of 1991, the value of Mutual Series's investment had approximately doubled on its books, according to the fund's own valuation of the equity. Price views the investment as one of the fund's all-time blockbusters. "We had to close [the acquisition] when the markets, the economy, rates were not looking good. We closed at a very difficult time. But boy we bought one of the cheapest things this fund has ever bought when we closed." How long would it keep its cash invested? "We're long-term investors," says Price. But surely they would take some profits. By 1992 they faced several choices. "The company has a reasonably structured capitalization," Davidson says, "which means if we want to do an IPO we can do an IPO [initial public offering of stock]. If we want to sell to a strategic buyer who, for whatever reason, lusts for this business we can do that, if we want to do nothing and dividend out a ton of money every year, we can do that. We have deliberately kept our options open, starting with the assumption that we decided that whatever we did we aren't going to piecemeal it out. This company is a unit. There are synergies between the different businesses." At the end of 1991 Sunbeam-Oster was Steinhardt Partners' largest equity holding.

Japonica and its investors were shrewd in Allegheny. But they were also lucky. They came along at precisely the right time to take advantage of a group of creditors that was thirsting for cash. "It's opportunity meeting preparedness or whatever they call luck," says Price. "We were real lucky in Allegheny. But what we brought to the table was, one, how to understand financial statements of bankrupt companies; two, how to understand how managements hide things in bankruptcies; three, how to buy bank loans cheaply; four, how to write a plan and design a capital structure; five, how to negotiate with all these adverse interests. So we brought a lot of knowledge. We had the capability and the cash, but that's what gets you the luck."

There are not likely to be many more Allegheny Internationals. The aggressive tactics of Japonica were highly unusual because Japonica Partners themselves are highly unusual people. The history of the company and its bankruptcy, too, were atypical, as was the unrecognized sterling value of the Sunbeam-Oster franchise. But although they may not happen in just the same way, hostile takeovers of companies in bankruptcy are more likely now that Japonica has shown the way.

Throughout 1992, Sunbeam-Oster continued to post higher sales and income. In August, the company went public with 20 million shares of stock, raising $250 million, which still left 77 percent in the hands of Mutual Series, Steinhardt and, as a minority partner, Japonica. An analyst's report called Kazarian "one of the most energetic and hardworking CEOs we have come across."

It turned out he was too energetic for his own good. In January of 1993, Lederman told the board that Kazarian had been unreasonably demanding of top officers, who were ready to walk out. After an investigation, the directors dismissed the young CEO.

He had one more battle to fight, however, as a partner in Japonica with Lederman and Setrakian. By January, Mutual Series and Steinhardt had taken out about $30 million apiece and had paper profits of more than $1 billion; Japonica's interest in that was $200 million. Lederman and Setrakian filed suit against Kazarian, seeking two-thirds of that sum, while Kazarian insisted he owned 99 percent. And so, the two men who were once called the twins had become bitter enemies.

9

Convenience in Bankruptcy Shopping

Now, my son, see to what a mock are brought
The goods of Fortune's keeping, and how soon!
Though to possess them still is all man's thought.
For all the gold that is beneath the moon,
Or ever was, never could buy repose
For one of those souls, faint to have that boon.

—*DANTE'S INFERNO*

How many lifetimes can a corporation live? In 1990, the Southland Corporation was at the end of its second and struggling for a third chance. During that effort, a throng of vulture investors descended on the company, not to fight to own it but to reap the rewards of a successful financial restructuring. The vultures ranged from one of the most famous of all investors, Carl Icahn, to one of the more obscure individual bankruptcy specialists, Ben Walsh. And in between were a number of familiar and unfamiliar names including Martin Whitman, R. D. Smith, and Deltec Securities. In this case, the vultures would receive a major bonus—an unusually brief bankruptcy reorganization—achieved through the first use of a prepackaged bankruptcy at a multibillion-dollar company. It would be the first example of vulture investors cooperating with a major company management to achieve a prepack, which not only gave the vultures a quick return on their money but benefited all creditors and the company as well by cutting out the high costs of a prolonged bankruptcy.

This was not the first time vulture investors profited from troubles at Southland. The company started out in 1927 as a chain of ice stores abiding in Texas and before long began selling milk, bread, cigarettes, and canned goods in the winter off-season. The convenience store was born. But just as the young company was blossoming, the stock market crash cut its life short and it plunged into bankruptcy. The president of the firm, Joe C. Thompson, Sr., hoisted the company out with cash, buying control of Southland at the marked down price of seven cents on the dollar. He then returned the company to the road of prosperity, introducing gasoline, cold beer, and other items to the stores he named 7-Elevens and building a chain of convenience outlets that his sons would expand into an empire.

Under the Thompson family's leadership, Southland fully bloomed. By the mid-1980s, Joe Thompson's son John and his brother Jere were chairman and president, respectively, of a company that was perhaps best described as a bazaar, consisting of 8200 of the 7-Eleven convenience stores, which were scattered nationwide, and a hodgepodge of about ten other businesses from auto parts to videotape rentals to oil refining, and marketing. Actually there was rationality in this assortment, since all but auto parts were built or bought to support 7-Elevens. In 1986, John earned $860,000 in cash compensation, and Jere took home $795,000.

In the spring of 1987, John Thompson was contacted by Samuel Belzberg, the Canadian takeover tycoon, and they got together to talk business. Belzberg said he owned 4.9 percent of the company's stock and was interested in exploring the possibility of doing a leveraged buyout at $65 a share—perhaps with the Thompsons. Recently, the stock had been trading at $47. After several meetings, Thompson told Belzberg that the family wasn't interested in Belzberg's proposals. Together with Southland's board, the Thompsons had been investigating some way to improve share-holder value on their own. (Or, at least that's what they said later.) But that didn't get rid of Belzberg, who told the Thompsons that he might buy more shares. In the feverish takeover environment of the 1980s, rumors of a potential acquirer drove up Southland's stock to new heights near $70 a share in early July. The Thompsons weren't about to surrender their father's legacy, let alone their lucrative salaries, to a raider. But now they had to do something.

To protect their kingdom from insurgents, John, Jere, and their brother Jodie, a director, hurriedly assembled their own plan to take the company private. They settled on a strategy to buy out Southland's stock at a staggering cost of $4.0 billion, rising to almost $5.0 billion when including retirement of debentures, refi-nancing of existing debt, and fees. In the days when anything seemed possible, handling the new debt burden was considered a mere matter of selling off some assets and running a tight ship. By August 1987, the Thompsons had used loans to tender for two-thirds of the common stock and all of the preferred shares, and planned to refinance a large chunk of those loans and buy the rest of the shares with a junk bond offering for $1.5 billion. Shareholders were scheduled to meet on November 5 to cast their final votes on the leveraged buyout plan.

But on October 19, Southland got sucked into the whirlpool of a stock market crash for the second time in its history. It was the beginning of the end of the company's second lifetime. The junk bond market tumbled, touching off a frantic effort by Southland's underwriters to restructure the $1.5 billion junk bond offering to make it more palatable to investors. On Wall Street, the transaction soon became derisively known as "the Texas Chain-Store Massacre." Despite market concerns about Southland's ability to carry the heavy debt, the sale of junk bonds sweetened by higher interest rates and stock warrants (options to buy stock at a named price) sailed through, and the buyout won resounding approval from shareholders. Thousands of Southland employees and 7-Eleven franchisees and licensees could now breathe easier. For them and for the Thompson family, however, the victory would prove to be all too brief. Because the family and its investment bankers and investors had blithely accepted a monstrously large debt load, the leveraged buyout was really the beginning of two desperate years to keep the company alive.

Eventually, the Thompsons would become enmeshed in another struggle for control, this time with the holders of the very bonds that were now saving their necks. But in December 1987, the Thompsons thought they were in the clear; all they had to do now was pay off the debt. But try as they might, they just weren't up to the job. Their efforts were as pathetic as someone trying to stopper a volcano with a wine cork.

In 1988 the Thompsons began selling off pieces of Southland—a total of about 1000 of the 7-Eleven stores, a milk-processing and distribution group, a videotape rental distribution company, an auto parts chain, an ice division, a snack foods operation, and a maker of cash-handling devices. They actually received better than expected prices. But with the onslaught of new competition coupled with an inability to raise its capital spending, the company still could not live up to the cheerful projections for the convenience store retailing business issued at the time of the buyout, and wallowing in a $216 million loss for 1988, it couldn't afford to pay interest on its remaining debt. It didn't help that Southland's forty-two-story Cityplace headquarters tower, a $475 million monument to the 1980s, which was the first part of a planned 160-acre office and residential complex in Dallas, was still under construction and wouldn't be completed until the following year.

Early in 1989, the Thompsons slashed Southland's interest tab by exchanging nearly $1 billion of outstanding 18 percent bonds (issued at a deep discount, they were by then worth $453 million) for about $500 million of shorter-term bonds with a 13.5 percent coupon rate but that were more senior in standing than any other class of bonds (meaning that they would be paid off first in a bankruptcy). It was their first experience practicing the art of negotiating with debt holders, but hardly their last or most difficult. Because the swap didn't provide quite enough debt relief, the company made a painful decision. It would sell a prized possession: its 50 percent stake in Citgo Petroleum. The company had sold the first half to Petroleos de Venezuela, the government-owned oil concern, back in 1986, and now approached its South American business partner to ask it to take the other half as well. In early November, Southland announced they had reached an agreement to complete the sale in January 1990.

Although the transaction would bring in a shipment of $675 million in cash, Wall Street securities analysts still wondered whether even that would be enough to keep the company afloat given the shrinking profit margins of the brutally competitive convenience store business and the big interest bill looming on the 1991 horizon. Behind the scenes, Southland began looking for a buyer. Shamrock Partners, Roy Disney's investment group, made a bid to bolster the company with $200 million in new cash in return for a large chunk of stock. They even signed a letter of intent to complete the deal. But before that became final, Southland began discussing a similar deal with Ito-Yokado, which controlled the licensee for 7-Eleven outlets in Japan and Hawaii. Because Ito-Yokado was offering more money, Southland paid a $5 million breakup fee to get rid of Shamrock. Southland's various junior and senior bonds were trading in a range of twenty-five and forty cents on the dollar—and falling.

THE IDEAL BANKRUPTCY

In the fall of 1989, Marty Whitman got a call from his friend Jerome Kohlberg. Kohlberg, once a senior partner with the star of all leveraged buyout firms, Kohlberg, Kravis, Roberts & Company, had left the firm in 1987 when his fellow partners decided to pursue much larger deals. The risks did not appeal to him, especially because he expected a credit crunch would stifle new LBO business. So while his ex-partners went on to snare companies like RJR Nabisco in their nets, Kohlberg teamed up with his son Jim, content to continue doing the somewhat humbler deals that had made him millions. Kohlberg had been watching Southland, and when it announced its intention to sell its half-interest in Citgo to Venezuela, he became intrigued. He went to his vulture investor friend Martin Whitman and asked him whether Southland was a good investment. On the Kohlbergs' behalf, Whitman took a serious look and concluded that the Citgo sale would hardly be the company's savior. Indeed, he was certain that Southland was destined for bankruptcy court. But to a vulture investor that prospect was reason to look further. If cash from the sale was used to pay off bank debt as intended, he reasoned, there would be less bank debt to satisfy in the bankruptcy before the bondholders got their recoveries. And that was the worst case.

The best case, as he saw it, was for Southland to be reorganized in a swift, prepackaged bankruptcy. Of course, this had been Whitman's hope for Public Service Company of New Hampshire two years earlier, but it never came to pass. Southland had a multilayered financial structure—bank debt, senior unsecured bonds, four junior classes, preferred stock, and common stock. But Whitman believed that if management wanted to do a prepack, it could pull it off without much trouble. It had enough cash to keep it from falling into a regular, what Whitman calls "uncontrolled," bankruptcy while management and creditors thrashed out the reorganization plan. He could only hope that the company realized the advantages of opting for the "controlled," prepackaged type of bankruptcy, because he was convinced that an out-of-court exchange offer would never work.

At the time, the professional bankruptcy community was just starting to discuss the prepackaged bankruptcy as a solution to a worsening problem of stubborn bondholders who were capsizing exchange offers. Companies often required that, for an exchange offer to go through, holders of the vast majority of outstanding bonds—more than 80 percent—trade in their bonds for bonds with less onerous terms. But a growing contingent of opportunistic bondholders wanted to be among the 20 percent who continued holding the old bonds and receiving their high current interest and principal payments. Indeed, once the exchange offer went through, the creditor quality of the company would improve and the holdouts would see their securities rocket in value. Trouble is, it's a game of chicken. Everyone can't be a holdout, and if everyone tries, exchange offers go down.

MAKING THE MOLD

Whitman knew a good prepack candidate when he saw one, having recently engineered one of the first such reorganizations at

Anglo Energy Corporation. Anglo was a New York–based oil services outfit that had failed in 1983 after swallowing more acquisitions than it could digest. During three years of bankruptcy proceedings, Whitman served on the shareholders' committee as a favor to some friends, owning only a small position. He didn't like the plan the company and its creditors agreed to in September of 1986, but as a minor shareholder there was not much he could do about it. "It was a stupid deal, never had a chance of flying, too much debt," recalls the veteran investor. In his view, Anglo would eventually sink back into the swamp of bankruptcy. Even so, Whitman saw black gold in the just-reorganized company's bank debt, which was selling at thirty cents to forty cents on the dollar and was secured by the company's assets. Some quick calculating told him that there was enough collateral in the company's Alaskan oil rigs to protect an investment in the case of another bankruptcy. What's more, he thought that the CEO at the time was competent and had a business with strong potential. So he started buying bank debt, a little here, a little there.

During his shopping spree, however, the board of directors fired the CEO, and Whitman's confidence in the value of the company deflated. There was no way out. "Buying bank debt is a Roach Motel℠—easy to check in, impossible to check out. It's not liquid," he says. "So I thought I'd better get control of the company." That way, he could fashion a restructuring the way he wanted and save his investment. He cranked up the speed on his bank debt purchases and also started buying the stock in the market. Soon, Whitman, through entities he controlled, laid claim to some 45 percent of Anglo's common stock and a large helping of the secured debt. His $14 million investment effectively put him in control of the company.

All along, Whitman had been discussing the Anglo situation with Gene Isenberg, an old friend from Princeton days who became a refinery officer with Exxon and later bought a construction products company with Whitman's assistance. He was in semiretirement, but when Whitman cast his net around Anglo in 1987 Isenberg expressed a desire to lead the company out of the depths as its next CEO. Now all that was needed was a debt restructuring to supply the company with a new financial framework. Easier said than done, because creditors were not instantly willing to bow to Whitman's plan. So Whitman and Isenberg decided to copy a precedent-setting deal completed by Crystal Oil early that year in which a majority of creditors holding two-thirds of the debt in each class assented to a preapproved reorganization plan, which allowed the company to enter bankruptcy for the brief time it took for the judge to confirm that plan. Dissenters were forced to go along.

At Anglo, Isenberg and Morgan Guaranty Trust Company, a bank creditor, peddled a debt-for-stock deal to the creditors and won over enough support to file a prepackaged Chapter 11. As a result, the company idled in bankruptcy for only four months, from February to May 1988, emerging debt free. Whitman was Anglo's largest shareholder with a 26 percent stake, which later fell to 23 percent, and he renamed the company Nabors Industries after its principal breadwinner, the Alaskan subsidiary. Powered by surging cash flow, the value of the shares gushed like a newly drilled well, from $1 a share at the time of the reorganization to $6 a share three and a half years later. Whitman's original $14 million investment had become a gleaming $100 million.

THE $400 MILLION SOLUTION

So it was no surprise that toward the end of 1989, as Southland began considering a financial restructuring, Whitman discussed the idea of doing a prepackaged bankruptcy with the Kohlberg father-and-son team. By injecting Southland with some new capital, Whitman explained, the Kohlbergs could easily recapitalize the company. It was just a matter of convincing the Thompson brothers to sell them a major equity stake and then doing a prepackaged Chapter 11. Intrigued, Jerry and Jim Kohlberg flew to Dallas to talk the idea over with the Thompsons. But the Thompsons weren't interested in selling out—or at least that's what they said at the time, because they were already negotiating with Ito-Yokado.

Still, Whitman thought Southland was a worthy investment, and in late February 1990 he slowly began gathering a position in the unsecured, senior class of bonds paying 13.5 percent interest. As was his usual practice before investing, Whitman calculated the value that the bonds would likely recover in an average three- to five-year bankruptcy proceeding and determined that his return would be more than adequate for what looked like a small risk. "I thought it was very hard to screw these bondholders," he says. Of course, he continued to hope for a prepackaged bankruptcy that would bring in a markedly better return on his money. And at the beginning of 1990, the idea of using the prepackaged bankruptcy on a widespread basis suddenly became more attractive as out-of-court exchange offers became less attractive. (A New York court ruled that if a holder exchanges his bonds for new bonds with the same face value and if the company then enters bankruptcy, the bondholder's bankruptcy claim is lower than the face value of the new bond he holds; it equals the market value of the old bond on the date of the exchange. That ruling was later reversed on appeal.)

It had been only two years since the Thompson family had struggled to bring $1.5 billion in junk bonds into the world. Those bonds had allowed the family to cling to control of Southland, but they also were ensuring its downfall. Now the Thompsons were realizing that their effort had failed and that to keep Southland alive it was imperative that they relinquish control.

Southland was due to make a $69 million interest payment on one bond issue on June 15, 1990, and bondholders were not sure that the company could afford the expenditure. On March 22, Southland confirmed their suspicions when it announced its restructuring plan with Ito-Yokado. The Japanese 7-Eleven operator agreed to inject $400 million into the company in return for a 75 percent equity stake. But that cash infusion was contingent on 95 percent of bondholders accepting an exchange offer that would slash the face value of Southland's $1.8 billion in bond debt nearly in half. For trading in their holdings, bondholders would receive zero-coupon bonds that pay no interest but increase in value over time and 10 percent of the restructured company's stock. The Thompson brothers would keep only 15 percent of the equity in the company founded by their father.

The cash from Ito-Yokado and the savings from the debt swap would finance store remodeling, state-of-the-art computer systems, and new advertising and promotion that would help revive the company's fortunes. But persuading the current bondholders to go along with this plan was going to be the Thompsons' hardest task yet.

Even for an initial offer, this one was hideous to bondholders, even vulture investors who had bought their securities at a steep discount, because they had counted on much greater returns. As John Gordon, the president of Deltec Securities and a Migratory breed of vulture investor, told *The Wall Street Journal,* "I'd be hard pressed to think of an initial exchange offer that could be more offensive." Bondholders complained about the severity of the principal reduction and the fact that the bonds paid no interest. They were also incensed that the Thompsons were getting more equity than they were, even though the company was broke and in a bankruptcy bondholders are the ones with priority over old stockholders. Even more infuriating to the bondholders, the Thompsons would continue to manage the company and would receive interest-free loans from Ito-Yokado. Some bondholders reacted to the announcement of the exchange offer by saying they would take the company into bankruptcy before accepting the proffered deal.

But to Whitman and other advocates of the prepack, this was good news. Bondholders hated the proposal and would not go along with it. And even if the terms were improved, many bondholders would soon see the advantage of holding out—not exchanging their bonds; that advantage was that Ito-Yokado's $400 million infusion of capital would give the restructured company a better credit quality and holdouts would see their bonds soar in value. Most likely, so many holders would want to hold out that the exchange offer would fail. Surely, the company would realize that to avoid a prolonged bankruptcy it had no choice but to propose a prepack to force dissenting creditors into the deal. At least that's what Whitman hoped would happen. He and other bondholders intended to urge management to pursue that alternative. First, however, both sides had to settle on a deal that at least two-thirds of creditors would accept.

It was around this time that the company discovered Carl Icahn's interest in its misfortunes. As a 1980s raider, Icahn had taken on USX, Texaco, and TWA—even acquiring TWA—and he had recently begun turning to distressed securities in a big way while at the same time trying to keep his airline aloft. One of Icahn's associates phoned Southland's investment banker Kenneth Moelis—a Drexel, Burnham, Lambert alumnus who had only recently joined Donaldson, Lufkin & Jenrette and gotten this assignment—and invited him to lunch at TWA headquarters, a small set of white egg-carton–like buildings in suburban Mount Kisco, New York. "I thought he was calling to chitchat," he says. But when he arrived, Icahn surprised him. As they sat down, Icahn said, "You know, I've got some of those Southland bonds." Knowing that Carl Icahn doesn't often invest passively, Moelis was taken aback. "You do? How much?" he inquired, well aware that Icahn rarely reveals the size of his positions. But to his amazement Icahn pulled out a sheet of paper listing all of his positions in distressed-company debt and added up his Southland investment: He refrained from giving Moelis a peek at the other items on the list, revealing only that he had accumulated bonds with a total face value of about *$1.5 billion.*

Since the end of 1989, Icahn had picked up Southland senior bonds at an average price of about thirty-five cents on the dollar and junior bonds for an average of ten to fifteen cents on the dollar. He owned $170 million worth of the senior bonds, 34 percent of the class—the same class Whitman held. When Ito-Yokado came along with its acquisition and exchange offer, Icahn was convinced that it was going to succeed, in part because by buying control of Southland Ito-Yokado would save money on royalties for 7-Eleven Japan. Like the other bondholders, Icahn didn't like the initial offer Ito-Yokado was making to them. But he didn't complain to Moelis, because he knew that this was just the beginning of what would be the usual drawn-out negotiation process. And he also knew that as holder of 34 percent of the senior bonds—a blocking position—he would have considerable clout in that process. He wouldn't even have to take much of an active role because, with his substantial holding, the company would have to come to him with an offer that made him happy. Moelis went away from that meeting knowing that Icahn was going to be a force to be reckoned with.

ORGANIZING FOR ACTION

The very day after the company's announcement of its exchange offer, March 23, Wilbur Ross, Wall Street's dean of restructurings at Rothschild, and David Strumwasser, a prominent bond-holders' attorney, called Deltec Securities's John Gordon. Gordon had started buying Southland junior bonds in earnest at the end of 1989 at a low of eighteen cents on the dollar, and by spring Deltec owned $36.2 million worth. He had worked with these two advisers several months earlier when he was chairman of the bondholders' steering committee for the out-of-court restructuring of Fruehauf Corporation, the Detroit maker of truck vans and auto parts. Today, they wanted to know if he owned any Southland bonds. When they learned that he indeed owned a generous portion, they offered to treat him to breakfast the following morning at the Intercontinental Hotel to discuss the possibility of working together once again.

At one time the establishment of a bondholders' committee before a bankruptcy filing was unheard of. But in the 1980s, two developing trends changed that. For one thing, the holdout phenomenon was foiling companies' exchange offers. And many bondholders realized that the exchange offers that did go through were often not fixing the companies. In the past, companies that had run aground hastily arranged debt swaps in back rooms with one or two large bondholders. Everyone got what they wanted. Bondholders got new higher-rate, shorter-term bonds and did not have to mark down their bonds on their balance sheets as they would have to do in the case of a bankruptcy; the company got to issue the bond with relatively short maturities and deferred payment; equity holders retained the bulk of their stake; and management stayed in place. In fact, however, these Band-Aids℠ were not nearly large enough to treat the wounds. Band-Aid restructurings tended to fail and fail again until the companies ended up in Chapter 11. In the late 1980s, a growing community of large bondholders felt cheated both by lame restructurings and by the short-term opportunism of fellow bondholders who were holdouts in exchange offers. So, at a sign of an impending default on their bond interest payments, angry investors started banding together in informal committees, hiring advisers to research the company's true value, devise a viable restructuring strategy, and negotiate with management, and insisting that the debtor pay for their advisers. Not surprisingly, it became a growth industry as lawyers and investment bankers began to initiate the committee organization process.

In a conference call with dozens of large bondholders on April 3, 1990, Wilbur Ross and David Strumwasser delivered their pitch for a Southland committee headed by Deltec's Gordon. The following day, George Varughese and James Casey of Kidder, Peabody hosted another conference call.

The day after Kidder, Peabody's meeting, Gordon decided to get the bondholders organized, the advisers hired, and the action rolling by holding his own conference call. "I was frankly really pissed about the offensiveness of the exchange offer, number one, and, number two, because I honestly thought that there was dramatically greater value inherent in the business than management was letting on. I just thought that everybody had to go to battle stations," he says. He put together a list of bondholders who had partaken in the other two conference calls, including Icahn. With seventy institutions on the line, Gordon led a discussion that resulted in the appointment of a steering committee that would represent the bondholders in negotiating with the company. The largest of the members were Kemper Corporation, the Chicago insurance company, and the Prudential Insurance Company, but the committee elected Gordon as chairman. "It wasn't a highly sought-after position," he says. But it was an influential one.

UPPER-CRUST CHAMPION OF THE UNDERDOG

The blue-eyed, forty-three-year-old Gordon is president of Deltec Securities, which is owned by a firm that has a unique history. Deltec Securities is the New York investment management arm of Deltec Panamerica, a financial house founded by a man named Clarence Dauphinot, who took his business to places few men had gone before. Fresh out of Princeton in the thirties, Dauphinot, a New York native, got a job as a runner delivering messages at Kidder, Peabody. He finally graduated to the trading desk and soon latched onto the market for foreign government bonds that were in default. After World War II, he pursued his love at the source, moving to Brazil and founding Deltec Panamerica, S. A., a banking, trust and investment company concentrating on Latin

America. By the 1960s, Deltec Panamerica, now headquartered in the Bahamas tax haven, had local operations in all of the major Latin American countries where it would, with a local partner, provide all types of financing from bank loans to private placements. Then at a time when only a few of the world's largest banks were making hard currency loans to Latin American borrowers of all types, Deltec strode into that business. Using its local partners as a credit check, it would lend in amounts ranging up to $10 million and then turn around and sell pieces of the loan to commercial banks in the United States and Europe. When, in the seventies, more banks began lending directly to Latin America, the spreads between lending cost and selling price narrowed. "It got to the point that it didn't make much sense anymore for us to tie up our own capital," says Arthur Byrnes, who as chairman of Deltec Securities works alongside Gordon. "It got too competitive. Everyone was doing it directly." Deltec Panamerica pulled out of that business at the end of the 1970s, as luck would have it just before the first major Latin American loan defaults and just as the real estate investment trusts began to collapse, which presented Deltec with a new subject for its contrarian tastes. Based in New York, Deltec Securities has placed its funds into several offbeat areas including REITs and distressed and bankrupt companies. Meanwhile, Dauphinot, at seventy-eight years old, still runs the parent organization in Nassau.

Gordon is the son of the man who gave Dauphinot his first job on Wall Street, former Kidder, Peabody chairman Al Gordon. Raised in Manhattan, the younger Gordon lived in the rarefied atmosphere of upper-crust society, attending St. Paul's boarding school in New Hampshire, Harvard University, and the Harvard Graduate Business and Law program. Favoring business over law, he had several offers from Wall Street houses but went to Kidder, Peabody out of family allegiance and a preference for a firm that although not hurting had some catching up to do. After ten years in corporate finance at Kidder, Peabody, he decided to leave, concluding that "Gordons had done everything there that Gordons could do. I had to branch out and do something different." But when in 1986 Kidder, Peabody was rocked by the departure of corporate finance star Martin Siegel for Drexel, Burnham, Lambert and then by the insider trading scandals, Gordon felt a family obligation to stay on a while and help steady things. But within two years he left for Deltec, a place that combined his desire to manage money with his preference for working with underdog companies.

After interviewing six investment banking firms, the Southland bondholder steering committee chose Kidder, Peabody as its financial adviser, and for its legal adviser James Spiotto of Chapman and Cutler in Chicago, who has a reputation as a pit bull. The company objected, but Gordon was unrelenting: "The company said you're reducing the chances of us being able to work something out because this guy is so combative, pugnacious. And actually that sounded pretty good to us." Kidder, Peabody then went off to examine the asset value of the company and arrive at its own valuation.

Neither Carl Icahn nor Marty Whitman had any desire to join the steering committee. Unlike Gordon and other vulture investors who willingly serve on committees, big investors like Icahn and Whitman prefer to do their own negotiating. "We go on committees when we can't get control otherwise," Whitman says of his firm, Whitman, Heffernan & Rhein. Besides, he says, committee members have to stop trading, they don't get paid for their work, and they have a fiduciary obligation to represent whole classes of debt, not just their own positions.

Southland soon embarked on a nationwide series of visits with investors to garner support for its Japanese-sponsored exchange offer. But management and its advisers met little success in convincing bondholders that the exchange offer was a good deal. As the "road show" toured the country, steering committee members watched and waited, and continued to trade in and out of the bonds. So did Whitman. By the end of May, Whitman, Heffernan & Rhein and its partners—who included a small clan of British investors and George Soros, the celebrated world-class investor—owned just under 30 percent of the senior class, $158 million worth bought at an average price of about thirty-five cents on the dollar.

ICE-CREAM-CONE POLITICS

On May 23, Kidder, Peabody and Chapman and Cutler met with the steering committee to report their findings. They assembled in a small auditorium at Kidder, Peabody's downtown headquarters, just after the firm's sales staff had filed out from their morning research meeting. The advisers delivered their astonishing conclusions: Southland was much more valuable than management was claiming. By Kidder, Peabody's analysis, Southland was worth $3 billion as opposed to the $2.2 billion management was claiming—actually Kidder, Peabody had arrived at the $2.2 billion by extrapolating from Southland's offer to bondholders. The value that Kidder, Peabody reckoned bondholders should receive in a restructuring, more than $700 million, was more than double the value indicated by the company's restructuring proposal. What's more, Kidder, Peabody showed the gathering a document that Southland had filed with the SEC in November, which contained seven-year cash flow projections that were 25 percent higher than those the company had given four months later when it presented its exchange offer. By Kidder, Peabody's analysis, the November projections were much closer to reality. Based on that information, the group put together a restructuring counterproposal that Kidder, Peabody's team leader, George Varughese, says was "just as outrageous as the company's plan was." On a conference call with the company and its advisers, he says, "We basically said, 'We want par for all of our bonds.' " Immediately after that call, Southland's financial adviser, Kenneth Moelis, called Varughese back. According to Kidder, Peabody's James Casey, "Our counterproposal drove Moelis crazy. Ken was swearing, telling George, 'I am going to sue you for financial malpractice.' "

Now face-to-face talks began. Gordon and Kenneth Urbaszewski, a Kemper junk bond mutual fund manager who held $100 million worth of senior- and junior-class bonds, took an active role in conferring with the advisers and, at times, participated in direct negotiations with the company. The negotiating teams had a month and a half before their first deadline, the June 15 due date for a $69 million interest payment. If the parties failed to reach agreement by then, the company had a thirty-day grace period. Then, if there still was no pact and if, as seemed likely, Southland could not make the payment, it would be officially in default, and by law any three creditors would have the right to tip it into bankruptcy—uncontrolled, without a prepackaged reorganization plan in hand. If that happened, the Japanese investors might very well abandon ship and Southland would be back to zero. Because July 15 was a Sunday, Monday, July 16, became D-Day—at precisely 10:00 A.M., Dallas time.

The talks proceeded slowly at first, through phone conferences and meetings. The parties often met at Shearman & Sterling, Ito-Yokado's New York law firm in midtown that had an entire floor of conference rooms, and sometimes at Skadden, Arps, Slate, Meagher & Flom, the company's attorneys, or at the midtown offices of Merrill, Lynch, Ito-Yokado's investment bank. The first time the bondholders met the company in person was in a conference room at Skadden, Arps. Appearing for the company was chief financial officer Clark Matthews, a tall Texan whose optimism was enhanced by his cowboy twang and broad smile, and DLJ's Ken Moelis, whose intense energy level led one committee member to describe him as a "whirling dervish" and others to suspect that he might try to pull a fast one. Investment bankers from Merrill, Lynch represented Southland's suitor, Ito-Yokado. When the committee hammered on the company to explain the discrepancy in the November and March sets of cash flow projections, Southland said its view of the industry's prospects had changed to a less sanguine one. "We didn't believe any of that," sniffs Kidder, Peabody's Casey. As far as Kidder and the steering committee were concerned, the company was worth more than the company indicated and bondholders should, therefore, get a larger recovery. And, by the way, they should also get a big helping from what the exchange offer put on the Thompsons' plate.

Lingering on this theme, Gordon introduced the concept of the ice cream cone to illustrate the principle of rank in bankruptcy. Like the scoop at the top, the fattest recovery goes to the most senior securities, and like the bit melted into the bottom tip of the cone, the least amount of recovery goes to the last-ranked securities—namely, the common stock. In Southland's restructuring proposal, Gordon pointed out, these roles were reversed. "But, the Thompsons are equity," he told Matthews, Moelis, and Philip Bowers of Merrill, Lynch. "They're at the bottom, so they're the tip of the ice cream cone. If you present to me a restructuring proposal where I can visualize an ice cream cone with those guys at the bottom, I'm going to be willing to at least seriously consider it and probably endorse it." Southland's advisers dismissed that argument, countering that the family created the company in the first place and has considerable expertise in the convenience store business. Besides, the Thompsons had brought Ito-Yokado and its money into the picture. If they did not get a good deal, the Japanese would pack up their money and go home. Gordon was unyielding. His cool response: "I've already lost enough money and the other bondholders have already lost enough money [the market price had gone down] so that frankly the incremental amount to be lost [if they were to leave] isn't that great, and therefore, I much prefer to deal with intangible issues of principle like fairness. And if there's no fairness, there's no deal."

Finally, the bondholders said that there was no way that a restructuring could get done without a prepackaged bankruptcy. Varughese and Casey had only recently finished advising Republic Health Corporation, an acute-care hospital company, in the first prepackaged bankruptcy of a company with multiple layers of debt, and they saw no reason why Southland couldn't do the same. What's more, Varughese had recently flown to Tokyo to meet with Ito-Yokado senior officials and asked them whether they would agree to do a prepack if Southland and the other parties agreed to do one first. As Varughese reported: "The answer from them was, if the company and its advisers agree, we don't have a problem with it." But the company refused to consider it.

The steering committee, however, was certain that the required 95 percent of bondholders would not accept the exchange offer. And at that first meeting it told the company straight out that if management lowered the requirement just to complete the deal, it would not recommend that the bondholders swap their holdings. Lowering the hurdle would only fix the company temporarily. And even worse to the committee members, it would allow bondholders who held onto their bonds to receive a windfall at the expense of those who made a sacrifice by exchanging them. So the steering committee concluded that the company should do a prepack because the exchange offer would fail and the only alternative would be a long and deep bankruptcy. "We said ninety-five or prepackaged," recounts committee member Kenneth Urbaszewski.

The company soon realized that the negotiations needed a

jump start. Just before the June 15 interest payment deadline, Bowers, the Merrill, Lynch investment banker who was advising Ito-Yokado, called a meeting of all bondholder representatives in New York to explain the desperate nature of the company's situation. Then he hopped on a plane to Tokyo and persuaded his clients to allow Southland to offer a better deal to the bondholders. On June 14, the company announced a revision of the exchange offer that would fatten the bondholders' take by $200 million in the form of new, cash-paying bonds and an 8.5 percent slice of equity taken from the Thompsons, whose stake would shrink from 15 percent to a mere 6.5 percent. "We didn't have anyone's agreement that if we bumped up the price, they would sign onto the deal," says Bowers. "But we had put on some cat-and-mouse game in New York where we had acted really depressed and soul searched." Yet, the bondholders' committee still wanted more.

PUSHING THE PREPACK

As the days wore on, the committee kept up the pressure to do a prepack. And other vulture investors began to join in. Whitman was not the only one who believed a prepackaged bankruptcy was the best way for this restructuring to go. James Bennett also thought the proposed exchange offer was dead on arrival without a controlled bankruptcy. Bennett was formerly the CEO of the vulture brokerage firm R. D. Smith & Company who had gone back to sales the year before, in 1989, so that he could have the time and flexibility to set up a vulture investing fund. His Restructuring Fund had been buying junior-level Southland bonds since December 1989. Between his fund and R. D. Smith's brokerage customers, Bennett spoke for investors representing more than 5 percent of one issue of Southland junior bonds. "We knew it was going to be one of those knockdown battles to get the bonds [exchanged] and ultimately the deal wouldn't get done in an exchange offer format," he says. Arguing for a prepackaged plan, he was told only that Ito-Yokado would never consent, given the Japanese aversion to bankruptcy of any kind. As time passed and Southland's advisers continued to demur, however, he began to understand from what they were saying that they were not absolutely rejecting the idea. He surmised that their public repudiation of a prepackaged bankruptcy was meant to reassure suppliers who were extending credit to Southland businesses. Just to make sure they would not rule it out, Bennett told them that he and R. D. Smith's customers were not going to go along with an exchange offer. They would not surrender their bonds.

The July 16 deadline was fast approaching. Over the latter half of June and first week of July, the interchange of proposals and counterproposals continued like an endless point in a tennis match until the final days were at hand. By the week of July 9, DLJ's Moelis believed he finally had worked out the framework for an agreement with the bondholders' committee on an exchange offer. Higher principal amounts on their bonds and another 6.5 percent in equity—for a total of 25 percent—resulting from a cut in the Thompsons' stake to 5 percent and Ito-Yokado's to 70 percent, gave them something they could live with. At Deltec's offices, Moelis and Southland's CFO Matthews sat with Gordon at a round glass table overlooking the East Side and reviewed the new package. "Now do you see the ice cream cone?" Moelis asked Gordon. "Yes"—he smiled at the reference to his own metaphor—"now, I see the ice cream cone." What remained was the matter of dividing the spoils among the different classes of bonds. In their discussions, they were circling around forty-five cents on the dollar in cash, stock and bonds for the seniors and thirty to forty cents for the juniors in stock and bonds.

COMBINING FORCES

But Whitman was not happy with these numbers. "These are crazy exchange offers," he said. In his view, the seniors deserved much more, and he invited the company over to hear him out on Wednesday, July 11. Before the meeting he decided that he wanted to be speaking on behalf of half the senior bonds—or at least give the impression of doing so. Why was he worrying about a 50 percent position when anything more than 5 percent would have been plenty to block an exchange offer requiring 95 percent approval? According to the terms of the senior notes he owned, a majority of the holders could reduce the rank of any of those voting against an exchange offer. "With more than fifty percent, there was no way you could get screwed," says Whitman's partner Jim Heffernan. Adds Whitman, "I wanted mathematical certainty."

He wanted to join forces with another major bondholder, namely Carl Icahn. Icahn owned about 34 percent of the senior bonds that had captivated Whitman; together they would control more than 60 percent. The day before the scheduled session with Southland, Whitman happened to be attending a meeting at TWA headquarters. He was wearing his investment banker's hat as the financial adviser to the TWA pilots union during particularly contentious discussions with Icahn. After that meeting, Whitman asked Icahn for his help in the Southland situation.

"I want to talk about a position we both own," Whitman said.

Treating this as a game, Icahn tried to guess. He grinned, then took out pen and paper and scribbled, "Leaseway," referring to Leaseway Transportation Corporation, an Ohio trucking concern then involved in an effort to restructure its debt.

Whitman shook his head. "No, Southland. I'm meeting with the management tomorrow. I'm going to hold out for seventy cents." They talked a bit. Icahn said he was concerned that a higher recovery for the senior debt would eat into the recovery due to go to the junior bonds he held. But he wasn't really all that worried, because the bulk of his holdings was in seniors.

Icahn walked Whitman down the stairway and out to the parking lot. "You can't tie up my bonds," said the gravel-voiced Whitman, implying that if Icahn didn't let him speak for half the bonds he would be powerless.

Icahn gave Whitman the go-ahead to demand seventy cents. But he asked that Whitman not mention his name at the meeting.

The meeting the next day convened on Whitman's turf, a fifth-floor suite of offices on the corner of Third Avenue and Forty-eighth Street in midtown Manhattan. The office is decorated in what could be called liquidation-modern: utilitarian, none-too-comfortable gray and black chairs, a drab wood conference room table, a few simple black-stained bookcases, here and there a droopy palm plant. The only splashes of color in the place are the Garudas—statues representing Balinese gods that are grotesque fusions of man and vulture painted in vivid strokes of gold, blue, and red. Standing about two and a half feet tall, the figures appear to be personifications of horrific ferocity with their two-inch fingernails, horned feet, curved open beaks and long spines fanning out from their shoulders. Acquired in Bali in 1987 while Whitman was visiting his son Tom, who was studying Indonesian music on a fellowship, the Garudas appear to be strategically placed throughout the offices. One greets visitors in the reception area, another occupies a corner in Whitman's office, and two glare at a conference table—presumably for inspiration of the whole group.

Whitman and his partner Heffernan, Matthews, Moelis, and Bowers huddled around that conference table during an amiable, four-hour discussion. The two vulture investors started by telling their guests that they would never get the required percentage to vote for the exchange offer and instead should go for a prepack. Says Whitman, "We told them, 'You've gotta go prepackaged. Watchyer doin' isn't gonna work.' They told us that Chapter 11 was impossible." Moelis and Bowers insisted that the Japanese would never go for it.

Getting back to the exchange offer, Whitman set down the price that he would accept—seventy cents, not the proposed forty-five cents. "I'm in touch with over half of the bonds," Whitman told them without mentioning Icahn's name. Of course, the company knew about Icahn's substantial position in the senior bonds, and Moelis assumed that he and Whitman were allies.

As far as where the company got the extra twenty-five cents, Whitman and Heffernan didn't care if it came out of the hides of Ito-Yokado or the junior bondholders. Together, the investment bankers Moelis and Bowers went through the numbers. The bottom line was, if the seniors took seventy cents, the whole deal would come up $30 million short. It looked as if the junior holders would have to take a big hit to accommodate those ranked above them.

DIALING FOR DOLLARS

Thursday afternoon, July 12, Moelis phoned the bondholder's steering committee to alert them to Whitman's demands. The committee members had been meeting all day and had decided that the recovery they had tentatively agreed to the week before was still not enough. So when Moelis called with his news, they were none too receptive.

"We're $30 million short," Moelis reported. And because Ito-Yokado had given all it had to give, that left one alternative: to take something from the four levels of junior bonds and give to the senior bonds. Moelis thought $3 a bond would do the trick—3 cents on the dollar—there being many more junior than senior bonds. The major senior holders appeared to have the holders of the lower classes over a barrel. They had the clout to take the case into bankruptcy by rejecting the exchange offer, and under the bankruptcy code they would be entitled to receive 100 cents on the dollar before any junior bondholder saw a cent. Now, without resorting to bankruptcy court, they were willing to take only 70 cents and give the juniors something.

The bondholders' committee scoffed at this prospect. Gordon, for one, was annoyed with the seniors' stubborn position. What irked him most was the fact that the senior bonds existed only because of the exchange offer the Thompsons performed in 1989 whereby holders of its most junior security were given these new senior bonds. To Gordon and others, the senior class had unfairly leapfrogged over all the others. The response they had to the bankruptcy argument was, he says, "If you want to get into a bankruptcy context, we will guarantee to you that the first issue that's going to get litigated is whether that new senior bond shouldn't be put back at the end of the line again."

Besides, the committee said that it wanted more money for all of the debt classes, which it would then divide up as it saw fit. As one committee member recounts, Moelis asked, "How much more do you want?"

"One hundred twenty million dollars," replied the committee member.

"Fuck you," snapped Moelis.

"For one hundred and twenty million you can fuck me all you want," the other replied.

Kidder, Peabody called Bowers and told him to inform his Japanese client that the bondholders still were not satisfied. To Moelis, these demands were not all that surprising; the bondholders were testing the limits of the Japanese. During the weeks of wrangling, Ito-Yokado officers stayed in Japan, negotiating by phone through Merrill, Lynch. To Gordon and others, this gave the Japanese the upper hand, whether intended or not. "When you meet somebody face to face you can get an appreciation for how interested they are in doing a transaction," he says. "Here it was just 'the Japanese' six thousand miles away and twelve hours time difference away so that there was this mysterious quality to it." Ito-Yokado had already given up some equity. The issue was, how far were they willing to reduce their percentage ownership and increase the take for the bondholders?

Thursday night Moelis and Bowers decided to give the Japanese a try after all. They placed a call, explained their dilemma, and in the end got what they were looking for. If everyone signed onto a deal, Ito-Yokado would agree to plug the $30 million gap. Next, Moelis and Bowers divided up the $30 million so that the senior holders got the bulk of it, but the juniors got a little too. The seniors would then end up with sixty-one cents on the dollar—not the seventy cents Whitman wanted, but much more than originally had been offered. Moelis and Bowers decided not to tell the bondholders' committee for now. They weren't going to reveal the extra $30 million until the seniors signed onto the deal first, because without them there would be no deal.

Friday morning, July 13, Moelis took care of that. On a conference call, he hooked up the three largest holders of senior bonds, Icahn, Heffernan, and Kemper Corp.'s Urbaszewski, who was the only committee member with a substantial stash of senior bonds. "If I can get thirty million dollars out of Japan, is it done?" Moelis posed to the trio. They talked for a while. That being the day the stock market cracked the 3000 mark, Icahn was on and off the call throughout the conversation as he tracked the market and the high-flying airline stocks. As Urbaszewski recalls, Icahn's bottom line was, "If it's okay with Heffernan and with you, it's okay for me." All appeared to be in agreement, and the Japanese came through, raising their contribution from $400 million to $430 million.

The process makes an important point about the power of the vultures. "There are a lot of good things and bad things about dealing with people like Carl and Marty," Bowers says. "The good part about them is you've got a guy who owns a large slug of bonds, so you can talk to him. You know who he is, you can sit down with him, you can meet with him, you can go over stuff with him, you can show him why what you're offering or what you're willing to offer is a better deal than he'll get in bankruptcy or a better deal than he'll get from anyone else. The bad part about it is you know that to get him to agree you're going to have to pay top dollar, whereas if you had a bunch of small bondholders, they would probably settle at something less than top dollar. But you could never reach them all, you could never find them to sit down and talk to them. And they would lack the sophistication to know the nuances of what would happen in bankruptcy and what would happen in terms of the market for the paper that we would be giving out. [The vultures] know what the market value is, so they know how to value the offer. So it's definitely a two-edged sword. In my opinion, it's better to know who your opponent is. In this case they actually helped."

After tying things up with the senior holders, Moelis and Bowers met the committee at Ito-Yokado counsel Shearman & Sterling law firm offices to reveal what they had accomplished: the $30 million boost in value and the distribution. The committee was not pleased to hear about the behind-their-back negotiations that had gone on. Gordon and some of the other members went into another conference room to let off steam. "We were astonished as to what was going on," Gordon says. "They were negotiating a deal with the bondholder community, and they went around the steering committee." A few revealed long-held suspicions they'd harbored about Ken Moelis, because he'd come from Drexel, Burnham, Lambert, the firm that had fallen after pleading guilty to insider trading in the junk bond market. But in the end, the committee bought the deal, and in fact, later some actually praised Moelis for putting it in place. There was one more item the bondholders insisted on, however. They wanted SEC documents prepared for a prepackaged bankruptcy in case the exchange offer failed. The committee remained certain that the company would not get 95 percent of the bondholders to swap their bonds and that bankruptcy was inevitable. But Southland continued to insist that the exchange would work and that the Japanese considered bankruptcy, prepackaged or not, simply out of the question. "Moelis was saying ninety-five percent was doable," says Casey. "It was a lie. Even novice investors understood the enormous economic incentive of holding out." Furthermore, Varughese himself had heard the Ito-Yokado officials say that if Southland opted to go with a prepack, they would not stand in the way.

But even today Moelis insists that 95 percent approval was feasible, for two reasons. First of all, there was no other choice. "The company believed the Japanese might not buy the company if it went into Chapter 11," he says. And second, the industry was pointing in a downward direction. "I thought this deal was one of the best recoveries ever," he maintains. "It was doable if people understood the downside of not doing it."

As for Bowers, he believed all along that the exchange offer was doomed to fail. And he also believed that the Japanese were not the chief stumbling block to a prepack. Back in March, when the company was devising its restructuring strategy, management told its advisers that it could not do a prepackaged deal because suppliers and other business associates would flee at the sight of a Chapter 11 filing. "We operated under the assumption for a long period of time that we weren't going to try it because *the company* didn't want to try it," says Bowers. But the Japanese's well-known aversion to bankruptcy "was a convenient excuse to give the bondholders." If there ever was a prayer of completing the exchange offer, this argument could help convince the bondholders that bankruptcy was not an alternative. But Bowers was almost certain that it would work and large numbers of holdouts would make a prepack the preferred option. "We thought that it would become clear in the end that the company would have to do it," Bowers says. With that in mind, he began educating Ito-Yokado about prepackaged bankruptcy early on, because if and when the company said go to a prepack, the big Japanese equity investor would have to sign on the next instant.

By mid-July, neither Southland management nor the Japanese were yet convinced. But the company's advisers decided to heed the bondholders' demands for the preparation of SEC documents for a prepack anyway. "That helped the steering committee have the confidence to agree to the economic terms that we put in the exchange offer at that point in time," says Bowers. "We didn't have agreement at that point in time from the Japanese or the company to have been able to use it, but we said that we'd work on it. We would prepare it in case we'd ever have to use it." It was late Friday—the thirteenth. Moelis boarded a flight to return to his home in California, and everyone else left the law office, leaving the attorneys to draw up the agreement by Monday morning.

UP-TO-THE-LAST-MINUTE SUSPENSE

Over the weekend the steering committee had second thoughts. The members met with Merrill, Lynch representatives in a large conference room at Shearman & Sterling. Still not sure that the deal was fair, the committee wanted to study the numbers further. On Sunday, committee advisors Varughese and Casey concluded that they could not balance all of the different interests and demanded that Merrill, Lynch deliver more to the first level of junior bonds by way of a sinking fund—which is an accelerated payment of interest—and also modify some covenants (the terms of the new bonds).

Now everyone had to pace the floor while Bowers called his Japanese clients for yet another request. Early Sunday evening, Bowers reemerged to announce that the Japanese had reached their limit. They would not grant the sinking fund payment or the covenant modifications. There was no more to discuss. The committee's advisers, Casey and Jim Spiotto, then had it out with Southland's Clark Matthews, Bowers, and Dan Turk, a Merrill, Lynch managing director from the Tokyo office. "It was probably the most hostile conversation we had during the case, a yelling match," Casey recalls. "I said, 'You're willing to walk away from a three billion dollar [his value for the company] deal for a lousy twenty-five million sinking fund payment? I'm going to go back and tell the committee to hold their ground. I don't believe the company can't afford it.'" Matthews responded by instructing all of the company's attorneys and investment bankers to go home, and then he went back to his hotel. Says Bowers: "I went home knowing the

phone would start ringing at around nine o'clock and that hopefully we could patch something together."

It took a bit longer than that. Casey and Spiotto stayed on a
while to confer with their clients. "Do you want to risk putting
Southland in bankruptcy?" the advisers asked the committee. The
members agreed that they did not, but that they would let the
company and its advisors stew a few hours. At around midnight,
everyone went home or back to their hotels. There was a flurry of
phone calls. In California, Moelis heard that the meeting had
broken up. Thinking that any lapse in the momentum could be
disastrous, he felt determined to get the negotiations back on track
as soon as possible. He called Bowers. Bowers then spoke with
George Varughese, who said, "If somehow I took care of the
covenants that you don't like, would you agree to the sinking
fund?" Bowers said yes, and they agreed that if the Japanese provided the sinking fund there would be a deal. Bowers then called
Ito-Yokado in Tokyo, where it was Monday morning, and got the
go-ahead. But what about Moelis, who said the company didn't
want to pay the sinking fund? Varughese played a little trick on
him. He called and said, "If somehow I got rid of the sinking fund
you don't like, would you agree to the covenants?" And Moelis
said yes. So the advisers to Ito-Yokado and Southland agreed to
get back together with the committee's advisers to work out the
details, not knowing that Varughese had promised two different
things to them.

It was two A.M., Monday, July 16. Moelis and Bowers phoned
all of the advisers and told them to get back to the Shearman &
Sterling office at once so as to make sure to get the agreement down
in ink by the deadline, which was now nine hours away. Someone
went out to get coffee and donuts. Spiotto was furious for having
to come into the office in the middle of the night. In the room were
four Shearman & Sterling lawyers, four Skadden, Arps lawyers,
three Chapman and Cutler lawyers, a couple of commercial bank
lawyers, Matthews, Bowers, Varughese, Casey, and a representative of DLJ. Moelis was on a speaker phone and when the parties
split up to discuss specific issues, he had three lines going at once—
one to Southland, one to the bondholders, and one to Bowers.
Varughese's deception worked. The group worked through the

covenants item by item for five hours, and by the time they got to the sinking fund issue they didn't have enough energy left to debate it for long. "I knew that neither point was so important that they would break a deal over it," Varughese boasts. "I knew that in a rational moment they would know it too."

Committee chairman John Gordon had gone to bed Sunday night, leaving the details to be worked out by the various company and committee advisers. The last he knew, Bowers was going to call the difficult and mysterious Ito-Yokado about the committee's latest request. The next morning, he rode in on an early train. "As I was coming in I had no idea whether there was an agreement or not, because they'd had to go back to the Japanese one last time. So I got in here at eight o'clock and still didn't know." He went over to the law firm offices where everyone had been meeting and found the exhausted group winding up a final agreement.

PREPACKAGED, FINALLY

Over the next two months, the scenario that Whitman, Gordon, the Restructuring Fund's Bennett, Bowers, and others had envisioned finally came to pass. The company tried to get 95 percent approval of the exchange offer three times. Each time, Icahn, Whitman, and the committee members supported the plan and even lobbied other bondholders to vote in favor. But to no avail. Many bondholders held out. When solicited, some even denied that they held any bonds so they would not be bothered. The company extended the mid-August voting deadline to August 23; when the vote fell short, management extended the deadline again to September 12; failing miserably, it extended the deadline a third time, to September 25. The repeated failures and the looming specter of bankruptcy began to weigh on Ito-Yokado's stock at home in Japan. Bondholders began to fear that the Japanese retailers would back out of their purchase agreement.

Meanwhile, Southland's finances were rapidly deteriorating. Since March, the company had lost $180 million in trade credit as suppliers became skittish about the company's prospects. Management raised cash by selling off planes, closing its aviation department, and borrowing $25 million from Ito-Yokado—but it had no luck selling the monstrous Cityplace Center development adjacent to its headquarters in downtown Dallas, now complete. By the end of September internal forecasts indicated that Southland's cash reservoir would be sand dry by the end of October. "We didn't know where we would get any additional cash," CFO Matthews later testified in court. Reaching the point of desperation, on October 22 the company presented the bondholders with a plan consisting of two parts—a yes or no on the exchange offer and then a yes or no on a prepackaged bankruptcy, each with the exact same financial terms. The exchange offer lost again, but the option for a prepackaged bankruptcy passed.

Votes in hand, the company and its Japanese acquirer agreed to stop trying for the exchange offer and to resort to a controlled bankruptcy—with conditions. The reorganization would have to be signed and sealed by the end of March 1991. And if war broke out or the Dow Jones Industrial Average or the Nikkei Average declined by 25 percent, Ito-Yokado could abandon the deal. These were hardly far-fetched notions. In October 1990, Operation Desert Shield was in full gear and oil prices were spurting through the roof. If war erupted, the markets were sure to cower. Creditors could only cross their fingers and wait for the confirmation hearing on the reorganization plan, scheduled for December 14 before Judge Harold Abramson in Dallas.

A BIG THREAT FROM SMALL-TIME VULTURES

Vulture investors can be big and powerful like Marty Whitman or Carl Icahn or they can be small and powerful. The small-timers most often exercise their influence by edging their way onto creditors' committees. Or they file litigation that delays a reorganization indefinitely, prompting other parties to throw them a morsel just so they'll go away. It's even conceivable that these vultures will win over enough support to gain control of the vote on a reorganization plan. After all, the required acceptance is two-thirds in amount *and one-half in number* of those voting. These vultures know what they are doing, and in Southland they crept up and began to unravel the neat package the company and its major bondholders had so painstakingly wrapped and tied.

The group was led by David Glatstein, president of the Dallas-based securities firm Barre & Company, who had always recommended high quality bonds until January 1990. "We'd been watching the high-yield bond market through the last decade," he says. The first month of the new one he decided to take a chance on Southland's very low quality bonds. Between itself and its customers, Barre & Company spoke for some $30 million worth of junior-level bonds. In Glatstein's opinion, when Southland filed its prepack bankruptcy the Thompsons were still getting too much out of the deal, even though their stake had been whittled down from 15 percent in the original exchange offer to 5 percent. Some individual investors agreed. One of them was Anthony Ben Walsh, a headstrong New York investor in his seventies. Walsh—who walks with a severe limp as a result of a skiing accident years before in which he was buried by an avalanche—had made a career out of playing the gadfly in bankruptcies. He was notorious for buying small amounts of debt, getting himself appointed to creditors' committees, and then holding fast to his demands.

The dissidents wanted to be appointed to the official Chapter 11 creditors' committee, but the U.S. Trustee decided simply to turn the prebankruptcy bondholders' committee into the official Chapter 11 creditors' committee. Undeterred, the dissidents declared the formation of an "unofficial" committee of five co-chaired by Glatstein and Walsh. Another well-known bankruptcy agitator, Howard Leppla, an amiable, bow-tied investor from Minnesota, was not on the committee but was a vociferous supporter of it and frequented Southland proceedings. Because the court would not recognize their official status as a negotiating party, the dissenters' chief tactic would be to throw tacks under the wheels of the prepackaged plan. The weapon they hurled was a claim that Southland had not followed proper procedure in soliciting votes. In late November, the dissidents went to court and filed a formal objection to the confirmation of the prepackaged plan and began an intensive investigation that included an examination of ballots and depositions of several witnesses.

Among the unofficial committee's complaints: the solicitation materials were confusing (they measured 16 by 33 inches and were described in hearings as a "tablecloth"); the company did not give creditors sufficient time to vote (eight business days); it did not count the votes of bondholders whose bonds were held in the name of a trustee bank but counted only the vote of the trustee; and errors were made in the tabulation of votes including ballots that were not counted. Addressing the plan itself, the unofficial committee griped that it did not adequately pay bondholders and awarded too much to stockholders—namely, the Thompsons. All of these points turned up as objections to the plan's passage at the hearing for plan confirmation commencing on December 14. Two weeks later, Judge Abramson, who throughout his career has championed the causes of small investors in corporate affairs, disqualified the vote that had approved the prepack back in October, and he ordered that a new vote be held. "I'm not going to have a case where we have a few playing God and deciding what's best for everyone," he asserted in court. Suddenly, the entire plan was in jeopardy. If the revote delayed the reorganization past mid-March, the Japanese would be able to withdraw their commitment.

In the market, Sothland's bonds had been cascading as the balloting issue threatened to undo this unprecedentedly large prepackaged bankruptcy. At the end of December and in the first part of January 1991 the bonds hit a low of eleven cents on the dollar. At the Restructuring Fund, Jim Bennett added to his position, but knew that he was taking a risk. "I was really concerned because if this thing got derailed at this point in time I was in trouble. If it worked, all our valuation analysis said it was worth twenty-five cents on the dollar."

By January 12, the revised voting materials were set. At the same time, however, the judge approved the dissidents' draft of a letter to be sent out along with the ballots, urging creditors to reject the plan. Although the company easily had the vote of two-thirds in amount of claims in each class, the dissenters hoped to recruit enough negative votes to block the plan under the requirement that a majority of creditors in each class vote in favor. The company and the other creditors, meanwhile, were pulling out their hair. "This is all going on in the context of the stock market going down and everyone being concerned about Iraq," Gordon says. "So it was extraordinarily upsetting. From October through the middle of January the dissidents engaged in what I would call guerilla warfare trying to change the restructuring package."

The voting materials *and the dissidents' letter* were to be mailed out at five P.M. Tuesday, January 22. The week before, from his office in Los Angeles, Ken Moelis began scrambling to negotiate. He called Peter Wolfson, the unofficial committee's chief attorney. "Why don't we sit down?" he offered. Wolfson said the dissenters wanted $100 million more. "Absurd," replied Moelis. So Wolfson suggested Moelis call dissident leader Ben Walsh and negotiate directly with him. He did, and the next day, Thursday the seventeenth, Walsh and his wife came to town. The three had dinner at The Bistro—one of Beverly Hills's primary power dining spots. There, Moelis discovered that what Walsh really wanted was to get bonds that had a higher yield and lower principal value because they would be easy to trade in the market. It was eleven P.M. when Moelis left Walsh. He then called an associate and got him out of bed to do the calculations.

The next day he called the committee's advisers, Icahn, and Heffernan. "We're starting down toward settlement," he told Heffernan and asked him what he thought of the idea of adjusting the principal and interest on some of the bonds. Heffernan laughed: "If you had to call me to ask me that, I have lost some respect for you."

Soon, however, Moelis heard from Walsh's co-chairman Glatstein, who did not like the deal that the two men had cut. He wanted stock warrants thrown in for all bondholders that would be taken from the Thompsons' 5 percent stake. When Moelis informed the official bondholders' committee of this demand, its advisers responded that instead of warrants, the bondholders wanted more stock outright. But that would increase the overall cost of the restructuring. Moelis was outraged. "This is not a retrade of the deal," he objected. "This is to settle." Friday night, January 18, Moelis spoke with Bowers about the two changes the unofficial committee was requesting, but Bowers refused to take any changes to his clients in Japan. What at first seemed like two minor adjustments was turning into a major problem.

Saturday morning, January 19, Moelis called Clark Matthews. Matthews had heard from Bowers and had told him that he was still not intending to bring the latest changes to the Japanese for their approval. Furious, Moelis phoned Bowers and threatened to fly to Japan with Matthews and take the deal to Ito-Yokado themselves. Bowers hung up on him and went away for the weekend.

Moelis was on the phone almost nonstop from Friday night through Sunday negotiating with the various constituencies. The New York native did manage to watch the final New York Giants and San Francisco 49ers' league playoff game out of one eye, however—although it affected his negotiating somewhat. Just after one bad play by the Giants, Jim Spiotto, the creditors' committee attorney, called.

"You've got to give us the stock, not the warrants," he insisted.

"Jim, that's a total retrade," Moelis steamed. "You can't do this to us. We're in this to settle, not to retrade the deal. You want stock, you call the Thompsons. If you get it, great."

Spiotto paused before responding. "Ken, are the Giants losing?"

"Yeah."

"Fine. I'll talk to you later." And he hung up.

During the last ten minutes of the game, the Giants were behind thirteen to twelve, a mere two points away from the Super Bowl. The 49ers had the ball. With five minutes and forty-seven seconds left to play, the Giants' Erik Howard knocked the ball from the arms of opponent Roger Craig. Then the Giants' defensive linebacker Lawrence Taylor swooped in to pick it up and ran down the field until he was stopped at the forty-three yard line. In the final three minutes of the game, the Giants drove down the field. And at the twenty-four yard line with four seconds remaining, Matt Bahr tried for his fifth field goal of the day. Moelis was talking on three lines with Matthews and two others, and he put everyone on hold for the kick. Bahr cleared the goalposts, lifting the Giants to a fifteen to twelve victory.

That night, Moelis got the bondholders' committee on the phone and told them that there would be no more stock given out, only warrants. They agreed.

Monday morning, Moelis called Bowers and explained that the new deal did not add a cent. Would he call Japan? "Either you're calling or we're calling," he said.

Bowers talked to his client that day and then got back to Moelis. "They'll do it. But we need everybody signed up." So, they

scrambled to get the members of the official and unofficial committees and Whitman and Icahn to sign a document detailing the
agreement. On Tuesday, even as the ballots—*without* the unofficial
committee's hostile letter attached—were heading to the post office
in a truck, they finally got the last signatures.

The deal was struck. Bondholders would receive stock warrants—the right for five years to buy half of the Thompsons' stock
at $1.75 a share, potentially reducing the founding family's stake to
only 2.5 percent. Also, all of the bondholders in the classes the
dissidents were in would be able to choose between a high-value,
low-interest bond and a high-yield, low-principal value bond that
would be easier to trade. Two of the dissidents' attorneys appeared
on the business page of the *Dallas Morning News* toasting their
victory with 7-Eleven Big Gulp℠ cups. The small-time vultures
had had leverage, Gordon says, "because we were trying to do a
prepackaged bankruptcy which had never been done before with
such a big company. The whole reason for a prepackaged bankruptcy is to have things move quickly, so we were trying to get
things done in a couple of months. We hoped to be out of bankruptcy by the end of 1990, and because of the dissidents we had to
add another two and a half months."

Votes had to be in by mid-February. Before then, of course,
fighting did break out in the Middle East, giving Ito-Yokado the
chance to take their money and run. But the successful first-day
bombing strikes buoyed the markets, and Ito-Yokado stuck with
the deal. Southland creditors overwhelmingly approved the reorganization plan, and in March, the company emerged from bankruptcy after a stay of less than five months.

Deltec came out victorious in its effort to get what it felt was the
fairest deal for the creditors in the shortest amount of time. But the
vulture firm only broke even on its investment—and barely at that.
"I'd say the main reason is that we misappreciated the values
inherent in the business," Gordon reflects, his eyes averting for a
millisecond. "I misappreciated either the willingness or the capability of the Thompsons to cut costs. I honestly still think the values
are there, it's just that the Japanese are going to get the benefit of
them." For Gordon himself, however, the redeeming value of

Southland was in the experience of taking an active role in the turnaround. "It was a huge drain on my personal time," he says. "It took twenty percent at least for close to a year, so I wouldn't want to do a lot more of it. I'm very satisfied that I was able to have a part in the rehabilitation of a big company."

Bennett, the R. D. Smith salesman and manager of the Restructuring Fund, nearly tripled his investment in a year, from an average cost of 13.1 cents on the dollar to 30 cents when he sold out. "I focused on the junior bonds. A lot of people focused on the senior bonds. They were safer. The difference and the distinguishing factor was I thought the deal would get done and go through, and it wouldn't go into an uncontrolled bankruptcy. I was taking a fairly big risk in the juniors if the deal fell apart; instead of an average cost of thirteen point one it may still be in bankruptcy today and probably wouldn't be worth much more than that." Later in 1991, Bennett split off from R. D. Smith to avoid any conflicts of interest with the brokerage firm and renamed the fund the Bennett Restructuring Fund.

Whitman reaped a 74 percent return on his group's money in under two years. Over time after the reorganization, the returns on Icahn's investment surpassed 90 percent as the bonds and the 20.9 million shares of stock he received (a 5.1 percent stake in the convenience store chain) appreciated in value. By the start of 1992, his dollar profit was none too shabby at about $120 million. But as with most bankruptcies, those who were original bondholders sustained big losses in the value of their securities and did not receive much equity to ease the pain.

The Thompsons, meanwhile, ended up with virtually nothing. The pressure applied by the bondholders shrank the founding family's stake in the company their father brought out of bankruptcy down to a mere 2.5 percent and removed them from their management posts. Clark Matthews took the helm from them. As a rather hefty consolation prize, John and Jere Thompson became co-vice chairmen of the board and Ito-Yokado would furnish each with $960,000 in annual salary including $360,000 in bonuses for five years. Their brother Jodie would keep his directorship, and all three Thompsons received a $60 million interest-free loan from their Japanese saviors.

The greatest beneficiary of a prepackaged plan is the company itself. By doing the bankruptcy quickly, Southland avoided the usual megasize bills from lawyers, investment bankers, and accountants that show up at the end of a regular bankruptcy. And with the abbreviated process, Ito-Yokado's cash infusion began sprucing up the company's 6700 remaining 7-Eleven stores all the sooner. For the first nine months of 1991, Southland earned $117 million compared with a $278 million loss the year earlier. Yet as a result of the recession and bad times in the convenience store business, in the fourth quarter, earnings were running about $20 million short of what management had projected in the reorganization plan. Analysts say Southland (now part of Ito-Yokado) lost $54 million in 1991. In late 1992, they were estimating that year's loss at $47 million and projecting a profit for 1993.) Perhaps the company had been right back in March of 1990 when it scaled back its projections—although the bondholders' committee's advisers thought otherwise at the time. Perhaps Southland paid creditors too much. Then again, it was a recession, and Ito-Yokado had been spending money burnishing its stores for a payback in a few years. So it was too early to tell whether this was the rough beginnings of the company's third lifetime or its end, doomed from the start by an overly expensive restructuring. But it was certainly a milestone as the biggest and the best example to date of how vultures teamed up with a company and its creditors to accomplish a prepackaged bankruptcy.

10

Surviving at the Bottom

In life my spirit never roved beyond the narrow limits of our money-changing hole; and weary journeys lie before me!

—*JACOB MARLEY*

In business, one man's catastrophe is often another's opportunity.

—*DONALD TRUMP, SURVIVING AT THE TOP*

Donald Trump can thank vulture investors for saving his casinos. In the summer of 1990, things looked bleak indeed for the flamboyant prince of New York real estate. His empire of hotels, towers, casinos, airlines, and property, assembled during the Easy Money Decade, appeared to be swiftly heading the way of Rome. The tale was a familiar one: a company carrying heavy debt ravaged by a poor economy. Trump had more than $3 billion in debt to service at a time when the real estate and Atlantic City gambling markets were in the tank and the financial markets were closing their doors to high-risk borrowers. There were also trou-

bling questions about the enduring strength of the Trump name—
part of the currency that built the vast company—given his financial problems and his widely publicized breakup with his wife,
Ivana, and an affair with Marla Maples. All of this added up to a
crying need for cash. As "The Donald" himself then proclaimed:
"Cash is king."

Earlier that year, the king of self-aggrandizement had thrown
himself into a desperate search for cash throughout his realm. He
refinanced his first mark on the Manhattan skyline, the thirty-two-
story Grand Hyatt hotel built above Grand Central Terminal. He
also refinanced the Trump Tower, his Fifth Avenue showcase condominium and retailing complex where he himself lived in a fifty-
room apartment. And, he began looking around for someone to
buy the Trump Shuttle, which threaded among New York, Boston,
and Washington. But the shuttle didn't sell, the cash wasn't coming
in, and Trump's banks were starting to become downright edgy.

That spring of 1990 Trump, the author of *The Art of the Deal*
who was then working on the sequel *Surviving at the Top,* began to
seem like someone who would benefit from a book titled *The Art
of Making a Deal to Survive the Fall.* He initiated frantic negotiations with his bank lenders—ninety in all—to refinance his $2
billion in bank debt and avoid a bankruptcy filing. By the end of
June, they reached agreement. The banks would defer interest
payments and lend Trump $20 million and then $65 million over
five years; the $20 million allowed him to make a $43 million
payment to Trump Castle casino bondholders that was already
late. As part of the bailout, Trump was forced to curtail his personal budget from about $10 million a year, or $850,000 a month,
to a mere $450,000 a month in 1990, reduced to $375,000 a month
in 1991 and $300,000 a month in 1992. But the ink on the bank
accord was barely dry when Trump found himself short of cash to
pay the debt layered atop his casinos.

The Taj Mahal had just opened in April. And while Trump was
caught up in final touches, Atlantic City gambling slowed to a
crawl, and then crawled nearly to a stop. In 1990, Trump's other
two casinos, the Castle and the Plaza, suffered both from the poor
environment and the opening of the Taj, which was siphoning
business from them. The Castle was in particularly bad shape, due

in no small part to the style of its chief manager, Ivana Trump, which included costly redesign of almost 100 suites and a higher-than-average ratio of gambler complimentaries (such as free bus service) to revenues. Plus the casino was carrying more than $350 million in debt on which it owed $41 million a year in interest. Consequently, the Castle lost nearly $7 million in 1989 and would lose $43 million in 1990.

By mid-1990, the economics on the entire Trump trio were simply not working: The cash coming in the door was not enough to make interest and principal payments to lenders who were at the door. The first deadline Trump faced after his bank bailout was October 15, the due date for a $47 million payment to Taj Mahal bondholders. Beyond that loomed deadlines on Castle and Plaza bonds. In July, Trump and his advisers laid tentative plans to ask bondholders to forfeit some of their scheduled interest payments in return for a slice of equity in the gambling houses.

Over the next several months, two vulture investors came to the casinos' rescue—though hardly driven by altruistic notions. Carl Icahn, the arbitrageur of the 1970s and legendary corporate raider-cum-airline owner of the 1980s, agilely got into vulturing just as the economy began to list. He became a Heavyweight investor in Taj Mahal bonds and in a critical moment came to Trump's aid. Meanwhile, over at the Plaza, Fidelity Investments single-handedly staved off the need for a restructuring for a year and in early 1992 became the linchpin in a longer-term revamping. And after some delay, the Castle's bondholders agreed to follow the restructuring model set by the Taj Mahal.

CASH COWS

Donald Trump loves casinos. He once wrote, "I like the scale, which is huge, I like the glamour, and most of all, I like the cash flow." Trump acquired his three New Jersey casinos during the 1980s. The first, built on the Boardwalk with hotelier Holiday Corporation, was called Harrah's at Trump Plaza when it was finished in 1984. The following year, he bought another casino that had just been completed by Barron Hilton, the chairman of the Hilton Hotel Corporation. After the Casino Control Commission denied Hilton a gaming license because of his company's association with a lawyer who had alleged ties to organized crime, Trump offered to buy the new marina casino-hotel for $320 million—even though he had never even stepped inside the building. In June, he opened it as Trump Castle with Ivana Trump in charge of operations.

In 1986, Trump bought Holiday's half of the Harrah's casino and, to no one's surprise, it became the Trump Plaza Hotel and Casino. Now he had two casinos all his own. Lest he let a year go by without acquiring all or part of a gambling establishment, in early 1987 he bid to buy Resorts International from the Crosby family. The first to operate a casino in Atlantic City in 1978, Resorts was then five years and $500 million into the construction of a second casino, a Goliath to be called the Taj Mahal. Delays and the onerous costs of the project had severely damaged the entire corporation and would eventually put it into bankruptcy. The Crosby family awarded Trump controlling interest, in part because they believed he had the staying power to finally finish the Taj Mahal. At the time, Trump thought he could have the Taj in operation by the fall of 1988.

But when he tried to take Resorts private by offering to buy out the stockholders, Trump encountered formidable competition from television tycoon Merv Griffin. In April 1988, the two celebrities agreed to divide up Resorts between them, with Griffin taking the original casino and Trump taking the half-built Taj from him for $273 million. To complete work on his casino-resort masterpiece, Trump raised $675 million via a mammoth November issue of 14 percent bonds, borrowed $50 million from banks, and took $75 million from his own wallet. Now the target opening date was moved to March 1990, although Trump aimed to surprise the world by opening in December 1989.

He then embarked on a mission to make the Taj Mahal the grandest and most dazzling casino-hotel in Atlantic City, and he outdid himself. Featuring three candy-colored onion domes, the Taj is twice as large as its nearest competitor. It is built on seventeen acres, making it, as Trump says, "only a little smaller than the Pentagon." Its 120,000-square-foot gaming floor is the size of three football fields and features 2,900 slot machines and 165 blackjack, roulette, craps, baccarat, and other table games—all illuminated by 5,000-piece Austrian cut-crystal chandeliers purchased for $14 million. Seventy minarets fringe the side of the building that flanks the Boardwalk. In the entranceway, patrons are greeted by nine carved stone Indian elephants (this is the Taj Mahal, after all) and a lobby made of a year's output of the quarries of Carrara, Italy. Hotel guests have 1,250 rooms and ten restaurants to choose from, and an 80,000-square-foot exhibition hall/arena in which they can watch everything from boxing matches to concerts. Unfortunately, though, they'd have to crowd in on a daily basis for the baby-faced Trump to raise the nearly $100 million a year he would need to pay interest on the $675 million in bonds plus whatever millions were needed to pay contractors and banks.

In the process of creating a spectacle, he blew past the original $250 million completion estimate by some $300 million like a Hell's Angel cruising past a cop. Contractors went unpaid and walked off in the middle of the job. When the Taj finally opened on April 2, 1990, with a temporary license, the pool, sauna, theater, and restaurants remained unfinished. The first test run went well at the tables, but within minutes of the opening the army of slot machine gamblers had emptied the automated change makers nearby, and hundreds of other change machines elsewhere on the floor soon broke down. The second test run the following day was an unmitigated disaster. The casino's failure to track the previous day's transfers of money to the floor delayed the opening until 4:20 P.M. Over the following days, problems plagued both the casino and its hotel.

But the Trump hype kept them coming, and the Taj did a gangbusters business, raking in $1.2 million a day from April to June. It was a record for an Atlantic City casino. But it was still not enough for the extravagant gaming house to break even. And it was stealing much of its business from the city's eleven other casinos—including the two others owned by Trump. The Castle and the Plaza began to feel intense pain.

If Trump missed an October 15 Taj bond payment, as most of the bondholders believed he would, he would have a thirty-day grace period during which he could pay up before bondholders could file to force the Taj into bankruptcy. In August, a steering committee quickly formed to represent bondholders. Among the ten institutional investors on it were Loews Corporation, the company owned by the Tisch family; Executive Life Insurance Company, the Los Angeles insurer itself toppled by a portfolio overloaded with junk bonds and a frequent participant on bondholder and creditor panels; Caywood Christian Capital Management, a junk bond investment firm; and Manufacturers Life Insurance Company.

As its unofficial chairman, the group chose Hillel Weinberger, the short, mustachioed vulture investor for the Tisch family who managed a portfolio of junk bond investments in troubled companies at Loew's CNA Financial insurance company. A familiar figure in bankruptcy circles, Weinberger has been actively involved in the workouts at Texaco, LTV, Farley, and TWA, to name only a few. Weinberger doesn't talk publicly about his activities or even the performance of his portfolio. But given the spotlight that insurance regulators and rating agencies have been shining on companies with junk bond exposure in recent years, if Weinberger was not doing well the world would know about it by now. He reportedly bought $45 million in Trump Taj debt as the casino swooned.

On August 21, the committee members voted to hire the well-traveled Wilbur Ross as their financial adviser to do combat—negotiate—with Trump and his adjutants. The investment banker from Rothschild, Inc., had just finished working with a bondholders' committee involved in the Chapter 11 reorganization of Resorts International, the casino that not only once owned the Taj but was across the street and linked to it by a skywalk. In Ross's first strategy conference call with the broad group of 100 or so bondholders, many were ready to take Trump to the cleaners—that is, to go into bankruptcy and reclaim the property as theirs. They had the ability to do just that because the bonds were collateralized by the casino itself. And they wanted to do it because in their opinion, Trump deserved to be trounced. He had issued $675 million of bonds to the public based on information about exactly how much he was going to spend to complete the Taj, and then he went on a shopping spree that broke the budget.

WHAT'S IN A NAME?

On Friday, August 31, a Trump helicopter picked up Wilbur Ross and some Trump advisers at the heliport at Sixty-first Street and the FDR Drive bordering the East River. Trump was already aboard the military-style black helicopter, which was emblazoned on the side with his name in red-nail-polish letters as tall as a man. Also on board were Harvey Freeman, Trump's chief operating officer, and Stephen Bollenbach, his chief financial officer. They exchanged only a few pleasantries with Ross during the short flight. In Atlantic City, the chopper landed on the stub of the old Steel Pier, all that remained after a devastating fire in 1988. The Taj Majal casino was within sight, perhaps 150 yards away, its main, drive-up entrance on a side street off the Boardwalk. "On a bright sunny day in August, you'd think normal people would walk from the helipad into the casino," says Ross. "No. A stream of limos." As he recalls the scene today, he makes a sweeping motion with his hand to illustrate the arrival of four stretch limousines, their chauffeurs garbed in black shirts and white ties. Everyone climbed in, and the procession moved at about a half a mile per hour down the Boardwalk in front of the Taj as policemen shooed people out of the way. The level of electricity in the air was palpable as people screamed "Donny! Donny!" and eagerly shoved their cameras at his car. Ross imagined that this could not be much different from the return of a third world country's dictator from a trip abroad. The cars then turned down a driveway along one side of the casino and into the city streets, where they pulled up at the front entrance. As the small contingent of managers and advisers filed into the casino, the activity at the front of the gambling floor stopped. Everyone wanted to see the fabled Donald Trump.

Ross had come to begin his work researching the company for the bondholders' steering committee. His first discovery, made during that trip to the casino, that the Trump name was still worth its weight in gold, was a valuable one that he stashed away for future reference. He continued working on the due diligence through September and so he was prepared when on the twenty-seventh the management restructuring team made a formal presentation to the steering committee. They met back at the Taj.

Trump's management team, minus Trump, walked the committee through the proposed business plan. As Ross later described it, that plan was essentially business as usual until the recession ended, and then casino earnings would go up and away. Management also laid out its restructuring proposal in which bondholders would take a fourth of the stock and new bonds with a much lower interest tab. Ross and committee attorney Robert Miller were not impressed. They thought the business plan was unrealistic and the exchange offer unfair.

That fall, all three of Trump's casinos continued to suffer from a stagnant gambling market, and the Castle and Plaza suffered more than the average, partly because of the Taj's strong debut. Discussions now began with lenders and bondholders of both the Castle and the Taj. Trump officials predicted that the Castle would not be able to afford a December 15 interest payment—indicating that it was next in line to undergo a restructuring. The Plaza was prepared to make a payment due the same day, but if the downward trend continued, it looked as if a revamp would be necessary in the spring of 1991.

THE RAIDER WHO BECAME A VULTURE

During October, Ross started to speak regularly with one bondholder who was not on his committee: Carl Icahn. Icahn had slowly been acquiring the Taj Mahal bonds in the market and by then had accumulated about $150 million worth at an average price below forty cents on the dollar. Ross wanted to know what Icahn thought about the developing situation, and Icahn wanted to know the same from Ross. Icahn wouldn't be buying any more bonds, but he would soon become much more heavily involved in the restructuring negotiations. At the start, he had the manager of his high-yield portfolio, Mark Rachesky, listen in on bondholder conference calls. In October Icahn himself also began participating and talking to the advisers as he piled the last helpings of bonds onto his plate.

Like Trump himself, Icahn was born in Queens, although his origins were more humble. An only child, his father was a cantor until he had a heart attack in his fifties, his mother was a teacher, and they lived in a two-family house. Icahn majored in philosophy at Princeton, dropped out of medical school after two years, and joined the army. During the 1960s, he began working on Wall Street and carved a successful niche in what was then a fledgling market in options. He traded calls and puts, or the rights to buy or sell securities at a named price. At the same time, he also became known as an ace gambler. While he was in the army he'd won several thousand dollars playing poker, and now that he was in the professional world, he continued gambling both at home and at work—even, as reported in *The Predators' Ball,* playing Monopoly℠ for real cash.

Soon, Icahn founded his own brokerage firm, where he practiced arbitrage using the options market to protect him on the downside. In the mid-1970s, he shifted his arbitrage dealings to closed-end mutual funds, and he then acquired control of a real estate investment trust. It was after that purchase in 1978 that Icahn debuted as a corporate raider, waging proxy fights at companies he believed were undervalued to attract the attention of potential buyers. His targets got bigger as he amassed more money, often through greenmail—when managements bought his stock position at a premium to the market price just to get rid of him. Starting with Tappan, the stove maker, he raided Saxon Industries, Hammermill Paper Company, Marshall Field, American Can, Owens-Illinois, Dan River, Gulf + Western, and the railcar-leasing company ACF Industries, which he acquired. Drexel, Burnham, Lambert backed him in an $8.1 billion hostile bid for Phillips Petroleum in late 1984, but once the company improved a recapitalization program, Icahn sold his stock holdings. Finally, Icahn took over his second major company, Trans World Airlines, in a bitter fight in which the chairman, C. E. Meyer, Jr., called him "one of the greediest men on earth." He ended up joining hands with the union to take on the management's white knight, Frank Lorenzo, and he won control of the company in 1986. Over time, he replaced most of top management, but within a few years the airline was in a tailspin. Even so, according to *Forbes* magazine, Icahn is worth some $660 million and lives on an estate in Bedford, New York, near TWA headquarters.

By the time he invested in Trump Taj Mahal, the fifty-six-year-old Icahn already had tried his hand a few times at vulture investing. Never one to do things in a small way, he was a Heavy-weight vulture in Texaco stock during the big oil company's bank-ruptcy in late 1987. Icahn picked up his Texaco shares just after the October stock market crash, and by January 1988 had bought thirty-six million shares for about $1.2 billion. When the company emerged from bankruptcy in mid-1988, Icahn turned on Texaco, staging a proxy fight to acquire the company. Although he didn't succeed, he put enough of the fear of God into management that it engaged in a far-reaching restructuring of its assets.

In June 1989, Icahn sold his 17.3 percent stake in Texaco for $2.07 billion in cash, a $650 million profit, and the world waited for him to use that money to challenge another major corporation. He used some of it to stage a proxy fight against the steel-and-oil giant USX. But he put a large portion of Texaco profits plus borrowed funds into about $1.5 billion worth of bonds of distressed compa-nies including Gillett Holdings, Interco, E-II Holdings, Leaseway Transportation, Southland, Western Union, Trump Taj Mahal, and his own Trans World Airlines. He won't reveal what he spent but observers estimate more than $400 million. To other, more experienced, vultures, Icahn's charge into several very large invest-ments and not always in the safest, most senior classes of bonds was "cowboy" investing. But Icahn took the position that he could buy controlling stakes in junior classes of bonds at much cheaper prices relative to risk than he could obtain in senior classes, and could often end up with a slab of equity. His staff saw prices falling, and their fundamental research on the companies told them the prices were very cheap. For the most part, they did very well. By the end of 1991 returns on the whole portfolio were in the clouds at triple-digit levels.

In the spring of 1990, at the same time that he was buying the bonds of the careening Southland 7-Eleven convenience store chain, Icahn was picking up Western Union senior bonds. The negotiations on Western Union's restructuring provide one of the best illustrations of just how hard nosed a bargainer Carl Icahn can be. Bennett LeBow, the same New York investor who had tried to buy Storage Technology, had bought control of Western Union in 1987 and then merged the telex business of ITT into it, just as the revolution of the fax machine was making the telex obsolete. By 1990, the 140-year-old company, known both for the telegraph and for turning away the rights to the telephone, was sending an SOS. A load of $500 million in senior bonds was crushing the company; the bonds, due in 1992, had reset provisions that forced their interest rate up from 16.5 percent to an awesome 19.25 percent in June 1989. In April 1990, the company proposed trading those bonds for new lower-rate bonds and some equity, hoping to reach an agreement before June 15 when a $51 million interest payment was due.

That was when Icahn became involved. By summer, he owned $75 million worth. Average cost: about forty cents on the dollar. He then joined in the ongoing bondholder talks along with—but not as part of—the bondholders' steering committee. Balfour Investors's Harry Freund and Jay Goldsmith, who, also with about $75 million of the bonds and also not on the committee, met with Icahn at the TWA offices in Westchester. As Goldsmith recounts what Icahn told them: " 'If you don't pay me, it's my company. If you don't pay interest on my bonds, you get nothing. You get no salary, you get no stock. It's all mine, and none of it is yours. You get no yacht.' It's a very simple theory, and it's based on priority [of debt over equity in distressed situations]. You can't argue with it." Not that he wouldn't participate in a debt swap—but only on the right terms.

Pretty tough talk, especially from a man who socialized with the man running Western Union, Bennett LeBow. In fact, for a week the previous summer the two men and their wives had sailed together on LeBow's yacht in the Mediterranean. "So, I met him on a boat. So what?" Goldsmith recalls Icahn once saying. "Not just any boat," Goldsmith reminded Icahn, "Ben LeBow's boat."

Kenneth Moelis, a financial adviser to the bondholders from Donaldson, Lufkin & Jenrette, had a similar conversation with Icahn in which the famous investor professed to "own" the company. But Moelis pointed out that as a bondholder Icahn did not own Western Union; he owned the right to put the company into bankruptcy, and when it came out of Chapter 11, he might then own all or part of the company. That's when Icahn and Moelis began to devise a plan for a "delayed control switch." The bondholders would agree to give management one more chance to rejuvenate the company, and if it failed, control of the company would pass to the bondholders. Bankruptcy would be avoided altogether. Ultimately, this model was also used for the Taj Mahal restructuring.

On June 15, Western Union defaulted on the $51 million payment, but it still had a thirty-day grace period to meet its obligations. The negotiations with LeBow on an exchange offer centered on the amount of equity LeBow was going to give the bondholders and also the terms of the new lower-rate bonds they'd get, including the delayed control switch. Icahn and LeBow repeatedly reached agreements and repeatedly, Icahn says, LeBow would come back after talking to his staff and break them.

But then, the dynamics of this negotiation changed dramatically. At one meeting held in Icahn's offices, LeBow in a joking manner said something to the effect of, "Carl, you don't respect me. You're being too tough in this. What do you care? When we're done, I'm sure I'll be able to find a loophole."

"If you can figure out a loophole in this one," Icahn answered, *"then* I'll respect you."

They had been kidding around. But Icahn and his staff began to worry that underneath it all LeBow was serious. Inadvertently, LeBow had thrown down the gauntlet and Icahn responded vigorously by changing tactics. He would now try to close *all* the loopholes. "It was a challenge," he says. "I wanted to make it perfect, and I did."

As the talks intensified, and Icahn continued to hold out on his demands and bring up new points, the conference calls became longer and more frequent. In a few of the calls with management before the July 15 deadline, about twenty people continued negotiating for ten hours, and one call continued for two days. Icahn, the ace gambler, seemed to be enjoying himself immensely. "He remembered every number," says Balfour's Goldsmith. "He didn't miss a thing. There was nobody who was more up to speed than he was. The guy loves it. His wife would be calling and saying, 'It's time to come home for dinner,' and he would say, 'No, we have a call starting at nine o'clock.' It would go to two in the morning." He loved the process for the process, but he also truly believed he was fighting for important principles. For instance, why should LeBow collect any management fee for chairing the company if he was helping to drive the company into the ground? LeBow's company, Brooke Partners, was getting a $2.4 million annual advisory fee for helping to manage the company.

"Why are you paying Ben a fee?" Icahn inquired of the company officers who were on the line.

"He's incredibly helpful," explained one of the executives.

That hardly satisfied Icahn. "Ben," Icahn told the Western Union men, "is like the general who is leading his army and says, 'Charge the hill.' We all followed. We invested. Now the troops are all lying dead. And the general wants to go home and get a fee?"

Often when LeBow was participating in the negotiations, he was on the defensive. At one point he challenged Icahn, prophetically: "I own some TWA bonds. Maybe some day you'll get into trouble and we'll see what happens." Responded Icahn, calmly, "If I do, I'll pay, or you can have the company." In what seemed an attempt at making peace, LeBow invited Icahn and vice presidents Mark Rachesky and Richard Rubin onto his magnificent yacht for dinner. But Icahn's tactics didn't change.

Icahn appeared to be wearing LeBow down with his persistence. But he was wearing everyone else down too. Every time the participants thought they were done, Icahn would pipe up with, "There are just two more points I want to discuss." And groans could be heard over the line, even from the people on Icahn's side. The Balfour partners were as much fascinated as frustrated by his intransigence. "In any process of reorganization there is a minute when even the hardest fighter says to himself, 'Okay, I'm not going to get every last nickel that I want, and pragmatically speaking, it's enough now and I'll settle for it,' " says Freund. "There just didn't come that moment with Carl. Every time that he got what he wanted—and it was inevitable that he did—he wanted something new. And everything he wanted was perfectly rational, but there was no end. And the other human beings—and they are after all human beings—on the other side of the negotiation have to feel that there will be an end. Otherwise there can't be a negotiation."

Just after the grace period expired in mid-July, the company reached agreement with the steering committee on an exchange offer format. Four out of the five largest bondholders indicated they would tender their bonds—the holdout being none other than Icahn himself. Because the company needed 95 percent acceptance, Icahn with his 15 percent position in the bonds was blocking the way. The offer was extended and extended again until on November 13, Western Union announced that if it didn't get the required acceptance it would offer to buy out half the bonds at attractive, above-market prices, leaving the other half in the lurch. Icahn's lieutenant on his high-yield bond portfolio, Mark Rachesky, scrambled to call bondholders representing more than 50 percent of the bonds and convince them not to tender.

During one of the key conference calls directed at this effort, about thirty people were on the line, including Icahn and the bondholders' adviser, Ken Moelis, who was in London. The delay on Moelis's line, from the overseas connection, got Icahn wondering.

"Where's mollusk? Where's that fucking mollusk?" he wanted to know. (He always called Moelis by that name. It was in jest, although at the time he sounded so matter-of-fact that Moelis figured he was just getting his name wrong.)

"I'm in London, Carl," Moelis said over the line.

"What are you doing in London? This is an important deal."

"Carl," Moelis said patiently, "I've got other deals besides yours. I've got to be here. I'm doing Saatchi and Saatchi." (The giant advertising agency was then in bankruptcy.)

"Well, come back tomorrow," Icahn ordered. "Get a flight on TWA."

"The next TWA flight is not for two days," Moelis ribbed him. "And are you going to get me an upgrade?"

"Sure, I'll get you an upgrade, if you pay for it."

The bondholders got enough signatures to block the company's tender offer. Icahn and the other top bondholders wrote to the company on November 27, threatening that unless it remade its cash offer with good terms for the whole group, they would push the company into involuntary bankruptcy. In the letter they laid out six demands that would ensure them the greatest amount of cash possible, including no management fee paid to LeBow. Western Union agreed to it all. In the end, enough bondholders ten-

dered to keep the company from hurtling into financial oblivion—
at least temporarily. Icahn did not sell out, opting to keep his
investment in the company for the long term and possible future
sparring with management.

THE CONTROL THING

In the fall, while Icahn was in the middle of both the Western
Union and the Trump Taj dramas, he gave Wilbur Ross a personal
demonstration of his will to win. Icahn had a housewarming party
at his newly restored, twenty-odd-room stone house located on ten
acres of East Hampton Beach. Ross noticed the brand new tennis
court, and Icahn challenged him to a doubles match a week later.
Ross and his partner, Robert Nederlander, managing partner of
the New York Yankees, arrived to find that Icahn had invited the
former captain of the Vanderbilt College tennis team to be his
partner. Although that captain was now forty years old, he was still
plenty effective to beat the Ross-Nederlander duo. "That's just an
illustration of how competitive Carl can be," Ross maintains with
his amused smile. (But Ross is being a little bit disingenuous here,
because Robert Nederlander, albeit years ago, won the doubles
competition at Wimbledon.)

While Western Union was working on its first exchange offer,
negotiations with Donald Trump on the Taj Mahal restructuring
were in full swing. After rejecting management's September 27,
1990 initial exchange offer, the committee came up with its own.
On October 3, it presented a proposal to management in which the
bondholders would acquire 85 percent of the company's stock in
return for taking new lower-interest bonds. But without hesitation,
Trump spurned that idea and came forward with a second proposition on October 11. A meeting was held at the Plaza Hotel with the
committee and its advisers and Trump and his advisers, including
his newest addition, Moelis. (Moelis first met Trump back in July,
just after The Donald had signed his bailout agreement with the
banks. Trump told Moelis that he should come work for him, and
if he did he would be on the cover of *Newsweek* magazine. Trump
said he'd make sure of it.)

Management offered 19.9 percent of the stock in return for

lowering the interest payment from 14 percent to 9 percent, and only part of the 9 percent would be payable in cash. The committee liked this version even less than the first offer, which had offered 25 percent of the stock, and the members left the hotel grumbling about it. In fact, when Moelis left the hotel, Trump's bodyguard, who had been standing outside during the meeting, stopped him.

"Are you Ken Moelis?" the burly guard asked.

"Yeah," Moelis replied.

"Those guys really didn't like you," the guard said.

Wilbur Ross labeled management's proposal "unrealistic," and the next day he wrote a letter on the status of the negotiations and faxed it to the bondholders. In it, he declared that the latest offer from Trump was "significantly worse than the one rejected by the steering committee" two weeks earlier. "We are deeply concerned about the prospects for a consensual restructuring." The committee had several issues it wanted to resolve in negotiations, including a higher interest rate with a sizable amount of it payable in cash, a certain amount of the equity, a decision about whether Trump would continue to run the place, and under what circumstances Trump would lose control.

Still, the Trump team packaged its proposal into a formal restructuring blueprint and filed it with the Securities and Exchange Commission. That was a strategic move recommended by Moelis. "It was a change of pace from the behind-the-scenes discussions," he says. "We filed a document to get the momentum going."

The October 15 due date passed with no payment to bondholders. Talks continued every few days with the goal of reaching agreement on an exchange offer by midnight November 15, when the grace period on the bond interest payment was set to expire. Trump continued to resist giving up control of his beloved Taj to its bondholders. The parties agreed on one thing: Tax legislation passed on November 5 made a conventional exchange offer unattractive and a prepackaged bankruptcy the best restructuring alternative.

The week of November 12, the committee—and Icahn, who was by now becoming more intimately involved in the talks—came to an important realization. "We felt that in order to make the deal with Trump, we would need to leave him in control to begin with, and we would need to leave him with more or less half the stock," Ross explains. Why? First, the Trump name still added marketing value to the casinos. Also, the committee really wanted to avoid a bankruptcy, since gambling houses that operated in bankruptcy had not done well because of the suspicion, by high and low rollers alike, that the house will win more often than it would if the casino were solvent. Although he knew that the bondholders could put him into Chapter 11 if they wanted to, Trump was not willing to give up control of the casino. In effect, he called the committee's bluff, and the committee didn't do the deed. Instead, it decided to let him have half ownership. But given that, the bondholders wanted to be able to yank him out of power if the casino did poorly—the same arrangement that had been negotiated in Western Union.

Trump appeared to be amenable, but he wanted the opportunity to earn back 100 percent ownership with relative ease and he wanted to pay less than half of the new bonds' interest in cash. "It's too early for Christmas," Ross quipped to the *New York Times.* The bondholders were willing to allow him to earn back as much as 80 percent. But no more. And they wanted a higher interest rate with most of it paid in cash.

STOP AND GO NEGOTIATIONS

Trump broke off negotiations on Tuesday, November 13, when the committee told him that unless he agreed to its terms it would draw up documents for filing an involuntary bankruptcy. Accusing Wilbur Ross of being the chief spoiler, Trump told the *New York Times,* "We saw no point in going forward. Unfortunately, this case will be in court for many years to come. We are unable to make a deal with Mr. Ross and his group." In other words, the first bankruptcy in the Trump empire appeared almost certain. Ross retorted that the bondholders had no fear of bankruptcy court. "If they say they've broken off talks," he said, "that's their prerogative." Icahn had little hope left for a settlement—or at least that's what he said publicly. "I'm a friend of Donald's and I'm trying to avoid [bankruptcy]. But a number of members of the steering committee have dug in, and it will be very tough to keep it out."

Advisers got the parties back together Wednesday evening at the Plaza Hotel. At the meeting were Ross and Bob Miller for the committee and Freeman, Bollenbach, and Moelis for the Taj. Trump attended only parts of the session. Most of the negotiators quit late that night. But Ross, Icahn, and Trump continued on over the phone, breaking at about two Thursday morning as far apart as ever on the issue of how much equity ownership Trump could earn back.

On Thursday, the Trump contingent and the committee negotiated through the day and into the wee hours of Friday, November 16. They moved closer together. But although Trump, Icahn, and Ross again talked late into the night, they adjourned at two A.M. with no resolution. Two hours earlier, at midnight, the grace period had officially expired, and Trump was in default on his debt payments. By the bankruptcy code, when default occurs, any three bondholders can file a petition to push the company into an involuntary bankruptcy. This would end any hope of doing an abbreviated, prepackaged bankruptcy and eventually could remove Trump from control. The Taj and its creditors could be swamped in bankruptcy for years to come. Friday was turning into a cliffhanger.

8:00 A.M.: Ross arranged a conference call with the members of the steering committee and delivered the grim news that no agreement had been reached. Then the committee called a press conference for 12:30 P.M. to report the deadlock. It announced that the briefing would take place at the Macklowe Hotel, a brand new hotel and conference center located on West Forty-fourth Street about halfway between Ross's and committee attorney Miller's offices. "That in effect told the whole world we didn't have a deal with Donald because if we had a deal we wouldn't be doing it at the Macklowe, we'd be doing it at his place, the Plaza Hotel," Ross points out.

10:00 A.M.: Ross and Miller reported the latest to a broad group of about 100 bondholders. On the call were the representatives of the bulk of the bond issue, including Japanese holders that owned about 20 percent, retail brokers, and institutional investors.

<u>10:30 A.M.:</u> The call ended, and Ross and Miller decided to give Trump one more try. They got Icahn and Trump on the phone, and negotiations resumed in earnest. That morning Trump and his advisers had been talking about where they should give in. Should they demand 50 percent ownership with the opportunity to increase that to 80 percent? Or 50 to 85? Or 55 to 85? "Finally, that morning he went along with what we wanted," Ross says.

<u>12:30 P.M.:</u> They had a deal. The final agreement reduced bond-holders' interest rate to 12 percent in return for half of the equity in the company. Trump retained control of the board, but had to give it up to bondholders if he didn't meet a target of $85 million in cash flow in the first year and other targets each year thereafter. If he met those targets and paid off the bonds at their original rates, he could regain up to 80 percent of the equity. The steering committee members were promptly informed and gave their approval.

By now members of the media had shown up at the Macklowe Hotel for the originally scheduled 12:30 press briefing and were annoyed to find out that there was to be no presentation. Shortly afterward, however, the company announced that the conference would take place at four P.M.—and this time it would be held at the Plaza Hotel on Fifth Avenue and Central Park South.

ICAHN TURNS THE TIDE

But first, it was back to the broad bondholder group with the good news. This meeting was not called as just a courtesy. Neither was it called to make sure that the company and the committee had enough support to do the prepackaged plan.

There were two reasons for this conference call with the broad group of bondholders. First, Ross and Miller wanted to make sure that nobody would put the Taj Mahal into an involuntary bankruptcy. Any three bondholders, even holders of a few bonds, could do the deed. And if they did, says Ross, "it would blow up the whole thing. You don't want to announce a deal and then have someone put it into bankruptcy the next morning." He had no particular reason to think this would happen. "It didn't occur to us

there would be a problem," he says. "We had the steering committee unanimously in support." But he wanted to make sure everyone
was on board.

Second, the deal the committee had struck with Trump was
contingent on getting about $45 million in concessions from the
bank lenders and the Trump Taj Mahal contractors who were
waiting for their bills to be paid. That $45 million would help pay
the bondholders what they wanted. "We were afraid if the bondholder group looked splintered we would never get the concessions," says Ross.

Once all 100 or so people were on the line—a process that took
about twenty-five minutes—Ross explained the deal that had been
worked out. Surprisingly, the news did not go over well with quite
a few of the bondholders. This group had had little insight on what
was being negotiated during the past two months beyond what
sketchy information was reported in the press, and most of the
newspaper accounts indicated that the committee was demanding
a controlling stake in the casino. Because they were still allowed to
trade in Trump securities, these bondholders were not privy to the
same nonpublic, insider information as the steering committee
members who had formally restricted their trading. So their first
reaction on hearing that Trump was going to remain in control of
the gambling house was not favorable.

"Why settle for this?" one bondholder protested.

"This deal looks like we're running scared," another chimed in.

To Kaye Handley, a vulture investor on the call, the whole deal
seemed much too generous to Trump and dangerous for the casino
as well. She objected, first of all, that the deal piled even more debt
on the casino company, although at lower rates than before. In her
opinion, over a period of several years the Taj had the potential to
become the strongest casino/hotel in Atlantic City, due to both its
size and grandeur. But it needed to lighten its current debt load
significantly to realize that potential, and that would not be happening in the deal that was on the table. Even if the company were
to revive, Handley went on, bondholders would not be the ones to
reap the benefits. And she questioned the threat of a protracted
bankruptcy, believing that bondholders were in a stronger position
in this case than the vast majority of junk bond restructurings and

would be better off taking the Taj to court. Finally, from what she could see, the sparkle of the Trump name was fading fast. If the bondholders put Trump into bankruptcy and then took over and hired a new management, perhaps the image change would do the company good.

Handley asked Ross, "Is the Trump name an asset or a liability?"

Having witnessed the public's continuing romance with Trump first hand at the casino, Ross had a ready reply. "In my assessment and according to my staff who have been working in Atlantic City, the Trump name is still very much an asset and a big draw to people in Atlantic City. If new management were to come in, it would not be a friendly changing of hands." Still, some bondholders wondered silently whether the Trump name would draw crowds from *outside* Atlantic City.

Whether or not Trump was good or bad for the company, many bondholders insisted that because he had brought the casino to ruin, he should suffer retribution. "What these people were complaining about was not that the economics were bad," Ross says today. "They were complaining, why did we make a deal with him? Why didn't we blow him up? There was an emotional content to it. In fact, when my wife heard that we had made the deal, she didn't like the whole idea either." Suddenly what had seemed a remote possibility was more real than ever: There was now a relatively good chance that some three disgruntled bondholders would go to court to force Trump into a prolonged bankruptcy. The hope for a prepackaged approach would be gone.

Soon, a few of the bondholders began to wonder aloud why Carl Icahn was not on this conference call, because he'd been on some of the prior calls. Icahn was a tough negotiator. Had he sold them out? Was Carl Icahn coming to the rescue of Donald Trump because they were social friends? Actually, the reason Ross hadn't asked Icahn to participate on this call was because he thought the deal was so attractive—that it would be sure to boost the value of the bonds in the market—that the bondholders would quickly agree and that would be that. Now that temperatures were rising over the phone lines, Ross thought it would be wise to get Icahn on the call. "In fact, he is very anxious to speak to the group," Ross announced.

Once on the line, Icahn's talk to the bondholders, brief as it was, proved to be a critical point in the Taj restructuring. For about twenty minutes, in a firm tone, he explained that he agreed with Ross and legal adviser Miller that the bargain that had been struck was the best the negotiators could do. He went on to say that the prepackaged bankruptcy was preferable to a contentious Chapter 11 case that would benefit neither the casino nor the bonds. "Why go through all that if he's agreed to pay you?" And he was convinced that the reorganization plan was a viable one; Trump would be able to make the payments. It might even help the company to keep Trump in charge, he said, because the New Jersey Casino Control Commission would not have to rule on a change in ownership. In conclusion, Icahn affirmed that he was going to vote his bonds in favor of the prepackaged plan. "To Carl, this was just a good investment," says Trump financial adviser, Ken Moelis. "He had no need for revenge. The others had wanted a pound of flesh, but Carl wanted an economic deal."

One angry bondholder challenged him. "At what price did you buy your bonds? We paid par for ours."

Icahn responded calmly with an analogy. "We're both on a life raft right now. And it's sinking. It doesn't matter who got on first. We have to do something to save ourselves."

Icahn's monologue appeared to do the trick. Where before there was hostility in the air and talk of forcing Trump into bankruptcy court, now the group on the conference call posed questions that were friendly and concerned narrower issues like governance provisions. "Part of it was just his aura," bondholder Handley maintains. "People are a little in awe of Icahn. He's not the usual person on a bondholder call. He's famous, a big deal maker. We all knew the clout he had because of his large position, and I'm sure some people felt intimidated." The call ended with a trial vote, and the vast majority voted in favor of the plan.

The conference call had taken an hour and a half. There was no time to lose. As soon as Ross and Miller hung up, they put on their jackets and literally ran over to Trump's office in the Trump Tower on Fifth Avenue. Trump, Miller, and Ross initialed a four-page agreement and then they all walked across the street to the Plaza Hotel for the press conference. Now all that was left to do was draw up the prepackaged bankruptcy plan to submit to the court with a Chapter 11 bankruptcy filing, although that would not be as easy to do as it appeared.

THE CASTLE WALLS ARE FALLING

Trump's next challenge was fast approaching. This time, he owed Castle bondholders $18 million on December 15, and by early in the month bondholders of the loss-ridden casino felt certain that they were not going to see a dime. Trump waffled on whether he would pay or not, but he had until December 25 (when the grace period expired) to decide. Led by Putnam Companies, the Boston mutual fund group that had bought Castle junk bonds both at par and as a vulture investor at discount, the bondholders hired financial and legal advisers and began to huddle on strategy. When the payment deadline arrived, Trump defied all expectations and made the payment—but reportedly he did so with some help from his eighty-five-year-old father, Fred, who had made his fortune building moderate-income housing in New York City and whom Donald tended to call Pops or Daddy-O. On December 17, a lawyer representing the elder Trump strolled into the casino and bought $3.35 million worth of chips and then walked out without using them, effectively giving Donald a gift. Once made, the interest payment was enough to keep bondholders at bay for six months, when the next payment was due.

Even with the Castle's problems on hold, there was to be no rest for the weary Donald Trump. In mid-January 1991, as the Taj Mahal bondholders' committee and Icahn were negotiating the terms of the reorganization plan they'd agreed to in theory two months earlier, the wheels ground to a stop. Icahn wanted details set down describing how the board would make decisions; the budget Trump would have to work with; and if the company did poorly, when Trump would have to relinquish control to the bondholders.

To most of the committee members, this development was jarring. As far as they were concerned, the interest rate on the bonds they were going to get was the important victory and they'd already won it by getting 12 percent. But to Icahn, the technical aspects of governance were just as vital as the economic questions.

"The other holders weren't opposed to stricter governance," says Wilbur Ross. "It's just that they would have settled for a little bit less strict than Carl would. They were happy to get it if they could get it, but their position was they wouldn't blow the deal over it." Icahn, on the other hand, was willing to blow the deal—or at least he publicly said he would vote his bonds against it, which was not a blocking position, but given his sway with bondholders he could probably defeat the whole prepackaged bankruptcy plan. He wrote members of the steering committee a four-page letter outlining his reservations. And he kept pushing for very strict, very tight oversight, while Trump held out to get the most lenient conditions he could get. "I wanted it airtight because I didn't want people to say I'm favoring Trump because he's a friend," Icahn says.

Another argument developed over whether Icahn, as the largest post-bankruptcy shareholder with about 13 percent, should be able to appoint someone to the board. Some bondholders were concerned that Icahn would be easy on Trump because of their friendly social relationship. Icahn tried to reassure them, and Ross was one who stood in his defense. "I wasn't concerned," Ross says. "Having seen how hard he negotiated, I knew damn well he wasn't going to play favorites."

A PREEMPTIVE SAVE BY FIDELITY

While they haggled over details, an earnings report issued in mid-March 1991 for the Castle confirmed what many had long suspected: The Taj Mahal was cannibalizing business from Trump's other casinos. The report noted that in 1990 the Castle lost $43 million and its cash flow plunged by 60 percent. The Plaza was also losing money to the Taj. In fact, bondholders at the Plaza were thinking of suing the bigger casino because the Taj's management had taken customer lists from the Plaza. In 1990, the bonds fell in price from a high of around eighty cents on the dollar to a low of forty-four cents. With the Plaza's revenue growth stagnating, it was looking less and less likely that Trump would be able to foot a $25 million bill on Plaza bond service payments due in June. Yet another restructuring loomed on the horizon.

But long before anyone began talking seriously about a Plaza revamping, there was a surprise announcement from a Heavy-weight vulture who had become the Plaza's largest bondholder. Early in April, the Fidelity Investments Capital & Income Fund, which speculates in sick companies, stepped in to ward off the coming storm. Two managers were assigned to handle the more than $1 billion of assets invested in troubled-company debt and junk bonds. (It later grew to $1.5 billion.) One was Daniel Harmetz, a Harvard Law School graduate who had spent one year as a bankruptcy lawyer at the premier Los Angeles firm of Stutman, Treister & Glatt. He then moved on to help manage the junk bond portfolio at Columbia Savings & Loan, the largest junk bond investor in the thrift industry that foundered during the junk market's rout in 1989 and 1990 and was taken over by the government. He then left for Fidelity, which was converting a passive junk bond fund into an activist vulture player. His co-manager was David Breazzano, a recent recruit from the vulture fund at Baltimore mutual fund giant T. Rowe Price Associates. While there, Breazzano performed one especially neat trick. Early in 1989, when Eastern Airlines went bankrupt, he bought some Eastern bonds between forty and sixty cents on the dollar. Four months later he sold out for eighty cents, even though the airline was then proposing to pay creditors in full. But like some kind of morality play about greed, the other creditors not only didn't get paid in full, they suffered huge losses when the airline was forced to liquidate.

Early in 1991, the Fidelity vultures built up large positions in the bonds of MCorp, a Dallas-based bank, and Gillett Holdings, a company owned by Colorado mogul George Gillett that is a collage of television stations, meatpacking businesses, and the Vail ski resort. Gillett's refinancing negotiations with bondholders bounced up and down for a year, when, in late February 1991, the Fidelity vultures and two other Boston-based institutional investors filed to put Gillett into involuntary bankruptcy. Also in the spring of 1991, the Breazzano-Harmetz team blocked a prepackaged restructuring at Price Communications, another media company, because it felt the deal left too much debt, or leverage, on the books. Breazzano told *Pension & Investments,* "We're willing to become extreme activists if that's what it takes to de-lever these companies." The move forced Price to file for bankruptcy.

During that same period, early 1991, the two Fidelity vulture funds purchased as much as $50 million face value of Trump Plaza variable-rate bonds at around fifty-five cents on the dollar. Then they approached Trump with an offer to swap $25 million of the bonds for a new note secured by the casino's ten-story, 2650-space parking garage that had cost Trump $30 million to build. As for interest on the bonds, Fidelity wanted 11 percent the first year and 12⅝ percent thereafter. The deal was a no-lose proposition for Fidelity. Whereas the collateral behind the old bonds—the casino—was shared by other creditors, Fidelity had the parking garage all to itself. As for Trump, the swap allowed him to meet the scheduled $25 million payment. The Plaza still had its long-term problems, but Fidelity provided Trump with a port in his financial storm.

THE GOOD BANKRUPTCY

Meanwhile, Trump had continued negotiating with Carl Icahn and the other Taj bondholders through February, March, and the beginning of April. Another issue arose: Icahn didn't want to allow Trump to issue Taj Mahal stock to raise funds in the future. If Trump sold off his control of the Taj, Icahn reasoned, he might be inclined to work harder at the two casinos he still controlled, the Castle and the Plaza, and the Taj would lose market share to them. But Icahn agreed to allow a public offering of Taj stock if Trump offered equal amounts of stock in the other casinos at the same time or sold stock in them first.

Through characteristic tenacity, Icahn also finally won the strict governance provisions he'd been seeking, making it easier for bondholders to wrest control of the casino from Trump in the case of disappointing performance. One day Icahn and Trump's chief financial officer, Stephen Bollenbach, were negotiating the governance matters at TWA offices. According to Icahn: "Bollenbach said, 'There's no way we're doing this. If we do this and we don't perform, we're screwed.' So I said, 'You're correct. If you don't perform, you're screwed.' And I looked at him and he looked at me, and he agreed to sign the deal."

A few days after the agreement was struck, the New Jersey

Casino Control Commission renewed the Taj's gaming license for another year—provided that the Taj file its prepackaged reorganization plan by June 17 and that Trump finalize his bailout agreements with bank lenders over $535 million of debt, on his sundry real estate, airline, and casino assets, that he had personally guaranteed. As a result of those bank agreements, Trump shifted the focus of his business dealings to his casinos. Over the months that followed, many of his other prized possessions would become repossessions. The *Trump Princess* yacht sailed over to the Boston Safe Deposit & Trust Company. His stake in Alexander's department store was sold to Citicorp. Trump's 49 percent interest in the Grand Hyatt Hotel passed to Bankers Trust New York Corporation. And the Trump Shuttle became part of USAir. He was allowed to keep the Trump Tower, 51 percent of the Plaza Hotel in New York, an undeveloped site in Manhattan, his residences, and his interest in his three casinos. Trump was betting that he could rebuild his vast fortune by reviving those casinos, and he planned to direct his energies toward that goal.

First, though, he had to finish negotiating a trade-off with Castle bondholders. The Taj Mahal deal served as a model. At the end of May 1991, as the June 15 $41 million payment approached, Trump began intensive negotiations for a deal. Late on June 11, management reached a tentative pact with representatives of the broad bondholder group. As with the Taj, in return for accepting a lower interest rate on their debt, bondholders would claim ownership of half of the casino's equity. And Trump would be able to increase his stake if he paid back the debt within five years. The deal was confirmed by the steering committee on June 14.

But within days, opposition among the bondholders surfaced and threatened to scuttle the deal. During a two-hour conference call on Tuesday, June 18, a number of bondholders rejected the compromise. They wanted to put Trump into involuntary bankruptcy and see what they could get in court, and one of them, Randolph Goodman of Advest, began to organize the Trump Castle Bondholders Protective Committee that would negotiate on its own. Trump had not paid the $41 million he owed bondholders, and three bondholders could force Trump Castle into bankruptcy when the grace period expired on June 28. But when Trump failed to make the interest payment, they didn't stage any attack, and at the beginning of September, the casino commission renewed the Castle's license based on the tentative plan. (By the end of February 1992, both the Castle and the Plaza were set to file prepackaged bankruptcy reorganization plans. Fidelity saved Trump once again. When negotiations on a securities swap stalled, Fidelity agreed to provide a $10 million loan to make the deal work.)

In mid-July 1991, a bit late but good enough for the casino commission, the Taj filed for bankruptcy and expected to be out within a few months. On October 4 the casino was out of court and doing business as usual. Many analysts believed that Trump would meet his cash flow targets and retain control. But four days after the company emerged, one influential skeptic spoke up. Moody's Investment Service, the credit agency, issued a report questioning the Taj's ability to meet payments on the *new* debt. "The debt load of the company is not alleviated by the exchange offer and the operating performance is not expected to improve greatly due to slower-than-expected growth of the Atlantic City casino market and intense competition among operators," Moody's said. By mid-1992, the Taj Mahal and the other two casinos were showing substantially better revenues and profits. Whether they would do well enough to allow Trump to continue dealing the cards was something Carl Icahn was watching very closely.

POSTCRIPT: ICAHN ON THE OTHER SIDE

The postcript to this story is the role reversal Carl Icahn was forced into during 1991 when his airline began plunging toward bankruptcy. TWA defaulted on $75.5 million of bondholder debt early in February 1991, at the same time that Icahn was bearing down on the details of the Taj Mahal reorganization plan. In April he started talking about a possible bankruptcy filing. In July, he avoided a close brush with bankruptcy by offering secured bondholders better terms, and then reached agreement with all bondholders to do a prepackaged bankruptcy in early 1992.

The fact that Icahn knew how bondholders think made the negotiations a lot easier, says TWA bondholder adviser Wilbur Ross: "It made it a lot easier to deal with Carl in that it's always easier to deal with someone who's really professional and who really knows the process. Most debtors are first-timers in the process. So they don't know really how it works. And a lot of times their advisers give them unrealistic notions. But Carl, having been in so many deals, knew that his equity position as such was gone. So while he put up a little bit of a show about it, it was clear he knew that it was history."

Carl Icahn had owned 90 percent of TWA's stock. On January 31, 1992, TWA declared bankruptcy, and at a press conference held at the St. Regis Hotel in midtown Manhattan he predicted that the airline would be out of court in six months. He would give his stock to the creditors (in exchange for debt forgiveness) and the unions (for wage and work rule concessions). By November, however, he was still negotiating with one creditor: the federal pensions agency. But TWA's emergence from bankruptcy appeared imminent.

11

The Grave Dancers

Money is always there but the pockets change; it is not in the same pockets after a change.

—*GERTRUDE STEIN*

Take one look at Sam Zell and what you see is energy. It is coming from his hands, his bearded face, his compact athletic body, and his ideas. He is a person who is continually, almost compulsively, moving and testing his limits. Except on snowy, below twenty-degree Chicago winter days, the balding, fifty-year-old financier rides his Ducati motorcycle to his downtown office. For a couple of weeks every year, he leaves home and—having shipped his motorcycle abroad in a specially built oceangoing container—buzzes around some foreign country like Australia with five or six like-minded adventurers. And just for the challenge, every Saturday afternoon at his house in Sun Valley, Idaho, Zell hosts "War at Four." Anywhere from ten to twenty friends, associates, and acquaintances split into two teams and, armed with gas guns, shoot paint pellets at each other until they are too tired to stand.

Zell even describes his own job in terms of action. As the title for a 1976 article about his experiences buying distressed real estate, he chose "The Grave Dancer," and the name stuck. It's a graphic image, bringing to mind not just the naked opportunism that any vulture investor practices, but a creative and energetic opportunism. Zell made his first fortune by tap-dancing on the tombs of real estate projects that had departed for another world, and later he waltzed into corporate cemeteries. The products of Zell's performances are abundant. First with his college friend Robert Lurie and now alone with his staff, Zell built a vast collection of real estate holdings with a value approaching $4 billion. And through cunning and sheer maneuverability, Zell has strung several pearls on his corporate investing string—Itel Corporation and Nucorp Energy with Lurie, and more recently Clark Oil and the department store chain Carter Hawley Hale Stores with partner David Schulte, a turnaround consultant. Zell's personal wealth is said to exceed $400 million.

How he has done so much with such great success is something Zell finds easy to explain. "There is one consistent theme, and that is simplicity," he says, adding, with utter self-assurance, "I have the ability to simplify a problem and identify a solution." For instance, he often identifies an inefficiency in the pricing of a property, or a company—a market value that he realizes is idling below the true value. And he often then finds a fairly straightforward way that the true value can be extracted. These simple solutions derive in part from his confidence: He firmly believes that he knows where troubled corporations have gone awry and how they can be set right.

Blunt, sarcastic, sometimes profane, Zell indulges in his disdain for management bureaucracy. Sitting in the lobby of Zell's spartan Equity Financial and Management Company office is a life-size, five foot eight statue of a man in suit and tie who is tangled in red tape and features actual bureau drawers. The engraving on a metal plate nearby leaves no doubt as to the object of this art. It reads: *The Bureaucrat*. It was carved by Michael Speaker, a model maker for filmmaker George Lucas. A friend of Zell's spotted *The Bureaucrat* in a Santa Fe gallery and sent Zell a picture of it with the message, "This is *you*, and you've got to have it." Zell not only bought the statue, he commissioned Speaker to make two others. Across the company's lobby, encased in glass, is a model of the Parthenon, but carved into each column are tiny bureaucrats in suits with their pants pulled down to their ankles. Title: *Truth in Ruins.* And in his own office, Zell keeps yet another version in view, this one sitting naked in a black caldron engulfed in flames. One year he had hundreds of miniatures of the standing bureaucrat made and sent out as Christmas greetings to four hundred friends and associates.

You won't find Zell in a suit. He goes to work in dungarees, a sweater, and penny loafers. He makes a point of thinking independently as well, and of hiring people who do the same. "I look for people who in no way, shape, or form can be intimidated," he says. "My greatest fear is somebody telling me what they think I might want to hear."

He also insists that companies would be stronger if more of them were run by people who have an ownership stake, as he explained in a 1991 speech before a crowd of New York academics and bankruptcy specialists. "Deals work when they have owners," he said. "There are a lot of good companies that are rapidly turning into bad companies by virtue of inaction, inattention, lack of capital expenditures, and most important of all, lack of owners. Deals don't work when in fact the guy calling the shots does not have his proverbial . . ." His eyes roll upward for a few seconds and then he shrugs. ". . . I guess I was going to say tit in the wringer, but be that as it may, they don't work." The audience rumbles with some embarrassed laughter, but the flinty Zell doesn't pause even to smile.

And he doesn't spare the rod for the restructuring process. Investment banking advisers are "the people who brought you leprosy now selling you the cure." Lenders, believing that "a rolling loan carries no loss," approve unrealistic restructurings. Committees clog the process because "when you have committees you have to have meetings, when you have meetings you have to have lunch or dinner or both. Businesses are eroding while the lenders are fighting about where we're going to have lunch next and dealing with the investment bankers and the committees."

Of course, the prevalence of wasteful bureaucrats, reluctant managements, and poor restructuring advisers creates openings for Zell and his current partner Schulte to come in with their particular brand of medicine that helps the company while making piles of money for them. They are a Nest-Building breed of vulture investor, specializing in good businesses with rickety financial structures. Often, they contribute fresh capital to a distressed company as the catalyst for a restructuring. But whenever they approach a needy company, they will not put money down—whether for bonds or post-restructuring stock—until they are sure that they will end up with a large stock ownership position and a say in how the revamped company is run. Otherwise, the investment is simply too much of a risk. As David Schulte has put it, they are little old ladies in tennis shoes. Very wealthy old ladies wearing top-of-the-line tennis shoes.

OPPORTUNITY MAN

Zell is an entrepreneur at heart. His father was a Polish grain broker, a Jew, who fled for America the night before the surprise Nazi invasion of September 1939. On August 23 of that year, while the elder Zell was traveling by train for business, he picked up a newspaper and read about the just-signed treaty between Russia and Germany. Getting home as quickly as he could, he packed up and, with his wife and daughter, left Poland on the afternoon of August 31. The following morning at 10:30, the German Luftwaffe began bombing the train stations. Zell's family traveled the only way they could: east, through Poland and Russia, reaching Japan by May of 1941. From there they went to New York and finally to the commodities capital, Chicago, where Zell was born in September.

Raised in the Chicago suburb of Highland Park, Zell began to display a creative mind for business as a young teenager when he bought up dozens of copies of *Playboy* at fifty cents apiece and resold them to his friends on the school playground for $1.50. He also came up with the idea of taking photographs and selling them at the eighth grade prom.

In the mid-1960s, while a senior at the University of Michigan, Zell launched his career in property management. While classmates were learning the basics of economics, he and his fraternity brother Robert Lurie were managing and refurbishing off-campus student housing and other apartment buildings throughout southeast Michigan. Then, as Zell pursued law and Lurie engineering, they intensified their extracurricular money-making activities; each raked in about $50,000 a year with investments in urban residences. That part-time occupation later bloomed into the Equity Financial and Management Company, a business that managed down-and-out properties.

In a 1969 real estate deal he would rather forget, Zell led an investor group that bought a Reno, Nevada, hotel and apartment complex for $13 million. His brother-in-law, Robert Baskes, represented the sellers. A federal tax investigation of the sale resulted in indictments of both Zell and Baskes for conspiracy to defraud the U.S. government. The charges against Zell were dropped, but in 1976 Baskes was convicted and served two years in prison. It marks a blemish on the Chicago financier's long record of successes.

When the REITs ran aground in the 1970s, the pair of young real estate buccaneers were made for the task. Acquiring sick real estate from East Coast REITs by assuming debt rather than putting up cash, they would nurse them back to health and put the cash flow into new purchases. Zell played the role of the strategist, and Lurie was the behind-the-scenes operations man—roles that would continue as their empire grew.

As investors propelled real estate values into the stratosphere in the early 1980s, Zell and Lurie turned their attention to undervalued corporations. Staying at first within their realm of expertise, they took a look at Great American Management & Investment, Inc., a real estate investment trust that had just hatched from bankruptcy but whose future remained in question. Laden with debt, GAMI did have one thing going for it: $110 million in tax loss carryforwards that could offset income for enormous tax savings. Zell and Lurie perceived that the securities markets were not reflecting a recent government action to extend the life of net operating loss carryforwards, which enhanced their value considerably. "We recognized an inefficient market," Zell says, "which has been a driving factor in all our activities." They bought some stock in GAMI and built a 22 percent stake by early 1981, got on the board, and eventually took control of management. Once in charge, they refinanced GAMI's debt and sold off properties to raise funds. Then they went out to find income-producing businesses that would greatly benefit from the tax loss carryforwards. GAMI's first corporate acquisition was rather inauspicious. In 1984, it bought the Raines Tool Company, a Houston-based maker of couplings that connect oil-carrying pipes. But cheap imports wiped out its market and the company had to be liquidated. GAMI's loss: $13 million. For the ace motorcyclist and skier, it was a rare fall. Zell and Lurie went on to fill their cups to overflowing with eighty new companies that diversified GAMI into everything from ski jackets to fertilizer. In the process they learned a great deal about non-real estate businesses—how they work and how to take them over, knowledge that would prove quite useful in the very near future.

In the fall of 1984, Zell caught a big one. Itel Corporation, a railcar and equipment leasing concern, had just come out of bankruptcy, and Zell bought up 10 percent of the stock. As he saw it, this was an opportunity to acquire low-cost railroad cars before the market for them strengthened, which he believed would happen as the existing supply aged. But also, as with GAMI, Itel had riches of tax loss carryforwards weighing in at $355 million that the market had undervalued. The company could use these to make highly economical acquisitions. Zell hammered at the company's directors to put him on the board, meeting with them time and again to explain the management strategy he envisioned. Finally, with some reluctance, Itel appointed Zell to the board, but only after he promised that for ten months he would not make a bid to acquire the company's shares. In the meantime, however, he raised his stake, first to 16 percent when he bought shares from vulture broker Randall Smith, and then to 22 percent. And it was partly because he was the largest shareholder that the directors nominated him in early 1985 to replace the company's retiring seventy-six-year-old chairman.

It became Zell's challenge to acquire profitable companies that could benefit from Itel's wealth of tax loss carryforwards. Again, he went out and loaded up sacksfull of businesses, expanding Itel into high-tech wire and dredging equipment and growing its railcar inventory. By 1991 Itel was a vast conglomerate with $2 billion in annual sales, now 26 percent owned by Zell. That year too, Zell maneuvered out of a tight squeeze. Having used junk bond debt to finance Itel's growth, he'd ended up with some lofty debt repayment bills. A series of asset sales in 1990 and 1991 eased the burden considerably.

When the real estate market, like a bullet fired into the air, slowed and began racing back downward toward a scurrying crowd, Zell loped back into that familiar territory. Not that he had ever completely abandoned it, but he had been waiting for the right moment to invest aggressively again. In 1988, he decided it was time. He called Merrill, Lynch, and he found that their capital markets group was thinking along the same lines. Together, they went out to raise a $250 million real estate vulture fund. He went on the road to promote the Zell-Merrill Real Estate Opportunity Partners Limited Partnership and hardly reined in his usual blustery manner. As one participant in a meeting with institutional investors recounted to *Institutional Investor* in April 1989: "He came into the office. He wouldn't sit down. He even took off his boots as he paced up and down talking about this bastard or that." (Zell maintains, however, that the myth perhaps had overtaken reality, because he would never behave rudely or wear boots to a meeting with prospective investors.) Together, Merrill, Lynch and Zell raised $410 million, mostly from pension funds but also $30 million from the top dozen executives at Zell's Equity group and $10 million from Merrill, Lynch itself. Because that fund was such a hit, Merrill, Lynch and Zell soon went out on the road again looking for funds, and by August of 1991 had closed with $550 million from pension funds, endowments, and foreign investors. In 1990, *Barron's* reported that the Zell-Lurie real estate empire (Lurie, Zell's first partner, died that year and his interest was then controlled by his estate) had grown to include some twenty-three million square feet of shopping centers, fifteen million square feet of office space, thirty-five thousand apartments, and mobile home parks with thirteen thousand pads for a total value exceeding $4 billion.

THE WORKOUT MAN

It was during his rehabilitation of Itel that Zell met David Schulte. Zell was looking for a financial adviser to help him with the restructuring of Itel's railcar division when Warren Hellman, a San Francisco investment banker and an Itel director, introduced him to Schulte. A graduate of Williams College in Williamstown, Massachusetts, and the Yale Law School, Schulte had spent several years half-heartedly working in law and corporate management before he settled into the workout business. He'd served as a clerk to Supreme Court Justice Potter Stewart and had left to become special assistant to the chief executive officer of Northwest Industries, a conglomerate, and later, vice president of planning and acquisitions and finally executive vice president.

Along the way, he had to do workouts—in other words, restructure the finances—of some Northwest operating companies that had fallen on hard times. "I found that work very engaging, and I decided that I wanted to do that full-time. It was the first time in my life that I really knew what I wanted to do. But at the time while there were bankruptcy lawyers and accountants, there was not one investment banker doing workouts." He shopped the idea of a workout department at all the major Wall Street firms. But while some offered to put him in mergers and acquisitions where he might do some restructurings on the side, only one agreed to hire him as a workouts specialist. That was Salomon Brothers.

Salomon had already handled one major restructuring, of Chrysler Corporation, for which it won an $800 million bailout loan from the federal government. When Schulte came on in 1979, the world thought that Lee Iacocca's company was fixed and the new workouts specialist did not have many projects to tend to. "But as luck would have it, by the end of 1980 it needed money again," Schulte says. On December 12, the man who'd handled the first bailout, James Wolfensohn, called Schulte and said, "You say you want to do workouts. You'd better come to a meeting tomorrow." That meeting lasted ten weeks.

Ronald Reagan had just been elected president, but Jimmy Carter was still in office. The new administration was against government bailouts of business. "So we were in a footrace with Inauguration Day," Schulte recounts. Finally, the decision was made by the Carter administration to lend Chrysler $400 million, and the Reagan administration agreed to implement the bailout that February. Later, Schulte became the principal point man on Salomon's

Chrysler account and kept busy handling postworkout jobs for the automaker.

On leaving Salomon in 1984, Schulte started Chilmark Partners, a debt-restructuring boutique, and soon was hired by Zell to work on Itel. "When I first met Sam Zell, I didn't know what to make of him," Schulte says. "There before me was an exuberant Jewish leprechaun emitting lots of energy. I wasn't sure if he was real or a figment of my imagination." After reworking the debt of Itel's railcar division, which had not been properly repaired in the Chapter 11 reorganization, he and Zell collaborated in Itel's acquisition of the Evans Rail Car fleet from the bankrupt Evans Products Company and shared several other vulture investing adventures. Zell became Chilmark's best client. "I'm his biggest fan," raves Schulte, whose polished manner and dress contrasts sharply with Zell. "I really think the guy is sensational."

ORIGINS OF A VULTURE FUND

One deal they stumbled on convinced them that there were some big opportunities in corporate vulture investing, but that an awful lot of money would be needed for them to really pay off. Based on their experience in that case, they would later decide to go for broke and raise a billion-dollar fund to invest in the market of distressed companies.

That deal was the restructuring of Apex Oil. A privately owned oil refiner, trader, and marketer, Apex collided with trouble in the mid-1980s. Most of the St. Louis, Missouri, company's assets were held in a subsidiary called Clark Oil & Refining Corporation, which encompassed two refineries, thirteen product terminals, 946 service stations, and a ski resort. Weighing it all down was $545 million of secured bank debt. For two years, the company and its lenders were locked in bitter debt restructuring talks. At each meeting of the two sides, CEO P. Anthony Novelly would announce the imminent emergence of someone who was going to buy the company; he often described the person as a wealthy Arab investor. Over time as no buyer stepped forward, the jaded bankers began referring to the invisible buyer as "Tony's Sheik of the Week." At one particularly raucous session, Novelly ended the meeting by "getting to his feet and making an obscene gesture at the lender group representatives," according to a study of the case done later.

In 1987, Zell was introduced to Novelly through a mutual friend and held preliminary discussions with the banks about buying their loans. Zell had never before seen such "bad blood" and "mistrust" between a borrower and its lenders. In June of 1987, someone did step up to acquire the bulk of the Clark subsidiary's assets—the Getty Petroleum Company. But within a month that deal fell through because the banks would not agree to cover liabilities that might pop up in connection with those loans. In August, Zell reached a tentative agreement to buy Apex's bank debt and its assets for $447 million, but that deal also crumbled. Finally, in December of 1987 as it teetered on the edge of liquidation, Apex took shelter from its creditors by filing for bankruptcy court protection.

Zell continued to negotiate with the bank group in direct competition with Getty. He hired Schulte to help him, offering as compensation the opportunity to invest side by side with him. During the talks at the lead bank in St. Louis, Schulte was in one room and Getty Oil representatives were in an adjoining room, as the banks' negotiators played off one bidder against the other. In June 1988, Zell and Schulte netted the deal by offering to buy the $545 million in loans for $396 million. But they won not so much on the basis of price as for their willingness to take the debt without assurances from the banks that any liabilities tied to the debt would be covered. Why would they take on the potentially great risks of lawsuits arising from these loans? "It was a business judgment," Schulte explains. "We always intended to wrap this [purchase] into a total deal that would be blessed by the bankruptcy court." In other words, they hoped to use their position as holders of Apex's senior debt to negotiate a reorganization plan with the company that would give them control of the new Apex and cancel those liabilities.

What made life interesting was that at the time they negotiated to buy the debt, Zell and Schulte didn't have anything near the $396 million needed to pay for it. And although Zell had borrowing power, no bank would lend money for the acquisition of defaulted bank loans. Even if they had that kind of money themselves, both of these investors were too conservative to lay it down just on a hope and a prayer that they would have the influence to bring about the plan they had in mind. The linchpin of their strategy was an option contract. By putting down a mere $5 million in cash, they would reserve the right for three months to buy the $545 million in bank debt at the agreed-on price.

Obviously, the option ultimately would be worthless if they couldn't come up with the cash to exercise it. So, Zell and Schulte teamed up with a more moneyed buyer brought in by Apex's management. CEO Novelly was on the board of a company called Horsham Corporation, a Canadian gold mining concern. Horsham could borrow money at a rate of 2 percent against the gold deposits it owned. Novelly saw the potential and brought Zell and Horsham together in a proposed two-step scheme: Zell and Schulte would have the right to invest $10 million in Horsham stock and stock warrants, and Horsham would finance the acquisition of the bank debt. "That's how this partnership went forward. Sam's deal, Horsham's checkbook," Schulte says.

THE REVERSE LBO

All the strings were tied on the option by the end of June, 1988. Later Horsham extended the option out to November 30, 1988, by paying another $3 million. So now Horsham, along with Zell and Schulte had the right and the money to buy the bank debt. But before the senior creditors could take control of the company, they had to pay off the unsecured creditors—who had filed claims of $900 million—and come out of bankruptcy. The seniors had enormous leverage in determining what the shape of the final plan would be. But they knew that the judge in the case had his eye out for the little guys—small creditors like suppliers to Clark's gas stations. And however mightily the senior creditors threw their weight around, the judge could trip them up unless the others got what he and they considered a fair shake. So, says Schulte, "Instead of going the King Kong route, beating our chest and saying, 'Look at us. We've got the liens on the assets, so we decide,' " they constructed a transaction that was too good for the unsecured creditors to refuse and presented it in September 1988.

This is where the deal becomes really creative, yet, in Zell style, quite simple. Zell came up with the idea of canceling the entire senior tier of debt—the debt that Horsham intended to buy—in return for majority ownership of the valuable Clark Oil. That is, they would tear up the bank note representing their loans, wiping out $545 million of debt and its liens on all of the assets of Apex. Most important, they would give the junior creditors Apex, which without Clark was an oil-trading company with terminals, boats and working capital. Free of the liens on these assets, and with an additional $45 million in cash the senior group offered to contribute, junior creditors would have a viable business.

Bankruptcy watchers called it the first "reverse" leveraged buyout. In a leveraged buyout, the acquirer loads the company up with debt in order to pay less up front. In this case, the acquirers unloaded the debt in order to get the company and end up with a low-debt balance sheet. Apex agreed not to pursue any lawsuits that might come up in relation to the bank debt, which is exactly what Zell and Schulte had figured on when they bought the option without guarantees.

Schulte maintains that the success of the deal lay in the nonconfrontational approach he and Zell made to the unsecured creditors. "We don't believe you can successfully play winners and losers in the insolvency market where by definition everyone's already a loser. If you choose to do the macho thing, if you choose to grind people to the ground, if you choose to say 'Screw em, They'll get what I give em,' all you do is piss them off, make enemies, and make it take longer. There's no such thing as a lawyer trained in an American law school who is without something to say—ever. So if you let it run so that everyone is at loggerheads all of the time and they all instruct their lawyers to fight, it will never end."

Before the unsecured creditors and the judge had a chance to ponder the proposed innovative arrangement, however, Getty Petroleum reappeared. Its attorneys stood up in court in October and announced that Getty was prepared to pay exactly what the senior creditor group offered to pay, plus $50 million in cash. Everyone knows that more money snares the deal, right? But a closer look revealed that this offer was not more money after all. Remember, Zell, Schulte, and Horsham had contracted to buy the $545 million bank debt at a $150 million discount. Getty had not negotiated such a deal, and the bank group was not about to break its contract with the senior creditors. Getty raised its bid by $35 million and in last-minute negotiations Horsham and its partners had to raise their bid, and ended up paying $30 million more than they had planned.

So, Horsham got Clark, and Apex rose from the ashes of bankruptcy in November 1988. And Zell and Schulte? They got the right to buy $10 million of Horsham stock at the price at which it had been trading *before* teaming up with Horsham—$5.50 Canadian, compared with about $8 after the Clark acquisition. That turned out to be quite a deal. The refineries Horsham now owned started to spout money, and by the end of 1991, Zell and Schulte had more than doubled their money.

FUND-RAISING FOLLIES

"It was fun," says Schulte. "But, we had relatively small dough invested. So our percentage profit was high but our dollar profit was tiny compared to the value of the deal. We looked back over our shoulders and said, 'You know, this was really pretty good. If we're going to do this kind of thing, we ought to have our own source of equity.' " So they decided to raise assets from investors to put into desperate companies. A vulture fund.

Zell had just finished raising his first $400 million vulture real estate fund with the help of Merrill, Lynch, when he hit the money trail once again at the end of 1989 for the new vulture corporate fund, the Zell-Chilmark Fund. Zell and Schulte made more than 200 personal sales calls in the United States, Europe, and Japan over a seven-month stretch—an odyssey that included its share of travails. On one trip at the end of January 1990, the pair of vultures had set up a grueling schedule of Vienna in the morning, Basel for dinner, and Paris the following morning. Because that zigzag was impossible to do by commercial airline, they chartered a plane to ferry them around Europe. At first, the trip went smoothly. They took an overnight flight from Chicago to Vienna, where they held a series of meetings, then boarded the chartered plane for the hop to Basel.

But during the dinner meeting there, the pilots of the plane arrived to tell them that because of a hurricane that was barreling across Europe they wouldn't be able to fly to Paris. So, at midnight Zell and Schulte boarded a train for the six-hour trip to Paris. They retired to their *couchette* for the night. "The cabin was about as wide as my desk," Schulte recalls. "There were three bunk beds—hammocks, really—stacked vertically, and a guy was asleep on the bottom one." Zell and Schulte climbed into the top two bunks, but as they were settling to sleep Zell suddenly became worried that his wallet in his pants and his passport in his briefcase would be stolen. So clutching his pants and the briefcase in the tiny berth, he drifted off to sleep.

Presenting their fund proposal to prospective investors, Zell and Schulte explained that multitudes of companies that had taken on too much debt in the 1980s were being squeezed in the credit crunch and would be in dire need of new capital. As Zell told *Barron's:* "These days money talks, and BS walks." Their offering memorandum included annual rate of return projections of forty percent, but the number was there only because Merrill, Lynch insisted that they put one in—and a relatively high one at that. In actuality, Zell and Schulte do not predict rates of return because forecasts are "an invitation to self-deception." At sales meetings they did not deceive the prospective investors. "We told everyone that our financial objective was to not lose money, and the upside would take care of itself," says Zell. At the end of 1990, Zell sent holiday greetings to those who had signed up to invest in the new fund in the form of statuettes of a joker dancing on a grave. Along with them he sent a poem he'd penned titled, "The Year of the Grave Dancer." Here is an excerpt:

> *If it's Santa you was 'specting*
> *Well you better get down*
> *Cause it's the Gravedancers Redux*
> *Who are coming to town.*
>
> *Who asked them to the party?*
> *It's pretty plain to see*
> *The lenders and the spenders*
> *Made them hop with glee.*

Leverage was the beverage
That got this party cookin'
But the hangover's set in,
And now a Gravedancer's lookin'.

It's Gravedancer times
When there's panic in the land
When assets sell at costs that scream,
"Bail me out, man!"

PICKY SHOPPERS

In July of 1990, it was done: With $1 billion in ten-year capital commitments, mostly from American investors, Zell and Schulte went shopping. The key word here is commitments. The money didn't sit idle in a bank vault somewhere. All of the investors kept their funds until Zell-Chilmark found something to buy—although the investors did pay fees to Zell-Chilmark on the funds not yet invested. After all, finding the right low-risk, high-profit target can take some doing, and the promise the vultures had made to investors to make six to ten investments in six years was a tall order. Zell and Schulte started out with a list of more than 200 companies, which grew to 280 and were categorized as attractive, unattractive, or deals completed by someone else. They talked to managements at such companies as Interco, Inc., Harcourt Brace Jovanovich, Morningstar Foods, and the Equitable Life Assurance Society of America. Leveraged-buyout investors outbid them on Morningstar and HBJ.

Finally, Zell-Chilmark took a dive—and made a splash. Toward the end of 1990, Zell got a call from Philip Hawley, the chairman of West Coast retailer Carter, Hawley, Hale. The company, which owns the Emporium, Broadway, and Weinstock's department store chains, was suffering from the ailment of crushing debt that had been going around in the country. Actually, its troubles went back to 1986 when Carter, Hawley spurned an offer to be acquired by Leslie Wexner's powerhouse specialty store chain, The Limited. To keep the wolf from the door, in 1987 Carter, Hawley heaped $600 million of new debt onto its balance sheet and spun off its crown jewels, the Neiman-Marcus and Berg-dorf Goodman store chains. But, profits from the remaining units fell short of expectations and, although the company laid off one thousand employees in 1990, there was no money to pay the interest on $350 million of junk bonds on top of $453 million in secured debt.

Zell had known Philip Hawley for years, having worked with him on several property development ventures. Hawley called his old friend to just "tell me where he was at," Zell says. According to Schulte, Zell and Hawley discussed the possibility of an investment in Carter, Hawley by the new vulture fund, but the discussion produced no agreement. In February 1991, the once-proud retailer crawled on hands and knees into bankruptcy court, its $1.4 billion of liabilities eclipsing $1.2 billion of assets.

Early in May, the company and its advisers sat down to review the options for reorganization, and they decided that the best alternative was to find an outside investor to contribute cash in return for stock. Carter, Hawley and its advisers drew up a list of investors, with Sam Zell at the top. The company called him up, and this time he was interested. Zell signed a confidentiality agreement that allowed him access to the company's files and business secrets so that he could do the research needed to determine his level of interest and set a price. Now, the only question was how Zell would buy his equity stake. Jeffrey Chanin, a Carter, Hawley financial adviser with a Los Angeles firm bearing his name, suggested the idea of simply making a tender offer to buy out the bondholders. A year and a half before, Japonica Partners had made the first bid for public debt in a bankruptcy setting in the Allegheny case. But Chanin considered this "the lesson in how not to do a tender in a bankruptcy context," since Japonica was hostile toward the company and had already picked up a lot of Allegheny's other debt anyway. In Carter, Hawley, the tender offer was going to be the mechanism for doing a very friendly reorganization.

Late in July 1991, Zell-Chilmark offered to buy out holders of $550 million in the unsecured bonds and supplier claims of Carter, Hawley, Hale Stores. Their price: forty cents on the dollar. Their objective: to acquire 80 percent of the unsecured debt class. As Zell and the company had discussed, these bonds would be traded in for stock when the company emerged from bankruptcy. "I clearly have no intention of being a bondholder," Zell proclaimed. "If I'm going to make an investment, I'm going to be an owner of equity."

It took some doing to get the tender offer over the top. The bid was set to expire on September 5, but the creditors' committee insisted on having more time to consider it. The committee wanted time to look around for people who might be interested in buying the entire company and offer creditors a more attractive recovery than the vulture investors were proposing. On August 15, Zell-Chilmark extended the forty-cent tender offer to September 16 and expanded it to cover $50 million worth of disputed claims.

In the meantime, Carter, Hawley shareholders were steaming. The Zell-Chilmark offer did nothing at all for shareholders. If 80 percent of the creditors took the vulture fund's price and gave it control of the unsecured class of claims, Zell-Chilmark would be in a position to push through a reorganization plan without giving lower-ranking stockholders a farthing. "As it stands, the equity holders are being taken to the cleaners," one bankruptcy specialist told *Corporate Financing Week*. In August, one large shareholder asked and received the court's permission to organize a committee to negotiate a recovery in the reorganization with whomever ended up controlling the company.

Early in September, it appeared that the vultures were going to have competition for Carter, Hawley when the company opened its books to new parties, including Dillard Department Stores. But Zell-Chilmark did not move to raise its forty-cents-on-the-dollar price. And on Monday, September 10, 1991, five days before the deadline, the creditors' committee refused to endorse the Zell-Chilmark bid in the hope that it would be raised or a better one would happen along. Zell-Chilmark extended its bid to October 1.

A few days before the deadline, the offer seemed to be failing as the tenders coming in fell far short of the buyers' 80 percent goal. It was time for some serious negotiating action. On Sunday night, September 29, Schulte flew to San Francisco and the following morning breakfasted with a key member of the bondholders' committee. The committee member wanted to join Zell-Chilmark in its tender for bonds so that he also could receive stock, which was not something the vulture investors wanted. That night, Schulte flew across the country to New York and on the morning of Tuesday, October 1 met with two more committee members. All the while, calls were coming in from Zell, who was doing his own airport-to-airport marathon. Finally, the investors agreed to raise their offer to forty-seven cents and require only 70 percent approval, and because no competing bidder ever emerged, the committee agreed to endorse the Zell-Chilmark proposal. By a new deadline of October 16, Zell-Chilmark received 80 percent of the claims, $431 million worth. Plus it threw in another $23.5 million to cover disputed claims and a $50 million special line of credit for store refurbishing—a total of about $276 million plucked from their $1 billion vulture fund. What followed were negotiations with remaining creditors and stockholders to pay them off and end the bankruptcy.

Part of the reason the deal worked without many hitches was because of Zell and Schulte's high level of credibility. "They were viewed as strong," says Carter, Hawley adviser Jeffrey Chanin. "That was part of the reason someone else didn't come in to bid for the company." And another reason was Hawley and Zell's ability to work closely together, even though they are contrasting personalities—Zell gruff and profane, and Hawley so gentlemanly that he replaces the *p* with a *k* when he says he's "pissed off."

Of course, the Carter, Hawley investment still left a lot of money in the Zell-Chilmark fund's kitty. In October, the partners were actively trying to invest it by joining in the competition for the Executive Life Insurance Company of California. The insurer had been brought to ruin by a $6.4 billion face value investment portfolio rich in low-quality junk bonds, and it was that portfolio that proved most interesting to a number of bottom-fishing bidders. Anyone who got hold of Executive Life would have a foot in the door of many ongoing reorganizations of junk-financed companies, and could end up with substantial ownership stakes in many of them.

Warren Hellman, the man who had introduced David Schulte to Sam Zell in the mid-1980s, proposed the idea of making a bid together with him and Jack Byrne, head of the Vermont-based investment company Fund American Companies and the man who turned around insurance giant Firemen's Fund. In turn, Zell-Chilmark brought in one of its own investors, the General Motors pension fund. The four investors cobbled together a $750 million bid, later increased to $1 billion. Their hope was that eventually, they would be able to take part in workout negotiations at each of the troubled companies represented in the Executive Life portfolio, and they could assemble a collection of large equity stakes in major recovering corporations such as Charter Medical, Memorex Telex, and Days Inns of America. But by year end, the Hellman, Zell-Chilmark, Byrne, and GM group's bid lost out to Drexel, Burnham alumnus Leon Black and his partner, Crédit Lyonnais.

So Zell-Chilmark and its professional staff of eight continued their quest for companies. Zell and Schulte hoped that their work would benefit from their philosophy of caution. As Zell himself wrote:

As with any opportunity . . . there are substantial pitfalls. The decisions and structuring of specific deals must be made with care and sophistication. Grave dancing is an art that has many potential benefits. But one must be careful while prancing around not to fall into the open pit and join the cadaver. There is often a thin line between the dancer and the danced upon.

12

A Flash and a Star

I'll be glad to pay up—tomorrow. And I know my fellow inmates will promise the same. They've all a touching credulity concerning tomorrows.

—THE ICEMAN COMETH

In the summer of 1990, the country stood at the precipice of recession. More and more companies were defaulting on their debt payments and being wheeled into intensive care. Many of them went bankrupt. Some died. With the growing casualty list, perhaps it is not surprising that at virtually the same moment two new vulture investors arrived with big money and big ambitions. Both were of the Heavyweight breed, that is, they pursued the strategy of taking jumbo positions in a troubled company's bonds that enabled them to be a force in the workout. By the end of 1991, one of these newcomers was making history in the business world and the other was rapidly becoming history.

The survivor was Leon Black, the former chief of mergers and acquisitions at Drexel, Burnham, Lambert & Company, whose aggressive marketing of junk bonds gave rise to the frenzy of mergers and acquisitions in the 1980s. With $1.3 billion to work

with from Altus Finance, which is an affiliate of the French bank
Crédit Lyonnais, and other investors, Black invested in several
companies that were just treading water and then boldly used
major bond positions to help facilitate restructurings beneficial to
himself. At the end of 1991, his major funder and other investors
emerged victorious in the bidding war for the Executive Life Insurance Company of California. Actually, Altus and Black were not
going to own any part of the insurance company; the underwriting
operation and the healthy section of the insurer's investment portfolio would go to a group of French investors including a French
insurance company. Rather, Black was going to manage much of
Executive Life's legendary junk bond portfolio on behalf of Altus
and take a cut of the profits as well as management fees. Included
in the $5.3 billion collection were chunky portions of the bonds of
many troubled companies that were or would be restructuring. By
becoming involved in those workouts, Black could greatly influence the restructuring and bring about the maximum return for
himself, whether that be in the form of cash, bonds, or sizable
equity stakes in renewed companies. In short, this acquisition was
a vulture investor's dream come true.

By contrast, Goldman, Sachs & Company's much-ballyhooed
Water Street Corporate Recovery Fund performed a virtual disap-
pearing act in 1991. It had been run on a day-to-day basis by
Mikael Salovaara, along with four other Goldman, Sachs general
and limited partners. Salovaara had been a natural choice for the
position as the head of Goldman, Sachs's leverage group that dealt
in debt-heavy companies of both good and poor quality. In May
1991, Goldman, Sachs announced that it would close the fund by
year end. But Salovaara and another of the fund's supervising
partners, Alfred Eckert III, the co-head of merchant banking, decided to leave and solicit investors—including some Water Street
investors—to raise their own vulture fund. They started out in a
four-room office in midtown far from the canyons of Wall Street,
soon realizing they needed to search for larger quarters. At the
same time, they helped Goldman drain the Water Street fund,
paying off investors as securities in the portfolio were traded in
restructurings or sold off. The portfolio, initially $783 million in
assets, had dwindled to $450 million by the end of the year.

Laid side by side, the stories of Water Street and Leon Black illustrate the dynamics of vulture investing in the early 1990s. Those who were well-versed in the financing needs of indebted companies and had the entrepreneurial drive could raise huge sums of money to invest in workouts, as both Black and Goldman, Sachs did. So armed, success seemed to be a matter of combining good analysis with the judicious use of power. But for Goldman, the controversy of vulture investing became too much of a risk. Its vulture fund was back on the ground just as Black was beginning to soar.

THE SOFT TOUCH

Mikael Salovaara (his father's parents were from Finland) is an investment banker in his late thirties with a reputation as an aggressive negotiator but without the personality to match. Conservatively dressed in a two-piece suit and suspenders, he is low key, serious, with blue eyes and a reddish blond beard and mustache. His approach is soft-spoken steadfastness. "We're prepared to come this far and no further," he says with cool resolve. "We will not take something in the middle. We know what we want."

The son of a town manager, Salovaara was born in Pottsville, Pennsylvania, but spent most of his youth moving from one small city to the next. Now he lives in Brooklyn with his wife and two young children. Salovaara's college and graduate education was a decade long and as varied as the curriculum. He started out at Dartmouth with a double major in English and math, earning degrees in both in 1974. From there he traveled to Cambridge University for an M.A. in literature in 1976. And as a final flourish, he earned business and law degrees from the University of Virginia, both in 1980.

A career in business it was to be, and that year Salovaara joined Goldman, Sachs as a generalist in the corporate finance department. He worked mostly on mundane corporate fund raising through stock and bond underwritings but occasionally helped reconfigure a troubled company's finances to ease debt obligations. In fact, his very first assignment was as part of a four-man team that was trying to pull the Itel Corporation from some very quick quicksand. Itel is the railroad car and equipment financing company that eventually fell into the hands of vulture investor Sam Zell. The previous fall, the fall of 1979, IBM had introduced a leasing product that instantly obsoleted some of Itel's major product lines. The Goldman, Sachs team—which also included Salovaara's future partner in business Fred Eckert—recommended that Itel file for Chapter 11, because there were too many different creditors and shareholders to do a successful restructuring out of court. But Itel's board wanted Goldman, Sachs to try to convince everyone to go along with an exchange offer anyway. It was useless. "We tried for over a year, and then Itel filed for Chapter 11 and got a new adviser," says Salovaara.

In 1984, he leapt onto the accelerating leveraged buyout locomotive, as many a corporate finance type would during the decade—including most notably Leon Black. Alfred Eckert had become head of the LBO group and brought Salovaara into the fold. In that capacity, they served as advisers to managements that were borrowing scads of money and hoisting their companies' debt levels in order to buy up low-priced stock and take possession. Together, in 1986, the two LBO advisers raised a $250 million fund to invest in buyouts and placed the money in about twenty-two companies. By the end of 1991, those investments had delivered glittering annualized returns of 35 to 40 percent.

But by the middle of 1987, after the stock market had spiraled up 1000 points to 2700 in just a year, the LBO group began to run out of good low-priced prospects. And with the SEC's insider trading investigation mounting and Drexel, Burnham, Lambert implicated, Salovaara says, "I said to myself, 'This market is going to fall apart. These LBOs are going to have to be restructured.' " In anticipation of that development, the LBO department was broadened to include workouts and junk-bond underwriting—the common thread for all three being heavy debt—and Salovaara took over management of the operation.

GOING FOR BROKE

The crash of October 1987 appeared to be Salovaara's prediction come true, but the changeover from LBOs to workouts failed to occur as frenzied stock market investing soon resumed. Two years later when a number of buyouts encountered severe problems meeting debt payment obligations, Salovaara knew the era of restructuring had finally arrived. He broached the idea of raising another fund, this one to invest in distressed companies reworking their finances—or what amounts to the unwinding of LBOs as they were forced to reduce their debt. The management committee partners at Goldman not only liked the idea of a vulture fund, they decided to put $100 million of the firm's money into it. They would call it the Water Street Corporate Recovery Fund after a street one block from headquarters.

In April 1990, Salovaara and others began making one-on-one presentations to institutional investors in an effort to raise $400 million for the fund. Water Street's strategy, as stated in the offering memorandum, was to "invest the Fund's capital on a basis that may enable it to *influence,* directly or indirectly, the recapitalization of those companies." And the objective was annually compounded returns of 25 to 35 percent, achievable only, the memo continued, *"if the Fund assumes an active investment role, acquires substantial positions, and seizes initiatives when there are restructuring opportunities"* (emphasis added).

A burly investment house seemed to be the ideal purveyor of a large vulture fund, for it has the intellectual resources, mergers and acquisitions expertise, and capital raising apparatus that can help analyze good investment opportunities and engineer major restructurings. But there were also potential conflicts of interest for an investment bank practicing vulture investing. Hardly denying this problem, Goldman, Sachs listed nine potential conflicts of interest in its offering memorandum. For instance, it mentioned relationships with corporate and investing clients: "There may be certain [Water Street Corporate] Recovery Securities investments or certain investing tactics that Goldman, Sachs will not undertake on behalf of the fund in view of such relationships." And among its clients may be creditors and debtors involved in restructurings: "Such actions, for which the Firm may be compensated, may limit or preclude the flexibility that the Fund may otherwise have to buy or sell certain Recovery Securities."

Yet, besides the conflict-of-interest problem that was applicable to any investment bank, Goldman, Sachs itself didn't seem to be the ideal brokerage firm to fulfill the role of activist vulture investor. Although Goldman, Sachs did traffic in busted railroad bonds back in the 1940s, time and money had changed the firm. It had grown up and matured into a prestigious securities house with Blue-Chip, conservative clients—including both institutional investors who used Goldman, Sachs to handle their securities trading and corporations who called on the firm for corporate finance services. During the 1980s when corporate raiding and greenmail were prevalent, Goldman, Sachs made a point of distancing itself from such predatory practices by generally refusing to represent raiders. But, of course, as the consummate defender of the corporation under attack, Goldman, Sachs was involved in the fray, and alienating its institutional investing clientele to some degree. In that sense, the conservative firm had taken a controversial position—although one that was far less controversial than that chosen by Drexel, Burnham, Lambert and others.

Goldman was, therefore, prepared for the rough-and-tumble of vulture investing. It was aware of the conflicts that arise between owners and managers of companies. It knew that an activist vulture influencing restructurings is often a catalyst of hostility. (The firm had done some vulture investing, in Wheeling-Pittsburgh and others.) But Goldman also felt confident that, as in the merger era, it could take a stance that did not intimidate managements. After all, investing in bonds is not hostile behavior, Goldman reasoned; a bondholder has no vote that it can use to eject management. And saying no to a company's exchange offer and waiting for a better one to come along do not remove executives from their jobs. "Nobody at Goldman, Sachs was surprised by the nature of the business," Salovaara says. Vulture investing wasn't comparable to a raider trying to acquire a company against the wishes of its management and board.

Whether or not a vulture fund fit Goldman, Sachs's staid culture, during the spring of 1990 investors rushed for the opportunity to sign up and participate in the rapidly developing restructuring boom. Within a mere six weeks, Water Street had more than $500 million of commitments from institutional investors, and Goldman, Sachs decided to stop marketing the fund. Over the following few months, more commitments came in from investors Salovaara had visited, and finally he closed the fund with $783 million in committed assets, $100 million from Goldman, Sachs and the rest reportedly from the likes of Princeton, Cornell, and University of Pennsylvania endowment funds; the Gordon Getty trust; wealthy individual investors; and such corporate pension funds as Du Pont Company's.

Salovaara made his first investments in late June, starting small with purchases of a few bonds here and a few bonds there. Among Water Street's first sizable plays was G-I Holdings, the company that owns the chemical manufacturer GAF Corporation. The giant vulture fund swallowed half the company's bonds for approximately seventy-five cents on the dollar for a total investment of $100 million. The company then began talking up the idea of exchanging outstanding bonds for new bonds with easier terms. In response, Salovaara drew a bottom line that G-I Holdings could not mistake for something that was negotiable. "We said we would not be a participant at less than one hundred cents on the dollar."

Later, the company came back and said it would be able simply to reset the interest rate on the existing bonds. Okay, rejoined Salovaara. Just reset the rate so that the bonds trade at 100 cents on the dollar. G-I went off and issued stock in its crown-jewel subsidiary, International Specialty Products, a maker of specialty chemicals. This move improved G-I's image in the securities markets, allowing it then to reset the bonds as Goldman, Sachs had so firmly requested. The vulture fund ended up with a profit of $33 million on its $100 million investment in a little less than a year's time.

By January 1991, Water Street had invested $650 million of its money, lumbering like a great beast into the restructurings of Interco, USG Corporation, National Gypsum, Maryland Cable, Harcourt Brace Jovanovich, and others. At the time, the value of its holdings had dropped by some 5 to 8 percent below their cost, and observers began to refer to Water Street as the "Underwater Fund." Salovaara was far from gloomy, however. As the prices on his holdings went down, he simply bought more. What he had liked at one price, he liked even more at a lower price. And besides, his investors had given him four years to make the grade.

CONTROVERSY

But Water Street also pursued investments in companies with which Goldman, Sachs had a corporate finance relationship, and this was where the fund ran into conflict of interest problems—or at least conflict of interest *appearance* problems. Nine of the twenty-one investments the fund made in its brief lifetime were in companies that either were Goldman, Sachs clients or had once been clients. What's more, Salovaara had maintained his position as head of the leveraged finance department—creating the potential that he would come into contact with companies that were also Water Street investment targets. This seemed to violate the usual protocol of setting up a Chinese Wall between trading and investment banking departments to prevent the transfer of confidential information. Traders at competing firms joked that Salovaara had "a Chinese Wall in the middle of his brain."

One fairly new Goldman, Sachs corporate finance client that Salovaara was involved with was E. M. Warburg, Pincus & Company, a New York investment firm that controlled a number of companies including newspaper publishers. In 1990, Salovaara and other Goldman, Sachs investment bankers advised Warburg, Pincus on how to ease the debt burden at its Community Newspapers, Inc., but the proposed restructuring failed and Goldman, Sachs ended its work. At about the same time, Salovaara saw that another Warburg, Pincus-controlled newspaper company with balance sheet problems, the Journal Company, would make for a good Water Street investment. But while advising Community Newspapers, Goldman, Sachs had learned the internal earnings projections for the Journal Company—and with such insider information the firm would not be able to invest in the company's securities. There was a way, however, and the Journal Company agreed to it. The company distributed the internal projections to all bondholders and included in that mailing the flash that Goldman, Sachs and Water Street could soon be joining their ranks. Meantime, Journal Company bonds were plummeting in price.

So at very attractive prices Water Street moved in. Late in 1990 and at the start of 1991, it picked up roughly $50 million worth—

about a fourth of the total debt—for sixty cents to sixty-five cents on the dollar. The company was facing a $7 million interest payment on March 1 that it was not going to be able to make. It presented a swap offer to one of its largest bondholders, Executive Life; in exchange for the current bonds, Warburg, Pincus would give the insurer new bonds that carried a lower interest rate but also a shorter term and a first call on the assets if there were to be a bankruptcy. Executive Life turned the offer down.

Without knowing this, Salovaara went to Warburg, Pincus with virtually the same proposition. The company agreed and suggested that they both try to convince other bondholders to do the same swap. Before they had a chance, however, bondholders heard about the agreement the company had struck with Goldman, Sachs, and some of them—including Goldman, Sachs clients—complained that they didn't like the deal. The most strident complaints came from William R. Huff, the manager of more than $1 billion in junk bonds in Morristown, New Jersey. He drew up a written protest about Goldman, Sachs's dual role as adviser to and investor in Warburg, Pincus companies, and he distributed it to about sixty other junk bond investors, including other Goldman, Sachs clients. In all, about 40 percent of the bonds were swapped, including Water Street's—but not enough to put the Journal Company completely in the clear. Salovaara hung onto the new bonds, confident that if bankruptcy befell the company the senior position he'd negotiated would ensure a 100-cents-on-the-dollar recovery.

But the deal that really carved the fate of the Water Street fund in stone was the bid for the nearly broken toy maker Tonka Corporation. In September 1990, Salovaara got a call from John Vogelstein, the vice chairman of Warburg, Pincus. He was calling on behalf of yet another company Warburg, Pincus controlled, Mattel Inc. He asked the young investment banker/vulture investor whether Goldman, Sachs would be interested in advising Mattel on an attempted takeover of Tonka. Because Water Street had owned some Tonka bonds since late July, Salovaara turned him down but offered to work in partnership with Mattel to acquire Tonka. Instead, Mattel indicated in early October that it was not likely to make a bid for Tonka in the short term.

Still, when Water Street wanted to continue buying Tonka bonds, it obtained Mattel's permission as a courtesy. The fund made big purchases in November and December—directly from Lehman Brothers, Tonka's investment bankers. The fact that it could purchase its bonds from Tonka's investment bankers indicated that Tonka had no plans to sell, because anyone with inside information on a transaction would not be allowed to trade in the securities. And indeed, Mattel never made a bid. But in January 1991, Hasbro Inc. did bid, offering $470 million to acquire Tonka—including $7 a share and eighty cents on the dollar for one bond issue and seventy-five cents for the other. The value of Water Street's holdings shot up by 50 percent.

When other investors learned of this sequence of events they complained of unfair tactics. "Certainly, we would want to have had that information (about Mattel's interest in Tonka)," said a resentful David Breazzano, manager of Fidelity Investments's vulture fund, in the *Wall Street Journal.* If he had known that Tonka was a takeover candidate in the toy industry, he might not have sold his $10 million of Tonka bonds before the Hasbro bid.

Goldman, Sachs kept buying bonds in February until it owned just over half of each of the two bond issues. In all, Water Street spent $84 million at depressed prices of thirty cents to forty cents on the dollar. Salovaara then received a call from Barry Alperin, Hasbro's co-chief operating officer who had negotiated the acquisition of Coleco two years earlier, and Peter Smith, Hasbro's investment banker. They wanted to meet. At a session shortly afterward, Salovaara told them that Water Street was not going along with Hasbro's exchange offer. He explained that the fund had made its purchases with a view toward gaining an equity stake in Tonka, and that he believed that the exchange offer, as it stood, didn't stack up. Because Hasbro required that 90 percent of Tonka's bondholders take the deal, Goldman, Sachs was a definite spoiler. What Salovaara wanted was a ninety-cent-on-the-dollar swap and a few odds and ends, including a fee for Water Street using its majority positions to help Hasbro change the indentures, or terms, of the bonds.

The press went crazy over Water Street's seeming use of insider information. And Tonka directors complained about Goldman,

Sachs's hostility. In particular, Richard Schall, a former Goldman, Sachs client while vice chairman at Dayton Hudson Corporation and a stockholder in Tonka looking at the mighty good prospect of $7 a share with the Hasbro offer, called Goldman, Sachs head of investment banking Geoffrey Boisi at home to register his objection that Goldman, Sachs was interfering with the board's efforts to save the company.

For its part, Goldman, Sachs insisted that its operatives didn't know anything more than any other investor knew about the likely scenario for Tonka. After all, Mattel had told the world it was nosing around for a toy company and there were only a few obvious prospects. The SEC launched an investigation focusing on trades in Tonka's stock by parties dealing through brokers in the Far East, and Water Street never owned any stock of Tonka.

In April, Hasbro caved in. It offered another $43 million to bondholders—ninety-three cents for each class—while subtracting $2 a share from what it was willing to give shareholders. Although $5 a share was worse than $7 a share for stockholders, it was better than the possibility of getting nothing in a bankruptcy, and bankruptcy appeared to be inevitable for Tonka if the acquisition failed. The Water Street fund said that it expected to receive $155 million for its Tonka bonds—a return of 85 percent in well under a year.

DEATH OF A VULTURE FUND

But early in May 1991, Goldman, Sachs announced it was closing Water Street down after less than a year of operation. The decision came from the top, from the firm's senior partners Steve Friedman and Robert Rubin. "They said they wanted to get out because of the controversy involved and because the marketplace had changed—that junk was not as attractive as it once was," in the sense that cheap bonds would be harder to come by in a soaring junk bond market, Salovaara recalls. "They were also worried about corporate clients and trading clients who thought we were competing with them."

Fred Eckert and Salovaara, however, weren't about to let what they thought was an opportunity of a lifetime slip by. The era of vulture investing wasn't over just because Goldman, Sachs & Com-

pany decided to kill its Corporate Recovery Fund. Others had
come and gone—a prime example being Citicorp after the Public
Service Company of New Hampshire deal—and the profits to
those who remained kept on rolling strong. Eckert and Salovaara
now had two strong points in their favor: (1) They had a good
performance record, brief as it was; by the end of November 1991
after more than a year of operation, the fund had paid investors
back more than 60 percent of their $783 million and achieved
annualized returns in excess of 33 percent. And (2) the two up-and-
coming vultures had satisfied customers who were likely to follow
them. "We started to hear over the transom that 'Anything you're
doing we'll be interested in,' " Salovaara says. They asked Goldman, Sachs's management committee to waive the usual non-
compete clause for people leaving the firm, and they were granted
their request. Still, they continued to help wind down Water Street
in 1992 while they began raising $150 to $200 million for their new
fund. It was to be called South Street, after yet another byway in
the Wall Street district.

LEAVING HOME

While Mikael Salovaara was raising money for the Water
Street fund, in the spring of 1990, Leon Black was doing exactly the
same for himself. A philosophy major at Dartmouth, where he
graduated summa cum laude in 1973, Black shifted course to earn
an M.B.A. at Harvard. He was twenty-five when his father, Eli
Black, the chief executive officer of United Brands Company, took
his own life. In 1975, just before the public learned that United
Brands had been paying bribes in foreign countries, he leapt from
the forty-fourth floor of the Pan Am Building in New York.
Today, his son is forty years old, tall, and rumpled. He wears
steel-rim glasses and has an abundance of brown hair that falls
over his forehead and ears. During the 1980s, Black was one of the
forces that was turning Drexel, Burnham, Lambert into the
prodigy of Wall Street. Indeed, in *The Predators' Ball* Connie
Bruck reports that in a 1979 meeting about the future direction of
Drexel, Burnham's investment banking activities, Black suggested
that the firm identify the "robber barons" who were on their way

to becoming the owners of major companies. These would be the corporate raiders that Drexel, Burnham financed in the 1980s—Carl Icahn, Henry Kravis of Kohlberg, Kravis, Roberts & Company, Samuel Heyman of GAF Corporation, media magnate Rupert Murdoch, Ronald Perelman of Revlon, and others.

But early in the decade, Black specialized in financing then out-of-favor cable television and other media companies. Bored with that after three years, he put together a budding leveraged buyout group and spent a few years helping managements issue debt to take their companies private—junk bond debt traded out of Michael Milken's outpost in Beverly Hills. The LBOs led to the much more exciting—and controversial—mergers and acquisitions transactions of the mid-1980s. "Doing deals from the outside on a leveraged basis was not too much different from doing them on the inside," was his simple explanation of the transition to M & A from management buyouts of their own companies. As head of Drexel, Burnham's M&A department, Black was advising such raiders as Carl Icahn in the acquisition of ACF Industries and in the raid on Phillips Petroleum, William Farley in West Point Pepperell, and Nelson Peltz in the acquisition of National Can.

In fact, Black has the dubious distinction of being the man who invented the "highly confident" letter in response to a request from Icahn. When Icahn was considering a tender offer for Phillips Petroleum, he asked Drexel, Burnham to give him a commitment letter, as if it were a bank pledging a loan. Instead, Black suggested that the firm say it was "highly confident" it could raise the financing, which is what it did. That enabled Icahn to go forward with a hostile bid that, although it didn't succeed, forced the company to sweeten its own restructuring plan and gave him a handsome profit. From then on, the release of a Drexel, Burnham highly confident letter was taken as virtual certainty by the financial world.

In his role as junk bond M&A financial adviser, Black says that the vast majority of the transactions he personally worked on did not run into severe problems later on. In 1989 as co-director of the corporate finance department, he found he was working increasingly with companies that had credit problems because they were carrying excessive debt.

When Drexel, Burnham declared bankruptcy in February 1990, Black said good-bye to his home of thirteen years and, along with those colleagues who hadn't already found new jobs, took his leave. He wasn't exactly penniless, having just negotiated a $20 million bonus for 1989. Originally given $16 million in stock and cash, he complained loudly to Drexel, Burnham CEO Frederick Joseph that he wasn't getting what he was worth—especially considering the greater sums that a few in Milken's operation had received in the past. Joseph responded by increasing Black's award, giving him $16 million in cash and $4 million in Drexel, Burnham stock—although the stock was soon to be worthless. Later, Drexel, Burnham and savings-and-loan industry regulators recovered $300 million in bonuses paid to employees—including Black—just before the bankruptcy.

As for what Black was going to do with his life after Drexel, Burnham, he knew from direct experience that many overleveraged companies were starved for new capital. So he decided to get into the business of providing capital to troubled concerns; by taking large positions in the debt of distressed companies, Black could then use his influence plus extra capital to help companies restructure their finances, while also extracting a sweet return for himself.

How he was going to set up this operation was still a blur when he got a call from Thierry de la Villehuchet, the head of Crédit Lyonnais Securities, a New York division of the French-owned banking giant Crédit Lyonnais. "He called me a few times," Black recalls. "I didn't return the calls because I'd never heard of him." Finally, Villehuchet and Black did meet one day for breakfast, and the Frenchman asked Black to help Crédit Lyonnais build a U.S. mergers and acquisitions investment banking group. Black was low on the idea. Although he saw some M&A transactions arising from divestitures by companies that needed to raise cash, he believed that overall the M&A business was going to be sluggish. "The real opportunities," he told Villehuchet, "were on the principal side dealing in a depressed and severely shocked junk bond market."

Not only was Villehuchet interested in this idea, but he suggested that Black talk to a certain person affiliated with the bank who had already invested $400 million in the U.S. junk bond market. That person was Jean-Francois Hénin, the president of Altus Finance. Altus was once the financial arm of Thomson-CSF, France's state-owned defense-electronics group. It would take the cash coming in for arms contracts and invest it in the foreign exchange and derivatives markets. In 1990, Crédit Lyonnais bolstered Thomson-CSF in part by taking a 66 percent interest in the high-flying Altus. With approximately $20 billion in assets and close to $3 billion in equity, Altus diversified its money management activities in many directions, including U.S. junk bonds.

Black flew to Paris to meet with Hénin, and found that they were speaking the same language. They agreed that the restructuring field was wide open, and they decided to create two new pools of capital for Black to invest in troubled U.S. companies. There would be a $400 million portfolio (of new money) from Altus alone and another $400 million in an independent fund in which Altus would be a minority investor. The Altus piece was in place by July, and by August, Black had raised the money for the fund from European and American investors. He named his new company Apollo Investments after the Greek god of sunlight, music, and poetry. It seemed the perfect image: a universal force that uses its power to create harmony. Black established headquarters in Westchester and Los Angeles and opened an advisory office on the thirty-eighth floor of the Crédit Lyonnais building on the Avenue of the Americas. His spacious corner office had a sweeping view of northern Manhattan taking in Central Park and beyond.

Starting in September, Black put nearly $500 million of his new supply to work. Most of it went into twenty-five or so very low priced but good-quality junk bonds such as Revlon and RJR Nabisco, and as the junk bond market sprung upward at the end of that year and in 1991 those investments soared. In fact, by Christmas 1990 Apollo was doing so well that Altus asked Black to take another $500 million of its money under his wing.

In August 1990 William Farley turned to Black for help squeezing out of a cash crunch. Black had advised Farley during the 1980s when the financier used Drexel, Burnham-issued junk bonds to acquire Fruit of the Loom and West Point Pepperell. Now he was in trouble, and Black gave him about $43 million in return for 3.75 million of Fruit of the Loom shares—$11.50 a share. (The funds were neither Altus nor Apollo funds, but Black won't say whether he personally or other investors, or both, provided them.) The catch was that Farley had to repurchase those shares at a $3.94-a-share premium by July 1991 or else potentially lose his own Fruit of the Loom shares that he had put up as collateral. In April 1991, Farley did buy the shares back and then issued them to the public. The gain to Black was $14.8 million. Later that year, due to un-related events, Farley's fortunes worsened. He lost control of West Point Pepperell in a bankruptcy and was forced to reduce his stake in his holding company.

But of all the junk bond investments Black made that fall of 1990, only one was a major "activist" vulture play. That one was in Harcourt Brace Jovanovich. The Orlando, Florida, publishing house had overborrowed in 1987 to fend off a bid by British press magnate Robert Maxwell. Coming up in 1992, its noninterest-paying zero-coupon bonds were suddenly going to start paying interest. But in late 1990, it was already clear that HBJ wouldn't have the money. The company hired the Wall Street firm of Smith, Barney, Harris, Upham & Company to design a restructuring pro-gram and to look around for someone who might want to buy a book publisher.

SAFETY IN NUMBERS

To Black, HBJ presented an especially tantalizing buffet of securities. On the senior level, the company had $150 million of bank debt and $200 million of senior bonds. The terms of the senior bonds prohibited the company from carrying any more than about $350 million in senior debt—the amount that was already in place. The last rung of higher-level debt was $500 million worth of senior subordinated debt. These three components of HBJ's higher-level debt were completely covered by the company's asset value, estimated at between $1.2 billion and $1.6 billion, depending on how conservative the estimater.

Despite this ample degree of safety, the senior subordinated bonds were trading in the market at a 30 to 40 percent discount to par value. The worst case that Black could envision was that the publishing concern would tumble into bankruptcy court and would twist and turn there for a few years. But he surmised that no matter how long the process, in the end the bonds would still collect 100 cents on the dollar. "That was the downside," Black points out. "How could you lose?" He plunged in to the market and from September to January 1991 bought 40 percent of the senior subordinated class—$200 million worth for about $130 million.

Once he had done his shopping and ensured himself a seat at the negotiating table, he bought some of the lower-ranked, junior bonds as well. There were three classes of junior bonds adding up to $1 billion, as well as $500 million of preferred stock and the common stock. Although these bonds were not completely covered by the available assets, someone with the proper measure of clout could probably get himself a good payment, and Black had plenty of clout. He picked up 10 percent of the juniors at "relatively low prices."

While he was busily buying, Black heard that another voracious vulture investor was in the market. The Water Street Fund was harvesting senior and senior subordinated bonds and preferred stock, spending about $175 million on a few hundred million dollars worth of securities.

Once he had established his positions, Black moved quickly to become involved in accomplishing the workout. He hired publishing consultants to study HBJ. "The more we learned, the more excited we were about the business," he says. Then, he invited Peter Jovanovich, the president and chief executive and son of HBJ's founder, to dine at his Manhattan home and presented a possible approach to solving the company's problem: As part of an overall restructuring, Black would relinquish some or all of his debt holdings in exchange for a sizable stock position and a role in revitalizing the company. He reassured Jovanovich that this was not a hostile move on his part, because he believed the management was not doing a bad job. The problem with the company was clearly the financial structure, and the cancellation of so much debt would give HBJ the breathing room it needed. And Black reckoned that by having a hand in management he could help hoist the value of his new equity stake.

But a couple of weeks later, in late January 1991, a buyer came forward. The bidder was the Boston-based theater operator and retailer General Cinema Corporation, one of the companies that Smith, Barney had contacted on behalf of HBJ. General Cinema offered $1.4 billion for the company in the form of an exchange offer and gave bond and stock holders until March 15 to respond to its overture. Like many exchange offers, this one required acceptance by fully 90 percent of bondholders, as well as half of preferred shareholders and two-thirds of the common shareholders. HBJ Chairman John Herrington warned that if the takeover didn't go through, bankruptcy was the most likely scenario, but one "too gruesome to imagine."

The bid translated into ninety-three cents on the dollar for senior bonds; seventy-seven cents on the dollar for senior subordinated bonds; and forty-five cents, forty cents, and thirty-two cents for the three layers of junior bonds. For stockholders—including employees, who owned 20 percent of the stock through a benefits plan—General Cinema offered $1.30 for common stock then trading at ninety-four cents and the same for preferred trading near eighty cents.

First offers are usually considered just that: first offers, with more to come. In this case, bondholders were not pleased either with the proffered payment or with the kind treatment of the stockholders. Some sizable bondholders formed a negotiating committee, which included Kemper Corporation as its largest member with about $200 million worth of junior bonds bought mostly at par. Kemper's junk bond manager Kenneth Urbaszewski had four major complaints with the proposed deal. In order of importance, he believed the price offered bondholders was not high enough; equity holders were receiving way too much; two levels of junior debt were contractually equivalent but were receiving different prices, forty-five and forty cents on the dollar; and last, he wanted the option of receiving equity in the new company.

Both of HBJ's other two major bondholders also spurned the bid. Water Street's Salovaara wanted 100 cents on the dollar plus accrued interest for both the fund's senior and senior subordinated bonds, "and they couldn't do the deal without us," he says. Leon Black similarly dismissed the seventy-seven-cent offer for his bonds, demanding no less than ninety-four.

But at General Cinema's March 8, 1991, annual shareholders'

meeting, Chairman Richard Smith declared, "We have no interest in haggling over price." That stubborn stance failed to intimidate bondholders into swapping their bonds, however. By the March 15 deadline, only two percent of the bonds had been tendered—an insult to the 90 percent goal. The bondholders' committee requested more time to study the deal, and General Cinema granted a three-week extension. When only another 6 percent of bonds came in, General Cinema again extended its due date, this time to April 18. And when it then became obvious that its 90 percent acceptance requirement was a hopeless fantasy, General Cinema announced that it was breaking off talks completely. Behind the scenes, however, the company for the first time declared a willingness to increase its offer, and the following week raised its $1.4 billion bid by about $95 million. But that step failed to win over many large bondholders including Black, Water Street, and Kemper.

"We felt it was insufficient, and we said we'd never do the deal," says Kemper's Urbaszewski, who was the most vocal of the holdouts. General Cinema refused to consider a prepackaged bankruptcy that would have lassoed those bondholders who were not satisfied with the bid. The prospective acquirer was convinced that a prepack or any kind of bankruptcy filing would scare off state school officials who make the final decisions on textbook purchases, making commitments of as long as three years. To them, the B-word is anathema.

But to Kemper, a prepackaged bankruptcy would have corrected the exchange offer's greatest flaw: The amount. It would allow General Cinema to offer bondholders more money. "The advantages of a prepackaged bankruptcy were several," says Urbaszewski. "Number one, there are no holdouts by definition, and that saves a lot of money for the buyer, and number two, there are tax benefits available to them that they can't get unless they go bankrupt. General Cinema could pay more to bondholders if they did a prepackaged bankruptcy." He uses the junior bonds to illustrate. He figured that if the requisite 90 percent of the $1 billion face value of those bonds took a General Cinema offer of forty-five cents on the dollar, that left 10 percent with bonds still valued at par. But in a bankruptcy, all creditors receive the same recovery, and that leftover $100 million would also have to take the forty-five cents. Urbaszewski's conclusion was that by using bankruptcy rather than a tender offer, General Cinema could save $55 million on just the junior bonds.

At the end of April, General Cinema withdrew its offer for HBJ. But it left the door open, saying through a spokesman that "if somebody in that bondholder group can get their act together and get back to us, negotiations might be resumed."

SHUTTLE DIPLOMACY

The opposing parties didn't budge from May through July. His investment sitting idle, Black tried to restart the engines. Flying to Boston to meet with General Cinema's Richard Smith in the chairman's office, he asked how he might be able to help. He then got on the phone to talk with Urbaszewski about his list of gripes and with other committee members about their dissatisfaction with the price offered.

With this new information, Black held a second discussion with Smith in Boston. Black suggested that a way out of this bind was for Smith to talk to Urbaszewski and offer him the option of buying General Cinema stock after the acquisition. So, in a brief phone conversation with Urbaszewski at the beginning of August, Smith held out that offer of stock. "We said we could live with this if you change the prices somewhat, and then the prices got changed a bit," Urbaszewski says. Equity holders were to receive less and bondholders a bit more, and to make all the bondholders on the committee happy, the value of the whole package was increased from $1.4 billion-plus to $1.5 billion. "Leon apparently convinced Smith to allow equity to be held by other people besides General Cinema," says the Kemper bond manager. "He got General Cinema to create equity (to issue new General Cinema stock) for people to buy. So Leon made a big contribution by getting the ball rolling again."

The new agreement threw open the floodgates and HBJ bonds poured into General Cinema. Salovaara, Black, and Urbaszewski were all satisfied now. Yet by the end of September, not quite enough bonds had been tendered to complete the merger. Only one class met the 90 percent requirement while others were as low as 78 percent—not as bad as the 11 percent heights reached previously but still not good enough. Some bondholder holdouts thought the price was still too low, while others simply wanted to keep their bonds. After all, the old bonds paid high interest rates and General Cinema would continue to service them at those rates after a successful acquisition. For junior bondholders holding out was especially attractive; they were slated to get forty-eight cents on the dollar in the tender offer, but if they held on, the value would rise to 100 cents once the acquisition was complete and they could sell in the market.

The offer was extended by one week and then another and another. In mid-October General Cinema Chairman Smith threatened that "if we fail to reach the required 90 percent . . . we will permit the tender offers to expire and terminate the merger agreement." But come the next deadline, Monday October 21, Smith extended the offer to Tuesday at two P.M. and on Tuesday he extended it again to five P.M. By then, all but one of the five classes of bonds had reached the ninety percent threshold—one of the junior-level classes.

Black was not about to let what he called a "dream deal" collapse. So what he did was buy a few million face amount of junior bonds at high prices near ninety cents on the dollar from specific bondholders in private transactions. Half of the bonds he sent over to General Cinema, pulling the class over the 90 percent mark. Of course, he received only forty-eight cents in exchange for those and so took a steep loss. But as a hedge, he held onto the other half of the bonds he'd purchased, and those rose in the market to 100 cents when General Cinema got its prize. So Black lost a couple hundred thousand dollars in the process, but by doing so he gained much more by getting the deal done.

On Saturday, November 23, 1991, fourteen months after Black began gathering HBJ bonds, the common and preferred shareholders voted on the acquisition. A majority of preferreds was needed, but many were opposed. The Resolution Trust Corporation, a major holder, caved in at the last minute and voted in favor. HBJ was independent no more. For its senior bonds, the Water Street fund received 100 cents on the dollar. The senior subordinated bonds that both Water Street and Leon Black held received ninety-one cents on the dollar. Black had paid about 65 cents for his bonds. Junior holders took home forty-seven cents on two classes and forty-seven and a half cents on the third.

TAKING STOCK, SOMETIMES

What Black did in HBJ was pure Heavyweight vulture investing. Go in, lend a hand, get out. Sometimes, however, he doesn't get out right away, but finds that the best possible return for his money lies in taking an equity stake in the new company. This does not make him a Nest-Building vulture investor, because his goal is not to own or control companies but rather to maximize his investment. Consider the case of Gillett Holdings. The company is a farrago consisting of television stations, meatpacking plants, and Vail, Colorado, ski resorts that was built by Denver entrepreneur George Gillett. With the help of Drexel, Burnham's junk bond machinery—although not Black personally—he had paid too much to build his television broadcasting empire during what was the decade of excess.

In March 1991, Black's Apollo Investments acquired $150 million of the most senior of Gillett's bonds. As it happened, he bought them from First Executive, the Los Angeles–based insurance company whose Executive Life of California would soon be taken over by insurance regulators, rendered insolvent by its underwater junk bond portfolio. At the time, Black was already talking with French investors about the possibility of acquiring the insurance company.

But first, he tried to fix Gillett, and by June he had arrived at a tentative solution with the company and its creditors. Black on behalf of the Apollo Investments fund agreed to contribute $40 million in return for a 52 to 55 percent stake in the company and a seat on the board. In addition, he agreed to split the senior class of bonds into two planks with him on the second level. The plan was for Gillett to raise cash with asset sales and pay off the top ranking senior bondholders first. For his second-tier bonds, Black would get some cash but also new bonds. And, of course, the stock. "We'll ride with the company as stockholders," he says. Carrying roughly $1 billion in debt, the company entered Chapter 11 that June to finish negotiating the plan. Almost all creditors were in agreement. The chief holdout was Carl Icahn, fellow vulture and a personal friend, who owned some $60 million of junior bonds, about 38 percent of the issue—a blocking position. An ad hoc committee on which Icahn and Drexel, Burnham were the largest members objected to the generosity of a bonus package for George Gillett's management company that included a $1.5 million salary and a veto on asset sales for three years, among other things.

Similarly, in Price Communications, Black agreed to turn in his senior bonds and assume some of the company's debt in return for a controlling stake in one of its properties, the *New York Law Journal.* In late May 1991 he bought 40 percent of the media company's subordinated bond issue convertible into stock, and he paid only a bit more than half-price for the $19.2 million face value. With that very large foot in the door, he negotiated his deal with the management and other bondholders.

With his staff of thirteen in New York and Los Angeles and the resources of Crédit Lyonnais, Black has been able to branch out from the usual vulture investing. For example, Apollo acquired a large part of a $400 million portfolio of distressed bank loans from Wells Fargo and accomplished a number of joint ventures. Among them: Black bought a wholesale drug distributor with Chemical Bank Venture Partners, teamed up with LBO financier Thomas Hicks to acquire Occidental Petroleum's natural gas business, and partnered with cable mogul Ted Turner to take a 50 percent equity interest in cartoon maker Hanna Barbera.

As might have been expected, since he entered the vultures' domain, Black has taken a great deal of flak in the press for feeding off problems that aggressive corporate finance engineers like himself created in the 1980s. Only by chance, in his first year and a half of vulture investing, Black mostly avoided former Drexel, Burnham clients, two major exceptions being Farley and Gillett, and he did not personally work on Gillett's financings. And he maintains that relatively few of the projects he handled at Drexel have ended up in the repair shop. His usually soft-spoken voice suddenly solidifies. "I had a damn good track record there," he says.

So far, he can say the same of his new career. It has hardly been easy, but his greatest test would be tackling the former Executive Life Insurance Company's portfolio of junk bonds. And then? Maybe Black will continue with vulture investing. But judging from his past, he will probably evolve with the times. Whatever opportunity calls the loudest, Black plans to follow. It could be a resurgence of mergers-and-acquisitions business, or the return of leveraged buyouts or junk bonds. If it involves deal making and big money, Leon Black will be there.

Conclusion

At the start of 1992, the U.S. economy had just suffered through an achingly slow Christmas shopping season, and economic forecasters were predicting more bad weather just ahead. At the same time, though, the stock market was bounding along like a Triple-Crown champion. The common wisdom explained the boom as a precursor of the recovery to come—maybe. Or was it simply that investors, facing sharply lower returns on fixed-rate instruments like money market accounts and certificates of deposit, were seeking a haven in stocks? Or both? Somehow, with the daily announcements of losses and layoffs, a vigorous recovery didn't seem to be around the bend.

The forecast, as far as I could tell, was for clear flying conditions for vultures for awhile. More companies would default on their debt, and more would declare bankruptcy. In late January, the predictions became jarringly real. After months in which rumors of severe problems hovered over the R. H. Macy & Company, the venerable department store chain succumbed. Another failed leverage buyout, another fallen retailing giant. After the company filed bankruptcy, the various junk bonds of the company plunged into the fifties, twenties, and teens. It was like the diminishing pulse of a dying body. The vultures were circling.

And did they have money to spend. For one thing, as the numerous bankruptcies of the previous few years, like those of Revco, Interco, and Federated and Allied stores, began to wind up, the investors in them harvested their winnings. At the same time, institutional investors, wary of pouring assets into a raging, record-high stock market but unsure of what else to do in the sluggish economy, continued to funnel money to the scavengers. Confident of this, vultures continued to go out and solicit new funds. Shrugging off the difficulties that Goldman, Sachs encountered in this field, CS First Boston set out to raise $250 million. Marty Whitman and Fidelity Investments both launched new funds specifically for institutional investors like pension funds and endowments. Whitman aimed to raise $300 million and Fidelity thought it would start with $100 million and then think about whether to go for more.

Still, no matter how rich the pickers and the pickings, the business of vulture investing remains as difficult and risky as charming a snake. If you don't know just what you're doing, if you don't pick the right snake to work with, at a time when he's in a good mood, and quit just before he gets annoyed, you're in big trouble. Vulture investing involves the skills of choosing the right security and class of claims to invest in, choosing them at the right time, and knowing if and when to take your profits and losses and get out. These are talents that come from years of work analyzing undervalued, debt-laden companies and understanding the bankruptcy process and the way the participants think as they make their way through it. More often than not, too, luck plays a frighteningly critical role. Japonica Partners, through a series of strategic moves interspersed with lucky developments, acquired Allegheny International a little more than a year after they became involved in the case and made huge profits for their backers. When luck goes the wrong way or one mistake is made, a vulture's wings can become caught in the very prickly brambles of a prolonged bankruptcy. Losses can be severe. In Revco, Global Marine, LTV, Manville, Interco, Wheeling-Pittsburgh, Eastern Airlines, and other cases, investors lost money and investors made money. What separated the winners from the losers was often one decision or one event that, say, brought them into the case earlier than others or took them out later.

In the spring of 1992 the hibernating economy began to stir and companies' profits started to slope upward once again. The vultures no longer had a seemingly endless supply of corporate woe to feast upon. But at the same time a lot of new money was chasing the limited number of deals. How would the vultures survive? Many investors who became vultures in the late 1980s and early 1990s will move on to whatever new opportunities call. Leon Black does not appear to be committed to vulture investing through thick and thin. His career has been a series of adventures with the common threads being corporate finance, primarily, and the corporate finance of companies that carry heavy debt, secondarily. To him, vulture investing is simply an opportunity thrown up by the recession to combine his knowledge of high-debt finance with his considerable resources in order to help distressed companies and profit along the way. When mergers and acquisitions or the use of junk bonds rebounds or some wholly new business develops, Black will probably pack his bags and move to the center of the action.

But many vulture investors are vulture investors forever who will not drift away as the economy improves. That crowd of diehards includes Marty Whitman, Ron LaBow, Balfour Investors, Shelley Greenhaus, Sam Zell, Jon Bauer, Mikael Salovaara, and Jim Rubin. Until Paradise arrives, there will always be enough misfortune and bad management to fill the appetites of this core of bankruptcy investors. They will lose some, but they will try to win more than they lose. The most cunning, and the luckiest, will survive and continue to wield their special kind of influence at troubled companies.

So, yes, they're here to stay, and yes, they're powerful. But the question remains, have the vulture investors been good for corporations? For the economy? The same was and still is asked time and again about the raiders who terrorized corporations in the 1980s. They were criticized for staging hostile raids on corporations just so the management would pay them a premium to the market price to go away—a payment that became known as greenmail. On the other hand, they were praised for shaking up tired managements who had not been able to realize the full potential of their companies.

A vulture is a different sort of animal, but the basic issue is the same: money versus the good of the corporation. Vultures are investors who like any investors are out to make a good living. They choose to enter a company at its most vulnerable point, when it can't pay its bills or is in bankruptcy, because they have the ability to recognize the value of a distressed business. Then they grasp for some measure of control over that company's fate. In many cases that means buying a hunk of securities or claims as a ticket to the reorganization negotiations.

Vulture investors are criticized for delaying reorganizations and restructurings for their own purposes. After all, they can reap better recoveries by forcing a case into limbo, and they sometimes do. The company and other creditors will fight them, but will also try to appease them and pay them more, just to get the darn thing done.

But the vultures are justifiably praised in many cases for their virtues. They bring liquidity to a bankruptcy, buying out creditors like suppliers and bondholders who need cash or who want to cut their losses and get out. And the activists become a new, puissant force trying to resolve the case. Vultures like Sam Zell, Leon Black, and others help push workouts along by contributing new capital to thirsting companies. Or vultures might bring financing of another kind. Ron LaBow reached a settlement with Wheeling-Pittsburgh creditors by offering to buy their stock after the bankruptcy. The mere fact that these investors effectively transfer a large amount of debt from many creditors to the hands of one person who becomes actively involved in negotiations can greatly simplify the process, reducing the time a company spends trammeled by debt.

To most of those involved in the field, the term *vulture* is a misnomer that indicates selfishness of the worst kind. Rather, the vultures see themselves as a type of value investor seeking value that has gone unappreciated by the markets. For the most part they are searching for companies that are not dying, but are merely in trouble and with their assistance have a chance to stabilize and thrive.

Notes

CHAPTER 1

p. 1–6 The account of Michael Price's Storage Technology investment is based on interviews with him on September 23, 1991, and with Ryal Poppa on September 22, 1991.
5 The description of Michael Price is from an interview with Harvey Miller on September 25, 1991.
6–8, 12–13 The profile of Michael Price is based on interviews with him on May 21, 1991, and September 23, 1991, and with Peter Langerman on August 2, 1991.
8–12 The account of Max Heine's life and career is based on interviews with Michael Price on May 21, 1991, with Seth Klarman in August 1991, and with Hans Jacobson on March 15, 1991; Dan Dimancescu, *Deferred Future* (Cambridge, MA: Ballinger, 1983), pp. 76–77; a speech given by Seth Klarman at the Max L. Heine Bankruptcy Symposium, New York, N.Y., on April 11, 1989; and press reports.
9–10 The account of Hans Jacobson's career and involvement in the railroads is based on an interview with him on March 15, 1991.
10 The account of the two traders' visit with Hans Jacobson is based on an interview with Arthur Byrnes on April 10, 1991.
11–12 The account of the Penn Central bankruptcy is based on interviews

with David Gillespie of Deltec Securities on April 10, 1991, and with Hans Jacobson on March 15, 1991; and press reports.

12 Max Heine's quotation appeared in Jeffrey Laderman, "Mutual Shares Finds Riches in the Darnedest Places," *Business Week,* December 8, 1986, p. 83.

12 Michael Price's quotation appeared in Richard Phalon, "Bear Market Blues," *Forbes,* January 21, 1991, p. 115.

13 The account of Martin Whitman's investment in Penn Central is based on an interview with him in December 1990.

13 The account of Goldman, Sachs's investment in Penn Central is from an interview with Robert Rubin by Henny Sender that appeared in "The Way It Was, An Oral History," 20th anniversary issue, *Institutional Investor,* June 1987, pp. 185–86.

13 The reference to Talton Embry's investment in Penn Central is from an interview with him on December 10, 1991.

13 The account of Balfour Investors's investment in Penn Central is based on an interview with Jay Goldsmith and Harry Freund on June 27, 1991, and press reports.

14–15 The story of the rise and fall of the REITs and of Deltec Securities's investment in them is based on an interview with Arthur Byrnes on April 10, 1991.

15 The account of Michael Milken's investment in REITs is from Connie Bruck, *The Predators' Ball* (New York: Simon & Schuster, 1988), p. 34.

15 The account of Carl Icahn's involvement in REITs is from Bruck, *The Predators' Ball,* pp. 154–55.

16–17 The account of the Nucorp Energy bankruptcy is based on an interview with Jay Goldsmith and Harry Freund on June 27, 1991, and press reports.

17 The account of the Petro-Lewis restructuring is based on an interview with Martin Whitman in December 1990.

18–19 The figures on corporate defaults and the size of the vulture market are from Edward I. Altman, Max L. Heine Professor of Finance, February 28, 1992.

19 Sandra Mayerson's quotation was given in an interview with her on June 24, 1991.

CHAPTER 2

21 Sam Zell's quotation appeared in Erik Ipsen, "Will Success Spoil Sam Zell?" *Institutional Investor,* April 1989, p. 90.

23 Harry Freund's quotation is from an interview with him on June 27, 1991.

24 Talton Embry's quotation is from "Is Now the Time to Buy Distress? (Scrapping with Shitheads)," a speech he delivered to the fall 1989 conference of *Grant's Interest Rate Observer,* November 14, 1989.

25 The account of the Creditors' Ball is from Alison Leigh Cowan, "Amid the Ruins, a Ball for the 90's," *New York Times,* August 15, 1991, sec. D, p. 1.

25 The reference to Ben Walsh is from interviews with several investors and attorneys.

27 Martin Whitman's quotation is from an interview with him in December 1990.

28 The account of Talton Embry's decision to leave the Allied Stores committee is based on an interview with him on March 22, 1991.

28 James Rubin's quotations are from an interview with him on July 11, 1991.

29 John Gordon's quotations are from an interview with him on April 10, 1991.

29 The reference to Talton Embry's holdings in the Allied Stores bankruptcy is from an interview with him on December 10, 1991.

30 David Schulte's quotations are from an interview with him on April 23, 1991.

CHAPTER 3

37–38 The description of the Seabrook groundbreaking is based on an interview with Robert Harrison on October 7, 1991.

38–39 The description of PSNH's developing debt problems is based on interviews with Charles Bayless on June 25, 1991, and September 4, 1991, and press reports.

39–42 Martin Whitman's quotations and profile are based on interviews with him on July 25, 1991, and in December 1990.

42, 43 Jim Heffernan's and Kirk Rhein's quotations are from an interview with Heffernan in December 1991.

44 The account of Martin Whitman's meeting with William Seidman is based on an interview with Jim Heffernan in December 1991.

44–45 The description of Martin Whitman's experience in the utility industry is based on an interview with him in December 1990, and on July 25, 1991, and a phone interview on December 26, 1991.

44–45 The references to Martin Whitman's report on utilities in bankruptcy are from his *Electric Utility Bankruptcy: Myths and Realities,* unpublished report, M. J. Whitman & Co., April 1985.

45 The accounts of Martin Whitman's investments in PSNH in 1985 and 1987 are based on an interview with him in December 1990.

45–47 The descriptions of CUC and of Martin Whitman's consideration of an investment in PSNH are based on interviews with Steve Davis on August 21, 1991, and with Whitman in December 1990, July 25, 1991, and December 26, 1991.

47 The description of talks within Citicorp about the PSNH investment is based on an interview with Steve Davis on August 21, 1991.

47–48 The accounts of the lunch with CUC and Citicorp, approval of the investment by Citicorp, the structure of the CUC/Citicorp team, and the investment are based on interviews with Martin Whitman in December 1990, on July 25, 1991, and on December 26, 1991, with James Heffernan in December 1990, and with Steve Davis on August 21, 1991.

48 The account of Robert Harrison's meeting with Governor John Sununu is based on an interview with Harrison on September 11, 1991.

49 The account of Martin Whitman's reaction to the PSNH exchange offer is based on an interview with him in December 1990.

49 The debate over the indentures is based on an interview with Martin Whitman in December 1990.

49–50 The account of Martin Whitman's call to Charles Bayless is based on an interview with Bayless on September 4, 1991.

50 The advertisement quoted is from *The* (Manchester) *Union Leader,* September 18, 1987.

50 Martin Whitman's quotation appeared in David Wessel, "Public Service New Hampshire Plans Debt Swap," *The Wall Street Journal,* September 21, 1987, p. 2.

50–51 The description of Martin Whitman's reorganization plan is based on interviews with him in December 1990, and on July 25, 1991.

51 The account of the dinner with Martin Whitman, Steve Davis, Robert Harrison, and Charles Bayless in New York is based on interviews with Harrison on September 11, 1991, with Davis on August 21, 1991, and with Whitman on July 25, 1991.

52 The account of the meeting at LeBoeuf, Lamb, Leiby & MacRae is based on interviews with Charles Bayless on September 4, 1991, and with Steve Davis on August 21, 1991.

52 The account of Charles Bayless calling the Edison Electric Institute is based on an interview with him on June 25, 1991.

53 The account of *The* (Manchester) *Union Leader* interview with Martin Whitman, James Heffernan, and Kirk Rhein is based on interviews with Steve Davis on September 30, 1991, and with Heffernan on September 30, 1991.

53 The account of Robert Harrison's reaction to Citicorp's involvement and letter to John Reed is based on interviews with Charles Bayless on September 4, 1991, and with Harrison on September 11, 1991.

53 The account of the Public Utilities Commission filing is based on John DiStaso, "Seabrook: The Final Battle Looms," *The* (Manchester) *Union Leader*, November 1, 1987, sec. A, p. 1, and an interview with Charles Bayless on June 25, 1991.

53–54 Martin Whitman's reaction to the charge that he was a raider is based on an interview with him on July 25, 1991.

54 The reference to Martin Whitman and Steve Davis's opinion that they would end up with majority control is based on interviews with Whitman on July 25, 1991, and with Davis on August 21, 1991.

54 The account of CUC/Citicorp's revised plan is based on an interview with Steve Davis on December 5, 1991.

54 The account of progress in negotiations with PSNH is based on Associated Press, "PSNH Discusses New Plan to Overhaul Debt," *The* (Manchester) *Union Leader*, November 7, 1987, p. 3, and John DiStaso, "PUC Seeking Supreme Court Opinion on its PSNH Rulings," *The Union Leader*, November 11, 1987, p. 9.

55 The account of Robert Harrison's meeting with Citicorp is based on an interview with Steve Davis on August 21, 1991.

55 The excerpt from the advertisement is taken from "An open letter to the citizens of New Hampshire," *The* (Manchester) *Union Leader*, November 12, 1987, p. 43.

56 The account of the CUC/Citicorp press conference is based on Robert Kinerk, "PSNH: Will Likely Default on an Additional Debt," *The* (Manchester) *Union Leader*, November 17, 1987, p. 3., and John DiStaso, "PSNH Bondholder Promises Better Deal," *The Union Leader*, November 19, 1987, p. 1, and an interview with Steve Davis on August 21, 1991.

56–57 The advertisement excerpted is from "What You Don't See About the NY Takeover of PSNH Should Worry You," *The* (Manchester) *Union Leader*, November 20, 1987, p. 46.

57–58 The account of the planned meeting with third mortgage bondholders is based on interviews with Steve Davis on August 21, 1991, and September 30, 1991.

57–58 The account of the lawsuit against CUC/Citicorp is from Robert Kinerk, "Public Service Files Suit to Stop Takeover Attempt by NY Firm," *The* (Manchester) *Union Leader*, November 26, 1987, p. 4, and John DiStaso, "Judge Blocks Meeting of PSNH Bondholders," *The Union Leader*, December 5, 1987, sec. A, p. 1, and interviews with Steve Davis on August 21, 1991, with Martin Whitman on July 25, 1991, with Charles Bayless on June 25, 1991, and with Robert Harrison on September 11, 1991.

58–60 The account of Balfour Investors's investment in PSNH and subsequent conversations with Robert Harrison and Martin Whitman is based on an interview with Jay Goldsmith and Harry Freund on June 27, 1991.

59 The article cited is Corie Brown, "Who Says Utilities Can't Be Raider Bait?" *Business Week,* November 23, 1987, p. 112.

60–61 The account of PSNH's new offer is based on press reports, and the meeting with Balfour is based on an interview with Robert Harrison on September 11, 1991.

61 The account of Citicorp and Martin Whitman's relationship is based on interviews with Steve Davis on August 21, 1991, and with Whitman on July 25, 1991, and in December 1990.

61–62 The account of the talks with PSNH and CUC/Citicorp and the meeting of Robert Harrison and George Skouras is based on an interview with Steve Davis on September 30, 1991. Harrison does not remember the meeting.

62 The account of the cause of the bankruptcy filing is based on press reports and interviews with Charles Bayless on September 4, 1991, and with Robert Harrison on September 11, 1991; Harrison's assessment is based on the same interview.

62–63 The account of Jay Goldsmith and Harry Freund in London is based on an interview with them on June 27, 1991.

63–64 The description of other PSNH investors is based on interviews with Talton Embry on December 10, 1991, with James Bennett on June 21, 1991, with Joel Zweibel on August 6, 1991, and with Charles Bayless on September 4, 1991.

64 The reference to Martin Whitman's withdrawal is from an interview with him on July 25, 1991.

64 The references to CUC/Citicorp's agenda are based on an interview with Steve Davis on August 21, 1991.

64–65 The assessment by Wilbur Ross is from an interview with him on October 9, 1991.

65 The assessment by Charles Bayless is from an interview with him on September 4, 1991.

65 The account of CUC/Citicorp's opposition to PSNH's exclusive right to file a plan is based on an interview with Steve Davis on August 21, 1991.

65 The account of CUC/Citicorp's talks with prospective bidders and regulators is based on an interview with Steve Davis on August 21, 1991.

65–66 Wilbur Ross's quotations are from an interview with him on October 9, 1991.

66 The reference to the committee's stance is from an interview with Joel Zweibel on August 6, 1991.

66 The account of creditors' committee meetings with state representatives is based on an interview with Joel Zweibel on August 6, 1991.

66 The account of the PSNH meeting with Governor John Sununu is based on interviews with Robert Harrison on September 11, 1991, and November 22, 1991.

67 The account of Robert Harrison's retirement is based on interviews with Charles Bayless on September 4, 1991, and with Harrison on September 11, 1991, and December 2, 1991. The assessment by Steve Davis is based on an interview with him on August 21, 1991.

67 The accounts of progress and problems for Seabrook are based on press reports.

67–69 The account of the meeting of all parties with Governor John Sununu is based on interviews with Charles Bayless on June 25, 1991, with Joel Zweibel on August 6, 1991, and with Steve Davis on December 5, 1991; and James E. Yacos, "In Re Public Service Company of New Hampshire, Amended Memorandum Opinion on Motion for Second Order Extending the Exclusivity Period," *Bankruptcy Reporter*, vol. 99 (March 22, 1989), pp. 168–70.

69–70 The account of Balfour Investors's decision to sell out of PSNH securities is based on an interview with Jay Goldsmith and Harry Freund on June 27, 1991.

70–71 The description of the PSNH proposed plan and competing plans is based on press reports.

71 The account of the exclusivity hearings is based on interviews with Steve Davis on August 21, 1991, and with Joel Zweibel on August 6, 1991, and on Yacos, "In Re Public Service Company of New Hampshire."

71–72 The account of the bidding war for PSNH is based on press reports.

72 Wilbur Ross's quotation is from Lawrence Ingrassia, "PS of New Hampshire Chapter 11 Case Draws Competing Reorganization Plans," *The Wall Street Journal,* September 18, 1989, sec. B, p. 9.

72 The reference to CUC/Citicorp's agreement with Northeast Utilities is from an interview with Steve Davis on December 5, 1991.

72 The account of the equity committee's role is from an interview with Wilbur Ross on October 9, 1991.

72 The description of CUC/Citicorp's profits is from an interview with James Heffernan on January 2, 1992.

73 The description of Martin Whitman's trophies is based on an interview with him in December 1990.

73 The account of the Whitman, Heffernan & Rhein fund raising effort is based on an interview with James Heffernan in December 1990.

74 Martin Whitman's quotations are based on an interview with him on July 25, 1991.

74–75 The account of Citicorp's exit from vulture investing is based on an interview with Steve Davis on December 5, 1991.

CHAPTER 4

76–79 The profile of James Rubin is based on interviews with him on August 19 and 22, 1991, and October 2, 1991.

79–80 The background on Coleco is based on an interview with Morton Handel on October 1, 1991, and press reports.

80 The references to James Rubin's holdings are based on interviews with him on July 11, 1991, and December 30, 1991, and with Morton Handel on October 1, 1991.

80–81 James Rubin's review of the balance sheet is based on an interview with him on July 11, 1991.

81 The account of the appointment of the creditors' committee is based on an interview with James Rubin on July 11, 1991, and court documents.

81–82 The account of the search for someone to buy the bank debt is based on interviews with Morton Handel on December 2, 1991, and with James Rubin on July 11, 1991.

82 The profile of Isaac Perlmutter is based on interviews with Sidney Dworkin on August 23, 1991, with Morton Handel on October 1, 1991, and with Wilbur Ross on October 7, 1991, and on press reports. Perlmutter and his attorney did not respond to calls requesting interviews.

83 The references to James Rubin's view of Isaac Perlmutter and Bernard Marden and Perlmutter's opinion of the estate's value are based on an interview with Rubin on July 11, 1991.

83–84 The description of the selection of attorneys is based on interviews with James Rubin on July 11, 1991, and with Marc Kirschner on August 15, 1991.

84–85 The account of the strategy session is based on interviews with James Rubin on July 11, 1991, and with Marc Kirschner on August 15, 1991.

85 The reference to the company's valuation of the proposed reorganization plan is from interviews with Morton Handel on October 1, 1991, and December 2, 1991.

85–87 The account of the development of the creditors' lawsuit is based on *Joint Application of the Debtors and the Official Committee of Unsecured*

Creditors for an Order Pursuant to Bankruptcy Rule 9019 Approving Settlement Agreement and Stipulation of Dismissal, filed at the United States Bankruptcy Court for the Southern District of New York, June 13, 1989, and interviews with James Rubin on July 11, 1991, and with Marc Kirschner on August 15, 1991.

86 The arguments backing the committee's charge that the payment to Coleco was made in bad faith is from *Joint Application of the Debtors,* pp. 19–20.

86 Marc Kirschner's view of James Rubin's role in the litigation is from an interview with Kirschner on August 15, 1991.

86 The account of the meeting of the creditors and the company about the fraudulent conveyance lawsuit is based on interviews with James Rubin on July 11, 1991, and with Marc Kirschner on August 15, 1991.

87 The reference to the company's response to the proposed lawsuit is based on interviews with Morton Handel on October 1, 1991, and with Marc Kirschner on August 15, 1991.

87 The account of the filing of the suit is based on an interview with James Rubin on July 11, 1991.

87 The reference to the company's reaction to the filing of the lawsuit is from an interview with Morton Handel on October 1, 1991.

88–89 The account of Coleco's preparation to put itself up for sale is based on interviews with Norman Brown on October 8, 1991, with Morton Handel on October 1, 1991, with James Rubin on July 11, 1991, and with Marc Kirschner on August 15, 1991.

89 The account of Coleco's initiation of talks with potential bidders is based on interviews with Norman Brown on October 8, 1991, and with Morton Handel on October 1, 1991.

89 The account of Coleco's decision not to sell is based on an interview with Morton Handel on October 1, 1991.

89 The account of Hasbro's initial contact with the committee is based on interviews with James Rubin on July 11, 1991, and with Marc Kirschner on August 5, 1991.

89–90 The references to the committee's hiring of Wilbur Ross and his role in the case are from court documents and an interview with him on October 7, 1991.

90–91 The accounts of Barry Alperin's meeting with James Rubin and Marc Kirschner and the theory of how to accomplish the acquisition are based on interviews with Rubin on July 11, 1991, and with Kirschner on August 15, 1991.

90–91 The accounts of Hasbro's bid for Coleco and the assembly of a joint plan of reorganization are based on court documents and an interview with James Rubin on July 11, 1991.

91 The account of the committee's decision to request placing Isaac Perlmutter's claim into escrow is from an interview with James Rubin on July 11, 1991.

91–92 The account of Coleco's revised reorganization plan is based on interviews with Morton Handel on October 1, 1991, and December 2, 1991.

92 The reference to the committee's valuation of the offer is from an interview with James Rubin on July 11, 1991, and press reports.

92 The account of the committee's actions announcing its agreement with Hasbro is based on an interview with James Rubin on December 30, 1991.

92 The accounts of the committee's efforts on Hasbro's behalf and the company's objection are based on an interview with Wilbur Ross on October 7, 1991.

92 The reference to Judge Abram's ruling is based on interviews with Marc Kirschner on August 15, 1991, with James Rubin on July 11, 1991, and with Wilbur Ross on October 7, 1991.

92–93 The account of the settlement of the litigation is based on interviews with Marc Kirschner on August 15, 1991, with James Rubin on July 1, 1991, and with Wilbur Ross on October 7, 1991.

93 The account of the recovery for the unsecured creditors is based on press reports and an interview with James Rubin on July 11, 1991.

93–94 The reference to Morton Handel's view of the unsecured creditors' recovery is based on an interview with him on October 1, 1991.

94 The account of Isaac Perlmutter's and Bernard Marden's recovery is based on court documents.

94 The account of the creation of Ranger Industries and the choice of management is based on an interview with James Rubin on July 11, 1991.

CHAPTER 5

95–96 The description of the strike poster is based on an interview with United Steel Workers officials on October 6, 1991.

97–98 The background to the Wheeling-Pittsburgh bankruptcy is based on press reports; the *Disclosure Statement Pursuant to Section 1125 of the Bankruptcy Code in Connection with Joint Plan of Reorganization dated July 11, 1990,* filed at United States Bankruptcy Court for the Western District of

Pennsylvania, and interviews with Paul Whitehead in December 1991, with Denis Cronin on January 3, 1992, with Lawrence Handelsman on October 30, 1991, and with William J. Scharffenberger on April 29, 1991, and October 8, 1991.

98 The reference to assets and liabilities is from J. Ernest Beazley, "Wheeling-Pittsburgh Steel Corp. Files for Protection under Bankruptcy Law after Union Vetoes Debt Plan," *The Wall Street Journal,* April 17, 1985, p. 3.

98 Judge Warren Bentz's quotation is excerpted from his ruling in Terence Roth and Thomas O'Boyle, "Wheeling Can Void Labor Pact, Judge Decides," *The Wall Street Journal,* July 18, 1985, p. 4.

98 The references to the savings on the pension plan termination and to the banks' objection to the labor contract are based on an interview with Denis Cronin on January 3, 1992.

99 The reference to "Saturday Night Massacre" is from an interview with Denis Cronin on January 3, 1992.

100 The description of Ronald LaBow's investment in Wheeling-Pittsburgh bank debt and his consultation with David Hains is based on an interview with LaBow on October 22, 1991.

100–101 The account of Ronald LaBow's competition with Oppenheimer on bank debt purchases is based on an interview with Jon Bauer on July 12, 1991.

101 The account of Jay Goldsmith's conversation with Ronald LaBow is based on an interview with Goldsmith on June 27, 1991.

101 The description of Ronald LaBow and David Hains's purchase of bank debt is based on an interview with LaBow on October 22, 1991.

101–2 The description of the partnerships is based on the *Disclosure Statement Pursuant to Section 1125,* p. 49, and on an interview with Ronald LaBow on October 22, 1991. The speculation over Michael Milken's involvement is based on interviews with David Strumwasser on October 18, 1991, and with Shelley Greenhaus on November 1, 1991.

102–3 The story of Todd Shipyards is based on press reports and an interview with Ronald LaBow on December 10, 1991.

102–3 The profile of Ronald LaBow is based on interviews with him on October 22, 1991, and with David Strumwasser on October 18, 1991, and press reports.

104 The profile of Jon Bauer is based on interviews with him on September 30, 1991, and October 30, 1991, and with Jeffrey Sabin on November 5, 1991.

104–5 The profile of Shelley Greenhaus is based on interviews with him on October 9, 1991, and with Jeffrey Sabin on November 5, 1991.

105–6 The account of the discovery and sale of the Maxus Energy claim is based on interviews with Philip Schaeffer on April 24, 1991, and with Maria Mendelsohn on September 6, 1991.

106 The account of negotiating the contract with Maxus is based on interviews with Jon Bauer on July 12, 1991, and with Jeffrey Sabin on November 5, 1991.

106 The reference to Balfour Investors's purchase is based on an interview with Jay Goldsmith on June 25, 1991.

107 The account of Ronald LaBow's increasing interest in the company is based on an interview with William Scharffenberger on April 29, 1991.

107 The account of Ronald LaBow and David Hains's early contact with the union and the union's stance is based on an interview with Lefty Palm on October 23, 1991.

107–8 The account of Ronald LaBow's negotiation with the PBGC is based on interviews with Thomas Mayer on October 24, 1991, and with Lawrence Handelsman on October 30, 1991.

108 Bruce McCullough's quotations are from interviews with him on October 8, 1991, and in December 1991.

108 The reference to the initiation of talks between Ronald LaBow and the creditors' committee is based on interviews with William Scharffenberger on April 29, 1991, and October 8, 1991.

109–10 The discussion of the debate over value is based on interviews with Lawrence Handelsman on October 30, 1991, with Robert Conway on October 15, 1991, and with Ronald LaBow on October 22, 1991.

111 The account of Oppenheimer's view of Wheeling's value is based on interviews with Shelley Greenhaus on July 1, 1991, and with Jon Bauer on October 30, 1991.

111 The description of the December 1988 plan is based on press reports and corporate documents.

112 The account of Lloyd Lubensky's stock sale to Goldman, Sachs & Company is from press reports. The reference to the offer to Oppenheimer and Balfour Investors is based on an interview with Jon Bauer in December 1991. The account of Lubensky's search for a restructuring strategy is based on an interview with William Scharffenberger on October 8, 1991.

112 Chriss Street's quotation is from Rick Wartzman, "Wheeling-Pittsburgh's Lubensky Resigns As Chairman, Sells His Stake in Company," *The Wall Street Journal,* January 30, 1989, sec B, p. 8.

113 William Scharffenberger's quotation is from an interview with him on April 29, 1991.

113 Ronald LaBow's quotation is from an interview with him on October 22, 1991.

113 The account of William Scharffenberger's encounter with Fred Cohen is based on an interview with Scharffenberger on October 8, 1991.

114 The account of Ronald LaBow's concern about the direction of the case is based on interviews with Bruce McCullough on October 8, 1991, and with Denis Cronin on January 3, 1992.

114 The account of William Scharffenberger's effort to give Goldman, Sachs time is based on an interview with him on October 8, 1991.

115 The account of Oppenheimer's purchase of the Hanna Mining affiliate is based on press reports, transcript of the court hearing on September 7, 1989, Case 85-793 PGH, United States Bankruptcy Court for the Western District of Pennsylvania, Judge Warren W. Bentz, pp. 81–100, and interviews with Shelley Greenhaus on July 1, 1991, and with Jon Bauer on October 30, 1991.

115 The account of the LaBow group's reaction to Oppenheimer is based on interviews with Thomas Mayer on October 24, 1991, and with Jeffrey Sabin on November 5, 1991.

115–16 The account of Goldman, Sachs's offer to Ronald LaBow is based on an interview with LaBow on October 22, 1991.

116 Denis Cronin's quotation is based on an interview with him on January 3, 1992.

116 The accounts of the meetings with Ronald LaBow and William Scharffenberger are based on an interview with Scharffenberger on November 4, 1991.

117–18 The account of Oppenheimer's negotiations with the committee is based on interviews with Shelley Greenhaus on July 1, 1991, and November 1, 1991, and with Jon Bauer on July 12, 1991.

118 The account of Oppenheimer's talks with Ronald LaBow is based on interviews with Shelley Greenhaus on July 1, 1991, and with LaBow on December 10, 1991.

119 The account of Oppenheimer's visits with Goldman, Sachs is based on interviews with Shelley Greenhaus on July 1, 1991, and November 1, 1991.

119 The reference to Oppenheimer's consideration of a takeover is based on interviews with Jon Bauer in December 1991, and with Shelley Greenhaus on November 1, 1991.

119 The reference to the Ronald LaBow group's strategy is based on an interview with Denis Cronin on January 3, 1992.

120–23 The accounts of the September 7 and September 21 hearings are based on the transcript for a hearing on September 7, 1989, Case No. 85-793 PGH, United States Bankruptcy Court for the Western District of Pennsylvania, Hon. Warren W. Bentz, pp. 99–100 and 105–113, and the transcript for a hearing on September 21, 1989, pp. 58–59, 63–64, and 65–68, and interviews with Thomas Mayer on October 24, 1991, with David Strumwasser on October 18, 1991, with Jeffrey Sabin on November 5, 1991, and with Shelley Greenhaus on July 1, 1991.

121–22 The account of the communications among Goldman, Sachs; William Scharffenberger; and Stan West is based on the transcript for the September 21 hearing, Case No. 85-793 PGH, United States Bankruptcy Court for the Western District of Pennsylvania, Hon. Warren W. Bentz, pp. 47–52, and interviews with Denis Cronin on January 3, 1992, and with Jeffrey Sabin on November 5, 1991.

123 The reference to Goldman, Sachs's securities offering is based on the September 21, 1991, hearing transcript, pp. 63–64, press reports ("W-P Outlines Reorganization Plans," *The Pittsburgh Press,* April 4, 1990, sec. B, p.3., and others), and an interview with Denis Cronin on January 3, 1992.

124 The reference to the committee's rejection of Goldman, Sachs is based on an interview with Lawrence Handelsman on October 30, 1991.

124 The account of Balfour Investors's mediation is based on interviews with Shelley Greenhaus on July 1, 1991, and with Jay Goldsmith and Harry Freund on June 27, 1991, and September 12, 1991.

124–25 The reference to Oppenheimer's strategy is based on an interview with David Strumwasser on October 18, 1991.

125 The account of the status conferences is based on interviews with Thomas Mayer on October 24, 1991, with Denis Cronin on January 3, 1992, with union officials in December 1991, with Shelley Greenhaus on July 1, 1991, and November 1, 1991, and with David Strumwasser on October 18, 1991.

125–26 The reference to Oppenheimer's offer to Goldman, Sachs is based on an interview with Jon Bauer on July 12, 1991.

125–26 The references to Oppenheimer's attitude toward Goldman and Shelley Greenhaus's conversation with Douglas Dethy are based on interviews with Greenhaus on July 1, 1991, and November 1, 1991.

126 The account of William Scharffenberger's view of the union is based on an interview with him on October 8, 1991.

127 The account of the union's goals and the October 12 meeting is based on an interview with Paul Whitehead in December 1991.

127 The account of the union's hesitance to negotiate and its meetings with

Goldman, Sachs is based on interviews with Lefty Palm on October 23, 1991, and October 30, 1991, and with Paul Whitehead in December 1991.

128 The account of the LaBow group's meeting with the union is based on interviews with Scott King on October 24, 1991, and with William Scharffenberger on October 8, 1991.

128 The account of the union negotiations is based on interviews with Lefty Palm on October 23, 1991, and with Joseph O'Leary on October 25, 1991.

129 The reference to the recovery amount offered to Oppenheimer is based on interviews with Shelley Greenhaus on November 1, 1991, and with Ronald LaBow on December 10, 1991.

129 The account of the lawsuit filed against Oppenheimer is based on interviews with Jeffrey Sabin on November 5, 1991, and with Bruce McCullough on January 2, 1992.

129 The account of negotiations between the LaBow group and Oppenheimer is based on interviews with Jeffrey Sabin on November 5, 1991, and with David Strumwasser on October 18, 1991.

129 The account of the presentations to the board is based on the transcript for a hearing on March 15, 1990, at United States Bankruptcy Court for the Western District of Pennsylvania, Case No. 85-793, PGH, Hon. Warren W. Bentz, pp. 9–11.

129–30 The reference to Judge Bentz's order is excerpted from *Memorandum and Order,* February 27, 1991, United States Bankruptcy Court for the Western District of Pennsylvania, Case No. 85-793, PGH, Hon. Warren W. Bentz, reprinted in Jeffrey S. Sabin, Carol A. Weiner, Andre Weiss, "Trading in Claims and Taking Control of the Chapter 11 Debtor: Allegheny Revisited" (prepared for distribution at the Trading in Claims Against Chapter 11 Debtors: Investment and Control Issues Program, March 11, 1991, New York City, Practising Law Institute), 1991, p. 224.

130 The description of the LaBow group's reaction to the order is based on an interview with Denis Cronin on January 3, 1992.

130 The description of the two plans is based on press reports.

130 The reference to the LaBow group's concern about Oppenheimer is based on an interview with Denis Cronin on January 3, 1992.

131 The reference to Jon Bauer's concerns about the LaBow group negotiations is based on an interview with him in December 1991.

131 The reference to Ronald LaBow's concessions is based on interviews with Shelley Greenhaus on November 1, 1991, and with LaBow on October 22, 1991.

131–33 The excerpt of the exchange among Lawrence Handelsman, Jeffrey Sabin, Arthur Field, Judge Warren Bentz, Denis Cronin, and David Murdoch is from the transcript for the hearing on April 5, 1990, at the United States Bankruptcy Court for the Western District of Pennsylvania, Case No. 85-793 PGH, Hon. Warren W. Bentz, pp. 70–95.

133 The account of the final agreement with Oppenheimer and the issue of the Goldman, Sachs's plan's viability is based on an interview with Jeffrey Sabin on November 5, 1991, and the transcript for the hearing on April 5, pp. 70–95.

133 The reference to negotiations between the LaBow group and Goldman, Sachs is based on interviews with Denis Cronin on January 3, 1992, and with Ronald LaBow on October 22, 1991.

133–34 The account of the negotiations with the pensions agency is based on interviews with Joseph O'Leary on October 25, 1991, and with Thomas Mayer on October 24, 1991.

134 The account of the company's stance toward the labor negotiations in late February is based on the transcript for the hearing on March 15, 1990, at the United States Bankruptcy Court for the Western District of Pennsylvania, Case No. 85-793 PGH, Hon. Warren W. Bentz, pp. 43–45.

134 Lefty Palm's quotation is from Thomas Buell, Jr., "USW Accuses Wheeling-Pitt of Nickel-and-Dime Deal," *The Pittsburgh Press,* March 13, 1990, sec. E, p. 1.

134–35 The account of the union's response and press conference is based on the transcript of the March 15, 1990, hearing, pp. 46–50, and press reports.

135 The account of the union's connection of fees to the duration of the case is based on an interview with Lefty Palm on October 30, 1991.

135–36 The account of the exchange among union members and the judge at the March 15, 1990, hearing is based on the transcript for that hearing, pp. 71–75, and on interviews with Denis Cronin on January 3, 1992, and with David Strumwasser on October 18, 1991.

136 The account of the union rally and response are from press reports.

136–37 The account of the steelworkers' claims is from *Amended Summary Disclosure Statement Pursuant to Section 1125 of the Bankruptcy Code in Connection with Amended Joint Plan of Reorganization dated October 18, 1990,* United States Bankruptcy Court for the Western District of Pennsylvania, Case Nos. 85-793 PGH through 85-799 PGH, Hon. Warren W. Bentz, pp. 4–5.

137 The discussion of a strike is based on press reports.

137 Lefty Palm's quotation is based on an interview with him on October 23, 1991.

137 The account of the suspension of labor talks and the settlement with the

LaBow group is based on interviews with Lefty Palm on October 23, 1991, and with Ronald LaBow on October 22, 1991, and December 10, 1991.
137 The account of the USWA's encounter with Carl Icahn is excerpted from John P. Hoerr, *And The Wolf Finally Came* (Pittsburgh: University of Pittsburgh Press, 1988), p. 543.
138 The account of the LaBow group's final negotiations with the committee is based on interviews with Lawrence Handelsman on October 30, 1991, and with Bruce McCullough on January 2, 1992.
139 Joel Gross's quotation is from an interview with Thomas Mayer on October 24, 1991.
139 The reference to Vega Partners is from Marlene Givant Star, "By Any Name, Profits Still Sweet," *Pensions and Investments,* November 25, 1991, p. 10.
139 The reference to Jon Bauer's latest responsibilities is from an interview with him in December 1991.
139–40 The account of the debate on the increased recovery is from interviews with Lawrence Handelsman on October 30, 1991, with Jon Bauer on October 30, 1991, and with Denis Cronin on January 3, 1992.

CHAPTER 6

141 The breakdown of the drugstore business is from a telephone interview with Gare Vineberg (an analyst with Dean Witter Reynolds) on April 29, 1992.
141–42 The history of Revco's growth, its problems, and the leveraged buyout is based on Karen H. Wruck, "What Really Went Wrong at Revco," *Journal of Applied Corporate Finance,* vol. 4, no. 2 (1991), pp. 79–91; an interview with Sidney Dworkin in January 1992; and press reports.
142 The reference to Salomon Brothers's miscalculation is from George Anders and Amy Dockser Marcus, "Revco Can Sue Its Ex-Advisers Over Buy-Out," *The Wall Street Journal,* January 3, 1991, sec. A, p. 3.
142 The reference to liability payments for infant deaths linked to a vitamin E supplement is from an interview with Sidney Dworkin in January 1992.
143 Boake Sells' quotations are from Gregory Stricharchuk, "Revco Doesn't Pay Interest on Bonds, And Buy-Out Fails," *The Wall Street Journal,* June 16, 1988, p. 9.
143 The description of the restructuring plan and the standstill agreement is from press reports.

143 The account of Talton Embry's investment in Revco is from press reports, and from an interview with him on March 5, 1992.

144 Talton Embry's demands and the account of his encounters with Boake Sells and Nathan Meyohas are from Gregory Stricharchuck, "Strong Stand by Revco's Bondholders Helped Push Firm's Bankruptcy Filing," *The Wall Street Journal,* August 1, 1988, p. 20.

145–47 The profile of Talton Embry's life and career, including investments in Manville and Federated/Allied, is based on interviews with him on March 22, 1991, and December 10, 1991.

146–47 The fraudulent conveyance lawsuit was never filed, although the creditors' attorneys prepared it and believe it gave them leverage in negotiations on bankruptcy recoveries.

147 The description of Magten's strategy is from *The Tenets of Value Bond Investing,* unpublished report, Magten Asset Management Corporation.

147 The reference to Talton Embry's 80-cent goal in the Revco investment is from Stricharchuk, "Strong Stand by Revco's Bondholders," p. 20.

147 The account of Talton Embry's reasoning behind his investment expectations is from an interview with him on March 22, 1991.

148 Talton's Embry's quotations are from Stephen Phillips, "Revco, Anatomy of an LBO That Failed," *Business Week,* October 3, 1988, pp. 59–61.

148 The accounts of Talton Embry's plan of reorganization and the equity holders' plan are based on Wruck, "What Really Went Wrong at Revco," p. 89, and Linda Sandler, "Revco Bankruptcy-Law Case Tests Advantage of Junk-Bond Holders Over Stockholders," *The Wall Street Journal,* September 27, 1989, sec. C, p. 1.

148 The accounts of Talton Embry's and the other creditors' fight against the equity holders' plan of reorganization and Embry's letter to the board are from Sandler, "Revco Bankruptcy-Law Case Tests Advantage," sec. C, p. 1.

148 The account of the committee's adviser's talks with potential bidders is based on an interview with Joel Friedland on January 29, 1992.

148 The reference to the Acadia Partners bid and the response of creditors is from Wruck, "What Really Went Wrong at Revco," pp. 89–90.

149 The account of Revco's asset-sales program is from *Disclosure Statement in Support of Creditors' Revco Plan of Reorganization and Proponents' ANAC Plan of Reorganization,* United States Bankruptcy Court for the Northern District of Ohio, Case Nos. 588-1305 through 588-1321, November 4, 1991, p. F-15.

149 The reference to Acadia's purchases of Revco's stores is from Wruck, "What Really Went Wrong at Revco," p. 90.

149 The reference to Jack Eckerd's purchases of Revco's stores is from

"Revco Unit to Sell Stores to Jack Eckerd of Florida," *The Wall Street Journal,* June 6, 1990, sec. A, p. 6.

149 The account of the investigation into Revco on fraudulent conveyance issues is from press reports.

149 The account of the creditors' effort to end exclusivity is from press reports.

149 The account of the trade creditors' lawsuit is from *Disclosure Statement in Support of Creditors' Revco Plan.*

150 The reference to Barry Zaretsky's opinion is from Anders and Marcus, "Revco Can Sue Its Ex-Advisers Over Buy-Out," sec. A, p. 3.

150 The account of Balfour Investors's involvement in Revco is based on an interview with Jay Goldsmith and Harry Freund on December 9, 1991.

150–55 The profile of Balfour Investors is based on an interview with Jay Goldsmith and Harry Freund on June 27, 1991; "Balfour Investors Inc. Schedule of Securities Performance," Balfour Investors, New York, N.Y., March 31, 1989; and Douglas Martin, "The None-Too-Gentle Art of the 'Bankruptcy Boys,' " *New York Times,* July 18, 1988, sec. D, p. 1.

155 The reference to Revco's financial results is from press reports.

155 The references to declining asset values and David Schulte's quotations on that are from George Anders, "Revco Saga: Or How Buy-Out Bonanza Became a Frenzy of Fees in Chapter 11," *The Wall Street Journal,* May 16, 1991, sec. C, p. 1.

155 The references to Boake Sells's complaints and the creditors' response are from George Anders, "Chapter 11 System Provokes Outburst from Revco's Chief," *The Wall Street Journal,* June 28, 1991, sec. A, p. 5.

155–56 Talton Embry's quotations are from George Anders, "Revco Creditors Propose Plan to Reorganize," *The Wall Street Journal,* September 10, 1991, sec. A, p. 3.

156 The account of David Schulte's contacts with potential bidders is based on interviews with him on December 18, 1991, and with Joel Friedland on January 29, 1992.

156 The account of Jack Eckerd's informal offer to Revco and Revco's rejection is based on an interview with Jay Goldsmith and Harry Freund on December 9, 1991, and on Dana Milbank, "Eckerd Offers $969.6 million to Get Revco," *The Wall Street Journal,* September 24, 1991, sec. A, p. 8.

156 The reference to the Revco plan is from *Disclosure Statement for Debtors' Plans of Reorganization,* United States Bankruptcy Court for the Northern District of Ohio, Case Nos. 588-1305 through 588-1321, Doc. No. 2547, June 6, 1991.

156 The reference to the creditors' preparation of a plan is from an interview with Joel Friedland on January 29, 1992.

157 The account of Balfour Investors's view of the proceedings, the search for potential bidders, and the view of Jack Eckerd's bid is from an interview with Jay Goldsmith and Harry Freund on December 9, 1991.

157–58 The account of Stewart Turley's visits to Balfour Investors and the Balfour partners' argument that Jack Eckerd should make its bid public is from an interview with Jay Goldsmith and Harry Freund on December 9, 1991.

158 The account of Jack Eckerd's continuing discussions with creditors is based on an interview with Jay Goldsmith and Harry Freund on December 9, 1991.

158 The accounts of the bondholders' new reorganization proposal and Eckerd's reorganization proposal are based on press reports.

158 The account of the creditors' reaction to Jack Eckerd's proposal is from press reports and an interview with Jay Goldsmith and Harry Freund on December 9, 1991.

159 The accounts of Rite Aid's offer, the subsequent bidding, and Judge White's order are from press reports.

159 The account of Balfour Investors's sale of its holdings is from an interview with Jay Goldsmith and Harry Freund on December 9, 1991.

160 The account of the rivals' advertisements is from press reports.

160 The account of Leon Black's involvement is from press reports and an interview with him in January 1992.

160–61 The account of the committee's efforts to bring in Zell-Chilmark is based on interviews with Joel Friedland on January 29, 1992, and with Sam Zell on January 28, 1992.

161 The account of Talton Embry's profits is from an interview with him on March 5, 1992.

CHAPTER 7

162–63 The account of Michael Lederman's visit to Allegheny is based on interviews with him on May 1, 1991, and November 4, 1991.

162–63 The reference to the CNG Tower is from William C. Symonds, "Big Trouble at Allegheny," *Business Week,* August 11, 1986, pp. 56–61.

163–64 The account of Allegheny's downfall is based on press reports, in particular, Symonds, "Big Trouble at Allegheny."

164 The reference to "the case from hell" is from Bernie Kohn, "Japonica

Tried to Take Over AI, Lenders Charge," *The Pittsburgh Press,* June 14, 1990, sec. B, p. 12.

164–65 The account of the multiple parties interested in buying Allegheny and in the decision to do a stand-alone plan is from press reports and interviews with all major parties in the bankruptcy.

165 The reference to "the Twins" is from an interview with Don Smith of Houlihan Lokey Howard & Zukin on April 12, 1991.

166–68 The profile of Paul Kazarian is based on interviews with him on April 30, 1991, and November 5, 1991, with Michael Lederman on May 1, 1991, and with Herbert Minkel on April 30, 1991.

167–68 The profile of Michael Lederman is based on interviews with him on May 1, 1991, and June 20, 1991.

168–70 The account of the raid on CNW is based on press accounts and interviews with Charles Davidson and Michael Lederman on May 1, 1991, and with Paul Kazarian on November 5, 1991.

169–70 The reference to Charles Davidson's call to Japonica and the account of his initial interest in Allegheny is based on an interview with him on May 1, 1991.

170 Wilbur Ross's quotation is from an interview with him on April 11, 1991.

170–71 The account of Paul Kazarian's initial investigation into Allegheny is based on an interview with him and Michael Lederman on April 9, 1991.

171 The account of the exploratory offer is based on press reports and an interview with Charles Davidson and Michael Lederman on May 1, 1991.

171 Bruce McCullough's quotation is from an interview with him on January 2, 1992.

171–72 The profile of James Milligan is based on an interview with him on May 19, 1991.

172 The description of James Milligan's advisory work to the Allegheny board is based on interviews with him on May 19, 1991, and with Lewis Davis on April 15, 1991.

172 The account of Joseph Cosetti's actions is based on an interview with Bruce McCullough on April 15, 1991.

172–73 The account of Harry Jones's role and actions in the case is based on an interview with him on May 10, 1991.

173 Charles O'Hanlon's quotations are from an interview with him on April 16, 1991.

173 The reference to Wilbur Ross's encouragement of Harry Jones is from an interview with Ross on April 11, 1991.

173–74 The account of the meeting at Milbank, Tweed is based on an interview with Lewis Davis on April 15, 1991.

174–75 The account of Paul Kazarian's presentation at the U.S. Trustee's office is based on interviews with John Mueller on April 3, 1991, with Harry Jones on May 10, 1991, with Wilbur Ross on April 11, 1991, and with Lewis Davis on April 15, 1991.

175 The reference to Michael Lederman's and Paul Kazarian's visit to the company and their perspective on it is based on an interview with them on April 9, 1991.

175 The description of James Milligan's business plan is based on interviews with Lewis Davis on April 15, 1991, and with Milligan on May 19, 1991.

175–76 The reference to cutting off Japonica is based on an interview with Lewis Davis on April 15, 1991.

176 The reference to the decision to develop a stand-alone plan and the description of that plan is based on interviews with Lewis Davis on April 15, 1991, with Joy Conti on April 16, 1991, and with Bruce McCullough on January 2, 1992.

176 The account of Michael Lederman's presentation at the U.S. Trustee's office is based on an interview with him on November 4, 1991.

176–77 The account of the collapse of the Allegheny plans is based on interviews with Lewis Davis on April 15, 1991, and with Joy Conti on March 16, 1991.

177–81 The account of the development and placement of Japonica's second bid is based on Paul J. Reiferson and Steven R. Fenster, *Allegheny International, Inc.,* Harvard Business School, unpublished case study, N9-291-052, June 1991, and interviews with Paul Kazarian on April 9, 1991, with Michael Lederman on April 9, 1991, May 1, 1991, and November 4, 1991, with Peter Langerman on August 2, 1991, and with Herbert Minkel on April 30, 1991.

178 The account of Japonica's hiring Herbert Minkel is based on an interview with him on April 30, 1991.

178 Michael Lederman's quotation about Herbert Minkel is from an interview with Lederman on June 20, 1991.

179 The account of Japonica's decision to increase its equity financing is based on an interview with Paul Kazarian on November 5, 1991.

179–81 The account of Michael Price's involvement in Allegheny is based on interviews with him on April 9, 1991, with Peter Langerman on August 2, 1991, and with Paul Kazarian on April 9, 1991, and November 5, 1991.

181 The creditors' reaction to Japonica's bid is based on an interview with Joy Conti on April 16, 1991.

181–82 The account of the equity committee's interest in Japonica is based on an interview with John Mueller on April 3, 1991.

182 The account of Japonica's effort to meet the board is based on interviews

with Michael Lederman on April 9, 1991, and May 1, 1991, with Herbert
Minkel on April 30, 1991, with Bruce McCullough on January 2, 1992, and
with James Milligan on May 19, 1991.

182 The reference to letters Japonica wrote the directors is based on an
interview with Herbert Minkel on April 30, 1991.

182 The reference to Japonica's reporting Bruce McCullough to the disciplinary board is from *Japonica's Opposition to Debtor's Motion for Examination,* exhibit B, United States Bankruptcy Court for the Western District of
Pennsylvania, Case No. 88-448, Doc. No. 6565, February 8, 1990, and
McCullough's assertion is based on an interview with him on January 2,
1992.

182–84 The account of Michael Lederman's meeting with Bruce McCullough is based on an interview with McCullough on April 15, 1991.

184 Michael Lederman's version of the meeting with Bruce McCullough is
based on an interview with Lederman on May 1, 1991.

184 The account of the board's rebuff to Japonica is based on interviews
with Michael Lederman on May 1, 1991, and May 17, 1991.

184–85 The account of the final agreement on the Allegheny stock plan is
based on interviews with Lewis Davis on April 15, 1991, with Joy Conti on
April 26, 1991, and with Charles O'Hanlon on April 16, 1991.

185–86 The account of Japonica's decision to start buying bank debt is
based on interviews with Paul Kazarian, Michael Price, and Michael Lederman on April 9, 1991, and with Charles Davidson and Michael Lederman on
May 1, 1991.

186–87 The account of Japonica's preparations to buy bank debt and early
negotiations is based on interviews with Paul Kazarian on April 9, 1991, with
Michael Price on April 9, 1991, and May 21, 1991, and with Michael Lederman on April 9, 1991, and May 1, 1991.

187 The description of Japonica's deadline to file a plan is based on interviews with Michael Lederman on April 9, 1991, and with Herbert Minkel on
April 30, 1991.

187–88 The account of the development of Japonica's reorganization plan is
based on interviews with Michael Lederman on May 1, 1991, and with
Herbert Minkel on April 30, 1991.

188 The account of the filing of Japonica's plan and the description of the
plan are based on interviews with Paul Kazarian on April 9, 1991, and with
Michael Lederman on April 9, 1991, and May 1, 1991.

189 The account of the company's reaction to the filing is based on an
interview with Lewis Davis on April 15, 1991, and on the transcript for the
January 25, 1990, hearing at United States Bankruptcy Court for the Western District of Pennsylvania, Case No. 88-448, Hon. Joseph L. Cosetti,
p. 238.

189–90 The account of Japonica's attempt to visit with the board is based on *Japonica's Opposition to Debtor's Motion;* Bernie Kohn, "AI Brushes Aside Japonica Offer; Ready for Reorganization Vote," *The Pittsburgh Press,* January 30, 1990, sec. D, p. 3; the transcript for the March 13, 1990, hearing at United States Bankruptcy Court for the Western District of Pennsylvania, Case No. 88-448, Doc. No. 6839, Hon. Joseph L. Cosetti; and an interview with Joshua Angel on April 22, 1991.

190 Paul Kazarian's view of Buchanan, Ingersoll is based on an interview with Herbert Minkel on April 30, 1991, and on *Japonica's Opposition to Debtor's Motion,* exhibit C.

190 The account of Michael Lederman's resumption of bank loan purchase negotiations is based on interviews with him on April 9, 1991, and May 1, 1991.

190 The bank loan sales are based on Judge Joseph L. Cosetti, *Memorandum Opinion,* United States Bankruptcy Court for the Western District of Pennsylvania, Case No. 88-00448, Doc. No. 7900, July 12, 1990.

190 The description of Michael Lederman's recollection of his methodology is based on an interview with him on November 4, 1991.

190–91 The description of Charles O'Hanlon's version of Michael Lederman's methodology is based on an interview with O'Hanlon on April 16, 1991.

191 Joy Conti's quotations are from an interview on April 16, 1991.

191 The description of the value of Japonica's plan is based on *Japonica Partners, L. P. Fourth Amended Disclosure Statement and Joint Plan of Reorganization,* United States Bankruptcy Court for the Western District of Pennsylvania, Case No. 88-448, Hon. Joseph L. Cosetti, April 5, 1990, and Cosetti, *Memorandum Opinion.*

191 The account of Charles O'Hanlon's dinner with Japonica is based on an interview with O'Hanlon on April 16, 1991.

191 The account of Charles O'Hanlon's meeting with Japonica at the Atrium Club is based on interviews with O'Hanlon on April 16, 1991, and with Paul Kazarian on April 9, 1991.

192 The description of the meeting at Bankers Trust is based on an interview with Paul Kazarian on April 9, 1991.

192 The creditors' view is based on an interview with Joy Conti on April 16, 1991.

193 The description of the scene at Bankers Trust and Japonica's introduction of its research is based on interviews with Joy Conti and Charles O'Hanlon on April 16, 1991.

193–94 The account of the confrontation at Bankers Trust is based on an interview with Charles O'Hanlon on April 16, 1991.

194 Michael Lederman's version of the confrontation is based on interviews with him on April 9, 1991, and May 1, 1991.

194–95 The account of Charles O'Hanlon's meeting with Dick Daniel is based on an interview with O'Hanlon on April 16, 1991.

194 Joy Conti's quotations are based on an interview with her on April 16, 1991.

195 Wilbur Ross's quotations are based on an interview with him on April 11, 1991.

195 The account of Charles O'Hanlon's meeting with Michael Lederman is based on an interview with O'Hanlon on April 16, 1991.

CHAPTER 8

196–97 The description of Japonica's desire for information and frustration in getting it is based on *Japonica's Opposition to Debtor's Motion;* a letter to Judge Joseph Cosetti from Herbert Minkel, dated January 30, 1990; *Motion of Japonica Partners, L.P. Compelling Financial Information from Debtors and to Appoint Independent Counsel to Debtor,* filed March 12, 1990, United States Bankruptcy Court for the Western District of Pennsylvania, Case No. 88-448, Doc. No. 6781; the transcript for the January 25, 1990, hearing, United States Bankruptcy Court for the Western District of Pennsylvania, Case No. 88-448, pp. 238–250; and interviews with Paul Kazarian on April 9, 1991, and with Michael Lederman on May 1, 1991.

197 The reference to Bruce McCullough's request for deposition is from the transcript for the February 9, 1990, hearing, United States Bankruptcy Court for the Western District of Pennsylvania, Case No. 88-448, Doc. No. 6595, Hon. Joseph L. Cosetti, p. 15.

197–98 The references to the subpoena servers' visits to Japonica's office and to the fact that they were told Michael Lederman and Paul Kazarian were not in were based on an interview with Lederman on May 1, 1991, and on *Notice of Attempts to Serve Process on Michael G. Lederman and Paul B. Kazarian of Japonica Partners, L.P.,* filed March 8, 1990, United States Bankruptcy Court for the Western District of Pennsylvania, Case No. 88-448, Hon. Joseph L. Cosetti, Exhibits A-F.

198 The account of Japonica's avoidance of service is based on *Notice of Attempts to Serve Process,* Exhibits A-F, with quote from Exhibit D, and an interview with Michael Lederman on May 1, 1991.

198 The account of Bruce McCullough's service on Michael Lederman is based on an interview with McCullough on April 15, 1991.

198 The reference to the reason few could attend the February 28, 1990, depositions is based on interviews with Bruce McCullough on April 15, 1991.

198 The account of the February 28, 1990, depositions is based on transcripts of the depositions of Paul Kazarian and Michael Lederman, United States Bankruptcy Court for the Western District of Pennsylvania, Case No. 88-448, February 28, 1990.

199 The description of the reaction to Japonica's purchases is based on interviews with Lewis Davis on April 15, 1991, and with Bruce McCullough on April 16, 1991.

199 The account of Paul Kazarian's decision to crash the Tampa meeting is based on an interview with him on April 9, 1991.

199 The reference to James Milligan's desire to move the company to Tampa is based on press reports.

199 The reference to James Milligan's position as Sunbeam CEO is from an interview with him on May 19, 1991.

200 The explanation of the reason for the Tampa meeting is based on interviews with Lewis Davis on April 15, 1991, and with Charles O'Hanlon on April 16, 1991.

200 The explanation of the failure to invite Japonica is based on interviews with Lewis Davis on April 15, 1991, and with James Milligan on May 19, 1991.

200 This account of Paul Kazarian's call to James Milligan is based on interviews with Kazarian on April 9, 1991, and with Bob Setrakian on March 6, 1992.

200–201 This account of Paul Kazarian's call to James Milligan is based on an interview with Milligan on May 19, 1991.

201-2 The accounts of Paul Kazarian's and Michael Lederman's depositions are based on the transcript for the *Deposition of Paul B. Kazarian,* United States Bankruptcy Court for the Western District of Pennsylvania, Case No. 88-448, Hon. Joseph L. Cosetti, p. 7, March 12, 1990, on an interview with Herbert Minkel on April 30, 1991, and Clare Ansberry, "Takeover Mayhem. When Will Somebody—Anybody—Rescue Battered Allegheny?" *The Wall Street Journal,* April 19, 1990, sec. A, p. 1.

202-3 The account of Michael Lederman's bank purchases, the lack of interest from Chase Manhattan, and frustrating negotiations with Morgan Guaranty is based on interviews with him on April 9, 1991, and May 1, 1991, and with Paul Kazarian on April 9, 1991.

203 The description of GKH Partners's activities is based on interviews with Charles O'Hanlon on April 16, 1991, with James Milligan on May 19, 1991, with Lewis Davis on April 15, 1991, and with Lawrence Schloss and Norman Brown from Donaldson, Lufkin & Jenrette on March 20, 1991.

204 The account of the Swiss group's invitation to the company is based on an interview with Robert Martin and Nicholas Sakellariadis on May 8, 1991, and on Cosetti, *Memorandum Opinion.*

204–5 The account of Japonica's decision to fly to Switzerland is based on interviews with Herbert Minkel on April 30, 1991, and with Michael Lederman on May 1, 1991.

205 The reference to Michael Lederman's remark to Tony Munson is based on an interview with Lederman on November 4, 1991.

205 The account of DLJ's encounter with the Swiss noteholders is based on an interview with Robert Martin on May 8, 1991.

205 The account of Michael Lederman's negotiations with the Swiss note-holders is based on an interview with him on May 1, 1991.

206–7 The account of Japonica's bank purchases is based on Cosetti, *Memorandum Opinion,* and interviews with Joy Conti on April 16, 1991, and with Michael Lederman on May 1, 1991.

207 The reference to James Milligan's call to Paul Kazarian is from an interview with Milligan on May 19, 1991.

207 The reference to Michael Lederman's comments to bank representatives is from an interview with Joy Conti on April 16, 1991.

207 Michael Lederman's explanation of Japonica's vote is from an interview with him on May 1, 1991.

207–8 The account of the company's lawsuit against Japonica is based on interviews with Bruce McCullough on April 15, 1991, and with Charles O'Hanlon on April 16, 1991, and on Cosetti, *Memorandum Opinion.*

208 The reference to Japonica's motion to disqualify votes is based on *Objection to Confirmation,* filed by Japonica on April 5, 1990, and Cosetti, *Memorandum Opinion.*

208 The account of the banks calling Michael Lederman is based on an interview with him on May 1, 1991.

208 The account of poor morale is based on an interview with James Milligan on May 19, 1991.

209–10 The account of Japonica's research efforts inside the company is based on interviews with Paul Kazarian on April 9, 1991, and with Michael Lederman on April 9, 1991, and May 1, 1991.

209–10 The account of the company's problems with Japonica while Japonica was doing its research is based on an interview with Lewis Davis on May 13, 1991, and Cosetti, *Memorandum Opinion.*

210 Michael Lederman's response is from an interview with him on May 1, 1991.

210 Charles Davidson's response is from an interview with him on May 1, 1991.

211 Paul Kazarian's quotations about Allegheny's results are based on an interview with him on April 9, 1991.

211–12 The account of the disclosure statement hearings on the Japonica plan is based on interviews with Herbert Minkel on April 30, 1991, and with Michael Lederman on November 4, 1991.

211–12 The account of arguments posed at the hearings is based on an interview with Herbert Minkel on April 30, 1991, and transcripts for the March 13, 1990, hearing at the United States Bankruptcy Court for the Western District of Pennsylvania, Case No. 88-448, Hon. Joseph L. Cosetti.

212 Odyssey Partners's quotation is from *AIA Objection to Japonica Disclosure Statement and Plan,* filed February 22, 1990, United States Bankruptcy Court for the Western District of Pennsylvania, Case No. 88-448, Doc. No. 6645.

212 The reference to the continuing efforts by the bank creditors is based on an interview with Joy Conti on April 16, 1991.

212 Wilbur Ross's quotations are from an interview with him on April 11, 1991.

212–14 The account of Japonica's tender offer is based on interviews with Herbert Minkel on April 30, 1991, with Paul Kazarian on April 9, 1991, with Michael Lederman on May 1, 1991, and May 17, 1991, with Charles Davidson on May 1, 1991, and with Wilbur Ross on April 11, 1991.

213–14 The account of Paul Kazarian's conversation with Mike Halpern is based on an interview with Kazarian on April 9, 1991.

214–15 The account of the strategy session with the banks and insurance companies is based on an interview with Lewis Davis on April 29, 1991. The 40 percent includes 8 percent resulting from the exercise of warrants.

215 The reference to Japonica's motivation to recruit James Milligan is based on an interview with Michael Lederman on May 1, 1991.

215–16 The accounts of the meeting at Nemacolin and the lunch the following day are based on interviews with Lewis Davis on April 16, 1991, with Paul Kazarian on April 9, 1991, with Michael Lederman on April 9, 1991, and May 1, 1991, and with James Milligan on May 19, 1991, and January 29, 1992.

216 The account of continuing discussions with the banks is based on interviews with Michael Lederman on May 1, 1991, and May 17, 1991, with

Charles Davidson on May 1, 1991, and with Herbert Minkel on April 30, 1991.

216–17 The account of Japonica's purchase of the insurance companies' claims and the insurance companies' attempt to change their votes is based on interviews with Paul Kazarian on April 9, 1991, with Herbert Minkel on April 30, 1991, with Bruce McCullough on April 15, 1991, and with Joy Conti on April 16, 1991.

217 Japonica's decision to suggest an orderly transition process is based on an interview with Michael Lederman and Paul Kazarian on April 9, 1991.

217 The account of Michael Lederman's call to Lewis Davis is based on an interview with Davis on April 29, 1991.

217 The reference to Joy Conti's interpretation of Japonica's move is from an interview with her on April 16, 1991.

217–18 The account of Bruce McCullough's action to expel Japonica from the building, including the conversation, is based on an interview with him on April 15, 1991.

218 The reference to Bruce McCullough's instructions to Earl Maxwell is from an interview with Paul Kazarian on April 9, 1991.

219 The reference to Paul Kazarian's insistence that he didn't challenge McCullough is from an interview with Kazarian in December 1991.

219 The reference to Michael Lederman's recollection of the confrontation with Bruce McCullough is from an interview with Lederman in January 1992.

219 Michael Lederman's quotation about leaving the building is from an interview with him and Paul Kazarian on April 9, 1991.

219 The excerpt from Japonica's memo to AI is from Japonica Partners, "Working Group Memorandum," June 12, 1990.

220 The account of Michael Lederman's discovery of the banks' lawsuit is based on an interview with him on May 1, 1991.

220 The account of the banks' dilemma and their lawsuit against Japonica is based on an interview with Joy Conti on April 16, 1991.

221 Judge Joseph Cosetti's quotation is from Len Baselovic, "Creditors Reject Japonica Proposal," *The Pittsburgh Press,* June 22, 1990, sec. D, p. 6.

221 The account of Japonica's negotiations with the banks is from interviews with Michael Lederman on May 1, 1991, and May 17, 1991, with Charles Davidson on May 1, 1991, and with Herbert Minkel on April 30, 1991.

221 The reference to Joseph Cosetti's rulings is from his *Memorandum Opinion.*

221 The account of Paul Kazarian's reaction to the ruling is based on an interview with him on April 9, 1991.

222 Joy Conti's quotations on the consequences of Japonica's stock being held in trust are from an interview with her on April 16, 1991.

222 Herbert Minkel's quotations are from an interview with him on April 30, 1991.

222 The account of Japonica's strategy is based on an interview with Herbert Minkel on April 30, 1991.

222–23 The account of the banks' views and offer to Japonica is based on an interview with Joy Conti on April 16, 1991.

223 The account of Japonica's negotiations with the banks is based on an interview with Joy Conti on April 16, 1991.

223 The reference to the choice given to unsecured debtholders is based on an interview with Wilbur Ross on April 11, 1991.

223 The account of the company's final negotiations with Japonica is based on an interview with Lewis Davis on April 29, 1991.

223 The explanation of James Milligan's severance is based on interviews with him on May 19, 1991, and January 29, 1992.

223 The account of the directors' severance is based on the transcript for the August 2, 1990, hearing at the United States Bankruptcy Court for the Western District of Pennsylvania, Case No. 88-448, Hon. Joseph L. Cosetti, p. 73, and interviews with Bruce McCullough on April 17, 1991, with Herbert Minkel on April 30, 1991, and with Michael Lederman and Charles Davidson on May 1, 1991.

224 The account of the August 2 hearing is based on interviews with Bruce McCullough on April 17, 1991, and with Herbert Minkel on April 30, 1991.

224 The reference to $270 million in cash is from the transcript for the August 2, 1990, court hearing, p. 42; it includes all available cash, including cash from operations and from the sale of assets.

224 Japonica's fears about delay are based on an interview with Herbert Minkel on April 30, 1991.

224 The account of Herbert Minkel's view of Bruce McCullough's statement to the court is based on an interview with Minkel on April 30, 1991; the excerpt is drawn from the transcript of that hearing, on August 2, 1990, pp. 13–14.

225 The reference to the NRC licence is from information supplied by Herbert Minkel in February 1992.

225 The account of Bruce McCullough's call to Herbert Minkel about the NRC license issue and the resolution of that problem is based on interviews with Minkel on April 30, 1991, with McCullough on April 17, 1991, with

Paul Kazarian on April 9, 1991, and with Michael Lederman on November 13, 1991.

226 The reference to calls to Michael Steinhardt are from an interview with Charles Davidson on May 1, 1991.

226–27 The account of the closing of the acquisition is based on an interview with Paul Kazarian on April 9, 1991.

227 The account of Japonica's outlay is based on interviews with Paul Kazarian and Michael Price on April 9, 1991, and with Michael Lederman and Charles Davidson on May 1, 1991.

227 Michael Price's and Paul Kazarian's quotations about the deal are from an interview with them on April 9, 1991.

227 The reference to the shrinkage in employees is based on interviews with James Milligan on May 19, 1991, with Paul Kazarian on April 9, 1991, and with Michael Lederman on May 1, 1991, and November 13, 1991.

228 The account of the move from Pittsburgh to Providence is based on an interview with Michael Lederman on November 13, 1991.

228 The description of compensation arrangements is based on interviews with Paul Kazarian on April 9, 1991, and with Michael Lederman on November 13, 1991, and press reports.

228 The account of new product introductions is based on an interview with Paul Kazarian on April 9, 1991.

228–29 The account of Japonica's discovery of the Paris office is from an interview with Paul Kazarian on April 9, 1991.

229 The reference to Michael Price's view of managements in Chapter 11 is from interviews with him on April 9, 1991, and May 21, 1991.

229 The reference to Mutual Series's profits from the investment is from an interview with Michael Price on December 10, 1991. The quotations are from interviews with him on April 9, 1991, and May 21, 1991.

229 Charles Davidson's quotations are from an interview with him on May 1, 1991.

230 Michael Price's quotations are from an interview with him on May 21, 1991.

CHAPTER 9

232 The reference to John and Jere Thompsons' salaries is from the 1987 Southland Corporation proxy statement, filed with the Securities and Exchange Commission, October 26, 1987.

232–33 The history of Southland is from Joe Simnacher, "Southland Weathered Bankruptcy Before," *Dallas Morning News,* October 25, 1990, sec. D, p. 2.

232–33 The account of John Thompson's meetings with Samuel Belzberg is from press reports.

233 The description of the leveraged buyout strategy, the restructuring of the strategy, and the completion of the buyout is from press reports.

233 The reference to "The Texas Chain-Store Massacre" is from press reports.

234 The account of the asset sales and the reference to the Cityplace Center are from press reports.

234–35 The account of the exchange offer is based on press reports.

235 The account of Shamrock Partners's deal to buy Southland and how that deal fell apart is from Judge Harold C. Abramson, *Memorandum Opinion Invalidating Acceptance of Pre-Packaged Plan of Reorganization,* filed February 28, 1991, United States Bankruptcy Court for the Northern District of Texas Dallas Division, Case No. 390-37119-HCA-11, and an interview with with Kenneth Moelis on December 3, 1991.

235–36 The account of Martin Whitman's contacts with Jerome Kohlberg about Southland and his view of Southland as a prepackaged bankruptcy are based on interviews with Whitman in December 1991 and on November 20, 1991.

236–38 The account of the Anglo Energy prepackaged bankruptcy reorganization is based on an interview with Martin Whitman in December 1991.

238 The description of the New York court ruling on exchange offers is based on an explanation of the *Chateaugay* case in Marc S. Kirschner, Dan A. Kusnetz, Laurence Y. Solarsh, and Craig S. Gatarz, "Prepackaged Bankruptcy Plans: The Leveraging Tool of the '90s in the Wake of OID and Tax Concerns," *Seton Hall Law Review,* vol. 21 (1991), p. 645.

238 The account of Southland's restructuring plan and exchange offer and the description of the expected use of proceeds are based on press reports.

239–40 The account of the bondholders' reaction to the offer is based on press reports and on interviews with John Gordon on June 7, 1991, with James Casey on July 15, 1991, and with James Casey and George Varughese on January 13, 1992.

240 John Gordon's quotation is from Karen Blumenthal, "Southland Approaches 2 Crucial Dates In Plan to Rearrange $1.8 billion in Debt," *The Wall Street Journal,* June 4, 1990, sec. B, p. 5.

241–42 The account of Kenneth Moelis's visit with Carl Icahn and the description of Icahn's holdings are from interviews with Moelis in July 1991 and on December 3, 1991, and with Mark Rachesky and Richard Rubin on January 30, 1992.

241–43, 244 The account of the bondholders' organizing activities is based on an interview with John Gordon on June 7, 1991 and court documents, including *Report of the Official Bondholders' Committee Regarding Formation of Pre-Petition Ad Hoc and Steering Committees of Security Holders, Selection of Financial Advisors and Legal Counsel, Results of Due Diligence Investigation, and Negotiation of Exchange Offer and Prepackaged Plan,* filed November 22, 1990, United States Bankruptcy Court for the Northern District of Texas Dallas Division, Case No. 390-37119-HCA-11, Hon. Harold C. Abramson.

242–43 The history of informal bondholders' committees is based on a speech by Wilbur Ross to the Fixed Income Analysts' Society, February 27, 1991.

244–45 The history of Deltec and the profile of John Gordon are based on interviews with him on June 7, 1991 and September 25, 1991, and with Arthur Byrnes on April 10, 1991, and September 25, 1991.

245 John Gordon's characterization of James Spiotto is based on an interview with Gordon on June 7, 1991.

245 Martin Whitman's quotations about joining creditors' committees is from an interview with him on November 20, 1991.

245 The reference to Southland's road show is from an interview with John Gordon on June 7, 1991.

245 The description of Whitman, Heffernan & Rhein's investment group and its investment is from interviews with James Heffernan in December 1990.

245–46 The account of the creditors' committee's first meeting with Kidder, Peabody is based on interviews with John Gordon on June 7, 1991, and with Jim Casey and George Varughese on January 13, 1992, and on *Report of the Official Bondholders' Committee.*

246 The reference to Kemper Corporation's holdings is from an interview with Kenneth Urbaszewski in July 1991.

247 The account of the talks through June are from interviews with John Gordon on June 7, 1991, with James Casey on July 15, 1991, and with James Casey and George Varughese on Janury 13, 1992, and on the *Report of the Official Bondholders' Committee.*

248 The description of George Varughese's view of a prepackaged bankruptcy and the account of his trip to Japan are based on an interview with him on January 13, 1992.

248 The account of the steering committee's demands to hold the requirement to 95 percent is from interviews with George Varughese and James Casey on January 13, 1992, and with Kenneth Urbaszewski in July 1991, and Abramson, *Memorandum Opinion.*

249 The account of Philip Bowers's effort at a jump start of the negotiations and the revised offer is from an interview with him on July 8, 1991, and Abramson, *Memorandum Opinion.*

249 The account of James Bennett's view of prepackaged bankruptcy is from an interview with him on June 21, 1991.

250 The reference to Kenneth Moelis's view that he'd worked out a framework of a settlement is from an interview with him in July 1991.

250 The account of Kenneth Moelis's meeting with John Gordon in Gordon's office is based on an interview with Gordon on June 7, 1991.

250 The reference to the tentative cents-on-the-dollar exchange offer amounts is from an interview with John Gordon on September 25, 1991.

250–51 The account of Martin Whitman's negotiation of the exchange amount for the senior bonds, including his visit with Carl Icahn, is based on interviews with Whitman in December 1990 and November 20, 1991, and with James Heffernan in December 1990.

252 The reference to Kenneth Moelis's assumption about Martin Whitman and Carl Icahn and the account of the calculation that the deal would come up short are based on an interview with Moelis in July 1991.

252–53 The account of Kenneth Moelis's report to the committee is from an interview with him in July 1991.

253 The account of the bondholders' reaction to Kenneth Moelis's news is from interviews with James Casey on July 15, 1991, and with John Gordon on June 7, 1991.

253 The account of the committee's demands for more money is based on interviews with Kenneth Urbaszewski in July 1991 and with an anonymous participant in the negotiations on July 21, 1991.

254 The reference to John Gordon's view of Ito-Yokado is from an interview with him on June 7, 1991.

254 The accounts of the call to Ito-Yokado and the decision on the amounts that would go to seniors and juniors are based on an interview with Philip Bowers on July 8, 1991.

254 The account of the phone call with Carl Icahn, Kenneth Urbaszewski, and James Heffernan is based on interviews with Urbaszewski and Moelis in July 1991.

254–55 Philip Bowers's quotations are from an interview with him on July 8, 1991.

255 The account of Kenneth Moelis's and Philip Bowers's meeting with the committee is based on interviews with James Casey on July 15, 1991, with Moelis in July 1991, with Kenneth Urbaszewski in July 1991, and with John Gordon on June 7, 1991, and September 25, 1991.

255 The reference to Kenneth Moelis's view of a prepackaged bankruptcy is from an interview with him on December 3, 1991.

256 The account of Philip Bowers's view of a prepackaged bankruptcy and the agreement to file papers for one is from an interview with him on July 8, 1991.

256 The account of the committee's problems with the deal is based on interviews with Kenneth Urbaszewski in July 1991, with James Casey on July 15, 1991, and with Philip Bowers on July 8, 1991.

257–59 The account of the committee's last night of negotiations on the preliminary deal is based on interviews with Kenneth Urbaszewski in July 1991, with James Casey on July 15, 1991, with Philip Bowers on July 8, 1991, with Kenneth Moelis in July 1991, and with James Casey and George Varughese on January 13, 1992, and Abramson, *Memorandum Opinion.*

259 The account of John Gordon's discovery that the preliminary deal was done is from an interview with him on June 7, 1991.

259 The account of the failed exchange offers and the successful prepackaged bankruptcy vote are based on press reports, Abramson, *Memorandum Opinion,* and an interview with John Gordon on June 7, 1991.

259–60 The account of Southland's deteriorating finances is based on Abramson, *Memorandum Opinion,* and David LaGesse, "Southland Financial Officer Describes Firm's Cash Crunch," *Dallas Morning News,* December 25, 1990, sec. D, p.3.

261 The account of David Glatstein's involvement in Southland bonds is based on an interview with him in June 1991.

261 The account of Anthony Ben Walsh's involvement in Southland bonds is based on *Unofficial Committee of Debentureholders' Application with Memorandum for Order Allowing and Awarding: (A) Reimbursement of Expenses of Certain Committee Members Pursuant to 11 U.S.C. #503(b) (3); and (B) Compensation and Reimbursement of Expenses of Counsel Pursuant to 11 U.S.C. # 503(b)(4),* filed May 23, 1991, United States Bankruptcy Court for the Northern District of Texas Dallas Division, Case No. 390-37119-HCA-11, Hon. Harold Abramson, and an interview with Kenneth Moelis in July 1991. Walsh declined to be interviewed about Southland.

261–62 The account of the formation of the unofficial creditors' committee and its objections to the prepackaged plan is based on *Unofficial Committee* *of Debentureholders' Application,* Abramson, *Memorandum Opinion,* and an interview with David Glatstein in June 1991.

262 Judge Harold C. Abramson's quotations are from David LaGesse, "Southland Told to Rehold Vote," *Dallas Morning News,* December 22, 1990, sec. F, p. 1.

262 The reference to more purchases by James Bennett is from an interview with him on June 21, 1991.

262 The reference to the dissenters' letter is from *Unofficial Committee of Debentureholders' Application.*

262 The account of the dissenters' hopes is based on an interview with David Glatstein in June 1991, and *Unofficial Committee of Debentureholders' Application.*

262 The account of the creditors' fears that the dissenters would hold the case up is based on an interview with John Gordon on June 7, 1991.

263–64 The account of Kenneth Moelis's effort to negotiate with the unofficial creditors' committee is based on interviews with him in July 1991 and on December 3, 1991.

265 The photograph of the dissidents' attorneys appeared in David LaGesse, " 'Little Guys' Get Theirs," *Dallas Morning News,* February 24, 1991, sec. H, p. 1.

265 The account of the deal with the dissenters is from *Unofficial Committee of Debentureholders' Application.*

265 John Gordon's quotations are from an interview with him on June 7, 1991.

265–66 The account of Deltec's returns and John Gordon's reward from the reorganization is from an interview with him on June 7, 1991.

266 The account of James Bennett's returns is based on an interview with him on June 21, 1991.

266 The reference to Martin Whitman's return is based on interviews with him and James Heffernan in December 1990.

266 The account of Carl Icahn's holdings is from "Icahn Stake in Southland," *New York Times,* March 15, 1991, sec. D, p. 3.

266 The reference to Carl Icahn's profit is from an interview with Mark Rachesky and Richard Rubin on January 30, 1992.

266 The reference to a $960,000 annual salary for each of the Thompson brothers for five years is from David LaGesse, "Thompsons Give Up Roles in Southland," *Dallas Morning News,* December 11, 1990, sec. A, p. 1.

266 The reference to the $60 million loan to the Thompsons is from an interview with Kenneth Moelis on December 3, 1991.

CHAPTER 10

269 Donald Trump's quotation is from Chris Welles, "Welcome to the Nineties, Donald," *Business Week,* May 14, 1990, p. 118.

269 The accounts of Donald Trump's efforts to find cash and his bank refinancing are based on press reports.

269–70 The account of problems at Donald Trump's casinos is from press reports and John R. O'Donnell with James Rutherford, *Trumped!* (New York: Simon & Schuster, 1991).

270 Donald Trump's quotation is from O'Donnell, *Trumped!*, p. 15.

270–71 The reference to the Hilton Hotel Corporation's alleged ties to organized crime is from O'Donnell, *Trumped!*, p. 27.

271 The account of Donald Trump's acquisition of three New Jersey casinos is based on O'Donnell, *Trumped!* and Donald J. Trump with Charles Leerhsen, *TRUMP Surviving at the Top* (New York: Random House, 1990).

271–72 The description of the Taj Mahal is based on Trump Taj Mahal Funding, Inc., Trump Taj Mahal Associates, Taj Mahal Holding Corporation, *Prospectus and Solicitation of Plan Acceptances,* issued to bondholders, June 5, 1991; O'Donnell, *Trumped!;* Trump, *TRUMP Surviving at the Top,* and Neil Barsky and Pauline Yoshihashi, "Trump Is Betting That Taj Mahal Casino Will Hit Golden Jackpot in Atlantic City," *The Wall Street Journal,* March 20, 1990, sec. B, p. 1.

272 The reference to Donald Trump's expenditures on the Taj Mahal is from O'Donnell, *Trumped!*.

272 The reference to unfinished contracting work is from press reports.

272 The account of the Taj Mahal's opening is based on O'Donnell, *Trumped!*.

272 The reference to the Taj Mahal's daily revenue is from Neil Barsky, "Trump to Ask his Bondholders for Debt Relief," *The Wall Street Journal,* July 26, 1990, sec. A, p. 3.

272 The reference to the Taj Mahal's cannibalizing business from other casinos is from O'Donnell, *Trumped!*.

272 The bondholders' expectations concerning the interest payment is based on an interview with Wilbur Ross on October 9, 1991.

273 The reference to the bondholders' committee and its members is from Trump Taj Mahal Funding, *Prospectus and Solicitation.*

273 The description of Hillel Weinberger is based on interviews with Wilbur Ross on October 9, 1991, and January 6, 1992.

273 The references to Wilbur Ross's employment by the bondholders' committee and his involvement in Resorts International are based on an interview with him on October 9, 1991.

273 The account of the first strategy conference call is based on an interview with Kaye Handley on October 11, 1991.

274 The account of Wilbur Ross's visit to the Taj Mahal is based on an interview with him on October 9, 1991.

274–75 The account of management's presentation to the steering committee is based on an interview with Wilbur Ross on January 6, 1992.

275 The reference to management's restructuring proposal is from press reports.

275 The reference to Wilbur Ross's and Robert Miller's reactions to management's presentation is from an interview with Ross on October 9, 1991.

275 The description of the Castle's and the Plaza's problems is based on press reports.

275 The references to Carl Icahn's developing involvement in the Taj Mahal case and his investment position are based on interviews with Wilbur Ross on October 9, 1991 and January 6, 1992, and with Mark Rachesky and Richard Rubin on January 30, 1992.

275–76 The account of Carl Icahn's childhood, education, early career, and corporate raiding activities is based on Bruck, *The Predators' Ball,* and Asra Q. Nomani, "Turbulent Times, Trying to Save TWA, Carl Icahn Is Facing Intractable Problems," *The Wall Street Journal,* April 29, 1991, sec. A, p. 1.

276 The reference to Carl Icahn's net worth is based on Harold Seneker with Dolores Lataniotis, editors, Jody Brennan, Lisa Coleman, Evan McGlinn, Wendy Tanaka, Jason Halperin, "Forbes 400," *Forbes,* October 21, 1991, p. 214.

277 The account of Carl Icahn's investment in Texaco is based on Allana Sullivan and Randall Smith, "Icahn's 'Midas Touch' as Investor Intrigues Would-Be Imitators," *The Wall Street Journal,* February 9, 1989, sec. C, p. 1, Allana Sullivan, "Star of Restructured Texaco Shines Again," *The Wall Street Journal,* July 8, 1991, sec. B, p. 6, and an interview with Carl Icahn on January 29, 1992.

277 The reference to Carl Icahn's investments in USX and in a number of distressed companies is from Linda Sandler and George Anders, "Icahn is Treading on Treacherous Terrain," *The Wall Street Journal,* November 29, 1990, sec. C, p. 1, and an interview with Mark Rachesky and Richard Rubin on January 30, 1992.

277 The background information on Western Union and its troubles is based on press reports.

277 The reference to Carl Icahn's purchase of Western Union bonds is from interviews with him on January 29, 1992, with Jay Goldsmith and Harry Freund on June 27, 1991, and with Mark Rachesky and Richard Rubin on January 30, 1992.

278 The account of Balfour Investors's meeting with Carl Icahn and the reference to Bennett LeBow's boat are based on an interview with Jay Goldsmith and Harry Freund on June 27, 1991.

278–79 The account of Kenneth Moelis's meeting with Carl Icahn is based on an interview with Moelis on December 31, 1991.

279 The reference to the negotiating points is based on an interview with Kenneth Moelis on November 15, 1991.

279 The reference to the change-of-control arrangement is based on an interview with Jay Goldsmith and Harry Freund on June 27, 1991.

279 The account of the confrontation with Bennett LeBow on loopholes is from an interview with Carl Icahn on January 29, 1992, and with Mark Rachesky and Richard Rubin on January 30, 1992.

279 The reference to the conference calls is based on interviews with Kenneth Moelis on November 15, 1991, and with Jay Goldsmith and Harry Freund on June 27, 1991.

280 The account of the conversation about the fee is based on interviews with Kenneth Moelis on November 15, 1991, and with Jay Goldsmith and Harry Freund on June 27, 1991.

280 The account of Bennett LeBow's remark to Carl Icahn is from an interview with Jay Goldsmith and Harry Freund on June 27, 1991.

280 The account of the dinner on Bennett LeBow's boat is based on an interview with Mark Rachesky and Richard Rubin on January 30, 1992.

280 The reference to the prolonged negotiating sessions is from an interview with Jay Goldsmith and Harry Freund on June 27, 1991.

281 The reference to Carl Icahn's block of the exchange offer is based on an interview with Kenneth Moelis on November 15, 1991.

281 The account of the change in the offer to bondholders is based on press reports.

281 The account of the bondholders' effort to block that offer is based on interviews with Kenneth Moelis on November 15, 1991, and with Mark Rachesky and Richard Rubin on January 30, 1992.

281 The account of the conference call is based on interviews with Kenneth Moelis on November 15, 1991, and December 31, 1991, and with Jay Goldsmith and Harry Freund on June 27, 1991.

281–82 The account of the bondholders' letter to management and Carl

Icahn's decision not to sell out is based on press reports and on interviews with Mark Rachesky and Richard Rubin on January 30, 1992, and with Jay Goldsmith and Harry Freund on June 27, 1991.

282 The account of Wilbur Ross's tennis match with Carl Icahn is based on interviews with Ross on October 9, 1991, and with Icahn on January 29, 1992.

282 The account of negotiations between Donald Trump and the bondholders' committee is based on press reports and an interview with Wilbur Ross on January 6, 1992.

282 The reference to Donald Trump's remarks to Kenneth Moelis is based on an interview with Moelis on December 31, 1991.

282–83 Management's offer to the bondholders is based on press reports.

283 The bondholders committee's reaction to the offer and the bodyguard's quotation to Kenneth Moelis are based on an interview with him on December 31, 1991.

283 Wilbur Ross's quotations about the management proposal, including the excerpts from the letter to bondholders, are from Neil Barsky, "Bondholders Reject Trump's Exchange Offer," *The Wall Street Journal,* October 16, 1990, sec. A, p. 8.

283 The list of issues the bondholders wanted to address is from an interview with Wilbur Ross on January 6, 1992.

283 The reference to the SEC filing is from an interview with Kenneth Moelis on December 31, 1991.

283 The reference to Donald Trump's resistance to giving up control is from press reports, specifically Neil Barsky, "Trump's Talks Over Taj Bonds Break Down," *The Wall Street Journal,* November 14, 1990, sec. A, p. 3.

283 The reference to an agreement on prepackaged bankruptcy is from an interview with Kenneth Moelis on November 15, 1991.

283–84 The reference to the bondholders' decision to leave Donald Trump in control is based on an interview with Wilbur Ross on October 9, 1991, and with Kenneth Moelis on January 29, 1992.

284 The reference to Donald Trump's demands and the bondholders' demands are from an interview with Wilbur Ross on January 6, 1992, and Richard D. Hylton, "How Trump Got a Second Chance," *New York Times,* November 22, 1990, sec. D, p. 2.

284 The reference to the committee's threat of an involuntary bankruptcy filing and Carl Icahn's comments are from Barsky, "Trump's Talks Over Taj Bonds Break Down."

284–85 Donald Trump's quotation and Wilbur Ross's retort are from

"Trump Ends Talks on Debt," *New York Times,* November 14, 1990, sec. D, p. 2.

285 The account of the Wednesday negotiating sessions is based on interviews with Wilbur Ross on October 9, 1991, and January 6, 1992.

285 The account of negotiations on Thursday are based on an interview with Wilbur Ross on October 9, 1991.

285–86 The account of the events on Friday morning to 10:30 is based on an interview with Wilbur Ross on October 9, 1991.

286 The description of Donald Trump's discussion with his advisers is based on an interview with Kenneth Moelis on December 31, 1991.

286 The account of the deal bondholders reached with Donald Trump is based on press reports and an interview with Wilbur Ross on October 9, 1991.

286–87 The explanation of the reasons for the conference call with the broad bondholder group is based on an interview with Wilbur Ross on October 9, 1991.

287 The account of the conference call and the bondholders' initial reaction is based on an interview with Wilbur Ross on October 9, 1991.

287–88 The account of Kaye Handley's perspective and Wilbur Ross's remarks about Donald Trump's image is based on interviews with Handley on October 11, 1991, and January 14, 1992.

288 The account of bondholders' demands and Wilbur Ross's quotations on them are from an interview with him on October 9, 1991.

288 The reference to the bondholders' questions about Carl Icahn is based on an interview with Wilbur Ross on October 9, 1991.

289 The account of Carl Icahn's presentation to the bondholders is based on Hylton, "How Trump Got a Second Chance," and interviews with Wilbur Ross on October 9, 1991, with Kaye Handley on October 11, 1991, and with Mark Rachesky and Richard Rubin on January 30, 1992.

289 Kenneth Moelis's quotations are from an interview with him on November 15, 1991.

289 The bondholders' reaction to Carl Icahn's comments is based on an interview with Kaye Handley on October 11, 1991.

289–90 The account of the signing of the four-page agreement is from an interview with Wilbur Ross on October 9, 1991.

290 The account of Donald Trump's interest payment to Castle bondholders is based on Neil Barsky, "Donald Trump Gets $3 Million in Chips Off the Old Block," January 21, 1991, sec. C, p. 13, and O'Donnell, *Trumped!.*

290 The reference to Pops or Daddy-O is from Trump, *TRUMP Surviving at the Top.*

290–91 The account of Carl Icahn's governance and other demands in the final negotiations are based on interviews with Wilbur Ross on October 9, 1991, and press reports.

291 The account of The Castle's loss is from press reports.

291 The references to The Plaza bondholders' lawsuit and the casino's worsening results are from press reports.

292 The profiles of Dan Harmetz and David Breazzano are from press reports.

292 The accounts of Fidelity's investments in MCorp and Gillett are from press reports. The account of the investment in Price Communications is from Marlene Givant Star, "Fidelity Pulls Plug on Packaged Deal," *Pensions & Investments,* April 1, 1991, p. 4.

293 The account of Fidelity's deal with Trump Plaza is based on press reports.

294 The accounts of the agreement on the Taj Majal, the renewal of its gaming license, and Trump's final agreements with his banks are from an interview with Carl Icahn on January 29, 1992, and press reports.

294–95 The accounts of the final deals with Castle and Plaza bondholders is from press reports.

295 The accounts of the Taj Mahal's emergence from bankruptcy and the Moody's report are from press reports.

295 The background information on TWA is based on press reports.

296 Wilbur Ross's quotations about Carl Icahn as a debtor is based on an interview with Ross on October 9, 1991.

CHAPTER 11

297 The description of Sam Zell's motorcycle trips is based on an interview with David Schulte on December 10, 1991.

297 The description of War at Four is based on an interview with Donald Phillips on December 2, 1991.

298 The reference to Zell's personal wealth is from Seneker, Lataniotis, Brennan, Coleman, McGlinn, Tanaka, Halperin, "The Forbes 400," *Forbes,* October 21, 1991, p. 244. The following quote appears in the article: "Zell manages empire worth over $800 million; split with Lurie's wife, 6 young children.

298 The reference to Sam Zell's simple approach to problems is from an interview with him on January 28, 1992.

298–99 The description of the three sculptures is from an interview with Sam

Zell on January 28, 1992, and Erik Ipsen, "Will Success Spoil Sam Zell?" *Institutional Investor,* April 1989, p. 90.

299 Sam Zell's quotations about the people he hires are from an interview with him on January 28, 1992.

299 Sam Zell's quotations on ownership stakes and ineffective workouts are from "Leverage, Workouts and Bankruptcy: How to Capitalize on Business and Investment Opportunities in a Troubled Economy," talk given at Rutgers Graduate School of Management conference held in New York City, June 28, 1991.

300–302 The profile of Sam Zell and description of his early career are based on an interview with him on January 28, 1992, Ipsen, "Will Success Spoil Sam Zell?" p. 90, Jonathan R. Laing, "The Vulture Capitalist," *Barron's,* July 30, 1990, p. 8, Lois Therrien, "Sam Zell, the Perpetual Dealmaking Machine," *Business Week,* June 26, 1989, p. 88, Eric N. Berg, "Building a Lost-Cause Portfolio," *New York Times,* October 23, 1991, sec. D, p. 1.

301 The accounts of the investment in Reno and the conviction of Robert Baskes are from Therrien, "Sam Zell."

301–2 The account of Sam Zell and Robert Lurie's investment in GAMI is based on an interview with Zell on January 28, 1992, and Laing, "The Vulture Capitalist," Therrien, "Sam Zell," and Berg, "Building a Lost-Cause Portfolio."

302 The reference to the Raines Tool Company investment is from an interview with Sam Zell on January 28, 1992, and Therrien, "Sam Zell."

302–3 The account of Zell's involvement in Itel Corporation is based on interviews with Jay Goldsmith and Harry Freund on June 27, 1991 and January 2, 1992, and Berg, "Building a Lost-Cause Portfolio," Roger Lowenstein, "Itel Tests Zell's Well-Known Taste For Turnarounds," *The Wall Street Journal,* February 4, 1991, sec. C. p. 1, James P. Miller, "Itel Will Sell Dredging Unit to Blackstone," *The Wall Street Journal,* August 19, 1991, sec. A, p. 5B, Christina Duff, "Itel Plans to Sell Its 15% Holding in Santa Fe Pacific, *The Wall Street Journal,* September 4, 1991, sec. A, p. 7, Laing, "The Vulture Capitalist," and Therrien, "Sam Zell."

303 The account of raising Zell-Merrill Real Estate Opportunity Partners is from Ipsen, "Will Success Spoil Sam Zell?"

303 Sam Zell's quotations about his image are based on an interview with him on January 28, 1992.

303 The reference to the second Zell-Merrill fund is from an interview with Sam Zell on January 28, 1992.

303 The reference to the Zell-Lurie empire is from Laing, "The Vulture Capitalist."

304–5 The profile of David Schulte and the description of his early involvement with Sam Zell is based on interviews with Schulte on April 23, 1991 and December 18, 1991.

305–6 The history of Apex Oil and its difficulties is based on press reports and Chaim J. Fortgang and Thomas Moers Mayers, "Trading Claims and Taking Control of Corporations in Chapter 11," *Cardozo Law Review,* vol. 12, no. 1, (1990), pp. 171–174.

305–6 The quotations about Anthony Novelly are taken from *Examiner's Report On Good Faith and Fair Dealing: Section 363 Issues Raised by Motion for Approval of Asset Purchase Agreement Between Debtors and AOC Acquisition Corporation and Objections Thereto* (October 10, 1988) filed in Apex Oil Co., Case No. 87-03804-BKC-BSSD, excerpted in Fortgang and Mayers, "Trading Claims and Taking Control," p. 172, Note 503.

306 The account of Apex's fall into bankruptcy and Sam Zell's early involvement with Apex is based on press reports, an interview with David Schulte on December 18, 1991, and Fortgang and Mayers, "Trading Claims and Taking Control."

306–9 The accounts of Sam Zell and David Schulte's negotiation of the bank loan purchase via an option, the negotiation of the agreement with Horsham, the negotiation of the reorganization plan, and the challenge from Getty are based on press reports and interviews with Schulte on April 23, 1991, December 5, 1991, and December 18, 1991.

309–11 The account of Sam Zell and David Schulte's campaign to raise a fund is based on interviews with Schulte on April 23, 1991, December 5, 1991, and December 18, 1991.

310 The *Barron's* quotation is from Laing, "The Vulture Capitalist."

310 The reference to the statuettes and the poem is from an interview with Sam Zell on January 28, 1992.

311 The description of the Zell-Chilmark fund is based on an interview with David Schulte on December 18, 1991 and press reports.

311–12 The background on Carter, Hawley, Hale's debt problems is from press reports.

312 The information on Sam Zell's relationship with Philip Hawley and Hawley's request for help is based on an interview with David Schulte on December 18, 1991.

312 The account of Philip Hawley's search for investors and link-up with Zell is from an interview with Jeffrey Chanin on December 3, 1991.

312 The account of the tender offer is based on press reports and Sam Zell's quote is from Francine Schwadel, "Zell 'Vulture Fund' Offers Investment In Carter Hawley," *The Wall Street Journal,* July 25, 1991, sec. B, p. 9.

313 The anonymous bankruptcy specialist was quoted in "Carter Hawley Shareholders Seek Delay on Zell Bid," *Corporate Financing Week*, August 19, 1991, p. 5.

313–14 The account of the final negotiations is from an interview with David Schulte on December 18, 1991.

314 The assessment of Sam Zell and David Schulte's effectiveness is from an interview with Jeffrey Chanin on December 3, 1991.

314 The account of the attempt to acquire Executive Life of California is from press reports.

315 The excerpt is from Sam Zell, "The Grave Dancer," *Real Estate Review*, 1976.

CHAPTER 12

317 The description of Crédit Lyonnais's acquisition of Executive Life of California is based on press reports.

317 The account of the Water Street Fund's demise is based on press reports.

317 The account of Mikael Salovaara's new effort is based on an interview with him on December 3, 1991.

317 The reference to the size of the Water Street Fund is based on an interview with Mikael Salovaara on January 17, 1992.

318–19 The profile of Mikael Salovaara's life and career is based on an interview with him on December 3, 1991.

319–20 The account of Goldman, Sachs's decision to launch a vulture fund and the fund's strategy is based on an interview with Mikael Salovaara on December 3, 1991, and *Private Placement Memorandum, Water Street Corporate Recovery Fund, L.P.*, distributed to potential investors, April 1990.

320–21 The account of Goldman, Sachs's design of the Water Street Fund, its awareness of potential conflicts of interest, and its intentions to take a stance that was not hostile to managements is based on *Private Placement Memorandum*, an interview with Mikael Salovaara on December 3, 1991, and press reports.

321 The account of raising the money for the fund is based on an interview with Mikael Salovaara on December 3, 1991.

321–22 The list of investors is based on "Hasty Retreat, How Goldman Scored with a 'Vulture Fund' Yet Decided to Kill It," Randall Smith, *The Wall Street Journal*, June 4, 1991, sec. A, p. 1.

322 The account of Water Street's investment in G-I holdings is based on press reports and an interview with Mikael Salovaara on December 3, 1991.

322 The reference to the decline in the value of Water Street's holdings is from Linda Sandler, "Is Goldman Sachs's Water Street Fund Sinking Fast?" *The Wall Street Journal,* January 6, 1991, sec. C, p. 1.

322 The reference to the Water Street Fund's response to that decline is from an interview with Mikael Salovaara on January 17, 1992.

323 The description of conflict of interest appearance problems is from Smith, "Hasty Retreat."

323–24 The account of Water Street's investment in the Journal Company is based on press reports and on interviews with Mikael Salovaara on December 3, 1991, and January 17, 1992.

324 The account of William Huff's protest is from Smith, "Hasty Retreat."

324–25 The account of Water Street's investment in Tonka bonds is based on press reports and on interviews with Mikael Salovaara on December 3, 1991, and January 17, 1992.

325 The account of various complaints about Water Street's investment in Tonka is from Randall Smith, "Goldman Bought Bonds of Tonka Knowing Mattel Had Mulled Bid," *The Wall Street Journal,* March 8, 1991, sec. C, p. 1, and Smith, "Hasty Retreat."

325 David Breazzano's quotation is from Smith, "Goldman Bought Bonds."

326 The reference to Goldman, Sachs's defense is from Smith, "Goldman Bought Bonds," and an interview with Mikael Salovaara on January 17, 1992.

326 The account of the decision to close down Water Street is from Randall Smith, "Goldman Plans to Shut Down 'Vulture' Fund," *The Wall Street Journal,* May 3, 1991, sec. C, p. 1, and an interview with Mikael Salovaara on December 3, 1991.

326–27 The reference to Water Street's performance record is from an interview with Mikael Salovaara on January 17, 1992.

327 The reference to potential clients for South Street is based on an interview with Mikael Salovaara on December 3, 1991.

327 The account of the suicide of Eli Black is from Bruck, *The Predators' Ball.*

327 The account of Leon Black's suggestion that Drexel, Burnham, Lambert pursue "robber barons" is from Bruck, *The Predators' Ball.*

327–29 The account of Leon Black's career while at Drexel, Burnham, Lambert is from an interview with him in December 1991.

328 The references to Leon Black's advisory clients and his invention of the highly confident letter are from Bruck, *The Predators' Ball.*

328 The account of Leon Black's work with overleveraged companies is from an interview with him in December 1991.

329 The account of Leon Black's negotiation of his bonus is from Kurt Eichenwald, "S.E.C. Report Attacks Big Drexel Bonuses," *New York Times,* October 4, 1991, sec. D, p. 6, and an interview with Black on January 20, 1992.

329 The account of Drexel, Burnham, Lambert's and regulators' efforts to reclaim bonuses is from Kurt Eichenwald, "Drexel Suit to Recover Bonus Pay," *New York Times,* February 12, 1992, sec. D, p. 1, and Wade Lambert, "Drexel Seeks to Recoup Employee Bonuses," *The Wall Street Journal,* February 12, 1992, sec. B, p. 5.

329 The account of Leon Black's ideas about a career in vulture investing is based on an interview with him in December 1991.

329 The accounts of Leon Black's discussions with Thierry de la Villehuchet and Jean-Francois Hénin are based on an interview with Black in December 1991.

330 The account of Altus Finance's history and of the founding of Apollo is based on an interview with Leon Black in December 1991, and press reports.

330 The account of Leon Black's first investments and receipt of additional funds from Altus is based on an interview with him in December 1991.

330–31 The account of Leon Black's investment in Fruit of the Loom is based on press reports and an interview with him on January 20, 1992.

331 The account of Harcourt Brace Jovanovich's problems is from press reports.

331 The reference to Smith, Barney, Harris, Upham & Company's role is based on an interview with Leon Black in December 1991.

331–32 The account of Leon Black's decision to invest and investment in Harcourt Brace Jovanovich securities is based on an interview with him in December 1991.

332 The account of Harcourt Brace Jovanovich's capital structure is based on press reports and an interview with Leon Black in December 1991.

332 The reference to the Water Street Fund's investment in Harcourt Brace Jovanovich bonds is from an interview with Mikael Salovaara on December 3, 1991, and press reports.

332 The account of Leon Black's involvement in accomplishing the workout is based on an interview with him in December 1991.

332–33 The account of General Cinema Corporation's bid for Harcourt Brace Jovanovich is based on press reports.

333 The reference to John Herrington's warning is from Ron Suskind and Daniel Pearl, "General Cinema Corp. Breaks Off Talks With Harcourt Bondholders on Bid Price," *The Wall Street Journal,* April 18, 1991, sec. B, p. 3.

333 The account of the bondholders' reaction to the bid and the formation of a committee is based on an interview with Kenneth Urbaszewski on November 27, 1991.

333 The reference to Kemper Corporation's holdings is based on an interview with Kenneth Urbaszewski on November 27, 1991.

333 The account of Kenneth Urbaszewski's complaints about the bid is from an interview with him on November 27, 1991.

333 The account of Mikael Salovaara and Leon Black's rejections of the bid is from interviews with Salovaara on December 3, 1991, and Black in December 1991.

334 Richard Smith's quotation is from Gary Putka, "General Cinema Takes Tough Stance with Bondholders in Bid for Harcourt," *The Wall Street Journal,* March 11, 1991, sec. B, p. 6.

334 The accounts of General Cinema's failure to get the required bonds and its offer of a bit more are based on press reports.

334 The account of the rejection of the deal by Leon Black, the Water Street fund and Kemper is based on interviews with Black in December 1991, with Mikael Salovaara on December 3, 1991, and with Kenneth Urbaszewski on November 27, 1991.

334–35 The accounts of General Cinema's refusal to do a prepackaged bankruptcy and Kenneth Urbaszewski's reasoning in favor of doing one are based on an interview with Urbaszewski on November 27, 1991.

335 General Cinema's quotation is from Daniel Pearl and Joseph Pereira, "General Cinema Withdraws Its Offer of $1.1 Billion for Harcourt's Bonds," *The Wall Street Journal,* April 29, 1991, sec. A, p. 3.

335 The account of Leon Black's efforts to get the General Cinema acquisition bid back on track is based on interviews with him in December 1991, and with Kenneth Urbaszewski on November 27, 1991.

335–36 The account of the multiple attempts to accomplish the tender offer is based on press reports.

336 Richard Smith's quotation is from William M. Bulkeley and Daniel Pearl, "General Cinema Extends Offer for Bonds Of Harcourt, Threatens to End Its Bid," *The Wall Street Journal,* October 15, 1991, sec. C, p. 11.

336 The account of Leon Black's actions to save the acquisition bid is based on interviews with him in December 1991, and on January 20, 1992.

336–37 The account of the stockholders' acceptance of the bid is from press reports.

337–38 The account of Leon Black's investment in Gillett Holdings is based on interviews with him in December 1991, and on January 20, 1992, and press reports.

338 The account of Leon Black's investment in Price Communications is based on interviews with him in December 1991, and on January 20, 1992, and press reports.

338 The account of Leon Black's other investing activities is based on an interview with him in December 1991.

338 The reference to Leon Black's avoidance of Drexel, Burnham clients is based on an interview with him in December 1991.

Index